Literary Culture in the
Holy Roman Empire,
1555–1720

University of North Carolina
Studies in the Germanic Languages
and Literatures

Initiated by RICHARD JENTE (1949–1952), *established by* F. E. COENEN (1952–1968), *continued by* SIEGFRIED MEWS (1968–1980) *and* RICHARD H. LAWSON (1980–1985)

PAUL T. ROBERGE, Editor

Publication Committee: Department of Germanic Languages

For other volumes in the "Studies" see pages 291–92.

Number One Hundred and Thirteen
University of
North Carolina
Studies in the
Germanic Languages
and Literatures

Literary Culture in the Holy Roman Empire, 1555–1720

Edited by

James A. Parente, Jr.,

Richard Erich Schade,

and George C. Schoolfield

The University of North Carolina Press
Chapel Hill and London 1991

© 1991 The University of North Carolina Press

Library of Congress Cataloging-in-Publication Data

Literary culture in the Holy Roman Empire, 1555–1720 / edited by James
   A. Parente, Jr., Richard Erich Schade, and George C. Schoolfield.
     p.   cm.—(University of North Carolina studies in the Germanic
   languages and literatures ; no. 113)
     Includes bibliographical references and index.
     ISBN 0-8078-8113-9 (alk. paper)
     1. German literature—Early modern, 1500–1700—History and
   criticism.   2. German literature—18th century—History and
   criticism.   I. Parente, James A.   II. Schade, Richard E.
   III. Schoolfield, George C.   IV. Series.
   PT238.L58   1991
   830.9'004—dc20   90-12891
                                                                   CIP

Manufactured in the United States of America

95   94   93   92   91   5   4   3   2   1

329/73

Contents

Preface

This volume would not have been published without the generosity and support of many people. We should first like to thank Dr. Erich Markel of the Max Kade Foundation for granting the financial assistance to hold a conference on literary culture in the Holy Roman Empire 1555–1720 at the Beinecke Library of Yale University in March 1987. His generous support enabled us to invite an international roster of speakers and helped us to defray a considerable portion of the publication costs of this volume. We should also like to thank Dr. Christa Sammons, the curatrix of the Curt von Faber du Faur collection of German Baroque literature at the Beinecke Library, for sponsoring the conference and helping with the local arrangements for the participants. Liselotte Davis (Yale University) also expedited the last-minute preparations for the symposium. Finally, we are especially grateful to Professor Paul T. Roberge, the editor of the Germanic Languages and Literatures series of the University of North Carolina Press, for his invaluable advice at all stages in the publication process, and Mamie Gray (University of Illinois at Chicago), without whose indefatigable efforts the final typescript of this volume would have never been completed.

Unless otherwise stated, all translations into English or German were completed by the author of each essay.

Spring 1990   James A. Parente, Jr.
                                                        Richard Erich Schade
                                                        George C. Schoolfield

Abbreviations

BLVS	Bibliothek des litterarischen Vereins Stuttgart
CEH	*Central European History*
DVLG	*Deutsche Vierteljahrsschrift für Literaturwissenschaft und Geistesgeschichte*
GLL	*German Life and Letters*
GQ	*German Quarterly*
GR	*Germanic Review*
IASL	*Internationales Archiv für Sozialgeschichte der deutschen Literatur*
JEGP	*Journal of English and Germanic Philology*
JMRS	*Journal of Medieval and Renaissance Studies*
JWCI	*Journal of the Warburg and Courtauld Institutes*
MLR	*Modern Language Review*
NDB	*Neue deutsche Biographie*
OL	*Orbis Litterarum*
PMLA	*Publications of the Modern Language Association of America*

Literary Culture in the
Holy Roman Empire,
1555–1720

1. Literary Culture in the Holy Roman Empire: An Introduction

James A. Parente, Jr.

To the present-day scholar of early modern European literature, the cultural landscape of sixteenth- and seventeenth-century central Europe seems relatively bleak. In contrast to the masterpieces of Elizabethan and Stuart England, the *siglo de oro*, and late Renaissance France and Italy, literary writings in the Holy Roman Empire are remembered, if at all, as the products of obscurantist, bookish scholar-poets whose greatest works derived their inspiration not from native talent, but from more accomplished authors to the south and west. Despite the recent successful efforts of early modern historians to rehabilitate the textbook image of central Europe as a cultural backwater, the literature of the Empire has still not attracted the attention of many literary scholars working in those two most international of epochs, the Renaissance and the Baroque. To be sure, specialists in German-language literature have long held an affection for the seemingly uninteresting two hundred years between the death of Luther and the golden age of Lessing, Goethe, and Schiller, but much of their often quite excellent scholarship has rarely been viewed outside the parochial boundaries of their own discipline. Even within German studies, the study of the sixteenth and seventeenth centuries still requires a careful apologia.[1] Indeed, the Germanists' own misgivings about the aesthetic value of much of their early modern literature may well have deterred curious European Renaissance scholars from exploring the field with greater enthusiasm.

The purpose of this collection of essays is to dispel this misconception about the lackluster quality of literary culture in the Holy Roman Empire and to awaken the interest of other Renaissance and seventeenth-century scholars in literary writing in these unjustly neglected centuries. Such a need has been especially pressing since the 1960s as both Germanists and other European Renaissance scholars have discovered and reevaluated the significance of such early modern phenomena as emblematics and school rhetoric, which informed the composition of literary works in their respective disciplines.[2] This initial interest in the historical background of poetic writing has resulted, more recently, in a renewed emphasis on the social, political, and economic factors that influenced the early modern poets and their works. Renaissance and Baroque scholars of several lands from the Empire to England, France, and Spain are posing similar questions about the social role of the poet, the effect of early absolutism on literary production and poets' self-conceptions of their calling.[3] The essays in this book have been organized around four major issues in contemporary literary-critical writing about the Empire as well as about early modern European literature in general: the connections between humanism and the new scientific thought; the relationship of late sixteenth- and seventeenth-century literature to ancient and Renaissance European traditions; the social and political context of early modern writing; and last, the poets' self-consciousness about their work. In this way, it is hoped that this collection will not only provide the general Renaissance and Baroque scholar with some insight into the complex circumstances of literary production in the early modern Empire, but also represent the diversity of literary-critical methodologies that early modern scholars currently employ to analyze and understand the literary works of the leading writers of this often forgotten period.

In light of the scant interest that many literary scholars have shown toward the early modern Empire, it is worth reflecting briefly on the reasons for such indifference and the best way for Germanists to effect a rapprochement with them. Early modern literature in the Empire has often been neglected because of the Anglo-Romance orientation of much Renaissance and Baroque scholarship. Such an alliance is of course understandable not only because of the close ties between the four main Romance literatures—French, Italian, Spanish, and Portuguese—to each other and to England, but also because of the numerous vernacular masterpieces that writers in these lands produced. This viewpoint has in turn given rise to the notion that the Renaissance, generally understood here as the rediscovery of antiquity and the rise of an unified national culture, arose in the Mediterranean, gradually spread across northern Europe in the fifteenth and sixteenth centuries with ever-diminishing degrees of success, and eventually died out in the hostile confines of the barbaric Germanic north. Few contemporary early modernists would ever acknowledge such an unabashedly naive and antiquated view of the dissemination of Renaissance thought, especially in light of recent scholarship on humanism in the sixteenth- and seventeenth-century Empire. Nonetheless, this subliminal prejudice still seems to persist as European Renaissance and Baroque scholars continue to work with little regard for the supposedly arcane pursuits of the Germanists.

Recently, however, early modern intellectual historians have revealed the forgotten world of late humanism in central Europe in all its fascinating complexity. As a result of the efforts of scholars such as R. J. W. Evans, Notker Hammerstein, Michael Stolleis, Manfred Fleischer, and Anthony Grafton, we are now much more informed about Renaissance learning in several Imperial territories; sixteenth- and seventeenth-century legal, political, and historical thought; and the colorful careers of the polyhistors.[4] More important, this excitement about intellectual life in the Empire has taken hold of German literary scholars such as Wilfried Barner, Albrecht Schöne, Conrad Wiedemann, Wilhelm Kühlmann, and Gunter Grimm, whose detailed research has contributed greatly to our understanding of the social, political, and educational institutions in which early modern German literature was created.[5] The disciplinary boundaries between early modern historical and literary scholars of the Empire have now been so completely effaced that it is rare when the two groups do not meet together or collaborate on research.[6]

It is ironic, though not perhaps too puzzling, that the disciplinary limits have proven easier barriers for literary scholars to cross than national frontiers. A waggish Renaissance literary scholar might even dismiss such interdisciplinary cooperation between Germanists and historians as proof of the inherently antiquarian appeal of sixteenth- and seventeenth-century German literature. Yet many of these same researchers are now likewise turning to social and political history, albeit with a different emphasis, to reinterpret early modern literature. English Renaissance scholars such as Stephen Greenblatt, Stephen Orgel, and Jonathan Goldberg, for example, have argued for the politically subversive nature of much Elizabethan and Jacobean literature or drawn elaborate epistemological parallels between historical events and specific literary works.[7] Others such as Marc Fumaroli and Brian Vickers have significantly increased our historical knowledge of the rhetorical context in which many literary writings were fashioned.[8] This increasing historicization of early modern studies thus suggests a common ground upon which literary scholars of the Empire and other nations might meet. Instead of relegating the Empire to a secondary position in sixteenth- and seventeenth-century letters, scholars will now be able to regard its literature and the institutions that fostered it as part of the larger intellectual, sociopolitical and economic framework in which all literature was produced in early modern Europe.

The title of this collection, *Literary Culture in the Holy Roman Empire, 1555–1720,* has been specifically devised to reflect this current historical direction in early modern studies. In the first place, there is no mention here of the frequently baffling terms "Renaissance" and "Baroque" in reference to early modern German literature, nor does one encounter such familiar designations as "Reformation" and "Counter-Reformation." The former headings have in recent years been consistently eschewed by most early modern scholars who work in these two periods because of the difficulties earlier generations have had in agreeing on what types of writing these two words connoted.[9] It is a commonplace among Renaissance and Baroque scholars, especially the latter, to call themselves "early modernists" and, as in the following essays, to use these two terms primarily for heuristic purposes. Discussions about the nature of Renaissance and Baroque literature and of that equally troublesome category, Mannerism, have for the most part been consigned to the history of ideas and aesthetics, for there is little place for such generalized arguments in the present historically oriented research of this period.[10]

The terms "Reformation" and "Counter-Reformation" literature have been avoided in our title because of their religious implications. Literature in the Empire was neither exclusively Protestant nor Catholic, but consisted of writings from adherents of both churches. Moreover, both words have traditionally been used to suggest a particular aesthetic attitude inimical to the development of poetry. Although literary writing thrived under the auspices of both churches, the unmistakable religious bias of such works has been thought to have hindered the spread of Renaissance (i.e., secular) ideas among early modern German writers.[11] Underlying this judgment of course is the questionable assumption that the Renaissance was primarily a secular movement that brought about the liberation of emergent states from the hegemony of the medieval church. Since the Empire was racked by religious controversies from the early sixteenth century until at least 1600, so the argument runs, no national and, by extension, no literary consciousness could prevail until the settlement of these internecine conflicts. To be sure, many early modern Germanists are aware of the reductiveness of this nineteenth-century, anticlerical, nationalistic point of view, yet it has been extraordinarily difficult to suppress.[12] The woeful neglect of much German literature between the death of Luther (1546) and 1600 is in part due to the tacit presumption that the religious polemics of that era stifled the poetic impulse nurtured by humanism earlier in the century.[13] As a result, the lasting effects of Renaissance learning are still generally believed to have reached the

Empire only in the early seventeenth century with the establishment of the vernacular as a literary language capable of the same range of poetic expression as the other major European tongues.

To challenge this traditional stance—now being splendidly reevaluated by, among others, Wilhelm Kühlmann and Dieter Breuer—a much wider time frame, 1555–1720, has been chosen for the contributions to this collection.[14] The *terminus ad quem*, 1720, poses little problem, for early modern scholars have long acknowledged the influence of many aspects of seventeenth-century learning, for example, encyclopedism, normative poetics, and the education of the absolutist *Christianus politicus*, on early eighteenth-century writers.[15] Several of the following essays, especially those of Gerhart Hoffmeister, Ferdinand van Ingen, and Uwe-K. Ketelsen, carefully delineate the continuance and gradual modification of some seventeenth-century literary practices in the next century.

The *terminus a quo*, 1555, however, is intended to suggest a different approach to the period. The present state of much early modern literary scholarship unjustly excludes the late sixteenth century. Whereas most sixteenth-century literary scholars limit the extent of their investigations to the 1540s (i.e., Luther's lifetime),[16] seventeenth-century researchers likewise ignore much of the late sixteenth century in their debates about at what point their field begins. The arguments of the latter researchers center around three possibilities: 1624, the publication of Martin Opitz's *Buch von der deutschen Poeterey*, the first prescriptive poetics for German; 1617, the establishment of the first German language academy, the Fruchtbringende Gesellschaft; or still earlier in the 1580s and 1590s when the first signs of the new poetic styles of Petrarchistic lyric and the *Pléiade* appeared in German-language verse.[17] Besides the obvious presupposition that the Renaissance in the Empire only truly began around 1600, there are two major weaknesses with these points of origin. First, all these dates hardly account for developments in sixteenth-century Latin writing where the European Renaissance interest in the revival of the Greco-Roman past and the education of the learned and eloquent individual thrived for more than a century from the late 1400s until well into the 1600s. Despite the now classic study of Erich Trunz on late humanism and Karl Otto Conrady's investigation of sixteenth-century Neo-Latin lyrics, we are still inadequately informed about the course of the main literary genres of sixteenth-century Latin and the breadth of late Renaissance learning in the Empire.[18] Second, previous datings of the origins of the "Baroque" have been based almost exclusively on works written in the three traditional genres of post-Romantic literature:

lyric, drama, and fictional prose. Little consideration has yet been extended to other forms of early modern writing, be it in German or Latin, such as school orations, dialogues, sermons, biographies, history, political treatises, letters, essays, travel literature, and so on (*Fachprosa*), where the influence of European Renaissance learning may be much more extensive than hitherto supposed.[19]

Because of the vast amount of sixteenth-century Latin and German writing that still awaits analysis, it is premature to designate a particular date as the beginning of the "Baroque," especially if this date is based on an evaluation of literature alone. Consequently, in accordance with the sociopolitical direction of much contemporary research in the early modern Empire—and of many of the essays in the present volume—1555, the date of the Peace of Augsburg, was chosen, for this year marked a turning point in both Imperial political and religious history. With a temporary end to the religious wars of the mid-century and the Imperial acknowledgment of the confessional status quo of Protestantism, the *respublica litteraria* of sixteenth-century central Europe entered a long period of consolidation and self-definition in both the religious and secular spheres whose effects, as far as they have been explored, appear to have played a major role in the later cultural development of the Empire. With the establishment of a confessionally determined humanist curriculum throughout the Imperial lands and the rise of new, practical methods for the composition of poetry, the governance of a state, and the study of natural phenomena, the late sixteenth-century learned world ostensibly created the intellectual stage upon which the seventeenth-century *theatrum mundi* would be played.[20]

The revisionist emphasis of the title is further reflected in the explicit references to "literary culture" and the "Holy Roman Empire." The use of the first phrase is intended to suggest that the traditional conception of literary genres—drama, poetry, prose—has been expanded to include other forms of writing, such as classical philology and astronomy (Anthony Grafton) or the *approbationes* that the literary censor used to preface most early modern works (Dieter Breuer). "Literary culture" is also preferable to the more customary "Literature in Germany" or "German literature," for both these descriptions imply a political and philological dimension to the modern reader quite different from the actual circumstances under which early modern literature was produced. Such terms are of course still used by many early modern literary scholars for the sake of familiarity and convenience, but it is important to recognize their limitations. Because of the bilingual (Latin and German) nature of most sixteenth- and seventeenth-century writing, "German literature" does not accurately describe all literary texts of this period; nor can "German literature" properly be applied to all "German-language" works, for as scholars such as Dieter Breuer have shown, the early modern German literary language took on different forms in various regions of the Empire.[21] Many Catholic authors in the south, for example, such as Jakob Balde, Johannes Khuen, and Laurentius von Schnüffis, cultivated an elegant Bavarian dialect as equally learned and sophisticated as the Upper Saxon-Meissen dialect promulgated by Opitz and the Protestant *Sprachgesellschaften*.[22] Given such imprecision about the use of the word "German" and the territorial significance of much early modern language and literature, it seems therefore much more appropriate to introduce the standard political and legal term, Holy Roman Empire, when dealing with sixteenth- and seventeenth-century writing.[23] This historical designation has never gained much currency among literary scholars, perhaps because of the aura of Imperial Catholic hegemony it appears to emit. Yet, as historians such as R. J. W. Evans have shown, the Imperial ideal remained quite attractive to intellectuals in both Catholic and Protestant lands throughout the early modern period (1450–1750), and its political and legal institutions were still regarded as authoritative in most territorial disputes.[24] Moreover, as is well known, many of the leading Catholic and Protestant writers of the sixteenth- and seventeenth-century Empire sought the favor of the emperor and his Imperial ministers in order to advance both their literary and political ambitions. Consider, for example, the crowning of Nicodemus Frischlin and Martin Opitz as *poetae laureati* by the emperor, Daniel Casper von Lohenstein's panegyrics to Leopold I, and Duke Anton Ulrich von Braunschweig-Wolfenbüttel's conversion to Catholicism to gain favor at the Imperial court. By referring to early modern culture in the *Holy Roman Empire* rather than Germany, the literary scholar is thus reminded of the different territorial contexts in which specific works were created, be it Silesia, Alsace, or an Imperial city, and of the geopolitical reality in which many writers structured their careers.

Most of the essays in this volume were first presented at a conference held at Yale University in March 1987 commemorating the Curt von Faber du Faur collection of German Baroque literature in the Yale Beinecke Rare Book and Manuscript Library.[25] The conference also served to bring together several scholars from North America and Europe so that they could discuss current developments in early modern studies in the Empire. The papers, most of which have been revised and enlarged for publication, were read in three seminars whose topics, as mentioned earlier, correspond to the leading issues confronting both Germanists and their colleagues in general Renaissance studies. Early modern literature in the Empire is viewed here in the context of its relationship to other European literary traditions, the sociopolitical institutions under which its authors operated and the individual poet's self-conception of the poetic craft (Parts II–IV in this volume). In addition to these distinctly literary essays, Anthony Grafton examines a central problem in the intellectual history of the early modern Empire in his keynote address on the contrastive methodologies of science and humanist scholarship around 1600. As a historian among literary critics, Grafton calls for the removal of disciplinary boundaries between these two related fields and demonstrates the benefits of such cooperation in his analysis of Johann Kepler's career as both a philologist and a scientist.

Because of the limitations of the conference, this book does not strive for a comprehensive portrait of all aspects of early modern literary culture. Indeed, many important topics in sixteenth- and seventeenth-century literature, such as Protestant and Catholic religious lyric, opera, and the new "realist" prose of the late 1600s, have not been treated at all. Nonetheless, several contemporary arguments in early modern studies and contrastive literary-critical approaches are presented here. Moreover, despite the distribution of the essays among three different headings, there is considerable overlap between their main themes. Gerhart Hoffmeister's description of the fate of the Spanish fool in seventeenth-century literature and Gerald Gillespie's comparative treatment of French and German tragedy (Part II) can only be understood against the backdrop of the political ambitions of the Habsburgs (Parts I and III). Similarly, many of the essays on the early modern writers' conception of their work (Part IV) deal as well with the social and political role of the poet (Part III), for the authorial identity of a poet is often indistinguishable from the poet's public function.

The vexing question about the indebtedness of sixteenth- and seventeenth-century German writers to other contemporary European authors occupies the participants in the second part of the volume. Much of the comparative work completed since the 1970s has addressed the transformation of specific literary texts or topoi from other European traditions by seventeenth-century German authors.[26] Two of the chapters represent this practice. Gerhart Hoffmeister traces the various forms the character of the Spanish fool assumed in German works from the early 1600s until the late eighteenth century. In contrast to the English figure of the worldly-wise clown, the Spanish fool was used as the target of anti-Spanish sentiment and as a negative exemplum of social deportment. Similarly, Gerald Gillespie compares two distinct views of the Ottoman Empire by western Christian authors in his analysis of the Turkish plays of François Tristan L'Hermite and Daniel Casper von Lohenstein. Whereas the French author emphasized the destructiveness of the passions manifested by his Turkish characters, Lohenstein used the occasion to extol the Habsburgs' cultural superiority to their dangerous eastern neighbors. Building on these comparative methodologies, Thomas W. Best offers a complex, intertextual reading of Andreas Gryphius's *Cardenio und Celinde* and Greco-Roman theater. Instead of concentrating on Gryphius's relationship to his Spanish source, Best reveals the Silesian playwright's subtle imitation and criticism of elements from both Roman comedy and Greek tragedy in his new Christian play. Finally, in the wake of the ever-increasing number of comparative analyses, Peter Skrine warns his fellow early modern drama critics to assess the public context in which theatrical works were written and reproduced before formulating any interpretation of their meaning or aesthetic judgment about their literary quality.

The third part of the volume deals with the increasingly important sociopolitical context in which early modern works were created. George C. Schoolfield, Barbara Becker-Cantarino, and Michael M. Metzger examine the way in which the culture of the court shaped the works of three seventeenth-century authors. Schoolfield delineates the complex relationship of the Jesuit poet Jacob Balde to both Habsburg and Wittelsbach (Bavaria) in his political poetry; Becker-Cantarino investigates the allegorical masques of Duchess Sophie Elisabeth von Braunschweig-Lüneburg and demonstrates the close connection between literature and the visual arts in the early modern court; and Metzger traces the afterlife of a cause célèbre of the Palatinate ruling house in the heroic epistles of Lohenstein. Finally, Dieter Breuer argues for the use of the early modern censor's judgment about the political and religious acceptability of certain texts, such as the writings of several Bavarian and Austrian authors, as a key to understanding the poetological principles by which these books were both read and composed.

In the fourth section, the early modern poets' self-conceptions of their art and public personas are discussed from several different viewpoints. Richard E. Schade suggests that the frontispiece to early modern books, and especially those that the portray the author, provide a fundamental insight into the poet's public image and, more important, serve as an interpretive guide for the reader to the work that follows. Using the dedicatory letter as an example, Ulrich Maché illustrates the significance of that prefatory essay for each author's own view of the work and provides a useful typology by which the importance of such letters can be gauged. In contrast, Ferdinand van Ingen turns to seventeenth-century poetological handbooks and poetic practice as sources for understanding the extent to which the educated scholar-authors of the century betrayed their authorial individuality as they continued to subscribe to the prescriptive norms of poetic composition. Van Ingen's discussion of the rhetorical tropes and topoi of the humanist tradition that informed the composition of most early modern writing, especially the occasional poetry of the seventeenth century, is treated further by Barton W. Browning and Joseph Leighton. In his interpretation of poems by Paul Fleming and Andreas Gryphius in which the author appears to address himself, Browning reveals the fundamentally public rather than private nature of seventeenth-century lyric. Adopting an even more skeptical posture, Leighton takes issue with the application of the concept of authorial individuality to all early modern lyric. Having represented the inevitable social rather than private role of the occasional poet, Leighton demonstrates that even the most seemingly personal elements of a given work, such as Paul Fleming's "Grabschrift für sich selbst," can easily be read as well as familiar humanist topoi.

Judith P. Aikin extends the conclusions of van Ingen, Browning, and Leighton into the realm of drama. By introducing himself as a clown into his comedies, the poet-dramatist Caspar Stieler creates a fictional social role for himself through which he can safely criticize and entertain the intimate court circle to which he belongs. The disappearance of this intimate circle in which and for which many early modern writers produced their literary works is detailed in Uwe-K. Ketelsen's essay on the gradual transformation of the reading public in the Empire in the early eighteenth century. In his literary-sociological examination of the public reception of erotic poetry around 1700, Ketelsen shows that a poet's identity is no longer conditioned so much by the small elite circle for whom he wrote, but rather by the demands of the marketplace. With the growth of a large reading public unfamiliar with the life and circumstances of the poet, publishers were constrained to create a public image for the author—in this case Christian Hofmann von Hofmannswaldau—that would appeal to the less sophisticated, if not crude, expectations of the mass reading audience. In the final section, then, all of these essays suggest that the identities of the early modern authors cannot be divorced from the social circumstances in which their works were written and from the poetological norms and rhetorical tropes to which they, as scholar-poets, adhered.

The following essays will thus make plain the advantages for scholars researching the lost culture of the Empire of occasionally overstepping the traditional boundaries of the present academic disciplines to reconstruct and understand the learned world of early modern central Europe. The increasing historicization of sixteenth- and seventeenth-century studies requires that the interpretation of literature no longer be viewed as a separate intellectual exercise unrelated to the external circumstances (be they social, political, educational, religious, or economic) which determined the poets' conception of their art and the nature of the writings they created.

As this volume attests, much work has already been done on elucidating the literary and sociopolitical contexts in which early modern books were written. But even more challenging tasks await future researchers in the field: the charting of the unknown waters of much early modern Latin literary culture, not only in the Empire but throughout Europe; the sociopolitical examination of German-language literature within the specific context of the large states, territories, bishoprics, and free cities of the Empire from Pomerania to Austria; the problematic place of the large quantity of mystic, pansophic, and alchemical writing in early modern cultural history and its relationship to similar underground movements in other European lands; and the continuity or discontinuity of humanist philosophy, history, education, and political thought from the late sixteenth century until the early Enlightenment. As a result of the efforts of Curt von Faber du Faur and the other leading bibliographers of early modern German literature, Harold Jantz (1974), Martin Bircher (1977), and Gerhard Dünnhaupt (1980–81), the present-day researcher has a solid foundation for future explorations of these fields.[27] But despite these masterful achievements, still more philological work needs to be completed, and the temptation to construct hasty interpretations of the early modern Empire without a secure historical foundation looms ever larger in the face of the seemingly endless number of texts emerging from the archives after some three hundred years. Yet if scholars writing on this cosmopolitan literary culture continue to benefit from the methods and findings of their fellow researchers in allied disciplines—chiefly history, sociology, and philosophy, as well as the literary-critical techniques of scholars in other European literatures—then the *respublica litteraria* of the Empire will no longer remain a historical curiosity but at last be recognized as an integral part of early modern European intellectual life.

Notes

1. Harald Steinhagen, "Dichtung, Politik und Geschichte im 17. Jahrhundert: Versuch über die objektiven Bedingungen der Barockliteratur," in *Deutsche Dichter des 17. Jahrhunderts*, ed. H. Steinhagen and Benno von Wiese (Berlin: Erich Schmidt, 1984), pp. 9–10. For a more comprehensive analysis of the reception of German Baroque literature in Germany, see Herbert Jaumann, *Die deutsche Barockliteratur Wertung-Umwertung. Eine wertungsgeschichtliche Studie in systematischer Absicht*, Abhandlungen zur Kunst-, Musik- und Literaturwissenschaft, 181 (Bonn: Bouvier, 1975).

2. Critical literature on both Renaissance emblematics and rhetoric has grown enormously since these fields emerged in the 1960s. For an overview of earlier work in these two areas for both the Empire and other European lands, see Manfred Brauneck, "Deutsche Literatur des 17. Jahrhunderts-Revision eines Epochenbildes. Ein Forschungsbericht 1945–1970," *DVLG* 45 (1971) Sonderheft: 451*–68*. Two continually influential works in German sixteenth- and seventeenth-century scholarship remain: Albrecht Schöne, *Emblematik und Drama im Zeitalter des Barock* (Munich: Beck, 1964), and Wilfried Barner, *Barockrhetorik: Untersuchungen zu ihren geschichtlichen Grundlagen* (Tübingen: Niemeyer, 1970).

3. For a sampling of these and other recent trends in European Renaissance literature, see *Literary Theory/Renaissance Texts*, ed. Patricia Parker and David Quint (Baltimore: Johns Hopkins University Press, 1986). In Germany, these issues have been discussed by Gunter E. Grimm, *Literatur und Gelehrtentum in Deutschland, Untersuchungen zum Wandel ihres Verhältnisses vom Humanismus bis zur Frühaufklärung*, Studien zur deutschen Literatur, 75 (Tübingen: Niemeyer, 1983); Wilhelm Kühlmann, *Gelehrtenrepublik und Fürstenstaat. Entwicklung und Kritik des deutschen Späthumanismus in der Literatur des Barockzeitalters* (Tübingen: Niemeyer, 1982); H. Steinhagen, "Dichtung, Politik und Geschichte"; and in many of the essays in *Zwischen Gegenreformation und Frühaufklärung: Späthumanismus, Barock 1572–1740*, ed. H. Steinhagen [*Deutsche Literatur. Eine Sozialgeschichte*, ed. Horst Albert Glaser, vol. 3] (Reinbek: Rowohlt, 1985).

4. Of the numerous writings of each of these authors, see especially R. J. W. Evans, *Rudolf II and His World: A Study in Intellectual History 1576–1612* (Oxford: Clarendon, 1973), and *The Making of the Habsburg Monarchy 1550–1700* (Oxford: Clarendon, 1979); Notker Hammerstein, *Ius und Historie. Ein Beitrag zur Geschichte des historischen Denkens an deutschen Universitäten im späten 17. und 18. Jahrhundert* (Göttingen: Vandenhoeck & Ruprecht, 1972); Michael Stolleis, ed., *Staatsdenker im 17. Jahrhundert: Reichspublizistik, Politik und Naturrecht*, 2d ed. (Frankfurt a. M.: Alfred Metzner, 1987) and *Arcana imperii und Ratio status. Bemerkung zur politischen Theorie des frühen 17. Jahrhunderts*, Veröffentlichungen der Joachim Jungius-Gesellschaft der Wissenschaften Hamburg, 39 (Göttingen: Vandenhoeck & Ruprecht, 1980); Manfred Fleischer, *Späthumanismus in Schlesien. Ausgewählte Aufsätze* (Munich: Delp, 1984); Anthony Grafton, "The World of the Polyhistors: Humanism and Encyclopedism," *CEH* 18 (1985): 31–47.

5. Kühlmann, *Gelehrtenrepublik;* Grimm, *Literatur und Gelehrtentum;* Barner, *Barockrhetorik;* Albrecht Schöne, *Kürbishütte und Königsberg. Modellversuch einer sozialgeschichtlichen Entzifferung poetischer Texte,* 2d ed. (Munich: Beck, 1982); see also the essays of the numerous contributors to *Stadt-Schule-Universität-Buchwesen und die deutsche Literatur im 17. Jahrhundert,* ed. A. Schöne (Munich: Beck, 1976); Conrad Wiedemann, "Barocksprache, Systemdenken, Staatsmentalität. Perspektiven der Forschung nach Barners *Barockrhetorik,"* in *Dokumente des internationalen Arbeitskreises für deutsche Barockliteratur I [1973],* 2d ed., ed. Paul Raabe and Barbara Strutz (Stuttgart: Ernst Hauswedell, 1976), pp. 21–51.

6. In 1979, 1982, and 1985, the triennial conferences of the Wolfenbüttel *Internationaler Arbeitskreis für Barockliteratur* featured contributions from both Germanists and early modern historians. The proceedings of these three congresses have been published: *Europäische Hofkultur im 16. und 17. Jahrhundert,* 3 vols., ed. August Buck, Georg Kauffmann, Blake Lee Spahr, Conrad Wiedemann, Wolfenbütteler Arbeiten zur Barockforschung, 8–10 (Stuttgart: Ernst Hauswedell, 1981); *Literatur und Volk im 17. Jahrhundert. Probleme populärer Kultur in Deutschland,* 2 vols., ed. Wolfgang Brückner, Peter Blickle, and Dieter Breuer, Wolfenbütteler Arbeiten zur Barockforschung, 13 (Wiesbaden: Harrassowitz, 1985); *Res Publica Litteraria. Die Institutionen der Gelehrsamkeit in der frühen Neuzeit,* 2 vols., ed. Conrad Wiedemann and Sebastian Neumeister, Wolfenbütteler Arbeiten zur Barockforschung, 14 (Wiesbaden: Harrassowitz, 1987). North American meetings also have included several historians and literary critics, as in the 1986 Washington University (St. Louis, Missouri) "Literatur und Kosmos. Innen- und Aussenwelten in der deutschen Literatur des 15. bis 17. Jahrhunderts" conference. The proceedings of this conference have been edited by Gerhild Scholz Williams and Lynne Tatlock and appear in *Daphnis* 15/2–3 (1986).

7. For example, Stephen J. Greenblatt, "Improvisation and Power," in *Literature and Society,* ed. Edward W. Said (Baltimore: Johns Hopkins University Press, 1980), pp. 57–99; Stephen Orgel, *The Illusion of Power: Political Theater in the English Renaissance* (Berkeley: University of California Press, 1975); Jonathan Goldberg, *James I and the Politics of Literature: Jonson, Shakespeare, Donne, and Their Contemporaries* (Baltimore: Johns Hopkins University Press, 1983).

8. Marc Fumaroli, *L'Age de éloquence: Rhétorique et 'res litteraria' de la Renaissance au seuil de l'époque classique* (Geneva: Droz, 1980). Brian Vickers has written extensively on Renaissance rhetoric; see his *In Defense of Rhetoric* (Oxford: Clarendon, 1988), which also contains references to his earlier work in the field.

9. For example, the recent congresses of the Wolfenbüttel *Internationaler Arbeitskreis für Barockliteratur* have been devoted to sixteenth- and/or seventeenth-century literature, or the early modern period, rather than to the "Renaissance" or "Baroque." See note 6.

10. For a review of the European debate on the nature of the Baroque, see Brauneck, "Deutsche Literatur des 17. Jahrhunderts," pp. 389*–434*; see also Wilfried Barner, "Stilbegriffe und ihre Grenzen. Am Beispiel 'Barock,' " *DVLG* 45 (1971): 302–35. The major late nineteenth- and twentieth-century

writings on the concept of the Baroque can be found in W. Barner, ed., *Der literarische Barockbegriff*, Wege der Forschung, 358 (Darmstadt: Wissenschaftliche Buchgesellschaft, 1975). For a discussion of the Baroque versus Mannerism problem, see Gerald Gillespie, "Renaissance, Mannerism, Baroque," in *German Baroque Literature: The European Perspective*, ed. Gerhart Hoffmeister (New York: Ungar, 1983), pp. 3–24.

11. For an excellent example of the practical application of this view, see Richard Alewyn, *Vorbarocker Klassizismus und griechische Tragödie, Analyse der "Antigone"-Übersetzung des Martin Opitz* (1926; rpt. Darmstadt: Wissenschaftliche Buchgesellschaft, 1962).

12. Jan-Dirk Müller has outlined the transformation of secular Italian Renaissance ideals by sixteenth-century poets into *docta pietas*. Unlike previous critics, however, Müller distinguishes between the southwest Empire where the worldly Renaissance continued to thrive and the confessionally informed writing of Saxony. Jan-Dirk Müller, "Zum Verhältnis von Reformation und Renaissance in der deutschen Literatur des 16. Jahrhunderts," in *Renaissance-Reformation. Gegensätze und Gemeinsamkeiten*, ed. August Buck, Wolfenbütteler Abhandlungen zur Renaissanceforschung, 5 (Wiesbaden: Harrassowitz, 1984), pp. 227–53.

13. An interpretive history of German literature between 1540 and 1620 still needs to be written; the present vade mecum through these decades remains the purely informational volumes of H. De Boor and R. Newald's *Geschichte der deutschen Literatur:* Hans Rupprich, *Vom späten Mittelalter bis zum Barock. Zweiter Teil: Das Zeitalter der Reformation 1520–1570 [Geschichte der deutschen Literatur*, vol. 4/2] (Munich: Beck, 1973); Richard Newald, *Vom Späthumanismus zur Empfindsamkeit 1570–1750 [Geschichte der deutschen Literatur*, vol. 5], 6th ed. (1951; Munich: Beck, 1967). The literary-historical introduction of Könneker and Wiedemann to German Renaissance and Baroque literature also neglects the late sixteenth century: whereas Wiedemann concentrates on the seventeenth century, Könneker limits her essay to the mid-sixteenth century and suggests that few connections, if any, can be drawn between the two epochs: Barbara Könneker, "Deutsche Literatur im Zeitalter des Humanismus und der Reformation," in *Deutsche Literatur in Humanismus und Barock*, ed. B. Könneker and C. Wiedemann (Frankfurt a. M.: Athenaion, 1973), pp. 31–32.

14. Kühlmann, *Gelehrtenrepublik*; Dieter Breuer, *Oberdeutsche Literatur 1565–1650. Deutsche Literaturgeschichte und Territorialgeschichte in frühabsolutistischer Zeit*, Zeitschrift für Bayerische Landesgeschichte, Beiheft 11 [Reihe B] (Munich: Beck, 1979).

15. The 1984 collection of Steinhagen and von Wiese, *Deutsche Dichter des 17. Jahrhunderts*, contains essays on several authors who had been previously assigned to eighteenth-century literature: Barthold Hinrich Brockes, Christian Friedrich Hunold, Johann Gottfried Schnabel. Curt von Faber also included the early eighteenth century in his collection of German Baroque writers: C. von Faber du Faur, *German Baroque Literature*, 2 vols. (New Haven: Yale University Press, 1958), 1:391–458.

16. See most recently Herbert Walz, *Deutsche Literatur der Reformationszeit. Eine Einführung* (Darmstadt: Wissenschaftliche Buchgesellschaft, 1988).
17. Steinhagen, "Dichtung, Politik und Geschichte," pp. 14–16; Faber du Faur, *German Baroque Literature* (1:1–8) includes many late sixteenth-century poets whose writings were inspired by both French and Italian models in his collection of Baroque literature.
18. Erich Trunz, "Der deutsche Späthumanismus um 1600 als Standeskultur," in *Deutsche Barockforschung. Dokumentation einer Epoche*, ed. Richard Alewyn (Cologne: Kiepenheuer & Witsch, 1965), pp. 147–81 [first published in *Zeitschrift für Geschichte der Erziehung und des Unterrichts* 21 (1931): 17–53]; Karl Otto Conrady, *Lateinische Dichtungstradition und deutsche Lyrik des 17. Jahrhunderts*, Bonner Arbeiten zur deutschen Literatur, 4 (Bonn: Bouvier, 1962).
19. Barner, *Barockrhetorik*, and more recently, Kühlmann, *Gelehrtenrepublik*, and Grimm, *Literatur und Gelehrtentum*, have mined the vast corpus of oratorical and educational prose writing in their studies on rhetoric and late humanism. Similarly, Hugh Powell reveals many connections between seventeenth-century literary writers and contemporary political and scientific ideas through the examination of many different types of documents from travel, mathematical, and medical texts to broadsheets and other forms of popular culture. Hugh Powell, *Trammels of Tradition: Aspects of German Life in the Seventeenth Century and Their Impact on the Contemporary Literature* (Tübingen: Niemeyer, 1988).
20. For example, Kühlmann, *Gelehrtenrepublik*; M. Stolleis, *Staatsdenker im 17. Jahrhundert*; Evans, *The Making of the Habsburg Monarchy*.
21. Breuer, *Oberdeutsche Literatur*; more recently, Herbert Zeman, "Die österreichische Literatur—Begriff, Bedeutung und literarhistorische Entfaltung in der Neuzeit," in *Die österreichische Literatur. Ihr Profil von den Anfängen im Mittelalter bis ins 18. Jahrhundert (1050–1750)*, ed. H. Zeman with Fritz Peter Knapp (Graz: Akademische Druck- und Verlagsanstalt, 1986), pp. 617–40; and Peter Glatthard, "Die eidgenössisch-alemannische Schreibsprache in der Auseinandersetzung mit der ostmitteldeutsch-neuhochdeutschen Schriftsprache," in *Das Reich und die Eidgenossenschaft 1580–1640. Kulturelle Wechselwirkungen im konfessionellen Zeitalter*, ed. Ulrich im Hof and Suzanne Stehelin (Freiburg [Switz.]: Universitätsverlag, 1986), pp. 319–34.
22. Breuer, *Oberdeutsche Literatur*, pp. 1–21.
23. To be sure, literary writing in the Holy Roman Empire also consisted of works written in the vernacular (e.g., Czech, Hungarian) in other regions of the Empire that the Habsburgs controlled, at various times, during this period. The dominant languages of the Empire were, however, Latin and German. Since the vernacular writers of early modern southern and east-central Europe frequently associated these two languages with the Imperial idea, it is not inappropriate to regard literary culture in the Holy Roman Empire as primarily Latin and German. For a brief survey of early modern Czech literature, see Arne Novák, *Czech Literature*, tr. Peter Kussi, ed. William E. Harkins (Ann Arbor: Michigan Slavic Publications, 1976), pp. 45–85. Novák, writing

in the 1930s, emphatically dismissed the commonly held view that Czech literature between the Reformation and the early seventeenth century had entered a "golden age"; such a designation had arisen *ex negativo* because of the bleakness of the Czech literary landscape in the later seventeenth century. For a detailed overview of Czech literature in this period, see Zdeněk Kalista, *České baroko* (Prague: Evropský Literární Klub, 1941). On early modern Hungarian writing, see István Nemeskürty et al., *A History of Hungarian Literature*, ed. Tibor Klaniczay ([Budapest]: Corvina Kiadó, 1982), pp. 37–114.

24. Evans, *The Making of the Habsburg Monarchy*, pp. 275–308.

25. The essay of George C. Schoolfield was written specially for this volume.

26. For example, *Europäische Tradition und deutscher Literaturbarock. Internationale Beiträge zum Problem von Überlieferung und Umgestaltung*, ed. Gerhart Hoffmeister (Munich: Francke, 1973); *Deutsche Barockliteratur und europäische Kultur*, ed. Martin Bircher and Eberhard Mannack, Dokumente des internationalen Arbeitskreises für deutsche Barockliteratur, 3 (Stuttgart: Ernst Hauswedell, 1977); Hoffmeister, *German Baroque Literature*, pp. 87–193.

27. Faber du Faur, *German Baroque Literature*; vol. 2 of his catalogue appeared posthumously in 1969; Harald Jantz, *German Baroque Literature: A Descriptive Catalogue of the Collection of Harald Jantz*, 2 vols. (New Haven: Research Publications, 1974); Martin Bircher and Thomas Bürger, *Deutsche Drucke des Barocks 1600–1720. Katalog der Herzog August Bibliothek Wolfenbüttel* (Munich: Saur Verlag, 1977–), twenty-three of the planned thirty-seven volumes have already appeared; Gerhard Dünnhaupt, *Bibliographisches Handbuch der Barockliteratur: Hundert Personalbibliographien deutscher Autoren des siebzehnten Jahrhunderts* (Stuttgart: Hiersemann, 1980–81).

Part I. Late Humanism in the Empire

2. Humanism and Science in Rudolphine Prague: Kepler in Context

Anthony Grafton

In winter 1612 humanism and science confronted one another in Prague. Humanism took the solid and threatening form of Melchior Goldast, Saxon *Rat* and envoy; science took that of the Imperial mathematician Johann Kepler, once called a pretty boy by the Greek scholar Martin Crusius in Tübingen but now bowed by financial trouble, racked by bad eyesight, and tormented by his inability to complete his great Rudolphine Tables of planetary motion and to discover all the harmonic ratios that governed the motions of the planets. The confrontation went exactly as one would expect, as Goldast recorded in his diary:

> *Kepplerus Mathematicus* rühmbt sich, er habe ein newe Welt in dem Mohn gefunden, die solle viel grösser seyn, als orbis iste habitabilis. Er vermeint, darinn werden wir nach der auferstehung gesetzt werden. Aber ich allegirte ihm dicta scripturae: Coelum et terra peribunt etc. Er hat mir ein instrument gewiesen, damit solte ich in den Mohn sehen. Es hat der Mohn eine gestalt, als ob er an einem orth höcher were, als an dem andern. Das wolt er mich bereden, seyen berge und thal. Ich aber wolt es ihme lieber glauben, dann hinauff steigen vnd besichtigen.[1]

Here we see scientist and literary scholar trying to talk about a vital matter but kept apart like Pyramus and Thisbe by the thick intellectual brick and mortar that already separated the two cultures. Kepler is fired with enthusiasm by Galileo's discovery of the moons of Jupiter—a discovery first announced to him by his philosopher friend Johann Matthias Wacker, who was so excited that he shouted the news from his coach in the street outside Kepler's house.[2] Kepler imitates his Italian correspondent and turns a telescope toward the Moon. He finds, as Galileo had, that the Moon was not the regular and perfect sphere of Aristotelian cosmology but a bumpy and imperfect planet like Earth. Immediately he begins to see visions and to dream dreams of a new heaven and a new earth. Goldast, jurist, historian, book thief, and literary scholar, reacts to new discoveries about the universe by looking for enlightenment in old texts. The editor, among other things, of a collection of treatises on the power and precedence of the Holy Roman Empire, Goldast kept his vision fixed firmly on the past and on his books. Even a look through Kepler's telescope inspired in him nothing more profound than a feeble joke.[3]

The encounter seems freighted with meaning; it seems, indeed, to reveal two world views in collision. One is empirical, turned toward the direct study of nature, open to imaginative speculations that could go wherever the facts might lead. The other is literary, bounded by vast authoritative texts that made speculation difficult and deluded Rudolf II and many others into thinking that the old world of humanism and Empire that they knew was not slipping into dissolution. It took more modern men than Goldast, we think, to appreciate Kepler as we do—for example, that English traveler, diplomat, and dilettante Henry Wotton, now remembered for his famous and injudicious remark that an ambassador "is a good man sent to lie abroad for his country." When Wotton met Kepler in Linz in 1620, Kepler showed him a landscape drawing he had executed—"methought," says Wotton, "masterly done." Kepler smiled enigmatically and explained that he had drawn it "non tanquam pictor, sed tanquam mathematicus" [not as a painter but as a scientist]. "This set me on fire," Wotton wrote; and he gave Kepler no peace until he had explained and demonstrated the camera obscura he had devised, which Wotton promptly described in detail to an even more famous and modern correspondent in England: Francis Bacon. With characteristic initiative Wotton invited Kepler to come back to England with him.[4]

Such incidents—and others could be cited—seem to point up the backward and literary character of Imperial culture in those transitional years around 1600, as well as the isolation of an innovator such as Kepler in his German setting, and the peculiarly modern qualities of his mind and interests. We regret that he refused to abandon Linz for London because, as he quaintly explained to M. Bernegger in Strasbourg, a German like Kepler, someone who loved to have a whole continent around him and feared the narrowness and isolation of an island, could not possibly accept the invitation Wotton offered—far less drag along his *uxorcula* and their *grex* of children.[5] In doing so, however, we wrongly accept modern disciplinary divisions as eternal-

ly valid. The twentieth-century historian of literary culture has normally felt justified in leaving on the shelf the stately gray and white
volumes of Kepler's *Gesammelte Werke*, abandoning the historian of
science to decode their highly technical diagrams and tables—and
their highly elaborate Latin—unaided. And historians of science in
their turn have happily ignored such backward fellows as Goldast and
Herwart von Hohenburg, with whom Kepler spent time and exchanged letters, but who had no new data or theses to offer him. The
result, wished for by no one but brought about by many, has been a
distortion in our vision of the past. We have allowed the divergent
forms of scholarship that we now recognize and practice delude us
into reconstructing a past culture as fragmented as our own.

To be sure, the walls between these two separate histories have
begun to crumble in a few strategic spots. Robert Evans's and Thomas
DaCosta Kaufmann's powerful books on the cultural history of the
Habsburg lands have shown that the separation between scientists
and humanists was not nearly so sharp as Kepler's confrontation with
Goldast would suggest. The two men in fact formed part of a larger
but coherent social world, a Prague province of the *respublica litter-
arum*, which included scientists, scholars, brilliant, obsessive paint-
ers, and bold "heaven universal" philosophers among its citizens.
Readers of Raymond Lull and practitioners of artificial memory such
as Wacker and Hans von Nostitz tried simultaneously to explore the
details of the mundane world, to botanize and to observe, and to
enfold the new data they obtained into comprehensive systems as
inclusive as the inherited one of Aristotle but more up to date in their
factual content.[6] Indeed, we know that Goldast, Kepler, Wacker, and
von Nostitz all had lunch together one day in February 1612, though
sadly we do not know what they talked about (Kepler, *Ges. Werke*,
19:350). Friedrich Seck has taught us to appreciate Kepler's devotion to
such literary and humanistic enterprises as the writing of Latin verse;
Kepler, we now know, covered his scrap paper not just with thousands of computations and successive discarded models of planetary
movements, but also with successive drafts of Latin poems. He expressed his distaste for efforts to censor the theories of Copernicus in
a bold epigram:

Ne lasciviret, poterant castrare poetam,
   Testiculis demptis vita superstes erat.
Vae tibi Pythagora, cerebro qui ferris abusus,
   Vitam concedunt, ante sed excerebrant

[They wished to keep the poet away from whores
  So they castrated him, the awful bores.
Thus of his testicles bereft of force
  The poet could live, tormented by remorse.
Poor you, Pythagoras, to feel worse pain,
  The organ you abused was your great brain.
They took your brain out with their surgeon's knife
  And left you what it's wrong to call a life].[7]

Not Martial or John Owen, certainly, but a sincere addition to the treasury of abusive Latin epigrams, which draws its tribute from the fifteenth-century Italian humanist A. Panormita, the sixteenth-century English humanist Sir Thomas More, and the seventeenth-century German humanist Kepler. And to move from high style to high science, Nicholas Jardine recently focused attention on Kepler's efforts to reconstruct the history of mathematics and astronomy in the ancient world. Kepler, he shows, both re-created specific ancient innovations with a lens grinder's meticulous attention to detail and rooted these in their wider social and cultural settings with a historian's bold flair for generalization.[8]

I hope to push these pioneering investigations a little further. We will see that the confrontation I described earlier actually stands out for its idiosyncrasy in Kepler's life and world. The tall volumes of his works reveal his intense and lifelong devotion to the humanist enterprises of eloquence and exegesis. More surprisingly, Kepler's contributions to these fields show so high a level of creativity and learning as to establish him as one of the most distinguished humanist scholars of his time—one whose work demands the attention of humanistic scholars now. Our journey will be a difficult one, through the dusty Faustian studies of scholars grappling with forgotten scholarly disciplines, across rebarbative pages of that macaronic language, half-German and half-Latin in vocabulary, half-Gothic and half-Roman in script, in which the scholars of the old Empire debated. But I hope that we will see enough curious sights and win enough enlightenment to make this strenuous effort worthwhile.

We begin with Kepler himself. He was born in 1571 and educated at Tübingen, where he learned astronomy from an expert Copernican, Michael Maestlin. He engaged in all the standard practices of the late Renaissance arts student. He wrote mannered Latin on the Mannerist themes of physical curiosities and obscure emblems. He describes this phase of his life in the explication that he drew up for his own horoscope, one of the most revealing autobiographical statements by any Renaissance humanist:

> Homo iste hoc fato natus est, ut plerumque rebus difficilibus tempus terat, a quibus alii abhorrent. In pueritia fuit metrorum rationem aggressus ante aetatem. Conatus est scribere Comoedias, Psalmos elegit prolixissimos, quos mandaret memoriae. Grammaticae Crusii omnia exempla ediscere tentavit. In carminibus initio operam dedit ἀϰϱοστείχεσι, Gryphis, Anagrammatismis, postquam hos ex suo merito contemnere potuit convalescente judicio, aggressus est varia et difficilima lyricorum genera. Scripsit melos Pindaricum, scripsit dithyrambica. Materias complexus est insolentes, de Solis quiete, ortu fluminum, atlantis prospectu in nebulas. Aenigmatis delectatus fuit, sales salsissimos quaesivit, Allegoriis ita lusit, ut quae sunt minutissima persequeretur, et crinibus traheret.

> [This man was fated from birth to spend most of his time on difficult things that every one else shies away from. In his boyhood he precociously attacked the problems of metrical composition. He tried to write comedies, and chose the longest psalms to memorize. He tried to learn every example in Crusius's grammar, by heart. In his poems at first he worked on acrostics, riddles, anagrams; when his judgment became more mature and he could esteem these at their own small value he tried various difficult genres of lyric poetry; he wrote a song in Pindaric meter, he wrote dithyrambs. He treated unusual subjects: the sun at rest, the origin of rivers, the view from Atlas over the clouds. He took delight in enigmas, looked for the saltiest jokes, played with allegories in such a way that he followed out every minutest detail and dragged them along by their hair.] (Kepler, *Ges. Werke*, 19:328)

Kepler thus portrayed himself as the normal graduate of the late Renaissance arts course, a lover of obscurity and erudition, of emblems and hieroglyphics, rather like those Altdorf students whose graduation exercises, including long speeches decoding the elaborate medals coined for the occasion, have been brilliantly studied by F. J. Stopp.[9] And he long kept his delight in such pursuits. He never gave up his search for a sufficiently ingenious anagram for his name, even though his efforts included such euphonious and elegant pseudonyms as Kleopas Herennius, alias Phalaris von Nee-sek. And in writing his Pindaric poem on a friend's wedding, following the meters of the first Olympian (ἄριστον μὲν ὕδωρ) line by line, he showed how fully he shared the fascination of such contemporaries as the younger Joachim Camerarius and Erasmus Schmid with Pindar's difficult but dazzling rhetoric and meter.[10]

Kepler, then, was by the 1590s a practicing humanist of the most up-to-date Imperial style. He was also, thanks to Maestlin's influence, a practicing scientist, as the provincial astrologer in Graz, where he published yearly predictions and taught mathematics and astronomy. And after 1596 Kepler became a famous and influential member of the German scientific community, thanks to his first remarkable book, the *Mysterium Cosmographicum*. Here he tried to show that the Copernican world system was not only true in itself but also the key to a still deeper revelation: the very logic of geometrical proportion that had guided the Creator's hand. Kepler proved, so he and many readers thought, that God had used basic principles of geometry in laying out the planetary spheres. These could be shown to be separated by varying distances, in Copernicus's system, which in turn were exactly those that would have separated them if God had taken the five regular Pythagorean solids, arranged them in an aesthetically pleasing order, and interposed the spheres. Since there were five and only five such solids and six and only six planetary spheres, and since the correspondences were very close, Kepler felt certain that he had unlocked the Pythagorean logic that underpinned the process of Creation itself. And though such bold explanations and novel world systems were not uncommon in Kepler's time, the elegance of his geometry and the mastery of planetary theory that supported his philosophical and aesthetic arguments were so palpable that he found receptive readers across Europe. Even Galileo, though not very responsive, doodled some calculations modeled on Kepler's. Tycho Brahe, the great Danish observer of the heavens who was soon to take his vast collection of empirical data about the stars to Rudolf's Prague, was very impressed. Eventually he invited Kepler to join him in Prague, and thus made the astronomical revolution happen.[11]

Kepler must also be considered in terms of his environment—the encyclopedic intellectual world of the early seventeenth-century Empire that has found its sympathetic chronicler in Robert Evans. The old Empire—especially its Bohemian heart—was the *locus classicus* for the powerful agglomerative impulse that motivated so many late Renaissance scholars. Some of the monumental products of that world still inspire awe and attract attention: for example, Athanasius Kircher's impressive volumes on the monuments and hieroglyphs of Egypt, in which, as an eighteenth-century critic said, he labored "thro' half a dozen Folios with Writings of late Greek Platonists, and forged Books of Hermes which contain Philosophy not Egyptian to explain old monuments not Philosophical."[12] He also produced profusely illustrated tomes on other subjects as varied as the route followed by Noah's Ark and the early history of China.[13] His interests—and those of his contemporaries—sprawled across centuries and continents, genres and disciplines with what now seems terrifying abandon. The ability of seventeenth-century scholars to combine scientific and humanistic interests, to use Near Eastern languages as well as Western ones, to move with obvious intellectual comfort from history to law to moral philosophy, is more likely to inspire bewilderment than admiration in the modern reader. True, efforts were made toward the end of the seventeenth century to map this vast and inaccessible intellectual country. Daniel Morhof's *Polyhistor* and its savage parody, Johann Burkhard Mencke's *Orations on the Charlatanry of the Learned*, offer a vivid panoramic introduction to the mental world of the polyhistors. But no modern scholar has retained full control over this dizzying, Baroque plethora of theories and information.[14]

Yet it seems clear that Kepler—student of texts, music, perspective, astronomy, and mathematics; measurer of barrels; and writer of Neo-Latin poems—fits naturally, if not neatly, into this variegated intellectual scene. The comprehensive impulse of the encyclopedists appears in Kepler's desperate, lifelong effort to distill neat geometrical models—or at least neat algebraical formulas—from the apparent chaos of the astronomical data. And the scattershot, omnivorous quality of the polyhistors' interests characterizes many of his major and minor productions. Consider, for example, the tiny book that he dedicated to Wacker in 1611: his *Strena seu de Nive Sexangula*. Here Kepler describes himself as hurrying across the Karlsbrücke in Prague, desolate at his lack of an appropriate New Year's gift for Wacker, when snow begins to fall. Noticing that the drops are all hexagonal, Kepler wonders what secret logic of geometrical form or physical function can account for uniformity in so impermanent a material as snow. Two-dimensional hexagons lead to hexagonal solids, and soon Kepler is off onto a brilliant study of the advantages of hexagonal cells, their ability to be packed together without wasted space and their immense structural stability—both qualities preeminently visible in the beehive. Snow brings Kepler to geometry, geometry to bees, the combination of questions to the world's first essay on what might now be called crystallography and what was in its day a pioneering inquiry about natural processes that result spontaneously in geometrically regular products. All of this is wrapped, moreover, in a fine covering of Latin rhetoric, as Kepler divagates feverishly about the appropriateness of this present, an essay on insignificant snowdrops, to Wacker whom he calls a "lover of nothing"—that is, a reader of the Epicurean atomist Giordano Bruno: "Eia strenam exoptatissimam Nihil amanti, et dignam quam det mathematicus, Nihil habens, Nihil accipiens, quia et de caelo descendit et stellarum gerit similitudinem" [Here was the ideal New Year's gift for the devotee of Nothing, the very thing for a mathematician to give, who has Nothing and receives Nothing, since it comes down from heaven and looks like a star].[15] Kepler's birdlike hopping from subject to subject, his effort to find God's logic in the smallest and most evanescent of His creations, his strenuous efforts to cloak cogent and original argument about structures in the traditional strained conceits of Neo-Latin wit—all these characteristics mark him out as one of that breed of humanist-encyclopedists whose last and noblest representative was Leibniz, and whose brutal parody was Dr. Pangloss.

Yet we can, I think, go still further in teasing out the interrelationships between science and scholarship in Kepler's years in Prague, 1600–1612. In fact, much closer and more profound connections ran between his scholarly and his scientific pursuits than I have yet suggested. By pursuing some of these threads we will find ourselves drawn deep into the dark heart of the culture of the old Empire. As an astronomer, Kepler had to interact with humanists and humanistic studies in three very precise ways. He had to interpret references to celestial phenomena in classical texts. He had to use his astronomical expertise to date events in ancient history. And he had to apply the humanists' methods of exegesis to the classical sources of his own discipline—above all the greatest ancient astronomical work, Ptolemy's *Almagest*, and many collateral sources. In each field his work resulted in triumphant applications of—and remarkable improvements on—the philological *Wissenschaft* of the humanists.

The interpretation of astronomical bits in literary texts had preoccupied philologists since ancient times, and some of the problems Kepler was asked to solve were traditional. In 1599, for example, Maestlin asked Kepler to do a little job for Crusius. The dean had interpreted the encounters of the gods in Homer as favorable and unfavorable conjunctions of the planets named after them, and he wanted Maestlin to work out the technical details. Maestlin in turn claimed to find the suggestion reasonable but urged that it be carried out by an astrologer, not an astronomer—and that Kepler was just the astrologer to do it (Kepler, *Ges. Werke*, 13:330). In this case the basic problem Kepler confronted went back to the Hellenistic origins of literary scholarship. Maestlin cited an ancient commentator on Aratus to the effect that Homer had been an astronomer. And an ancient he did not cite, Heraclitus, recorded—and refuted—the suggestion of an unknown critic that the battle of the gods in *Iliad* 20 and 21 in fact represented a conjunction of all seven planets, of the sort that would occur at the end of the world.[16] Kepler replied by making fun of the whole enterprise. He urged Maestlin to take on the enormous and impractical job of computation:

> Quin tu potius Homerum totum pervolvis, historiae sedem in Chronologia certam assignas, cum etiamnum erret, colloquia singula ad suos dies refers, calculum adhibes, Ephemeridas 20 annorum condis?

> [Why don't you read all of Homer, assign his story the firm chronological place which it still lacks, fix the individual colloquies (of gods) to their calendrical dates, do the computation, and produce Ephemerides for twenty years?] (*Ges. Werke*, 14: 45)

And he promised that if Maestlin did the astronomy, he, Kepler, would happily do the astrologer's proper job of interpreting the planetary positions and predicting their effects. Evidently he was as unconvinced as Heraclitus or Plutarch that Homer had described precise conjunctions, and like them saw no need for elaborate counterarguments. Kepler's attitude was individual enough; in the Baroque Empire most scholars thought Homer a learned authority on everything from history to husbandry.[17] But Kepler's reaction was clearly inspired by—and did not transcend—the mild skepticism of the Greek students of Homer.

In other cases, problems and solutions alike were both more original in conception and far sharper in definition. Johann Herwart von Hohenburg, chancellor of Bavaria and a scholar of great energy—if little judgment—asked Kepler for enlightenment on what he considered a vital source for the early history of the Roman Empire. The text in question was not historical but literary; it formed the end of book 1 of *De bello civili*, Lucan's epic on the Roman civil wars, that vast poem which employs the meter of Vergil and the artistic sensibility of Roger Corman to give the fall of the Republic punch and drama. At the end of book 1, Caesar has crossed the Rubicon and Pompey has left Rome. Terrible omens appear: animals speak, women give birth to creatures monstrous in size and in the number of their limbs, and urns full of the ashes of dead men let forth groans. The Etruscan seer Aruns has a bull killed, but it leaks slimy liquid instead of blood and its flabby liver, streaked and growing a monstrous extra lobe, fills him with horror. Then a more reputable prophet comes on stage: Nigidius Figulus, Pythagorean astrologer and friend of Cicero. He too prophesies doom, but he uses up-to-date Chaldean astrology to do so:

> Extremi multorum tempus in unum
> Convenere dies. Summo si frigida caelo
> Stella nocens nigros Saturni accenderet ignes,
> Deucalioneos fudisset Aquarius imbres,
> Totaque diffuso latuisset in aequore tellus.
> Si saevum radiis Nemeaeum, Phoebe, Leonem
> Nunc premeres, toto fluerent incendia mundo
> Succensusque tuis flagrasset curribus aether.
> Hi cessant ignes. Tu, qui flagrante minacem
> Scorpion incendis cauda chelasque peruris,
> Quid tantum, Gradive, paras? nam mitis in alto
> Iuppiter occasu premitur, Venerisque salubre
> Sidus hebet, motuque celer Cyllenius haeret,
> Et caelum Mars solus habet. Cur signa meatus
> Deseruere suos mundoque obscura feruntur . . . ?

[The lives of multitudes are doomed to end together. If Saturn, that cold, baleful planet were now kindling his black fires in the zenith, then Aquarius would have poured down such rains as Deucalion saw, and the whole earth would have been hidden under the waste of waters. Or if the sun's rays were now passing over the fierce Lion of Nemea, then fire would stream over all the world, and the upper air would be kindled and consumed by the sun's chariot. These heavenly bodies are not active now. But Mars—what dreadful purpose has he, when he kindles the Scorpion menacing with fiery tail and scorches its claws? For the benign star of Jupiter is hidden deep in the West, the healthful planet Venus is dim, and Mercury's swift motion is stayed; Mars alone lords it in heaven. Why have the constellations fled from their courses, to move darkling through the sky?] (Book 1, lines 650–64, tr. J. D. Duff)

Herwart read these lines as a description of the configuration of the skies at a given time. He fixed this on general grounds as between 50 and 38 B.C. But how to gain greater precision? The humanist commentators, Giovanni Sulpizio and Ognibene da Lonigo, applied their normal dull-edged tools. They explained the names of the planets, paying special attention to the title of Mercury, Cyllenius. They named the signs of the zodiac and listed those that enhance the power of each planet. They tabulated the periods in which the planets make their way around the zodiac and found references to these in the text. And then they went on their way rejoicing, not having explained in more than the vaguest, most qualitative way what Lucan—or Nigidius—was actually saying about the position of the planets, or indeed when he said it.[18] Herwart did his best. He took Lucan as placing Saturn in Aquarius, the Sun in Leo, Mars near the end of Libra, and Jupiter in Scorpio. He found that they had indeed been in those positions toward the middle of 39 B.C. and thus could have presaged Augustus's victory in the civil wars. But he could not make sense of the positions of the inferior planets, Venus and Mercury, and turned to Kepler—as he also had to Tycho and Maestlin on similar problems—for help: "Quaeritur itaque cuinam tempori intra annum ante Christum 50. et 38. haec figura caeli, quam Lucanus designat, exacte competat?" [To what date between 50 and 38 B.C. does the celestial configuration that Lucan describes precisely correspond?] (Kepler, *Ges. Werke*, 13:393).

Kepler answered with a meticulous essay. In it he showed the philologist how to do philology:

> Ad enodationem propositae quaestionis, prius atque Calculus adeatur, et frustra in incerto mari duodecim annorum jactetur: considerentur primo omnia verba poetae, quibus constellationem describit. Si Saturnus (ait) esset in summo caeli, hoc est in cancro, quod est signum altissimum, atque ibi accenderet (hoc est conjunctione sua in effectum produceret atque cieret) nigros ignes (id est nebulosas stellas asellos et praesepe) tunc portenderetur diluvium. Dicit autem, fudisset Aquarius imbres, vel quia poeticae servit fictioni, nec aliud signum Zodiaci magis aptum est, quam Aquarius, describendae effusioni aquarum: vel quia Sol in Aquario eclipsin fuit passus, vel quia cum Sol in Aquario est, maxime pluit: De quo ultimo certi quid statuendum. Verum ex hac sequitur descriptione, poetam Saturnum neque in Cancro neque in Aquario reponere. Non in Cancro, quia hoc fingitur a poeta (secundum meam interpretationem), si fuisset in Cancro, pluiturum fuisse. . . . Sed neque in aquarium a poeta reponitur, sic ut dicat Saturnum in Aquario in MC: quia rursum haec a poeta per figuram fictionis proferentur: si Saturnus in Aquario esset: tunc Aquarius plueret. Quibus verbis inest vis negandi.

> [In explanation of the proposed question: Before we try calculations, and let these be tossed about to no avail in this uncertain ocean of twelve whole years, let us first examine the poet's de-

scription of the constellation word by word. If Saturn, he says, "were in the highest sign," that is, in Cancer, and there "kindled"—that is, brought into operation and aroused by his conjunction—"black fires"—that is, the rain-portending stars Aselli and Praesepe—then a flood would be portended. He says, "Aquarius would pour out waters" either for the benefit of his poetic fiction and because Aquarius is the zodiacal sign most appropriate to describing a flood (or because the Sun was eclipsed in Aquarius or because it rains most heavily when the sun is in Aquarius . . .). But it follows from this description that the poet is *not* putting Saturn either in Cancer or Aquarius. For what the poet feigns is—as I interpret it—that if it were in Cancer, there would be rain. . . . But neither is the poet putting it in Aquarius, so as to say that Saturn is in Aquarius, in the Mid-Heaven; for again the poet would be using a fictional figure; if Saturn were in Aquarius, then Aquarius would rain. These words imply negation.] (Kepler, *Ges. Werke*, 13:132–33)[19]

Kepler sees, as Herwart did not, that Lucan's constructions were contrary to fact. Accordingly, they gave positions that the planets did not occupy, not those they did. Moreover, the text as a whole made clear the general date of the prophecy, and here too philology, not astronomy, by itself showed Herwart to be wildly wrong. "Lucanus bellum civile inter Caesarem et Pompeium descripturus a primis orditur initiis, nempe a transito Rubicone, captoque Arimino. . . . Non igitur dubium est, quaerendam hanc constellationem anno ante Christum 49. 50. vel ad summum 51mo" [Setting out to describe the civil war between Pompey and Caesar, Lucan starts at the very beginning, the crossing of the Rubicon and the fall of Ariminum. . . . There is no doubt, then, that this constellation must be sought in 49, 50, or at the earliest 51 B.C.] (*Ges. Werke*, 13:134–35). Kepler then offered a possible solution to the problem Herwart had set him by determining when Mars entered Scorpio and setting out a possible version of Nigidius's horoscope for a date in January 50 B.C.

Herwart was not satisfied. He insisted that Nigidius must have drawn his figure to predict the civil wars of Augustus, not those of Caesar. He insisted that the text did describe Saturn in Aquarius and the Sun in Leo. And he explained the contrary-to-fact character of the description as referring not to the planets' position but to their effects—which would be neither a flood nor a fire, but war. That was what Lucan meant when he said that Mars alone lorded it in heaven (Kepler, *Ges. Werke*, 13:148). But Kepler stuck to his guns. He held that a close reading of Lucan's text revealed that he was offering either a horoscope for 51 B.C. or a purely imaginary one. And he now found the latter explanation likelier. After all, he pointed out, what Nigidius offered was actually a description of astrological theory of a very elementary kind. In each case, he predicted what would happen if the planet were in the zodiacal sign that was its *domus*, where it exerted its greatest influence. "Si Saturnus sit in domo sua, quae est Aquarius, ait diluvium futurum. Si Sol in domo sua, scilicet in Leone, incendium; si Mars in domo sua, scilicet in Scorpione, bellum" [If Saturn is in its house, which is Aquarius, he says there will be a flood. If the Sun is in its house, Leo, there will be a fire. If Mars is in its house, Scorpio, there will be war] (Kepler, *Ges. Werke*, 13:158). This was no description of the heavens but a set of elementary astrological doctrines, cobbled together from a manual without understanding. Competent astrologers know that no single planet produces overwhelming effects on its own. What bring about floods and fires and wars are conjunctions, oppositions, and other meaningful configurations of two or more planets at once, not the appearance of one planet in one place. And in any event planets had their benevolent and malevolent effects when in various signs, not only their own *domus*. Kepler's conclusion was lapidary: "Sed tyronem aliter loqui non decet" [This is the only appropriate way for a tyro to speak) (*Ges. Werke*, 13:158). Accordingly, his "facies Caeli," his configuration of the stars, was not to be sought for in the heavens or in human time.

Herwart did not drop his bad counterarguments. Indeed, two years later Kepler complained that Herwart still exhausted him with his continued inquiries. But he held firmly that Nigidius's horoscope of the Roman civil wars was as imaginary as the horoscopes of Plato, Paris, and other ancient heroes contained in the ancient astrological manual of Firmicus Maternus (Kepler, *Ges. Werke*, 14:46). For our purposes, what matters is first of all that Kepler was right. Twentieth-century commentators confirm his interpretation of Lucan's dramatic date for the horoscope, his contrary-to-fact reading of Lucan's verses on Saturn and the Sun, and his conclusion that the horoscope was imaginary and Lucan incompetent.[20] What matters even more is the way Kepler reached his conclusions. He did so, as he rightly said, not by computing expertly but by reading carefully, by sticking *mordicus* (with his teeth) to the words of his text. He practiced not astronomy here, but hermeneutics, and he did so so expertly as to prove himself the master of both cultures—or else, perhaps, to prove their basic unity. Kepler's works are strewn with less extensive but equally provocative discussions of ancient texts; it seems not only a pity but an injustice that they have not earned him a place in modern histories of classical scholarship.

Even more powerful are the interventions that Kepler made in another area of study where philology and science intersected. Technical chronology deals with the basis of ancient and modern calendars and the dating of ancient and modern events. It offers, especially for ancient history, the hard spine and skeleton of dates to which ordinary historians affix the analytical muscle and narrative skins of their accounts. Though now forgotten, it enjoyed immense prestige in sixteenth- and seventeenth-century Europe.[21] When someone confronted Philipp Melanchthon in hall at Wittenberg with the claim that formal study of chronology was superfluous, since the peasants on his estate could locate summer and winter without it, Melanchthon replied with open contempt: "Illa profecto non est doctoralis responsio. Ey das ist ein schöner doctor, ein grober narr, man solt im ein dreck ins paret scheissen vnd vffsetzen."[22] Everyone knew that chronology was essential to classical and biblical studies. And it required at every turn the active collaboration of the astronomer. Only the astronomer could date the eclipses and other celestial phenomena that provide absolute dates for past events. Kepler would not have agreed with his acquaintance Helisaeus Röslin that chronology was "ultimus finis astronomiae"— far less with Röslin's belief that he himself had, thanks to divine aid, made such progress "in sacro et prophano calculo mit Hülff Astronomici calculi . . . das mir nit ein scrupulus pleiben soll" (Kepler, *Ges. Werke*, 14:45). But Kepler studied chronology from early on in his academic career: "In historiis hebdomadas Danielis aliter explicavit. Novam Assyriacae monarchiae historiam scripsit, Calendarium Romanum investigavit" [In history he gave a different explication of Daniel's weeks. He wrote a new history of the Assyrian monarchy; he studied the Roman calendar]—so runs his horoscope of 1597 (*Ges. Werke*, 19:329). On Maestlin's recommendation he read Joseph Scaliger's *De emendatione temporum* as soon as it became available in the pirated Frankfurt edition of 1593—though, as he confessed in a sentence that he wisely deleted from his draft of a letter to Scaliger, the difficulty and idiosyncrasy of the first book made him so sleepy that he found it impossible to work through the text as a whole.

Kepler and his teacher corresponded as eagerly about chronological as about astronomical matters. It is engaging to hear Kepler confess that he and Maestlin had often spent days, and even weeks, worrying about the chronology of *Judges*. And it is instructive to watch Maestlin instruct Kepler about a major chronological problem: the eclipse that supposedly heralded Xerxes' crossing into Greece in 01. 75, 1 (480–79 B.C.):

> Ipsius [Xerxis] transitus in Graeciam fuit Anno. 1. Olymp. 75. Oportebat ergo eclipsin fuisse anno. 4. Olymp. 74. in vere, qui est annus 268. Nabonn. et 480. labens, ante Christum natum. Sed nulla tum fuit eclipsis. Quae anno 3. Olymp. 74. fuit ridiculum est, quod a nonnullis illa putatur, cum Sol 1. digito tantum defecerit, quem defectum miles in ordine militari nequaquam sentire potuit. Anno sane 2. Olymp. 75. Nabonn. 270 defecit Sol fere 10. digitis.

> [The eclipse must have taken place in 01. 74, 4 in the spring, in the year 268 of Nabonassar = 480 B.C. But there was no eclipse then. The notion that some have that it was the eclipse of 01. 74, 3 is absurd. The sun was eclipsed for only one digit; a soldier in a military formation couldn't even have noticed it. In 01. 75, 2 = Nabonassar 270 there was a solar eclipse of some 10 digits.] (Kepler, *Ges. Werke*, 13:127)

And this, Maestlin argues, must have been confused by historians with a prodigy that actually preceded Xerxes' expedition. This last thesis is perhaps fanciful. But the rest of Maestlin's comment shows that he could have given lessons to many of the modern scholars who still try to deal with the same data.[23] No doubt Kepler owed him much.

By his Prague years, however, Kepler had gone beyond his teacher. In a splendid letter to Scaliger, the monarch of the discipline, Kepler emended central tenets of the *De emendatione temporum*. Scaliger had laid great stress on Herodotus's report (1.32) of a conversation between Solon and Croesus, in which the gloomy Solon proved that a man had many chances of suffering ill fortune, given a life span of seventy years with 360 days per normal year (or 25,200 days—or, counting every other year as an embolismic one of 390 days, 26,250 days). Scaliger had used the passage in his own reconstruction of a nonlunar Greek calendar and then accused Herodotus of inventing a nonexistent calendar.[24] Kepler's response was devastatingly insightful: "Nec hic initur calculus aliquis dierum subtilior, sed summaria ratione rhetoricatur coram Croeso Solon, quam facile fieri possit, ut in tanto dierum numero unus aliquis ater sit" [No precise computation of days is undertaken here; Solon is using rounded numbers to show Croesus how easy it is, given this great sum of days, for one of them to be unfortunate] (*Ges. Werke*, 15:208). And yet this passage may have stung less than a later one. Scaliger had cited, among other texts that seemed to support the existence of a nonlunar calendar, Plutarch's *Camillus* 19.5. This seemed to set the battle of Naxos on the fifth day before the end of Boedromion *at full moon* (which, naturally, should fall at the middle, not near the end, of a lunar month).[25] Kepler simply advised Scaliger, "Velim tamen in emendato Plutarchi contextu requiras" [Please look the passage up in a correct text of Plutarch] (*Ges. Werke*, 15:209); for as he saw, and Scaliger failed to, Scaliger's theory rested solely on two independent clauses wrongly conflated in the Aldine edition of Plutarch. For want of a comma Scaliger had committed himself to a wrong thesis. Kepler thus triumphantly anticipated Dionysius Petavius's full-scale attack on Scaliger a few years later. To be sure, Kepler's positive efforts were less successful than his critical ones; he shared with Scaliger the erroneous belief that Attic months in Plutarch were not strictly lunar.

Though quantitative and technical enough for most of us, however, the chronology practiced in Habsburg Imperial circles was anything but a simply empirical or technical discipline. The Habsburgs liked universal claims and programs (for example, the claim to domination of the natural world advanced by the painter Arcimboldo in his famous portrait of Rudolf II as Vertumnus, Roman god of the changing year, where the vegetable ingredients of Rudolf's face powerfully express the analogy between divine rule of the cosmos and Habsburg rule of the Empire).[26] The chronologers they patronized had to devise original and impressive general theses like the staggeringly novel one advanced by Wolfgang Lazius in the 1550s. He argued that inscriptions in Hebrew found in Gumpendorf, outside Vienna, proved that the Austrians were directly descended from the Jews who settled Europe after the Flood.[27]

Chronologers also had to impose neat patterns on events, showing that these lined up in numerically elegant ways, were closely connected to celestial and other omens, and pointed explicitly toward Imperial hegemony in general and Habsburg power in particular. Thus the Austrian Freiherr Michael von Aitzing—later to win fame as the first author of political newsletters or *Zeitungen*—made his *Pentaplus regnorum mundi* (1579), which he dedicated to Rudolf, a key not only to the dating of events but to their inner providential logic.[28] His fabulously profuse and detailed tables illustrate both the variety of the causal systems he invoked and the inventiveness with which he fused them into a whole. One of them listed the so-called great conjunctions of Jupiter and Saturn that occurred at twenty-year intervals through all of history, providing the celestial omens that occurred most regularly. Another by contrast divided history up into the reigns of seven angels, each in charge for 792 years, the first five before Christ and the sixth and seventh after Him; these in turn are divided into twelve subsections corresponding to the signs of the zodiac, twenty-four subsections corresponding to the hours of the day, forty-two corresponding to the places where the Jews stopped between Egypt and Palestine, and so on.

The last conjunction falls in 1583, and the last angel runs out in 1584; all this to show that history will soon play the starring role in a crowd-pleasing death scene. Meanwhile, and for good measure, a splendid emblematic illustration (fig. 1) summed up the most important lesson of all. The letters above the two columns headed by the sun and moon are the initials of the biblical patriarchs from Adam to Noah; these, when rearranged by von Aitzing's instructions—and when Noah's name is given in its alternative Greek form, Ianus—spell out the name of Rudolf's father Maximilian. Meanwhile four beasts—the traditional ones of the Book of Daniel—represent the four Empires, the last of which is the Holy Roman Empire represented by the Habsburg double eagle. Here was a powerful skeleton key to history itself, and the door thus opened revealed the Habsburg monarchy at the very heart of things. Many others tried to forge and apply similar keys. Indeed, doing so was part of Kepler's job. His predecessor as Imperial Mathematician, Nicolaus R. Ursus, had written, supposedly in 1596, a work that conflated chronology with eschatology to show that the world would end "innerhalb 77 Jaren."[29] Kepler, accordingly, had to comment when, as in 1603, a particularly vivid great conjunction took place—especially as this one was followed by the appearance of a nova, a brilliant new star that seemed to portend some special change in human affairs.

Kepler did not drag chronology off the traditional rails, as he did astronomy. He took great interest in the old doctrine of the great conjunctions, compiling his own table of the correspondence between the beginning of the great conjunction cycle every 800 years and major changes in events. It runs from the first great conjunction, that of Adam in 4000 B.C., to that of 1603, which portended something for Rudolf, and as Kepler said, for "Vita, fata, et vota nostra" [Our life, our fate, and our prayers]. A final line pointed out that in A.D. 2400 still another cycle would begin. Kepler commented: "Ubi tunc nos, et modo florentissima nostra Germania? Et quinam successores nostri? an et memores nostri erunt? Siquidem mundus duraverit" [Where will we be then, and our Germany which is so prosperous now? And who

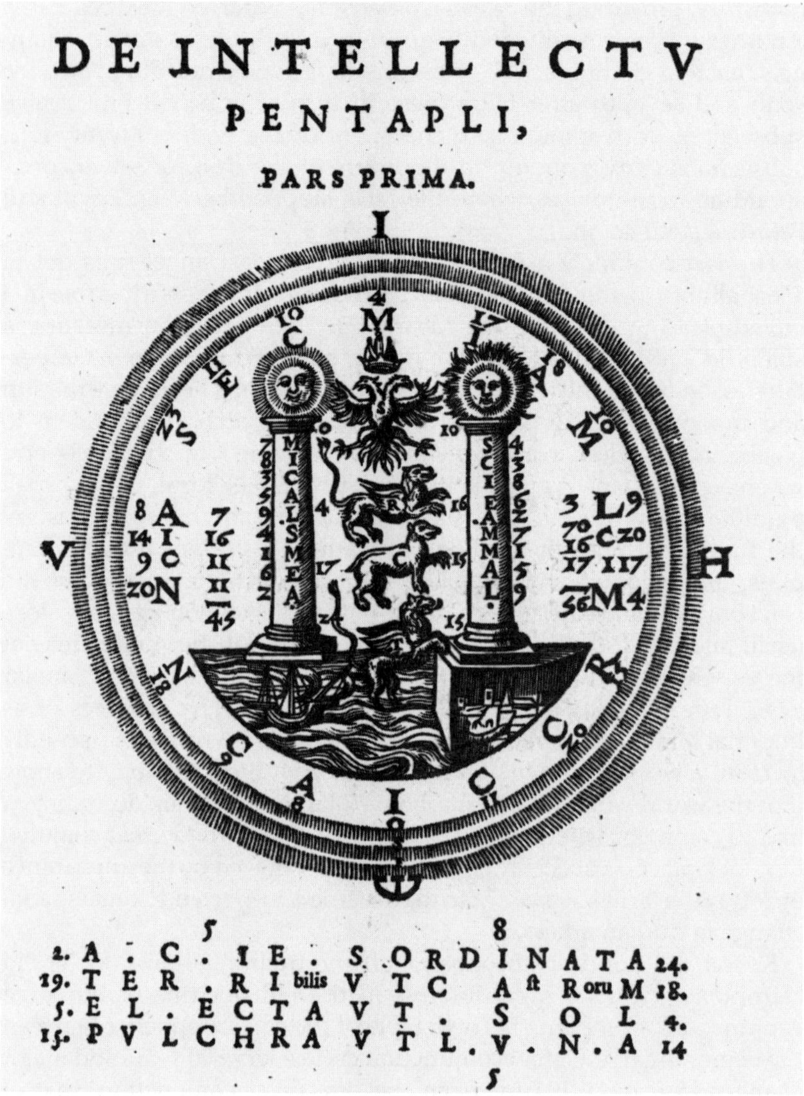

Fig. 1. *World History in Emblematic Form. From Michael von Aitzing,* Pentaplus regnorum mundi *(Antwerp: Plantin, 1579). (Rare Book and Manuscript Division, Princeton University Library)*

will come after us? And will they remember us? If the world lasts so long] (*Ges. Werke* 1:183). So far there was nothing novel in Kepler's sensibility or method, even if he did insist that he loved the next series of great conjunctions largely for the prosaic reason that it served as such a splendid mnemonic device for historical dates.

In other respects, however, Kepler's approach to chronology was as novel and elegant as his approach to Lucan. He argued, in the first place, that the great conjunctions were a useful tool for finding order in the past but not a valid guide to the immediate or distant future. The only prediction he felt able to make on the basis of the new star was that it portended "den Buchdruckhern grosse unrhu und zimlichen gewin darbey," since every theologian, philosopher, doctor, and mathematician in Germany would write about it (*Ges. Werke*, 1:398). He argued again and again that only God knew the date of the end of the world, and urged chronologers to study only the past. He thus separated the discipline's two traditionally related functions and deprived one of value or interest.

In the second place, and more striking still, Kepler used even the traditional doctrine of the great conjunctions in a novel way. Most chronologers packaged history neatly. They ignored structural differences between people and events in order to make recurrent celestial events line up as neatly as possibly with similar earthly ones. Chronology was for them not a means of discovering new facts or connections but a way of imposing an order on facts already known. And it constantly threatened to degenerate into a mindless, repetitive series of lists of names and numbers signifying nothing.

Kepler by contrast applied the theory of the great conjunctions heuristically rather than rhetorically. Did the conjunction of 1603 and the nova of 1604 portend a specially radical change? He was not sure. And so he examined other great conjunctions of the last two centuries. He argued that more prominent conjunctions than that of 1603 had occurred in the sixteenth century. He also argued that these had cumulatively had a special effect, one visible from the historical record. They had stirred up people's minds in uniquely powerful ways. Above all the invention of printing had transformed the intellectual world, creating a new community of scholars not confined to monastic orders:

> Typographia nata vulgati libri; hinc universi passim per Europam ad literarum studia se contulerunt: hinc natae tot Academiae; tot subito docti viri extiterunt; ut brevi caderet eorum, qui barbariem retinebant, authoritas

[After the birth of printing, books became widespread. Hence everyone throughout Europe devoted himself to the study of letters. Hence many universities came into existence, and at once so many learned men appeared that the authority of those who clung to barbarism soon declined.] (*Ges. Werke*, 1:330)[30]

Kepler connected this rise of a new "public domain of knowledge" with the discovery of the new world, the growth of rapid means for communicating goods and knowledge, and the development of modern techniques in every area from warfare to textual criticism.[31] And he explicitly contrasted the limited achievements of the ancients with the greater ones of the moderns: "Quid habet simile propior antiquitas hodiernae scientiae rei militaris?" [What did they have in antiquity that resembled present-day knowledge in the art of war?] (*Ges. Werke*, 1:331). The great conjunction and nova could not portend any very radical change, for the world had already been radically transformed by the cooperative interactions of the stars and human beings for the last century and a half.

Kepler never abandoned his belief that the configurations of the stars provided a constant and vital thread in the tapestry of the past; he redated Christ's birth to a few years before the outset of the Christian era in part because he could thereby bring it nearer to a great conjunction that might have been related to the Star of the Magi.[32] But he used this traditional doctrine in a novel way: to show that society and culture changed by accretion and development, not by a sudden seismic shifts engendered from on high. And he developed a penetrating insight into the fabric of society as well as into the movements of the stars. True, he was by no means the first humanist to venture such analyses of the reasons for rapid cultural progress or decline. Lorenzo Valla, more than a century before, had attributed the simultaneous flourishing of art, architecture, sculpture, and literature in ancient Rome to the existence of a common language, classical Latin, which had enabled people to communicate, to learn from and compete with one another, and therefore to devise powerful new inventions and try to surpass those of their rivals.[33] Although the two men differed on important points, Valla giving supreme explanatory power to language and Kepler to printing, they agreed on a crucial one: both invoked a medium of communication as a central factor in cultural change. Humanists, in short, thought deeply about the problems of historical explanation.

Chronologers, however, had always stuck to the skeleton of events rather than their meat and skin; they had always seen stars (and angels) as the decisive factors, and human beings and society as largely passive. Yet Kepler the chronologer cut the role of stars to mere stimulation. He constantly adjusted the celestial history of conjunctions to fit a messy human history that he studied field by field and decade by decade. And he thus raised chronology to the level of a powerful tool for studying social and cultural processes, one capable of using and enriching the maturest historical ideas of the humanists instead of ignoring these in favor of neat numbers.

Kepler's third transformation of the study of the past lay in his own special discipline of astronomy. Renaissance astronomers had always had to confront the work of their classic predecessors: the preserved work of Ptolemy, the *Almagest;* the lost works of Hipparchus that Ptolemy had used and quoted; and the large corpus of ancient anecdotes and shorter texts about astronomers. They used these materials as their primary sources of data, models, and techniques. And they also used them as something more: as the classical foundation, or pedigree, that gave astronomy legitimacy and dignity in their own time. But the very need for legitimacy that made astronomers study their ancient predecessors also made them depart from objective truth in their interpretations. After all, a substantial body of ancient anecdotage treated astronomy as the oldest and purest of the sciences—developed by Jewish patriarchs, virtuous Near Eastern priests, and Gallic Druids; preserved during the Flood by being engraved on stone tablets; gradually lost in later, less pure times by Greeks and Romans.[34]

When a late Renaissance scholar wrote the history of astronomy—as Henry Savile did in 1570, preparing for his Oxford lectures on Ptolemy—he tended to insist that the primeval astronomy of the patriarchs had been both simpler and more accurate than the developed astronomy of Ptolemy. He divagated at length about the astronomical achievements of such dubious luminaries in the field as Enoch, Seth, and Hermes Trismegistus, which could be reconstructed with great confidence primarily because not a scrap of evidence about them survived. And he described the purpose of astronomy in his own time as being to recover the lost wisdom of pre-Socratics, patriarchs, and other sages.[35] Such views were widely shared and long persisted; Newton himself was inspired by them to form his own unhistorical view of the history of astronomy, according to which Chiron the Centaur, no less, laid out the first constellations on a sphere for the use of the Argonauts.[36]

Kepler himself took a very different view. From early in his career he devoted attention to the ancient astronomers. Just arrived in Prague, he spent time unwillingly on what he considered a philological, not a mathematical, task: showing that his predecessor Ursus had misrepresented the history of ancient astronomy to claim that Tycho had derived his compromise system of the universe, in which the planets revolved about the Sun, and the Sun in turn about a stationary Earth, from classical sources. Already in his *Apologia* against Ursus, Kepler insisted on the primitive conditions in which the ancients had worked. In the teeth of a tradition that arranged all ancient sages genealogically into schools, Kepler pointed out that ancient astronomy had not really had an institutional base and that its chief developments came about through the discontinuous efforts of a few individuals.[37]

After leaving Prague, in the great *Tabulae Rudolphinae* of planetary motion that he compiled from Tycho's data, Kepler went much further. He began the work with a history of astronomy, and astronomical tables in particular, in which Seth, Enoch, and other early sages played no part. The first real developments he could trace fell in the third century B.C., when the Greeks gained access, under the Seleucid kings of Babylon, to a not very old corpus of Babylonian observations. Hipparchus, in the second century B.C., offered the first adumbrations of tables of the motions of the planets, which made rough predictions of their future positions possible; and Ptolemy, some three hundred years later, perfected the exact science of sciences and offered the world its first full tables. Other sections traced the later and even more sophisticated work of Alfonso of Castile, Johannes Regiomontanus, and Erasmus Reinhold. The message of the whole was clearly that astronomy had grown, by uneven increments, from primitive beginnings in the ancient world to modern perfection (Kepler, *Ges. Werke*, 10:36–41). And Kepler gave this thesis pictorial and poetic as well as technical and prosaic form. The title page of the Tables (fig. 2) represents an "Astro-poecilo-purgium," a "variegated-star-tower," or temple of astronomy. Here architectural orders drive home historical lessons. The Chaldean sage appears in the very back, sighting through his fingers at the stars and standing by a rough wood column, almost still a tree. Aratus and Hipparchus on the left, Meton and Ptolemy on the right, the heroes of Greek astronomy, have their names attached to plain brick columns. But the heroes of modern times, Copernicus and Tycho, dominate the foreground, and they receive the compliment of classical ornament. Copernicus sits by an Ionic column. Tycho, who is arguing with Copernicus—he points upward to the diagram of his own system on the roof and asks "Quid si sic?" [What if it's this way?]—has the most glamorous column of them all, a fine Corinthian creation. Thus modern culture is revealed

Fig. 2. The "Astro-poecilo-purgium." From Johann Kepler, Tabulae Rudolphinae *(Ulm: Saurius, 1627). (Rare Book and Manuscript Division, Princeton University Library)*

as older—that is, more experienced and sophisticated—than that of the so-called ancients, which was ignorant and primitive. And just in case any readers failed in their duty to decode this rich historical emblem, Kepler had the Ulm *Gymnasialrektor* Johann Baptist Hebenstreit provide a pedestrian *Idyllion* to explicate it, imaginary brick by brick.

In advancing this thesis, Kepler made his own a modern and perceptive view of the history of ancient astronomy. It was not entirely his own invention, to be sure. He owed parts of it at least to Giovanni Pico della Mirandola, whose *Disputationes contra astrologiam divinatricem* of a century before provoked and fascinated Kepler as did few other modern texts. Pico had incorporated similar arguments, likewise based on direct study of the sources, into books 11 and 12 of his great work. He had argued there, as Kepler would, that astronomy and astrology had no very ancient pedigree, and that the ancients' boasts of possessing records of observations stretching back for hundreds of thousands of years were not borne out by the facts: "Hipparcus et Ptolemaeus principes astronomiae, ubi pro dogmate statuendo veterum observationes afferunt, nullas afferunt ipsi vetustiores his quae sub rege Nabuchodonosor apud Aegyptios Babyloniosve fuere, post cuius regnum sexcentesimo fere anno floruit Hipparcus" [When the founders of astronomy, Hipparchus and Ptolemy, produce the ancients' observations in order to lay the foundations of their own doctrines, they cite none older than those made under Nabuchodonosor (Nabonassar) in Egypt or Babylon. Hipparchus flourished around the six-hundredth year after his reign].[38] Pico, like Kepler, located the beginning of mathematical astronomy near Nabonassar's accession in 747 B.C., and its perfection in the time of Hipparchus. He thus adumbrated Kepler's polemical history, and to the same end of puncturing the pretensions of astrologers and believers in the *prisca theologia*. And Kepler actually cited Pico's book in a letter in which he sketched a genealogy of ancient astronomy, though in a different context (Kepler, *Ges. Werke*, 14:285).

For all Kepler's traditional interests and beliefs, in following and developing Pico's ideas he challenged one of the deepest convictions of late Renaissance intellectuals in general and his Prague friends Wacker and von Nostitz in particular. They saw truth as residing in a primeval revelation, handed down in its purest form by God at the outset of human history and degraded ever since by contact with mere humans.[39] Pico and Kepler saw truth as the product of human effort, untidy and inconsistent, but gradually able to reach perfection over time. Kepler's *Tabulae Rudolphinae*, the last and most technical product of his Prague years, not only replaced ancient astronomy but also attacked ancient myths about the nature and origins of human culture.

The case of Kepler, then, offers by itself enough dynamite to explode any notion that the scientific and the literary cultures of the Empire existed in isolation from one another. The scientist could not perform the scientific function without being enough of a scholar to decode the classical texts that still contained the richest sets of data. The scholar could not read poems without having recourse to scientific concepts and methods. And in some of the most fashionable and attractive studies—such as astronomy and chronology—scholarship and science were necessarily fused into a single pursuit not identifiable with any modern discipline. Both cultures, in other words, formed parts of the same vast Mannerist garden, and a single wind could send pollen from each side to fertilize the other. Like a German court garden of the time—like those of Heidelberg, soon to be destroyed—they make a lurid, variegated, and alien spectacle to the modern onlooker. And yet, if we limit our explorations to the familiar we fail to understand the principles of order and the connecting links of method that bound science to scholarship and mathematics to letters in this singularly fascinating lost intellectual world.

Notes

1. J. Kepler, *Gesammelte Werke*, 20 vols., ed. Walther von Dyck, Max Caspar, and Fritz Hammer (Munich: Beck, 1937–88), 19:350. Further references to this edition are cited in the text.

2. R. J. W. Evans, *Rudolf II and His World: A Study in Intellectual History 1576–1612* (Oxford: Clarendon, 1973), p. 156.

3. On Goldast see B. Hertenstein, *Joachim von Watt (Vadianus), Bartholomäus Schöbinger, Melchior Goldast* (Berlin: de Gruyter, 1975), pp. 115–35.

4. L. P. Smith, *Life and Letters of Sir Henry Wotton*, 2 vols. (Oxford: Clarendon, 1907), 2:205–6.

5. Ibid., 2:205 n. 4.

6. Evans, *Rudolf II and His World*; Thomas DaCosta Kaufmann, *L'Ecole de Prague* (Paris: Flammarion, 1985). See also N. Mout, *Bohemen en de Nederlanden in de zestiende eeuw* (Leiden: Universitaire Pers, 1975).

7. F. Seck, "Johannes Kepler als Dichter," *Internationales Kepler-Symposium Weil der Stadt 1971*, ed. F. Krafft et al. (Hildesheim: Gerstenberg, 1973), pp. 427–50.

8. N. Jardine, *The Birth of History and Philosophy of Science* (Cambridge: Cambridge University Press, 1984).

9. F. J. Stopp, *The Emblems of the Altdorf Academy* (London: Modern Humanities Research Association, 1974).

10. See Seck, "Johannes Kepler als Dichter," for an exemplary treatment of these aspects of Kepler's writing.

11. Earlier technical treatments of Kepler's work are listed in the bibliography to B. Stephenson's elegant analysis of *Kepler's Physical Astronomy* (New York: Springer, 1987), pp. 206–8, which supersedes most of them. Much biographical detail can be found in the late E. Rosen's characteristically learned and cranky *Three Imperial Mathematicians* (New York: Abaris, 1986).

12. William Warburton, quoted by E. Iversen, *Obelisks in Exile*, vol. 1: *The Obelisks of Rome* (Copenhagen: Gad, 1968), p. 92.

13. See D. C. Allen, *The Legend of Noah* (Urbana: University of Illinois Press, 1949).

14. A. Grafton, "The World of the Polyhistors: Humanism and Encyclopedism," *CEH* 18 (1985): 31–47.

15. J. Kepler, *The Six-Cornered Snowflake*, ed. and tr. C. Hardie (Oxford: Clarendon, 1966), pp. 6–7. For Wacker and Bruno, see Evans, *Rudolf II and His World*, p. 232.

16. Heraclitus, *Problemata Homerica* 53; cf. Plutarch, *De audiendis poetis* 19E.

17. See in general the excellent survey of Th. Bleicher, *Homer in der deutschen Literatur (1450–1740)* (Stuttgart: Metzler, 1972). For Crusius's own views see *Diarium Martini Crusii 1598–1599*, ed. W. Göz and E. Conrad (Tübingen: Laupp, 1931), pp. 201–2, where he says that in his commentary "Posui ubique doctrinas Ethicas, Oeconomicas, Politicas, Physicas, etc. . . . Ex his commentariis demum intelligeretur: quantus sit Poëta Homerus, quantâ sapientia."

18. *Anneus Lucanus cum duobus commentis Omniboni et Sulpitii* (Venice: B. de Zanis de Portesio, 1505), fols. 23–24.

19. For a brief discussion of Kepler's views on Nigidius and Lucan see F. Boll, *Sphaera* (Leipzig: Teubner, 1903), p. 362 n. 1.

20. *M. Annaei Lucani Belli civilis libri decem*, ed. A. E. Housman (Oxford: Blackwell, 1950), "Astronomical Appendix," pp. 325–37; R. J. Getty, "The Astrology of P. Nigidius Figulus (Lucan I, 649–65)," *Classical Quarterly* 35 (1941): 17–22.

21. See in general D. J. Wilcox, *The Measure of Times Past* (Chicago: University of Chicago Press, 1987); A. T. Grafton, "From *De die natali* to *De emendatione temporum:* The Origins and Setting of Scaliger's Chronology," *JWCI* 48 (1985): 100–143.

22. *Melanchthoniana Paedagogica*, ed. K. Hartfelder (Leipzig: B. G. Teubner, 1892), p. 182.

23. P. Crusius had already pointed out that Xerxes' crossing into Greece in 480 B.C. could not have been accompanied by a solar eclipse; see his *Liber de epochis seu aeris temporum et imperiorum.* ed. I. Th. Freigius (Basel: S. Henricpetri, 1578), p. 57: "Non convenit synchronismus. Nam eclipsis illa [of 481 B.C.] toto anno praecessit expeditionem seu traiectum Xerxis in Europam."

This did not stop Joseph Scaliger from redating the crossing to Ol. 74, 3, on the basis of the synchronism between it and a solar eclipse attested by Herodotus. He concluded: "Beavit tamen nos Herodotus, qui characterem apposuit, ex quo illum annum dignosceremus" (*Opus novum de emendatione temporum* [Paris: Patisson, 1583], pp. 222–23).

24. Scaliger, *Opus*,15;47.

25. Ibid., p. 15.

26. See Kaufmann, *L'Ecole de Prague*, p. 217.

27. W. Lazius, *De aliquot gentium migrationibus . . . libri xii* (Basel: Oporinus, 1572), p. 23.

28. M. von Aitzing, *Pentaplus regnorum mundi* (Antwerp: Plantin, 1579); see G. N. Clark, *War and Society in the Seventeenth Century* (Cambridge: Cambridge University Press, 1958), pp. 134–40.

29. Evans, *Rudolf II and His World*, p. 280 n. 4.

30. I borrow the translation of Jardine, *Birth of History and Philosophy of Science*, p. 277; his discussion of the passage is excellent.

31. Ibid., p. 279.

32. See M. Caspar's comments in Kepler, *Ges. Werke*, 1:445; 462–64.

33. For the texts and a splendid analysis see M. Baxandall, *Giotto and the Orators* (Oxford: Clarendon, 1971).

34. See in general Jardine, *Birth of History and Philosophy of Science*, ch. 8; A. Grafton, *Joseph Scaliger*, 1 vol. to date. (Oxford: Clarendon, 1983–), 1: ch. 7.

35. Savile's *Prooemium mathematicum* is preserved in Oxford, Bodleian Library, MS Savile 29; a specimen is edited, with its chief sources, in Grafton, "From *De die natali*," pp. 138–40.

36. F. E. Manuel, *Isaac Newton, Historian* (Cambridge: Harvard University Press, 1963).

37. Jardine, *Birth of History and Philosophy of Science*, pp. 116–17; 181; 276–77.

38. G. Pico della Mirandola, *Opera Omnia* (Basel: Officina Henricpetrina, 1572), p. 715.

39. See for example M. Croll's genealogy of knowledge, discussed in O. Hannaway, *The Chemists and the Word* (Baltimore: Johns Hopkins University Press, 1975), pp. 18–20; 51. Andreas L. Libavius's critique of the Hermetic tradition, discussed on pp. 78 and 98–105, offers an interesting parallel to Kepler.

Part II. Imitation or Innovation: Early Modern German Literature and Europe

3. German Baroque Drama and Seventeenth-Century European Theater

Peter Skrine

As the seventeenth century drew to a close, John Dennis, the Augustan dramatist and critic, became involved in public debate on the subject of dramatic poetry. Championing it against the charge of immorality and profanity in his aptly entitled treatise *The Usefulness of the State, to the Happiness of Mankind, to Government, and to Religion* (1698), he produced what amounts to a pre-echo of Schiller's *Die Schaubühne als moralische Anstalt betrachtet* (1784/1802); in the course of it passing mention is made of Germany. Dennis wonders whether there can be any correlation between the stage and the general corruption of manners, that is, the low standard of public and private conduct, as some would claim. In Germany, he says, and in Italy too, the theaters are less frequented than in France or England: "For in *Italy* they seldom have Plays, unless in the Carnival; and in most of the little *German* Sovereignties, they have not constant Theatres. And yet in *Germany* they drink more." Manifestly, he says, it would be unthinkable "to derive the Brutality of the *High-Dutch* Drinking, from the Prophaneness of our *English* drama."[1] The remark is a curious one; what does Dennis mean? There is no reason to suppose that he was as well informed about seventeenth-century Germany as we are, and it is very doubtful that he knew anything about the antics of the *Englische Komödianten*. Yet his two interrelated references to conditions in Germany are not without relevance as we set about the task of surveying dramatic activity there to discover where it stands in relation to the practices and achievements of other countries.[2]

When Dennis was composing his most interesting and admired aesthetic study, the ablest, most productive, and arguably most neglected German playwright of the period was at the height of his powers. For Christian Weise's powers were considerable; he possessed imagination (though he would not have used the word, preferring to call the quality that I have in mind invention) as well as the technical know-how that nondramatic authors lack. The particular quality of Weise's dramatic writing may be shown by focusing on a specific episode in *Der Fall des Frantzösischen Marschalls von Biron* (1693).[3] Biron, the protagonist, has overreached himself; his swelling self-esteem, indeed his good fortune, forces his king, Henry IV of France, to take the decision to order his arrest. But what then? We have almost reached the end of the third act as Henry, torn between his impulse to display clemency and his obligation to be just, muses on his dilemma in soliloquy: "Wie schwer wird es einem Könige / der seine Gnade mittheilen wolte / gleichwohl aber sich benöthiget befindet die strenge Gerechtigkeit zu ergreiffen." If only Biron could have met the king halfway; but no, his stubbornness prevented him: "Doch das Unglück / das über ihn beschlossen ist / macht ihn hartnäckicht / daß er auch wider unsern Willen seinen Untergang suchen muß." There are pointers here to a conception of tragedy more akin to that of Heinrich von Kleist in *Prinz Friedrich von Homburg*. But such pre-echoes tell us little. Of much more immediate interest and significance is what Weise now chooses to do with his play, for this is the measure of his ability. As the king's soliloquy dies away to the ominous words just quoted, the scene opens (i.e., "Die mittelste Scene zeucht sich auff,") to reveal his queen, Marie de Médicis, sitting at a table: "Biron steht davor / ein Page mischt die Karten / sie spielen." The scene is intimate, but its familiarity is charged with terror, for as they play, "der König sieht eine Weile zu." The drama here is all in the grouping; the game of cards, deliberate and calculating, yet a game of chance and thus unpredictable; the watching king, alone in the knowledge that Biron's freedom, indeed his life, is measured in rapidly decreasing moments. Then, only then, is the silence broken as Henry casually inquires: "Herr Marschall / was haben sie vor einen Zeit-Vertreib?" Biron, startled, comes hurriedly forward toward the king: "Ein Spiel, Ihro Majestät." Henry: "Wir haben auch ein Spiel / das wollen wir bald gewinnen. . . . ADJEU BARON BIRON." Impassively he withdraws, leaving Biron to communicate his mounting anxiety to us, the audience, in an aside that skillfully fuses pride with apprehension, tragic blindness with tragic insight: "Was ist das / hat der König vergessen / daß ich ein Marschall bin? Soll ich so niedrig werden / und nicht mehr als ein BARON bedeuten? Ach ich fürchte mich vor meinem Untergange." Biron is losing his concentration; the queen has to call him back: "Beliebt dem Herrn Marschall nicht das Spiel zu vollführen?" They resume the game, and the queen of course takes the trick: "Der Herr Marschall ist höfflich und überläst uns das Glücke," she says most charmingly. He repays the compliment, but in words that betray his inner state of mind: "Das Glücke ist scharffsichtig / es weiß den Ausgang nach den MERIten zu urtheilen." She thanks him for his company and he reciprocates with profuse expressions of gratitude for her "hohe Gnade." The curtain closes. As he issues from the royal apartments, the blow falls: "Im Nahmen Ihr Königlichen Majestät begehre ich seinen Degen!" says the captain of the guard.

It is worth dwelling on this scene from act 3 of Weise's *Biron* because it graphically illustrates both Weise's dramatic sense and his effective use of stagecraft to arouse that *frisson* of tension that all genuine drama creates between suspense and conflict. It is genuine theater, one may unhesitatingly say, and as such it is equally alive to sight and sound, speech and silences, grouping, gesture, and movement and, of course, auditorium and stage. Yet the very words *stage* and *auditorium* raise problems. When we say that Weise was writing for the stage—or for that matter Andreas Gryphius or Daniel Casper von Lohenstein—what stage was he writing for, what auditorium? The simple answer is well known; it was a collapsible wooden structure put up in the town hall or sometimes in one of the larger rooms in his grammar school at Zittau; this, his "Zittauischer Schauplatz," as he liked to call it, was from 1678 to the turn of the century the effective center of serious theatrical activity in the vernacular in the German-speaking lands.[4] Yet this statement, too, raises reservations. Is it possible to talk about theatrical activity in a linguistic and cultural landscape that had no public playhouses in the full and accepted sense of the term until well into the next century, with the exception of the short-lived Ottonium in Kassel?[5] Accepted notions of auditorium and stage, audience and actors, have to be radically revised if what was written and produced ostensibly for the stage is to be assessed and understood with any degree of accuracy. Has it not struck us all, as we read the steady flow of academic studies devoted to German Baroque drama, that the actual conditions governing its composition are overlooked by scholars more intent on demonstrating their erudition than on undertaking the more humdrum and often painstakingly unproductive detective work without which the dramatic texts under discussion bear scant relationship to the plays that were written, rehearsed, performed, and responded to by an audience of spectators and readers about whom we know too little?[6] It is a pity there was no German Pepys.

Broadly speaking, most of what German speakers composed in dramatic form in their own language during the seventeenth century was specifically intended, indeed designed, for school consumption; this is a basic fact which must be realized in all its implications before one can go on to analyze Baroque Germany's achievement in relation to that of the other literate nations of Europe. The exceptions are few.

Occasionally, of course, a work might be taken up by the *Wanderbühne;* for instance, Lohenstein's *Ibrahim Bassa* was taken up by Paulsen's company.[7] Some of Gryphius's plays entered the repertoire of the company led by Joris Joliphus (alias George Jolly).[8] *Maria Stuarda*, the principal play by A. Haugwitz, may have been performed at the Saxon court; and his vanished *Wallenstein* was performed there by Johannes Velten's company just before the accession of an opera-loving new elector led to its dismissal.[9] Haugwitz's "Misch-Spiel" *Soliman* was clearly aimed at a different type of performance which represents the other main alternative to the general rule: it was, the author tells us, "vor vielen Jahren auff einer Universitet einer damahls von etlichen Studenten zu einiger Sprach = Ubung unter sich auffgerichteten Co-moedianten Compagnie zugefallen auffgesetzt."[10] Haugwitz, in any case atypical because of his superior social background, provides us with handy reminders of what other alternatives were open to the would-be German playwright, though few seem to have managed to take them up. Caspar Stieler was a notable exception with his *Rudol-städter Festspiele*, discussed in detail by Judith P. Aikin in chapter 16 of this book, as were the products of J. C. Hallmann's late creative period.[11]

Another interesting earlier alternative is provided by Josua Wetter (1622–56), who was a minor dramatic author and also something of an anomaly because he was Swiss. On the title page of his *Deß Weyland Großmächtigen und Großmühtigen Hertzogen / Carle von Burgund &c / un-glücklich geführte Krieg mit gemeiner Eydgenossenschaft . . . auch kläglicher Undergang vor Nancy*, Wetter provides a rare instance of conclusive evidence of performance by specifying that the play was "durch eine Junge Burgerschafft der Statt St. Gallen in einem offentlichen Schau-Spiel widerumb an das Tage-Liecht gebracht"—an event repeated a year later, in 1654, when this group produced his *Denckwürdiges Ge-fecht der Horatier und Curiatier*, or, later, Gryphius's *Leo Armenius* (1666) and *Papinianus* (1680). What else they produced in the interim is un-certain. Wetter's plays were posthumously published in Basel in 1663.[12] Now the published text of a performed play is clearly a valu-able document for the theater historian, as Ronald W. Vince has re-cently reminded us, but such texts are seldom true production docu-ments, that is, texts used as scripts during rehearsal or directly based on a specific production.[13] At most, students of German Baroque drama only receive a fleeting glimpse of a performance—a glimpse provided more often than not by a title page or a dedicatory preface.[14]

As for the place in which the performance was held, German edi-tions are coy. There were no playhouses as such, as we know already;

but—was it a sense of shame that suppressed the information?—few, tantalizingly few are the overt references to venues, let alone to the facilities would-be performers could draw on and which would tell us so much about the practical, tangible realities that circumscribed their concept of the stage. The De Witt drawing of the Swan Theatre in London is both literally and symbolically at the center of Elizabethan stage studies. But Germany, equally obsessed with the simile of human life as a play upon a stage, has no such central *Dingsymbol*, not even a drawing. Was its stage, then, just one of the mind, a topos that only now and then found its inadequate counterpart in reality? If that is so, this makes it almost impossible to compare Germany's seventeenth-century achievement in comedy or tragedy with that of France, England, Spain, or the Netherlands despite the shared delight in the spectacle of life's inherent drama, and some shared dramatic subject matter too—though rather less than one might at first suppose.[15]

In 1773 Lessing remarked to his brother that Weise had an occasional spark of Shakespeare's genius. We smile when we hear this, but we should bear in mind that Zittau grammar school was Weise's Globe and draw practical inferences from this juxtaposition. The pedagogic nature of German *Schuldrama* has often been stressed; but other important aspects may have more to tell us about his plays and those of several others—about the plays themselves, that is, and not their underlying educational strategies and academic objectives. If modern Germany still had an established tradition of school plays, its literary scholars might probably be more alive to certain practical factors and less prone to gaze beyond the text (the primary evidence we have that the play was ever given) in order to develop retrospective theories about their deeper meanings.[16] A school or undergraduate play production takes for granted a number of things that distinguish it from productions on the professional stage of any place or period: first, the audience; then, the cast. In seventeenth-century Germany's case, the audience consisted of an assembly of parents, relatives, and friends, plus school governors, staff, and local dignitaries, many of whom were Protestant clergymen—people who would probably never otherwise have attended a public playhouse, even if they had had the opportunity to do so. Respectability was assured. The actors they watched were schoolboys: is there any evidence of *Schuldrama* in girls' schools to set alongside Racine's *Esther* and *Athalie*?

On the other hand, apart from those two plays, where in French or English drama are the dramatized parables and Bible stories that constitute an important element in the German school tradition? The repertoire of Jacobean and Restoration England was almost wholly secular in subject matter and spirit, while that of France tended to look to classical antiquity for its subjects except for the brief vogue for plays on religious subjects between 1637 and 1645 associated with Jean Rotrou, Corneille, and Pierre Du Ryer. Although there are points of similarity (e.g., the vogue for "Islamic" subjects in all three countries during the early 1670s), the criteria governing the German play-wrights' choice of subject matter have yet to be fully investigated.[17] One may surely surmise, however, that in cases of close collaboration between dramatist and school (as was generally the case both in Bres-lau and Zittau) the choice was at least partly dictated by current em-phases in the school curriculum, and that some plays were therefore in fact dramatizations of episodes drawn from "set texts" being stud-ied by the senior boys who were also leading members of the cast.

If the circumstances and conditions governing play production in Germany differed from those elsewhere, this must also have been evident in actual performance. No neat parallels can be drawn with Elizabethan performing style or Jacobean acting practice. In Germany, boys' grammar schools thus provided the experience of legitimate theater. This makes the question of when the first woman appeared on a German stage both irrelevant and very hard to answer, for in Germany female roles were acted by schoolboys, whereas in England they were played by professional actors and therefore in due course by women when they were admitted to the acting profession. The perfor-mances attended by audiences in Breslau and elsewhere must certain-ly have been challenging displays of rote learning glorified. Not so in London, Paris, or Madrid, where the rapid turnover of plays catered to a limited audience in constant search of novelty. A school play, on the other hand, was generally an annual event put on by a group of mainly older pupils who in all probability would never meet again. In other words, the *Einmaligkeit* of German Baroque plays was not dictat-ed by the public's potential boredom but by the fact that they were written for a specific school year which, like a vintage, never comes again. Revivals were therefore almost invariably out of the question unless, like some of the plays of Gryphius and Lohenstein, they were taken up elsewhere.[18] It follows that there must have been some local performing traditions associated with particular institutions, though nothing that could be termed a national style such as we see develop-ing on the legitimate stage in Paris. The style lay in the text rather than in the performance. This bred in turn a further characteristic phe-nomenon, the learned poet-playwright, and as a corollary, the drama publication complete with learned notes, which paradoxically flour-ished in seventeenth-century Germany despite the virtual absence there of closet drama; for were any of these German plays specifically written to be read rather than performed? None comes readily to mind within our period.

Apart from various kinds of court entertainment and the published repertory of the *Wanderbühne*, almost all extant seventeenth-century German dramatic texts owe something to school performance—often their inspiration and very existence. School was not just the matrix of seventeenth-century German dramatic literature, as G. Spellerberg calls it—for that would apply equally well to France or England.[19] School was the common denominator of German Baroque drama. This disqualifies the plays of Lohenstein, Gryphius, Hallmann, and Weise from being designated as "theater," yet it underpins them all with a genuine performing situation—one that cared little and knew next to nothing about the performing arts in contemporary Europe but which must have developed some practical performing tradition of its own handed on from boy performer turned schoolmaster to his own pupils in each generation, about which we know very little.[20] The extant data are meager, and what there is has not been scrutinized with archaeological flair; it is significant that our most obvious source about Breslau, the diaries of Elias Major, the rector of the Elisabethanum during its heyday of dramatic activity, are not available in a modern critical edition and translation.[21] Indeed, how figuratively apt is his remark of 25 September 1658: "Theatrum pro ludis scaenicis exstructum, dissolvitur; eiusque partes sub tectum Gymnasii (Elisabetani) reconduntur" [The stage erected for the plays is dismantled, and its parts are stored away under the roof of St. Elizabeth's grammar school]. Both literally and figuratively, German Baroque drama was in the hands of its schools. From the point of view of Anglo-German literary comparisons, Major's vague but thought-provoking remarks should be collated with the dramatic productions he oversaw, the parallel happenings at Breslau's other grammar school, the Magdalenäum, and of course what we partially know about the *Englische Komödianten* there, not to mention the important contribution to the city's cultural life being simultaneously made by the Jesuits.[22] Then a picture, however incomplete, would emerge of what was actually taking place in one of the Holy Roman Empire's main literary centers during the decade or so that saw the interplay of Corneille, Racine, and Molière, the reconstruction of the Amsterdam Schouwburg, and the emergence in London's two patent theaters of what Robert D. Hume calls Carolean drama, which introduced major innovations such as the use of actresses, and the vogue for Spanish romance, heroic plays, and the Restoration comedy of manners.[23]

By 1669 that Breslau epoch was over. Time passes, new tastes emerge, and new requirements stimulate innovation. In the late 1680s, the Zittau plays of Weise pose different problems and display different aesthetic criteria. But within the ambit of German literature Weise's Zittau plays simply mark a further evolution of *Schuldrama*, whereas to the comparatist they reveal exciting parallels; for instance between his *Trauer = Spiel von dem Neapolitanischen Haupt-Rebellen Masaniello* (1682) and that isolated anomaly in the English context, Thomas Durfey's *Famous History of the Rise and Fall of Massaniello* (1699), an equally realistic picture of the lower orders raised to power, couched in flat, harsh prose and achieving a coarse mimetic realism found nowhere else at that time except in a remote corner of Germany. Indeed, the differences of occasion, purpose, and technical means are what make the obvious similarities between Durfey and Weise so fascinating.

A more or less coherent school of drama that often parallels the interests of the stage in other countries but whose raison d'être was quite different: this is my view of German Baroque drama; a half-tradition, rather, of which contemporaneous Jesuit drama in Latin represents the other component, one now much better known thanks to the work of E. M. Szarota, J.- M. Valentin, and F. Rädle.[24] Call it a dual tradition, then, which only now and then came into constructive contact with the more popular but more amorphous brand of entertainment provided by successive generations of strolling players. Its authors evolved a dramaturgy both practical and theoretical in keeping with the aesthetic of the age but molded to requirements quite different from those catered to by their Spanish, French, and English counterparts. Its origins went back to humanism and the sixteenth-century grammar school tradition, which was not quite so moribund as sometimes claimed. It was highbrow and male-dominated, but its Baroque tone and format were a response to the changes in taste governed by the Opitzian revolution and by other factors; for example Dutch, Italian, and Jesuit Latin drama, the reservations Gryphius may have had about Corneille, and maybe a pre-Lessingian instinct that German taste was more akin to that of England—as represented by its thespian exiles, the "histriones anglicani," whose competition Rector Major deplored. If this thesis has any validity—and I think it does—it may account for the difficulties literary historians have had in accommodating, for instance, Duke Heinrich Julius of Brunswick within the overall pattern—and thus for his quite unjustifiable neglect.[25] The century ended with attempts by schoolmaster dramatists to teach politics to the prospective civil servants of princes; its prelude had been that rare and short-lived episode when it pleased a German prince to bypass the earnestness of Teutonic education and learn his stagecraft from professional actors fresh from some of Europe's major theaters.

Notes

1. John Dennis, *The Critical Works*, 2 vols., ed. Edward Niles Hooker (Baltimore: Johns Hopkins University Press, 1939), 1:154; 155.

2. The evolution of German seventeenth-century drama has been ably charted by Judith Popovich Aikin, *German Baroque Drama* (Boston: Twayne, 1982), and by Barton W. Browning, "The Development of Vernacular Drama," in *German Baroque Literature: The European Perspective*, ed. Gerhart Hoffmeister (New York: Ungar, 1983), pp. 339–56. See also Hoffmeister's "The English Comedians in Germany" in the same volume, pp. 142–58.

3. Christian Weise, *Sämtliche Werke*, 10 vols. to date, ed. John D. Lindberg, (Berlin: de Gruyter, 1971), 3:181–411. The scene referred to occurs on pp. 322–24.

4. The outstanding treatment of the subject remains Walther Eggert, *Christian Weise und seine Bühne* (Berlin: de Gruyter, 1935).

5. See Hans Hartleb, *Deutschlands erster Theaterbau. Eine Geschichte des Theaterlebens und der Englischen Komödianten unter Landgraf Moritz dem Gelehrten von Hessen-Kassel* (Berlin: de Gruyter, 1936). Ingrid Schiewek points out the ironic fact that the 1606 Ottonium was soon converted into a school. See her article "Theater zwischen Tradition und Neubeginn," in *Studien zur deutschen Literatur im 17. Jahrhundert*, ed. Werner Lenk et al. (Berlin: Aufbau, 1984), pp. 145–251, esp. p. 153.

6. But see the pioneering work carried out by the distinguished theater historian Willi Flemming: *Andreas Gryphius und die Bühne* (Halle: Niemeyer, 1921) and *Einblicke in den deutschen Literaturbarock* (Meisenheim am Glan: Hain, 1975).

7. *Ibrahim Bassa*, first produced at the Magdalenäum, Breslau, in 1650(?), seems to have been the only Lohenstein play to have been taken up by the "alternative" professional stage; performances are documented in Nuremberg (1667) and Danzig (1669). See Alberto Martino, *Daniel Casper von Lohenstein*, 1 vol. to date. (Pisa: Athenaeum, 1975), 1:186–87; 197, and now Pierre Béhar, *Silesia Tragica. Epanouissement et fin de l'école dramatique silésienne dans l'oeuvre tragique de Daniel Casper von Lohenstein (1635–1683)*, Wolfenbütteler Arbeiten zur Barockforschung, 18 (Wiesbaden: Harrassowitz, 1989).

8. What could happen when a serious school drama was adapted to the requirements of the strolling players is shown by Barbara Drygulski Wright, "Kunstdrama und Wanderbühne, Eine Gegenüberstellung von Gryphius' *Papinian* mit der populären Bearbeitung," in *Literatur und Gesellschaft im deutschen Barock*, ed. Conrad Wiedemann (Heidelberg: Winter, 1979), pp. 139–54.

9. August Adolph von Haugwitz, *Prodromus poeticus, oder: Poetischer Vortrab* (1684), ed. Pierre Béhar (Tübingen: Niemeyer, 1984), pp. 33; 39.

10. Ibid., 80; Béhar speculates that this took place in Leipzig between 1675 and 1678.

11. See Peter Skrine, "An Exploration of Hallmann's Dramas," in *GLL* 36 (1983): 232–40.

12. Josua Wetter, *Karl von Burgund, Denkwürdiges Gefecht der Horatier und Curiatier*, ed. Hellmut Thomke (Bern: Haupt, 1980), p. 180.

13. Ronald W. Vince, *Renaissance Theatre: A Historiographical Handbook* (Westport, Conn.: Greenwood, 1984).

14. "Tatsächlich muß das gesamte szenische Erscheinungsbild des schlesischen Kunstdramas heute als unwiederbringlich verloren gelten," Harald Zielske observes (p.2) in his informative article "Andreas Gryphius' *Catharina von Georgien* auf der Bühne," *Maske und Kothurn* 17 (1971): 1–17.

15. Compare the wealth of material regarding the stage in England, Spain, France, and Italy recorded in Vince, *Renaissance Theatre*; see too J. A. Worp, *Geschiedenis van den Amsterdamschen Schouwburg 1496–1772* (Amsterdam: S. L. van Looy, 1920).

16. Secondary evidence is provided by the plot synopses that accompanied the original Breslau performances of plays by Gryphius, Lohenstein, and Hallmann. Interesting exploratory work has been done on some of these counterparts of the Jesuit *periochae* by Gerhard Spellerberg in his two articles: "Szenare zu den Breslauer Aufführungen Gryphischer Trauerspiele" and "Szenare zu den Breslauer Aufführungen Lohensteinscher Trauerspiele," *Daphnis* 7 (1978): 235–65; 629–45.

17. Helpful work is being done in this connection by Ilona Banet; see her article "Die Entwicklungstendenzen des Schulwesens der Stadt Breslau zur Zeit Daniel Caspers von Lohenstein," in *Virtus et Fortuna* (= Festschrift Roloff), ed. J. P. Strelka and J. Jungmayr (Bern: Lang, 1983), pp. 479–95.

18. For example, Gryphius, *Leo Armenius* at Regensburg in 1659–60; Gryphius, *Carolus Stuardus* at Zittau in 1665, and Lohenstein, *Epicharis* in Sion in 1710.

19. Gerhard Spellerberg, "Das schlesische Barockdrama und das Breslauer Schultheater," in *Die Welt des Daniel Casper von Lohenstein*, ed. P. Kleinschmidt, G. Spellerberg, and H.-D. Schmidt (Cologne: Wienand, 1978), pp. 58–69.

20. The most stimulating account is that by Florentina Dietrich-Bader, *Wandlungen der dramatischen Bauform vom 16. Jahrhundert bis zur Frühaufklärung* (Göppingen: Alfred Kümmerle, 1972).

21. One remains grateful to Max Hippe, "Aus dem Tagebuch eines Breslauer Schulmannes im siebzehnten Jahrhundert," *Zeitschrift des Vereins für Geschichte und Althertum Schlesiens* 36 (1901): 159–92.

22. C. A. Schimmelpfennig, "Die Jesuiten in Breslau während des ersten Jahrzehntes ihrer Niederlassung, aus den Akten des Stadtarchivs zu Breslau," *Zeitschrift des Vereins für Geschichte und Althertum Schlesiens* 24 (1890): 177–216; James A. Parente, Jr., "Andreas Gryphius and Jesuit Theater," *Daph-*

nis 13 (1984): 525–51; and Parente, *Religious Drama and the Humanist Tradition: Christian Theater in Germany and the Netherlands 1500–1680*, Studies in the History of Christian Thought, 39 (Leiden: Brill, 1987), pp. 175–98.

23. See Robert D. Hume, *The Development of English Drama in the Late Seventeenth Century* (Oxford: Clarendon, 1976).

24. See E. M. Szarota, ed., *Das Jesuitendrama im deutschen Sprachgebiet: Eine Periochen-Edition*, 3 vols. in 6 (Munich: Fink, 1979–87); Jean-Marie Valentin, *Le Théâtre des Jésuites dans les pays de langue allemande (1554–1680). Salut des âmes et ordre des cités*, Publications Universitaries Européennes, série I, 255/1–3 (Bern: Lang, 1978), and *Le Théâtre des Jésuites dans les pays de langue allemande. Répertoire chronologique des pièces représentées et des documents conservées (1555–1773)*, 2 vols., Hiersemanns Bibliographische Handbücher, 3 (Stuttgart: Hiersemann, 1983–84); Fidel Rädle, *Lateinische Ordensdramen des 16. Jahrhunderts, mit deutschen Übersetzungen*, Ausgaben deutscher Literatur des XV. bis XVIII. Jahrhunderts, 82 (Berlin: de Gruyter, 1979).

25. A. H. J. Knight's pioneering study, *Heinrich Julius, Duke of Brunswick* (Oxford: Blackwell, 1948), has recently been followed by a revival of interest in the duke's literary work. See Ingrid Werner, *Zwischen Mittelalter und Neuzeit: Heinrich Julius als Dramatiker der Übergangszeit* (Bern: Lang, 1976); Barton W. Browning, "The Manuscript Version of Heinrich Julius von Braunschweig's *Von einem ungeratenen Sohn*," in *Barocker Lust-Spiegel: Studien zur Literatur des Barocks*, ed. Martin Bircher et al. (Amsterdam: Rodopi, 1984), pp. 175–85; Richard E. Schade, "Zur Funktion der *Miles-Gloriosus*-Satire im *Vicentius Ladislaus* des Heinrich Julius," *Simpliciana* 6/7 (1985): 205–17, and *Studies in Early German Comedy 1500–1650*, Studies in German Literature, Linguistics and Culture, 24 (Columbia, S.C.: Camden House, 1988), pp. 123–46.

4. Gryphius's *Cardenio und Celinde* in Its European Context: A New Perspective

Thomas W. Best

Accompanied by two or more servants, Lysander returns to his home in Bologna from a trip to court. The time is shortly after midnight in act 4 of Andreas Gryphius's *Cardenio und Celinde*. One of the menials, named Storax, protests against the danger of traveling at such an eerie hour, especially on foot, for the party has led its horses through the neighborhood in order not to waken anyone. Storax, who fears an ambush, lacks Lysander's confident bravery, though he vows that he would risk his life defending Lysander and the latter's family. His arrival with his master and Lysander's welcome by Olympia, the wife for whose embrace Lysander has yearned, are Gryphius's inventions. They have no precedent in Juan Pérez de Montalbán's Spanish tale "La fuerza del desengaño," which was printed first in 1624, or in Biasio Cialdini's rather free Italian translation of it, which dates from 1628 and is relevant because Gryphius became acquainted with the *Stoff* in Italy. Directly or indirectly, his source must have been Cialdini rather than the pioneering Montalbán.[1]

Hugh Powell has speculated that Storax with his comic funk is modeled on Shakespeare's Falstaff or the garrulous porter in act 2, scene 3 of *Macbeth*. Supposedly Gryphius knew a variety of Elizabethan dramas through the productions of itinerant troupes in Holland and Germany. As evidence Powell cites the figure Poleh in the *Carolus Stuardus* of 1663. Poleh's name is an anagram of "Ophel," which is an abbreviation of "Ophelia," according to Powell.[2] Though Falstaff, as a variety of the braggart warrior and thus a distant cousin of Gryphius's Horribilicribrifax and Daradiridatumtarides, is cowardly, the porter in *Macbeth* is not, so far as we can perceive; and Karl-Heinz Habersetzer has demonstrated that "Ophel" is far less likely to come from "Ophelia" than from "Ahithophel," (or "Achitophel"), the name of King David's rebellious minister in 2 Samuel 15–17.[3]

Even if Gryphius had been introduced to Falstaff, a closer counterpart to Storax is Sosia in Plautus's *Amphitruo*. Sosia is a nocturnally timorous servant who was definitely familiar to educated people all over Europe in the seventeenth century. Carrying a lantern, he cautiously approaches Amphitryon's house at night as the Plautus play begins. He could be assaulted, but his principal fear is of being arrested, for he is only a slave. Like Storax, he complains about his master's impatience. Instead of waiting for daylight before sending him home with news of their victory in battle, Amphitryon has dispatched him as soon as possible. As the Theban general, Amphitryon is delayed by the settlement of various affairs, and he is eager for his dear wife Alcmena to learn not only of his imminent arrival but also of his exploits. In line 153 Sosia asks whether anyone could be bolder than he; but the god Mercury, who is standing guard at Amphitryon's door, waiting to drive him away, comments soon that no greater poltroon could be found (line 293).

The two scared lackeys forced by ardent masters to trudge home late at night are not the only similarity linking *Cardenio und Celinde* to *Amphitruo*. Another salient tie is that in each drama divinity masquerades as humanity, with salutary consequences. On the one hand, Jupiter adopts Amphitryon's guise, while Mercury pretends to be Sosia; and on the other hand, not only Olympia but also the deceased Marcellus is counterfeited by a supernatural being. The spirit posing as Olympia turns itself climactically into a menacing figure of Death, which terrifies Cardenio into reform. By seeming to reanimate Marcellus's corpse, the second ghost effects the same improvement in Celinde. Like both Celinde and Cardenio, if less pronouncedly, Amphitryon is reformed as a result of the epiphany in his life. Initially none of the three is religious enough to be mindful of divine intent.

Whereas Celinde is so obsessed with winning Cardenio's affection that she tries to cut the heart out of Marcellus's moldering body so that Tyche, the witch, can concoct a magic aphrodisiac, Cardenio is an egomaniac. He confesses to his confidant Pamphilus that in becoming a *uomo universale* he was deluded by success: "Der Dünckel nam mich ein," he says; "Ich glaubt, es könte mir kaum einer gleiche seyn" (1.59–60). Until he met Olympia he did not consider any woman worthy of him. He wanted her, but her father refused to let her marry him, because of his hot-tempered belligerence, which could inflict unhappiness on the family. When Olympia was compromised by Lysander, who sneaked into her bedroom unrecognized, so that her father relented, supposing the intruder to have been Cardenio, Cardenio disdained what he haughtily viewed as "eines andern Rest" (1.215). After Olympia has accepted Lysander as her God-appointed husband, Cardenio determines to kill his lucky rival for depriving him of the woman he covets. Only metaphysical intervention prevents him from at least attempting to slay Lysander and Storax in act 4. His desire for Olympia is selfish rather than altruistic, for which reason he scarcely exaggerates in 5.388–89, where he declares that, playing "toller Löw" to her "keusches Lamb," he has been her "grimmster Feind." Obtaining her became the principal way in which he sought to gratify his ego. Thus it is appropriate that the phantom posing as Olympia should also mimic Death. The lovely woman and the hideous allegory are logically conjoined by the fact that Cardenio's passion contributes mightily to his spiritual quietus. Death aims an arrow at him, but Cupid has already shot him with a potentially more lethal barb.

In his preface to *Cardenio und Celinde*, which he probably composed at least five years later than the drama itself, Gryphius announces what he claims to have been his purpose with the work he subtitled *Unglücklich Verliebete*.[4] "Mein Vorsatz ist zweyerley Liebe . . . abzubilden," he affirms. One kind of love is "eine keusche / sitsame vnd doch inbrünstige in Olympien," the other being "eine rasende / tolle vnd verzweifflende in Celinden." Apart from omitting Cardenio's fervor, that testimony does not do justice to the play, which teaches *amor fati* through the agency of all three principal characters. Whereas Olympia learns the lesson voluntarily, it must be forced on Cardenio and Celinde. The ultimate meaning of Montalbán's material is that our will should accede to God's, and the same message underlies *Amphitruo*. Plautus's protagonist cannot resist the will of Jupiter, however, whereas Gryphius's title figures are free to reject the guidance that has been thrust on them, if they are sufficiently obdurate. Both the pagan god and the Christian one demand obedience, but the latter is somewhat more permissive.

Celinde stoops to necromancy in an effort to captivate Cardenio again, and he for his own part sets about committing murder, whereas in Plautus's play Amphitryon incurs no guilt for any misdeed. Jupiter even calls him innocent (lines 894–95), yet the Theban general is so much a man of the world that he gives no thought to the gods. They are merely figures of speech or names for him to swear by, as in line 1051. Not realizing who has replaced him with Alcmena, he blusters there that he will break into his house, felling everyone he meets, and neither Jupiter nor any other gods will stop him. When Alcmena first informs him that he has already visited her, he suspects her of being crazy (line 696), then either silly or arrogant (line 709). When she insists that he came the day before and departed a little while ago, he assumes again that she is insane (line 727). When she relates that he gave her the golden bowl he had taken from his conquered enemy Pterelas, he surmises that she is possessed (line 777). When she describes how he dallied with her earlier, he fancies that a magician cuckolded him (line 830). After meeting his twin in act 4, he takes the fellow for a sorcerer (line 1043). Never, in what remains of Plautus's first four acts, does Amphitryon entertain so much as an inkling of his surrogate's Olympian nature.[5] Only when he has been struck by lightning and told that his wife has given birth to a pair of sons with no pain at all does he begin to understand that he and his family have been involved with higher powers (lines 1105–6).

After hearing that Jupiter fathered one of the boys, who immediately strangled two invading serpents, Amphitryon grows devout. In lines 1126–27 he orders sacrificial vessels for worshiping the king of the gods; like Cardenio and Celinde he has finally been converted to piety by a terrifying confrontation with the preternatural. In his case fright is occasioned by the thunderbolt that knocks him unconscious. "Jupiter's blast has left me paralyzed with fear" ("totus timeo, ita me increpuit Iuppiter"), he groans upon awakening in line 1077. He feels as if he were returning from the underworld (line 1078), and a monitory foretaste of hell is what not only Celinde's traumatic experience in the crypt amounts to but also Cardenio's awful moment in the "abscheuliche Einöde" at the mercy of Death. When Cardenio recovers, having fainted like Amphitryon, he wonders whether he might be in Hades (4.281–86). Apparently Celinde never loses consciousness throughout her ordeal, but she nearly does so when Marcellus, who supposedly is dead and certainly is in decay, addresses her and rises to his feet. "Ich sank auff seinen Sarg," Celinde reports in 5.330, with sibilants that imitate expiring life, and Cardenio remembers that she gasped for help "mit schier erstarrter Stimm" (5.260).

In *Amphitruo*, Sosia is evidently more aware of the gods and dutiful toward them than his master is. Early on (lines 180–84) Sosia suffers remorse because he was slow to thank them for his safe return from battle. Alcmena is mistaken in praising valor (*virtus*) as the *summum bonum*, or in her words the "praemium . . . optumum" (lines 648–53). Despite being blessed with plenty of valor, her husband subjects both her and himself to misery on account of his spiritual blindness. If he maintained proper regard for Jupiter, the omnipotent and notorious paramour, he would suspect that his *Doppelgänger* might be more than just a sorcerer. In the prologue to their play (lines 104–6), Mercury remarks that we must all be cognizant of what a philanderer his father is. Amphitryon, who can hardly be ignorant of Jupiter's amorousness, is so indifferent toward the gods that it does not occur to him.

Another passage in the prologue relates to a section of *Cardenio und Celinde*'s preface. In lines 50–63 Mercury jokes about the genre of *Amphitruo*. After terming it a tragedy, he labels it a comedy but then opines that it ought to be both. Because it mixes gods and high nobility with Sosia the lowly thrall, besides combining witticisms and slapstick with a marital crisis, Mercury pronounces it a tragicomedy. Despite denominating *Cardenio und Celinde* a *Trauerspiel*, Gryphius recognizes in his preface that its major characters, who belong to the upper bourgeoisie, are "fast zu niedrig" for classicistic tragedy and that "die Art zu reden ist gleichfalls nicht viel über die gemeine."[6] What the latter clause imports is that the drama's style is not so lofty as was customary in tragedy. Cardenio and Celinde will never marry —to the disappointment of many readers—but their story still ends happily, and it contains the moment of comic relief contributed by Storax, so that it qualifies to be categorized as tragicomedy, just like *Amphitruo*.

Consonant with the informal tone of *Cardenio und Celinde*, Gryphius included pleasantry in its preface. Alluding to the apparent revivification of Marcellus, he jests, "Ob jemand seltsam vorkommen dörffte / daß wir nicht mit den Alten einen Gott auß dem Gerüste / sondern einen Geist auß dem Grabe herfür bringen / der bedencke was hin vnd wieder von den Gespensten geschrieben."[7] Instead of presenting a deus ex machina, presumably up above, Gryphius proffers a ghost down below, in a subterranean crypt. He mentions only the specter that frightens Celinde because it brings about a starker contrast, thanks to its location, than the shade that leads Cardenio to a brighter future. The author is facetious, yet his drollery has a serious dimension, for he believed that spirits indeed exist, revealing what God desires.[8] Like angels, they partake of divinity and serve the Lord as messengers (except for those who are conjured up by necromancers, as is Jamblichus in act 4 of *Leo Armenius*). In his Latin preface to the 1663 edition of *Carolus Stuardus* Gryphius indicates the status that he accorded to wraiths who do not collaborate with Satan. Whereas Eumolpus in Petronius's *Satyricon* declares that poets employ the intervention of gods, Gryphius causes him to state that poets employ the intervention of gods *and ghosts*. (The phrase "per . . . Deorum ministeria" becomes "per . . . Deorum, spectrorum, Larvarumque ministeria.")[9] Therefore a spirit can operate as a deus ex machina, and it is by no means accidental that apparitions terrorize Cardenio and

Celinde. They intercede beneficently as instruments of providential grace despite their horridness, like Justina's spectral duplicate, which shrivels to a skeleton, preserving Justina's honor and Cipriano's soul in Pedro Calderón's *El mágico prodigioso* (initially published in 1663).[10] Tarasius's ghost, which predicts the demise of Gryphius's Leo Armenius, is likewise a blessing in disguise, for it alerts the emperor to prepare for meeting his Maker.

Elsewhere in the preface to *Cardenio und Celinde* Gryphius discloses that his initial intention was simply to draft a German version of the tale to which he had been introduced in Italy.[11] Friends to whom he had told it orally in Amsterdam had requested it in writing. Soon he changed his mind, however, and cast the *donnée* into dramatic form, perhaps persuaded by its kinship with *Amphitruo*. At any rate, because he ascribed divinity to ghosts, Cardenio's flirtation with a revenant that imitates Olympia must have reminded Gryphius of Jupiter wooing Alcmena in the guise of her husband; and the social level of Montalbán's characters must have recalled what Mercury utters about class differences in the prologue to *Amphitruo*. Gryphius is also likely to have noticed that Alcmena's true spouse resembles Cardenio and Celinde in becoming religiously sensitized through stressful interaction with deities, though on account of his vigorous Lutheranism Gryphius was surely impressed by the contrast between Jupiter's selfishness in the pagan comedy and God's generosity in the Christian narrative.

In "La fuerza del desengaño," Cardenio's pendant, Teodoro, is lured by a female figure calling itself Narcisa (the name of Olympia's equivalent) out of Alcalá (rather than Bologna) to an abandoned house in the country. There, by removing the creature's veil, he discovers an image of Death, which menaces him with a scythe instead of an arrow. The process unfolds continuously, without interruption, both in the Spanish original and in Cialdini's Italian.[12] In Gryphius's adaptation for the stage, Cardenio's encounter with the spurious Olympia is divided into two parts, the first of which concludes as the couple leaves the true Olympia's residence. After Lysander has safely returned with Storax and been admitted by his wife, the setting shifts to a luxuriant garden symbolizing the meretriciousness of earth's attractions. To that *locus amoenus*, rather than to Montalbán's "casería, que . . . apenas conservaba las paredes," the apparition then conducts Cardenio. In the same instant that his uncanny companion, a Baroque Frau Welt, metamorphoses from beauty to beastliness their location "verändert sich . . . in eine abscheuliche Einöde," as theater reinforces action. The sixty-four-line interval reuniting Lysander with the real Olympia serves three purposes. It provides Cardenio and the ghost with time enough to reach the magic park; it creates suspense through plot retardation; and it helps to prove that Olympia has acquired sincere devotion toward the husband she married out of spite, when Cardenio fastidiously sniffed that she was sullied.

Neither Montalbán nor Cialdini indicates that Lysander's equivalent, Valerio, is accompanied by any servants when he returns to Alcalá from a business trip to Madrid. Though the possibility that Valerio is escorted is not excluded, being single makes him easier prey for Teodoro. If the latter were faced with attacking a servant or two besides Valerio, Montalbán and Cialdini would probably comment on his predicament. Teodoro has routed several insulters of Celinde's counterpart, Lucrecia (Lucrezia in Italian), but they were not compelled to fight for their life. Their swashbuckling adversary was intent on nothing more than driving them away.[13] Not only does Storax lack a precursor in earlier versions of the *Cardenio und Celinde* material, as was noted at the outset of this chapter; the addition of him is also problematical, especially since he assures Lysander (4.179–80):

> mir ist die Seele feil,
> Mein Herr, vor seinen Leib vnd seines Hauses Heil.

Evidently Gryphius believed that a gentleman normally would not travel to court on horseback unattended and that Cardenio scorns whatever odds might be against him. After all, when he passes the church in which Celinde is desecrating Marcellus's corpse, Cardenio stalwartly confronts what he thinks are robbers.[14]

If these considerations account for the inclusion of Storax and an unnamed servant or two, they still do not explain why Storax is partially a clown. Though some dialogue between Lysander and a member of his entourage was needed to flesh out the previously nonexistent interlude, Gryphius did not have to center the conversation on a valet's fear of the dark. We may legitimately theorize that he remembered *Amphitruo*, in act 2, scene 1 of which the title figure marches home with a slave at night, after having sent that craven ahead in vain as the play begins. Mercury lurking at Amphitryon's stoop to pummel Sosia is even loosely comparable to Cardenio, who hides beside his rival's door. Convinced that Lysander's rescue by the seductive spirit justifies a humorous moment, which also anticipates his drama's happy end, Gryphius constructed a scene from both act 1, scene 1, and act 2, scene 1 of *Amphitruo*.

Since Storax is indebted to Sosia, a skeptic might wonder why his name is not "Sosia." We could answer that Gryphius also changed the names of Montalbán's characters, all of which Cialdini preserved. Our critic might argue, however, that either Gryphius forgot the names he perhaps only heard in Italy or they were already altered in his immediate source, which was a text later than Cialdini's translation. The challenger could assert that for Gryphius the names were not imaginary because in his preface to *Cardenio und Celinde* he maintains that in Italy "diese deß Cardenio Begebnüß" (not "diese deß Teodoro Begebnüß") was communicated to him ("mitgetheilet") as "eine wahrhaffte Geschicht."[15] Having accepted the incident's alleged veracity, Gryphius concluded his preface with other supposedly historical cases of corpses come to life. Because what its author recounts about the genesis of *Cardenio und Celinde* is so tenuous and vague that it permits conjecture and debate, let us concede for the nonce that our hypothetical adversary is right about Montalbán's names (i.e., that Gryphius forgot them if he ever knew them). We can defend the derivation of Storax from Sosia by observing that Storax is not Sosia, though he resembles the latter to some extent. Just the few lines spoken by Storax prove that he is more loyal to Lysander, for whom he is ready to die, than Sosia is to Amphitryon. Whereas Sosia obeys because disobedience can result in brutal punishment, Storax willingly follows orders, albeit sometimes with reservations.[16] Whereas Sosia is devout but sly and bibulous, while also being fond of wordplay, we never learn that Storax is. Thanks to his more extensive role, Sosia is endowed with a more developed personality.

Inasmuch as he and Storax are not identical, it is altogether proper that their names should differ. They are rather like Sulpice in Gryphius's *Verlibtes Gespenste* (1660) and Fabrice in Philippe Quinault's *Fantosme amoureux* (1657).[17] Both Fabrice and Sulpice, who are thought to be dead, pretend to be ghosts, reaching a lady by means of a secret passageway and frightening their respective antagonist (the Duke of Ferrara for Fabrice; Cornelia for Sulpice) into reform. Sulpice's goal is to bring Cornelia, his future mother-in-law, to her senses, however, as real ghosts sober Cardenio and Celinde, whereas Fabrice's aim is to save himself and Climene, the woman he loves, from the Duke. In spite of major discrepancies between the two plays, there is no good reason to doubt that *Fantosme amoureux* is a source for *Verlibtes Gespenste* and that Fabrice is the model for Sulpice. Gryphius even kept the name "Fabrice" but switched it to Sulpice's servant instead of assigning it to Sulpice himself. Whatever motivated Gryphius to substitute "Sulpice" for "Fabrice" was probably also his rationale for replacing "Sosia" with "Storax."

Presented with a copious supply of slaves' names in Plautus's and Terence's comedies and not being limited to those works, why did he select "Storax" for Lysander's servant? Why has that servant been christened after a pagan slave who is summoned to no avail at the opening of Terence's *Adelphoi* but who never appears and about whom nothing is said? In his *Historia Naturalis* (12.55.124) Pliny affirms that "Storax" (or its variant, "Styrax") is the name of a Syrian tree whose aromatic resin attracts insects that mar the wood by gnawing on it in the summer. Thus "Storax" possesses significance, and Gryphius was fond of self-reflective names for comic personages, such as "Horribilicribrifax," which hints at its owner's pompous and ludicrous bellicosity through its sound as well as its meaning. In the same play with him are Selene, who is moonlike in her inconstancy; Sophia, who is truly wise in her virtue; and Coelestina, who is heavenly in the sincerity of her affection for Palladius. Many names in Gryphius's comedies are in some way descriptive or suggestive, consonant with Renaissance tradition. Should the humorous figure in *Cardenio und Celinde* not be granted a commentarial appellation too? Gryphius may have associated Lysander's Storax with Pliny's sordid tree and its sticky but pleasant gum. When the servant's name is understood, in any case, his comicality increases.[18]

Tyche, Celinde's necromantic procuress, has an unquestionably meaningful name—the Greek word for luck or chance—and accounting for it will lead us to a second classical antecedent of Gryphius's tragicomedy. By instructing Celinde to cut out Marcellus's heart, Tyche causes her desperate client to become so traumatized emotionally that she forsakes her godlessness. Like the spirits impersonating Olympia and Marcellus, therefore, Tyche operates as a tool of holy grace, though the ghosts are good and she, a witch, is evil. Analogous to her are Leo's assassins in Gryphius's first *Trauerspiel*. They commit political murder for the sake of Michael Balbus, who is no more entitled to rule than Leo is, and they do so in the imperial chapel on Christmas morning, ignoring Christ's true cross; yet their sin conforms to the will of God, who has sentenced Leo to death.[19] Though Leo's killers will surely burn in hell, they unwittingly serve God as executioners. Either Gryphius or his immediate source, if that was not Cialdini, named Celinde's evil genius "Tyche" partly because she is exploited by God in a way that is comparable to His manipulation of luck or chance, personified as the goddess Fortuna, in some Renaissance cosmologies. Like Dante in the seventh canto of the *Inferno* (lines 73–96), the German Jesuit Jacob Bidermann, for instance, explicitly subordinated Fortuna to Providence while granting her sway over earth. In 1.3 of his Latin drama *Belisarius*, she proclaims herself superior to everything but Providence,[20] and in an epilogue to the same play she emphasizes that she rewards or punishes all mankind "on Providence's orders" ("ad nutum Providentiae," line 2076).

Evidence that Gryphius likewise imagined quasi-random events as ultimately God-ordained is furnished by his "Freuden-Spiel" *Majuma* (1653). In act 2, Mercury delivers Mars to Chloris, the goddess of flowers, so that she may avenge her suffering during the Thirty Years War. Mars defends himself by contending that he is subject to fate, which inflicts him on humanity as atonement for trespasses; he never acts on his own initiative:

Nein; das Verhängnüß / das härter als Eysen /
Schickt mich vom Himmel / wenn Menschliche Sünden
Meine Demantene Ketten entbinden,

he protests to Chloris.[21] Consistency requires, therefore, that in a Christian Weltanschauung Fortuna must be directed by the Almighty if her existence is posited. How could she be utterly capricious for Gryphius when her compeer Mars is obligated to heed a superior force?[22]

In his preface to *Cardenio und Celinde* Gryphius refers to the play as "der schreckliche Traur-Spiegel welcher beyden Verliebeten vorgestellet."[23] Though superficially a pun on "Traur-Spiel," the word "Traur-Spiegel" is pregnant with significance, for it echoes a sentence by Martin Opitz in the introduction to his 1625 translation of Seneca's *Troades:* "Dann eine Tragedie / wie Epictetus sol gesagt haben / ist nichts anders als ein Spiegel derer / die in allem jhrem thun vnd lassen auff das blosse Glück fussen."[24] Tragedy is always a "Traur-Spiegel," mirroring the irreligious, who depend on Fortuna rather than on Providence. For Gryphius martyrs were exceptions to this rule, but Cardenio and Celinde were not. Their implicit reliance on Fortuna in general is exemplified by Celinde's explicit reliance on a particular woman whose name means *Fortuna* in Greek. Not only is Tyche directed by God like Fortuna in *Belisarius;* she is also a mortal version of Fortuna, representing chance. Since, in addition, she "gibet Anschläge zu einer verfluchten Zauberey / vnd wil Liebe erwecken durch den Stiffter deß Hasses vnd Geist der Zweytracht," as Gryphius states in the preface to *Cardenio und Celinde*, we should infer that he conceived of chance as something devilish, such as a sorceress.[25] Because Celinde banks on Tyche instead of trusting in the Lord, her vicissitudes become a parable on the First Commandment, though the Old Testament's severity has been softened into New Testament benevolence. The true God still courts us, Celinde demonstrates, when we for our own part woo false gods. Luring us from faith to superstition and then making us either proud when it is good or despondent when it is bad, luck is insidious, so that we are justified in suspecting that "Tyche" as a name is supposed to remind us of the German word

Tücke.[26] In the *Reyen* to act 2 of *Leo Armenius*, Gryphius imputes *Tücke* to Fortuna, apostrophized as "Ewig wanckelbares glücke," and among his contemporaries he was not alone in deeming *Glück* to be *tückisch.*[27]

Our suspicion postulates that it was he who named the procuress, but in his immediate source she may have been called Tyche already, provided the source was not Cialdini's "La forza del disinganno." There she is innominate, as also in "La fuerza del desengaño," yet something that both Montalbán and Cialdini have Lucrezia say about her hints that she ought to be named either Fortuna or Tyche. In the Spanish novella, Lucrecia tells Teodoro, "Puse en manos de aquella mujer mi fortuna." In the Italian translation that clause became "Posi nelle mani dell'incantatrice Donna la mia fortuna."[28] In each case Lucrecia-Lucrezia reports that she placed her fortunes in the witch's hands. As the administrator of her luck, the hag can easily be identified with luck itself, and Cialdini doubled the connection. Whereas Montalbán has Lucrecia lament that she is "una mujer con poca dicha" (*Sucesos*, p. 86), with Cialdini Lucrezia cries that she is "colei, che fatta bersaglio di Fortuna non proua, che disastri, & angustie" (*Prodigi*, p. 116). No longer merely unfortunate, she has become Fortuna's dupe ("bersaglio di Fortuna") in "La forza del disinganno." Since what has reduced her to being the goddess's laughingstock is her pact with Tyche's pendant, to whom she has entrusted her welfare and who has caused her to experience only "disastri, & angustie," Lucrezia ties her counselor to Fortuna twice. Apart from the homophonic quality of *tyche* and *Tücke*, a reason to surmise that it was Gryphius indeed who named the sinister bawd is that in the Spanish and Italian tales she is not a figure about whom the authors narrate anything themselves. Lucrecia and Lucrezia only talk about her briefly, whereas in *Cardenio und Celinde* she becomes a participant who utters 125 lines. It was probably the dramatist Gryphius who, with staging in mind, fleshed her out sufficiently to merit a name.[29] If so, Lucrezia's "Posi nelle mani dell'incantatrice Donna la mia fortuna" supports the hypothesis that Gryphius drew directly from Cialdini after all. Being unmemorably incidental, moreover, the sentence suggests that Gryphius owned a copy of "La forza del disinganno." Perhaps his text was an anonymous transcription presented as fact instead of fiction, so he never knew that either Cialdini or Montalbán preceded him in contributing to *Cardenio und Celinde*'s history. Having renamed Teodoro himself would not prevent him from referring to the macabre story as "diese deß Cardenio Begebnüß."[30]

That τύχη is a Greek word can be important not only because it sounds like a certain German one; there is also a familiar tragedy by Euripides in which Celinde's mentor has a counterpart. *Hippolytus* is the dramatization of Aphrodite's scheme to punish Theseus's illegitimate son for stubbornly rejecting her in favor of austere Artemis. In hunting him down, as he hunts animals, having adopted Artemis's sport, Aphrodite plays with his father, with the latter's wife Phaedra, and with Phaedra's nurse as if they were pawns. The goddess sets the course of Euripides' play as surely as Jupiter determines the action in *Amphitruo*. Though for Hippolytus eroticism is taboo, Aphrodite infects his stepmother with a consuming desire for him that is comparable to Celinde's obsession with Cardenio. Like Celinde, who is narrowly saved from suicide in act 2 of Gryphius's play, Phaedra grows so melancholy over her unrequited passion that she refuses to eat, hoping to starve herself. When she confesses her sexual craving to her nurse, the latter betrays her to Hippolytus on the mistaken assumption that he will commiserate. Fearing public humiliation, Phaedra hangs herself. From beyond the grave she seeks revenge, while she also tries to protect her and her family's honor, by asserting in a mendacious suicide note that Hippolytus has raped her. Having promised the nurse that he would not divulge his stepmother's lust, the libeled ascetic refrains from discrediting Phaedra to his father, in spite of her damaging lie. Theseus considers him guilty, therefore, and angrily has him killed. Belatedly Artemis interrupts the action to disillusion Theseus, as Jupiter undeceives Amphitryon, and to rebuke Theseus for his temper, thereby reconciling him with his son before Hippolytus completely succumbs.

Tyche abets Providence by putting Celinde into a situation that will shock her out of her intoxication, and Phaedra's nurse helps Aphrodite by precipitating a crisis that fatally affects Hippolytus. She triggers a series of emotional explosions that proceed from Hippolytus to Phaedra and from Phaedra to Theseus. (Consequently, it is ironic that the nurse invokes the goddess's assistance as she goes to apprise Hippolytus of how he is clandestinely admired.) Like Plautus's Jupiter, Aphrodite differs from Christian Providence by being selfish, and the nurse reverses Tyche by being blameless. Whereas Hippolytus is irreverential toward a deity, and Phaedra is criminally dishonest and Theseus is blinded by fury, the nurse cannot be criticized for any lack of virtue. If her judgment seems poor, as she herself professes it to be in line 704, she is reduced to drastic measures to rescue Phaedra. Though morally the nurse is Tyche's opposite, each woman attempts to aid a victim of unreciprocated love, and the plans of each are divinely thwarted. In Tyche's case, for the better; in the nurse's, for the worse. Like Tyche, the nurse even proposes a charm (*Hippolytus* 509–15).[31]

As Celinde bewails her desertion by Cardenio shortly before Tyche prevents her from taking her life, she recalls her dreams about women in classical literature with whom she identifies. In 2.65–68 she specifies four of these older sisters in sorrow:

> Medèen seh' ich rasen;
> Ich seh auff Didus Brust von Blut geschwellte Blasen;
> Die bleiche Phyllis hangt von jhrem Mandelbaum
> Alcione sucht Ruh auff toller Wellen Schaum.

Her omission of Phaedra cannot be construed as evidence that Gryphius forgot Euripides' *Hippolytus*, because Medea, Dido, Phyllis, and Alcyone, like Celinde, have been loved by the men who forsake them. Phaedra belongs in a different category, since misogynous Hippolytus never dotes on her. Celinde's citing of Medea implies that Gryphius definitely did remember Phaedra, for Seneca and Euripides each composed a surviving tragedy about her and also one about the woman repudiated by Jason. Anyone who was as humanistically trained as Gryphius was, would have been bound to associate the queen and the princess fixated on hostile men. Phaedra joins Phyllis, Dido, and Medea, moreover, as a fictional contributor to Ovid's *Heroides*. Incidentally, Medea's successful sorcery can be seen as subtly coaxing Celinde to experiment with a philter; and Dido's suicide (at the close of book 4 in Vergil's epic) must encourage Celinde to end her life. Though Montalbán and Cialdini have Lucrecia or Lucrezia refer to her nameless witch as a Medea, neither the Spanish author nor his translator has her speak of the Carthaginian queen and attempt to kill herself.[32] Celinde as a Dido imitator is another of Gryphius's innovations.[33]

Plautus's *Amphitruo*, Euripides' *Hippolytus*, and Gryphius's *Cardenio und Celinde* are all religious plays, insofar as they are dominated by deities. In both of the ancient works, however, divinity abuses mortals for self-gratification, whereas in Gryphius's Baroque morality it pressures mortals to prepare for heaven. To some extent *Cardenio und Celinde* is an anti-*Amphitruo* and an anti-*Hippolytus*. Though a religious lesson can be read from *Amphitruo* (be mindful of the gods), as well as from *Hippolytus* (honor all the gods), Gryphius is likely to have felt that a drama preaching *memento mori*, like *Cardenio und Celinde*, should not be called a tragicomedy, even when it terminates joyfully after heading toward calamity, contains a bit of humor, deals with the middle class, forgoes stylistic grandiosity, and is reminiscent of Plautus's archetypal mixture of the tragic with the comic. Gryphius's dramatization of a godless couple's miraculous conversion can be thematically too noble and earnest, in spite of its untragic features, for the rubric jocularly proposed by Mercury in the prologue to *Amphitruo*.[34] Surely, moreover, Gryphius knew the influential lines from Ovid's *Tristia* (2.381–83) characterizing tragedy as the most serious type of literature yet one that always deals with love. Plays about Hippolytus are even cited as examples there:

> omne genus scripti gravitate tragoedia vincit:
>   haec quoque materiam semper amoris habet.
> num quid in Hippolyto, nisi caecae flamma novercae?

> [In weightiness tragedy surpasses every other kind
> of writing, but it never omits the theme of love.
> What destroys Hippolytus if not the passion of his
> blinded stepmother?]

In the preface to *Leo Armenius*, Gryphius denies that love is essential to tragedy, but Ovid's verses do apply to *Cardenio und Celinde*, which treats love very seriously—that is, in conjunction with redemption.[35] Thus the *Tristia* passage may have helped persuade Gryphius that *Cardenio und Celinde* ought to be elevated to the level of Euripides' *Hippolytus* by being styled as nothing less than a *Trauerspiel*. If tragedy is the gravest genre, salvation was for Gryphius the gravest subject. His classification of *Cardenio und Celinde* is another way in which this play negates *Amphitruo*.

Notes

1. See Gryphius's account of *Cardenio und Celinde*'s origination in the preface to the play, *Gesamtausgabe der deutschsprachigen Werke*, 8 vols., ed. Marian Szyrocki and Hugh Powell (Tübingen: Niemeyer, 1965), 5:99. All quotations from and references to Gryphius's works comply with this *Gesamtausgabe* (Tübingen: Niemeyer, 1963–72) except for some corrected punctuation. Citation references specify act number followed by line number; that is, 1.59–60 indicates "act 1, lines 59–60."

2. *Cardenio und Celinde*, ed. Hugh Powell (Leicester: University Press, 1961), p. lvi. See also *Gesamtausgabe*, 4:272, note to 5:157.

3. Karl-Heinz Habersetzer, *Politische Typologie und dramatisches Exemplum* (Stuttgart: Metzler, 1985), p. 39.

4. *Gesamtausgabe*, 5:100. See p. xii regarding the preface's date.

5. Three times during the Neo-Latin supposititious scenes usually includ-

ed in *Amphitruo* editions from the sixteenth and seventeenth centuries its title figure does acknowledge the possibility that his difficulties are due to the gods. See Ludwig Braun, *Scenae suppositiciae oder der falsche Plautus* (Göttingen: Vandenhoeck & Ruprecht, 1980), pp. 128; 130; 139, lines 56–57, 65; 149. Even so, Amphitryon fails to become religious prior to act 5.

6. *Gesamtausgabe*, 5:99.

7. Ibid., pp. 100–101.

8. Misunderstanding Gryphius, Walter Benjamin glorified his joke as a "wunderschöne Übertragung des deus ex machina." See Benjamin, *Ursprung des deutschen Trauerspiels* (Frankfurt a. M.: Suhrkamp, 1969), p. 144.

9. *Gesamtausgabe*, 4:56. Gryphius quotes, in italics, from Petronius's *Satyricon* 118.6. See also *Gesamtausgabe*, 5:101–3, where Gryphius disagrees with people who hold that eidola are "Tand vnd Mährlin oder traurige Einbildungen." Distorting this testimony, Harald Steinhagen has tried to persuade us that the false Olympia is just such a "traurige Einbildung"—a projection of Cardenio's guilt-ridden unconscious; see Steinhagen, *Wirklichkeit und Handeln im barocken Drama* (Tübingen: Niemeyer, 1977), pp. 158–59. Steinhagen goes on to criticize Horst Turk wrongly (p. 159) for viewing the false Olympia as a "Verkörperung des Überirdischen" and an "Eingriff der Vorsehung." See Turk, "Cardenio und Celinde Oder Unglücklich Verliebete," in *Die Dramen des Andreas Gryphius*, ed. Gerhard Kaiser (Stuttgart: Metzler, 1968), pp. 96; 98. It is illogical of Steinhagen to argue (p. 160) that Gryphius repudiated all supernatural intervention because he judged in "Fewrige Freystadt" that the fire destroying the town was started by natural means. In this regard, see Marian Szyrocki, "Andreas Gryphius' 'Feurige Freystadt,'" *OL* 25 (1970): 111 ("Im Gegensatz zum Volksgerede vertrat der Dichter die Ansicht, daß der Brand auf eine natürliche Art und Weise durch unvorsichtigen Umgang mit Feuer und nicht durch einen aus heiterem Himmel herabgefallenen Feuerball entstanden sei"); cf. Marian Szyrocki, *Der junge Gryphius* (Berlin: Rütten & Loening, 1959), p. 118. Steinhagen claims (p. 161) that by Gryphius's own avowal (*Gesamtausgabe*, 5:100) "das Gespenst" is no deus ex machina. Here Steinhagen misconstrues Gryphius's quip about there being no "Gott auß dem Gerüste" in *Cardenio und Celinde*. Finally, if the drama's phantoms were figments of imagination, they would not be numbered among the *Personen* as real entities (*Gesamtausgabe*, 5:105).

10. Calderón drew from Mira de Amescua's *El esclavo del demonio* (1612), in which ersatz Leonor becomes a skeleton, but not at God's behest. She is entirely the creation of demonic Angelio.

11. *Gesamtausgabe*, 5:99.

12. Juan Pérez de Montalbán, *Sucesos y prodigios de amor* (Madrid: Sociedad de Bibliófilos Españoles, 1949), pp. 83–85; Biasio Cialdini, *Prodigi d'amore, rappresentati in varie novelle dal Dottore Mont Albano* (Venice: Rescaldini, 1676), pp. 110–13.

13. Pérez de Montalbán, *Sucesos*, p. 80; Cialdini, *Prodigi*, p. 104. Cf. *Cardenio und Celinde*, 1.385–92.

14. See 4.308–16 and 5.245–46. In 5.52, however, Lysander is confident that he and his brother-in-law together are superior to Cardenio.

15. *Gesamtausgabe*, 5:99.

16. See *Amphitruo*, line 280 (Sosia was once left suspended all night after being beaten); line 446 (he discloses that his back is full of scars); line 1030 (Amphitryon threatens Mercury as Sosia with a whipping).

17. For confirmation of this date see Etienne Gros, *Philippe Quinault* (1926; rpt. Geneva: Slatkine, 1970), p. 774. Two editions of *Fantosme amoureux* appeared in 1657 and one in 1658. In literature on *Verlibtes Gespenste* one reads that the first edition of *Fantosme amoureux* dates from 1658 or 1659. In 1659 no edition whatsoever was issued. *Fantosme amoureux* is based on Calderón's *El galán fantasma*, which was printed initially in 1637. There Fabrice's counterpart is named Astolfo.

18. Another domestic created for *Cardenio und Celinde* is Dorus, Lysander's porter, whose name is fitting because of its phonic affinity with German *Tor*. Gryphius took this name from the dilapidated and emasculated slave in Terence's *Eunuchus*.

19. See *Gesamtausgabe*, 5:51, lines 85–87, which are spoken by the former patriarch Tarasius.

20. *Jakob Bidermanns 'Belisarius,'* ed. Harald Burger (Berlin: de Gruyter, 1966), p. 11, lines 60–67. Though written in 1607, *Belisarius* was not published until 1666.

21. *Gesamtausgabe*, 8:15, lines 154–56. See also lines 157–60. On presenting Mars to Chloris in 2.86–87, Mercury confirms that the god of war cannot act independently.

22. See Ferdinand van Ingen, "Wahn und Vernunft, Verwirrung und Gottesordnung in *Cardenio und Celinde* des Andreas Gryphius," in *Theatrum Europeum*, ed. Richard Brinkmann et al. (Munich: Fink, 1982), p. 287 n. 56, where he avers: "Es ist zwar richtig, daß die Fortuna immer mehr christianisiert wird, daß etwa im Mittelalter das *gelückes rat* auch die Providentia vertreten kann . . . aber hier [in *Cardenio und Celinde*] sind die Fortuna-Welt und die göttliche Providenz deutlich unterschieden." No; they are just not explicitly connected. Van Ingen overlooks Tyche. Without producing any evidence, Wilhelm Vosskamp rightly affirms that Gryphius subordinated Fortuna to Providence directly; see Wilhelm Vosskamp, *Zeit und Geschichtsauffassung im 17. Jahrhundert bei Gryphius und Lohenstein* (Bonn: Bouvier, 1967), p. 138.

23. *Gesamtausgabe*, 5:100, except that "beyden" is given as "bey den." See Peter Michelsen, " 'Wahn.' Gryphius' Deutung der Affekte in 'Cardenio und Celinde'," in *Wissen aus Erfahrungen*, ed. Alexander von Bormann (Tübingen: Niemeyer, 1976), p. 87 n. 30.

24. Martin Opitz, *Gesammelte Werke*, ed. George Schulz-Behrend, BLVS 301, vol.2, part 2 (Stuttgart: Hiersemann, 1979), p. 430. Rist paraphrases this passage in the *Vorrede* to his *Perseus;* see Johann Rist, *Sämtliche Werke*, 7 vols., ed. Eberhard Mannack (Berlin: de Gruyter, 1967), 1:121, lines 5–8.

25. *Gesamtausgabe*, 5:100.

26. Jean Ricci goes too far in contending "Tyché . . . signifie sans doute *Tücke.*" Ricci does not associate Gryphius's Tyche with Fortuna, even though he notes that her name possesses "une allure grecque." See Ricci, *L'Histoire de Cardenio et de Celinde dans le théâtre allemand* (Paris: Corti, 1947), p. 50.

27. See not only *Gesamtausgabe*, 5:46, lines 605–8, but also H. J. C. von Grimmelshausen, *Der seltzame Springinsfeld*, ed. F. G. Sieveke (Tübingen: Niemeyer, 1969), pp. 4; 66; and M. Opitz, *Geistliche Poemata 1638*, ed. Erich Trunz (Tübingen: Niemeyer, 1975), p. 100.

28. Pérez de Montalbán, *Sucesos*, p. 87; Cialdini, *Prodigi*, p. 119.

29. Febronia's "alte Hex" in Harsdörffer's story "Die Zauberlieb" (first published in 1649) is distinguished with a name, Affra, but "Die Zauberlieb" differs considerably from "La fuerza del desengaño," despite some similarities. See Georg Philipp Harsdörffer, *Der Grosse Schau-Platz jämmerlicher Mordgeschichte* (Hildesheim: Olms, 1975), pp. 120–24.

30. Szyrocki (*Der junge Gryphius*, p. 125) has doubted Gryphius's assertion that the tale was presented to him as a record of actual events, but Szyrocki reads *Cardenio und Celinde* as a confessional *drame à clef* potentially embarrassing to its author. Whereas Cardenio's age could indeed be an autobiographical touch, as Szyrocki contends, since both Montalbán and Cialdini omit Teodoro's age, Szyrocki's speculation otherwise defies belief. His reason for suspecting a "Mystifikation" is insufficient. Given his fascination with possible number symbolism elsewhere in *Cardenio und Celinde*, it is strange that he sees no significance in the fact that Cardenio gives his age by saying in 1.37, "Ich zehlte (wo mir recht) die zweymal eilfften ähren." Szyrocki observes, "Die 11 symbolisiert die Maßlosigkeit und die Sünde." (*Der junge Gryphius*, p. 61).

Though Gryphius was evidently not acquainted with Montalbán's *Sucesos*, Harsdörffer was, already in the 1640s. He had Vespasian mention it in the *Frauenzimmer Gesprächspiele*: G. P. Harsdörffer, *Frauenzimmer Gesprächspiele*, 8 vols., ed. Irmgard Böttcher (1641–49; rpt. Tübingen: Niemeyer, 1968), 1:287. See also 2:483. If Harsdörffer fashioned "die Zauberlieb" from "La fuerza del desengaño," as seems likely, it can scarcely be accidental that both he and Gryphius renamed Teodoro "Cardenio." Since "Die Zauberlieb" was published at the time when *Unglücklich Verliebete* may well have been composed, Gryphius must have taken "Cardenio" from Harsdörffer.

31. Gryphius was probably steeped in Seneca's *Hippolytus* at least as much as in Euripides', but Seneca's has less in common with *Cardenio und Celinde*. The nurse's role in furthering Seneca's plot is diminished, for Phaedra herself discloses her embarrassment to Hippolytus, as in Racine's *Phèdre*.

32. Pérez de Montalbán, *Sucesos*, p. 88; Cialdini, *Prodigi*, p. 120 (misnumbered 126).

33. In "Die Zauberlieb" (Harsdörffer, *Schau-Platz*, p. 121, section 5) the Celinde-like Febronia is compared to Dido, but Febronia is never self-destructive.

34. See Gerhard Kaiser, "Verlibtes Gespenste—Die gelibte Dornrose," in his *Die Dramen des Andreas Gryphius* (Stuttgart: Metzler, 1968), p. 261, where

he states: "In der barocken Tragödie des Gryphius ist 'Welt' das irdische Treiben . . . das durchdrungen werden muß, ehe die große Harmonie der göttlichen Ordnung und der sittlichen Werte bestätigt gefunden werden kann. Allein durch diese Perspektive, nicht durch Motiv und Handlungsablauf, wird
'Cardenio und Celinde' zum Trauerspiel. Das Stück zeigt das irdische Leben
als Trauerspiel, solange es dem Helden die Richtung auf Gott und die ewigen Werte verstellt." Since Cardenio and Celinde overcome the world,
however, Kaiser's rationale dictates that their play should indeed be called a
tragicomedy. Taking a cue from Gryphius's reference to the work as a "Traur-
Spiegel" (without linking it to Opitz's metaphorization of tragedy as a mirror), Michelsen proposes an explanation similar to Kaiser's for why *Cardenio
und Celinde* is designated a *Trauerspiel*. See Michelsen, "Cardenio und Celinde,"pp. 87–90. Some excerpts are "Nicht der Untergang: das Leben spiegelt
Trauer" (p. 87); at the drama's denouement, "immer noch Melancholie, nicht
Heiterkeit und frohe Zuversicht angesichts des Höchsten begleitet den
Menschen auf seinem neuen Wege" (p. 89); and Gryphius's "Lebenslehre ist
eine Thanatologie" (p. 90). To be sure, the drama's concluding words are
"denck jede Stund ans Sterben," but neither Cardenio and Celinde nor
Olympia and Lysander, who are gathered in the final scene, are melancholy.
Their closing twelve lines of enthusiastic beatitudes ("Wol dem / der . . .!")
testify to the contrary. All four personae do indeed display "frohe Zuversicht
angesichts des Höchsten," for each of them has found the path to joy forever. Gryphius, the author of "Kirchhoffs-Gedancken," would recommend
"Thanatologie" as a vitalizing "Lebenslehre," not a debilitating one. In
4.383–84 of *Cardenio und Celinde* Marcellus's ghost declaims: "O selig ist der
Geist / dem eines Todten Grufft den Weg zum Leben weist!" Marian Szyrocki, *Andreas Gryphius, sein Leben und Werk* (Tübingen: Niemeyer, 1964),
p. 95, alleges that the poet labeled *Cardenio und Celinde* a *Trauerspiel* because
"die Bezeichnung Schauspiel damals noch nicht bekannt war," but Szyrocki
is mistaken. See, for instance, Rist's 1634 preface to *Perseus* (*Werke* 1:123).
"Schawspiel" occurs twice already in Gryphius's *Leo Armenius* (2.92 and 423),
to cite just his earliest play.

35. *Gesamtausgabe*, 5:4: "Die jenigen welche in diese Ketzerey gerathen / alß
könte kein Trawerspiel sonder Liebe vnnd Bulerey volkommen seyn / werden hierbey erinnert / daß wir diese den Alten vnbekante Meynung noch
nicht zu glauben gesonnen." When he penned that sentence, Gryphius was
thinking of ancient dramatists rather than of Ovid, to whom his literary
Ketzer were loyal.

5. Passion, Piety, and Politics: Lohenstein's *Ibrahim Sultan* and Tristan L'Hermite's *Osman*

Gerald Gillespie

Fascination for the poet and dramatist François Tristan L'Hermite (1601?–55) has remained high since the important reassessments by A. Carriat, D. Dalla Valle, and C. Abraham in the 1950s and 1960s.[1] Thus it is curious that French Baroque scholarship has reveled in perceived spiritual affinities between Tristan and such post-Elizabethans as John Ford and John Webster, yet has ignored Daniel Casper von Lohenstein's (1635–83) tacit artistic rivalry with Tristan, although German Baroque experts, notably B. Asmuth, pointed it out by 1970.[2] Having myself compared Tristan's *La Mort de Sénèque* and Lohenstein's *Epicharis* elsewhere, I now turn to the relationship between the *Osman* and the *Ibrahim Sultan* which so far has commanded less attention even from Germanists.[3]

Clearly, however he came to Tristan—and we are not yet sure—Lohenstein could not have failed to admire the French author's gripping portrayal of forceful women.[4] The somber dignity of the revolutionary Epicharis runs as a binding thread through both Tristan's and Lohenstein's tragic visions of the collapse of the Roman Republican ethos; their sharing of ancient and modern sources (e.g., Tacitus, Desmarets de Saint-Sorlin, Gauthier Costes de La Calprenède) cannot fully explain the remarkable correspondences in their treatments of the subject. By the same token, their differences, too, furnish a valuable index to later critics. For instance, by making Seneca at best coequal in the failure to curb Neronian degeneracy, Lohenstein seems bolder than Tristan. Hence we may legitimately ask whether in the later *Ibrahim Sultan* (1673) the Silesian playwright accommodates himself to the logic of greater hope in German cultural leadership or even to a modern political myth of empire, which Judith Aikin argues is the basic thrust of his works.[5]

Lohenstein's departure from Tristan's *Osman* would be far-reaching and would have serious political implications if we concluded that his

Ibrahim Sultan indeed reverses the roles of "passion" and "piety." It is therefore natural to ask the twinned questions: does this seeming divergence mark a subsidence of Lohenstein's artistic experimental-ism of the early 1660s, or does something bearing resemblance to Tristan survive? Territorial distance from the actual Ottoman menace presumably enhanced Tristan's inner liberation from the standard Christian terms, whereas Lohenstein could hardly have circumvented the standard Germano-Austrian interpretation of the Turkish realm as a real historical threat to Europe and as a showplace of those forces that internally threatened Western civilization. Nonetheless, to state the matter bluntly, I do not agree with the assumptions I have just outlined. In my view, Lohenstein does not exhibit an unusual degree of dependence on Tristan's Turkish tragedy, and thus it is wrong, in the first place, to try to assess his play as a departure. Nonetheless, it is precisely Lohenstein's peculiar brand of independence that indeed bears some affinity to Tristan's, despite the considerable disparity in their cultural backgrounds.

In any case, it is unmistakable that Tristan daringly examines drives and motives, under Turkish garb, in psychodynamic terms. He por-trays his youthful Osman as a harsh idealist and genuine hero who refuses any concession to the all-too-human tendencies of the Otto-man aristocracy and military. Battle-weary and discontent, they favor politics and privilege over the demanding cause of the empire and their Islamic faith. In act 1, Osman has reached the decision to leave the corrupt capital on a religious pilgrimage and to form a new army in Asia for a rebirth of glory. At first attracted by her beautiful portrait, in act 2 Osman then abruptly rejects in person the "impérieux et grave" daughter of the Mufti as being "plus d'orgueil vingt fois que de beauté" (lines 433; 435).[6] Thus in Tristan's play the beleaguered Turk-ish monarch fails to embrace his true soulmate and squanders, simul-taneously, a brilliant political solution. In reciprocal blind pride, she sways her father, the supreme religious authority, to back the emerg-ing revolt. Osman's regal courage in act 3 in the face of mutiny is dazzling; and in act 4, he repeatedly refuses to sacrifice loyal ministers to placate his enemies. It is too late in act 5 when the passionate daughter of the Mufti is ready to sacrifice everything for the magnifi-cent, honorable, severe Osman; he already accepts his own death as a religious and cultural martyrdom and goes down fighting. She re-mains to deplore the outrage committed by "des monstres pervers" against "Le prince le plus grand qui fut en l'Vnivers" (lines 1571–72). In the cascading paradoxes of her guilt-crazed final speech, she kills herself to extinguish the life of "cet aimable inhumain" (line 1603) still pulsating in her own veins. Tristan's tight neoclassical focus on a few characters diminishes the cultural specificity of the setting and magnifies the invented roles of the Mufti's daughter and of the Sultan's likewise unnamed sister (discussed later).

I do not believe that Tristan's plot directly furnished Lohenstein with a framework, even though the underlying story was obviously on Lohenstein's mind. An encapsulated summary of the entire state crisis that culminated in the fall of Osman, based mainly on M. Bisaccioni's account, appears in the long annotation to lines 132–33 in act 5 of *Ibrahim Sultan*.[7] Among the precise and symptomatic details bearing on Osman's character, Lohenstein cites in the note to line 113–14 of act 2 the criticism against him for marrying only one wife. Missing in these many references from several contemporary historical sources, however, is any mention of any daughter of the Mufti who played anything like Ambre's crucial part in inspiring the coup d'état in the German play. As Asmuth has surmised, Lohenstein appears to have borrowed from Tristan the fateful effect of the portrait and the political activism of the Mufti's daughter, but to have reconstrued her motives and the function of her suicide within the plot. It is even more plausible, however, that Lohenstein recognized how Tristan, as dramatist, had transposed details from the widely known story of Ibrahim and had poetically altered them to suit Osman, Ibrahim's predecessor.[8] What is involved in the German playwright's version is at most a silent historical correction of Tristan's own poetic borrowing from later pages of the historical record, but certainly not an arbitrary plagiaristic rearrangement.

Not clear enough in Asmuth's commentary is the fact that Lohenstein's subsequent *reversal* of Tristan's reordering of historical details goes hand in hand with Lohenstein's shift of attention from the more attractive figure Osman II, who ruled 1618–22, to his dissolute younger brother Ibrahim I, who ruled 1640–48, for the antihero. The son of this latter monarch was Mohammed IV (Machmet in the German play), who was crowned sultan at age ten and was still ruling the Ottoman Empire at the time of Lohenstein's death. Thus not only was Ibrahim's story historically closer for him; an analysis of Lohenstein's annotations supports our reading his treatment of this story as a generalizing interpretation of contemporary Turkish culture. In contrast, Tristan's play exploits in bare outline the facts of the two coups d'état by which the preceding monarch's, that is, Osman's, short reign was bounded. In actual history, Mustafa I, Osman's uncle, had been imprisoned by Osman's father, Ahmed I (1603–17), and his sanity was impaired after many years in the dungeon. Upon Ahmed's death,

Mustafa was raised straight out of prison to the throne. But Mustafa was soon returned to the dungeon in 1618 in favor of his seventeen-year-old nephew Osman, only to be fetched out again in 1622 to replace Osman in turn, as in Tristan's play. And then, in 1623, Mustafa was deposed a second time, in favor of his then fourteen-year-old nephew, Murad IV. Murad, Osman's more successful younger brother, managed to stay on the throne from 1623 to 1640 by his ruthless assertion of authority. Upon Murad's death, a third brother, Ibrahim I, assumed the crown and then eventually fell from power in 1648 during another revolt of the janissaries, which the Mufti backed. Whereas Tristan's choice to develop a heroic personage out of the one brother, Osman, strains against the longer-term implications of such a sordid historical backdrop, Lohenstein instead focuses on Ibrahim and thereby returns our attention squarely to the more obvious generic aspects of Ottoman dynastic fortunes. The annotations to act 1 of the German play exhibit Lohenstein's tendency, from the inception, like Tristan's, to conflate information from various accounts and about several reigns and distill the historical essence. The annotations to act 2 are an especially striking reflection of his wide-ranging interest in Turkish customs and religious beliefs. The dramatic dialogue of the play *Ibrahim Sultan* is correspondingly saturated with references to historical precedents and the range of impinging cultural and political considerations. These matters enjoy far less prominence and coverage in Tristan's play.

In terms of Realpolitik, the rebellion makes sense in both dramas. But it is the human dilemma per se that dominates the selectivity of the French tragedy; Tristan's more concentrated representation of an antagonist camp accords not just with neoclassical norms but with what has aptly been termed his existentialist vision. In contrast, working closer to the purposes and scale of an Elizabethan history play, Lohenstein meticulously names some three dozen Turkish characters and classes and shows affairs of state in considerable complexity. For example, he painstakingly traces stages in the actual complot involving Kiosem, the Queen Mother, who secretly supports the Mufti's plan to replace the Grand Vizier Achmet with Mehemet and thus to undermine her own son Ibrahim's power. The chief conspirators maneuver thereby, in act 5, into the position where they can topple the Sultan. Committed to the dungeon in act 1 for having killed her son's favorite concubine, wheedling her way out of prison through Mehemet in act 2, fighting tenaciously throughout against the influence of the pandering courtesan Sechierpera, the redoubtable, ingenious Queen Mother ends up as one of the most influential persons in the realm. Kiosem's desperate decision is clearly formed in act 3 when the mentally disintegrating Ibrahim is at the point of murdering all his own sons under the delusion that this might be a means to win Ambre. The Grand Vizier Achmet intervenes, too, to save the royal princes because, as he warns, the military will not tolerate such an outrage. But the Vizier's miscalculation under pressure is to authorize the expedient seizure of Ambre to satisfy the Sultan's lust. Lohenstein criticism has by and large overlooked the impressive resolve of the royal women in opposing Ibrahim in act 3, even before Ambre is violated and humiliated and soon afterward, in act 4, rallies the nobles and officers who have gathered at the Mufti's residence. Lohenstein knows, as his annotations show, very important historical details beyond the moment staged in his play: in the actual course of events, as Mohammed IV matured, a complex political struggle ensued between the forces centered around the new Queen Mother and those around the Regent Dowager Kiosem. Slipping as if by necessity into the same crime against nature that Ibrahim committed in slaying two of his principal heirs, the brilliant Kiosem maneuvered to overturn her grandson in the hope of prolonging her own power, but her grip on the state was broken and she died nastily during a particularly horrible coup.[9] This implicit future highly conditions Lohenstein's portrayal of the Queen Mother.

Tristan excites our wonderment over the power of the passions per se as the underground forces that dictate the character and destiny both of individuals and societies. Under the duress of historical circumstances, Osman's prideful struggle against the baser expressions of life, his desire to reform the Turkish world, leads to a tragic misalignment, the insult to the embodiment of vitality, the daughter of the Mufti. Instead of a tragic logic that is individual, Lohenstein reveals a collective terrifying threat that is visible in the corrupt core of Turkey; it seems structurally inherent in its absolutism. From the statements of his Turkish characters who are themselves obsessed by the evidence, it is clear the German playwright is generalizing from contemporary accounts of the ills of Turkish culture. Among the points cited are disregard for Islamic prohibition of wine and pictures, constant political purges, lasciviousness, homoerotic practices, and vicious sectarianism. The central theme throughout Lohenstein's play is the violation of natural morality, which the sultanesses explicitly condemn when this directly threatens their interest, but which is inherent in the Turkish system. This curse is underscored by Ibrahim's attempted rape of his sister-in-law Sisigambis at the opening of act 1, as well as by his later menacing of his own children and his violation of

Ambre. Ambre's case comes as the extra shock that galvanizes the moral sense of the Turkish nobles, but to a large extent it also signals the level of the danger they themselves face and represent in their own society.

The function of the final chorus of *Ibrahim Sultan* celebrating the marriage of Leopold and Claudia Felicitas hardly requires commentary. The historical record amply justifies Lohenstein's praise for the leadership of the Holy Roman Empire as a happy contrast to Turkish depravity. But I would argue, in addition, that Lohenstein fluctuates creatively at the end of this tyrant drama between his desire to state firm conclusions as a philosopher of history and his poetic fascination for the anthropological facts in their own right. The two final scenes of his play exhibit this striking trait. The tumultuous moment when the rebel leaders confront Ibrahim is so laden with explicit references to the case of his brother Osman, which still haunts their memory, that it is not farfetched to discern here Tristan's influence on Lohenstein's imagination. (That Tristan goes unacknowledged in the annotations is not surprising; several relevant contemporary French authors are missing, and perhaps are not listed because they were not perceived as scholars.) True, unlike Tristan, Lohenstein does not dwell as intently on the personal, but rather stresses the societal roles that seem predetermined according to the baleful model of Osman's rise and fall. Nonetheless, the fact that the German tragedian affirms that a societal impulse will assert itself even in "Turkish" society to counteract gross departures from natural law inevitably leads us to one more step. We realize that, on another level, the philospher of history is saying something similar about the inevitable reassertion of balance among the constituent parts of a political system, whatever the system. He rivets our attention on the intricate position-taking by, and interaction of, the familial, military, political, and religious authorities. We hear the ceremonial language of this complicated political process, including such hard, unpleasant slogans as that covering the required payment to the troops, and we witness the ritual of translation of power and investiture of a new sultan in its full theatricality.

Lohenstein's eye is that of a poetic anthropologist. The ultimate scene plunges us from the splendor of the throne room into the horror of the dungeon where the deposed Ibrahim, expecting strangulation, the usual fate of high prisoners of state, cannot succeed in killing himself, slips into madness, and is beset by the accusing ghosts of Ambre and six Bassas who were his political victims. Above, in the naked light, Kiosem—who will herself be killed beyond the play's final curtain—has summed up the strange spectacle that reflects the consequences of the lust for power that infects almost every "Turkish" soul (5.690–91):

> Verwirrtes Trauerspiel! verkehrte Mitter-Nacht!
> Da ich den Sohn vergehn / den Enckel wachsen schaue.

A magnificently robed ten-year-old boy hears the ironic cry: "Daß Sultan Machmet müß unendlich blühn und leben" (5.724). Below, quite literally eclipsed, Ibrahim knows that "ein stets-wehrend Traum / / Den Kopf uns wüste macht" (5.729–30); he is in the "abyss" (5.807).

I suggest that more is happening in conjunction with this grim exposure of the Turkish system in a political spectacle. By penetrating into the oppressive abyss of the Turkish soul in the final scene, Lohenstein also transcribes in substance the "dreaming" of the Sultan's sister in Tristan's *Osman*. He does so in a way that inverts the metaphoric order of the French play. There the action seems as if spawned out of the prophetic nightmare of "La Svltane Soeur, dormante," who initially is the sole figure, a figure literally asleep, on stage as act 1 begins. The words "dream" and "lie" ("songe," "mensonge") and synonyms are woven throughout the play. Only the word "blood" ("sang") is more frequent. Out of the concern of the princess for her brother's welfare and her incisive analysis of the political impasse, we soon read another deeper message; it becomes apparent she loves him profoundly as a counterpart of her own self. Ironically, because her brother actually absorbs and reacts in line with her misgivings about the Mufti's daughter, the Sultane Soeur helps to bring about the realization of her own nightmare. Her passionate monologue opening act 2 is a prayer that the answer to the warning dream be granted and that Osman escape the dangers posed by his nobility and courage, but she still views the possible marriage as a fatal delay and, clutching at false hopes, she tries to use their mad uncle Mustafa's correct interpretation of her dream, as foretelling Osman's fall, to shock her brother into the proper response. The long monologue of the Mufti's daughter opening act 3 exhibits an analogous confusion of motive. The latter's adoration of the Sultan's virile beauty and her erotic energy are transformed into a political violence that matches the military hero's blind indifference to pain and suffering. This crossover of the principal French and German characters—Ambre assuming the nobility of Osman, and Ibrahim the sexual wildness of the Mufti's daughter—has a parallel in the configuration of the acts, if we regard the rampant sexuality at the very start of *Ibrahim Sultan* to be an inversion of the erotic raving of the Mufti's daughter, by which Tristan ends the French tragedy.

Besides transference or redistribution of the incest and suicide motifs, Lohenstein's treatment of lesbianism is further evidence of affinity between the plays.[10] In act 1 of the French tragedy, we quickly perceive that Fatime is more attached to serving the Mufti's daughter than her own mistress, Osman's sister. The very last line of act 5 confirms that Fatime has schemed to attract Osman's favor to the Mufti's daughter out of her own love for the proud girl; she begs to be buried with her: "Qu'on mette nos deux corps dedans vn monument" (line 1608). The Mufti's daughter has meanwhile recounted in 5.3 how the sight and sound of Osman instantly ravished her and how she has shared her secret suffering and desire with Fatime. Lohenstein's play sticks closer to the historical accounts when it portrays the Sultan's panderer, named after the actual Sechierpera (Italian spelling), as seeking to protect her own position at court by finding a replacement for Ibrahim's assassinated favorite, the Armenian Giantess, and thus deflecting his libido from his brother's widow. But Lohenstein induces us to sense yet another ulterior motive in Sechierpera's redirecting of Ibrahim's attention to Ambre. Her description of Ambre whom she has glimpsed at the baths (1.319–32)—lush even by Baroque standards—reveals that she herself is smitten by the beauty and wants to bring her into the seraglio out of personal infatuation. Ambre may experience revulsion for the Sultan's untrammeled lust, but she knows how to recruit Mehemet, the future Grand Vizier, as her fiancé and protector. Ambre may be resolved to resist her monarch on religious grounds, but in so doing she demonstrates a rich sexual vocabulary. She also manages to maneuver the lesbian Sechierpera into intervening on her behalf despite the considerable risk that entails. Sechierpera's more than maternal feelings are evident when, giving in, she addresses Ambre as "Du meiner Seelen Trost / Mein Augen-Apffel" (2.521).

In my remarks I have discussed the central displacement by which Tristan converts political drama in considerable measure into psychological drama. I have compared Lohenstein's anthropological penchant to depict the workings of a larger social system rather than a few psychological types. I have not pursued the implications of the various political arguments voiced by participants in the deposing of Ibrahim. But I do believe that the aggregate of political rationales in Lohenstein's tyrant play suggests a newer discourse that seeks to emerge out of the apparent Turkish hopelessness. The word "freedom" is constantly on Ambre's lips as she expresses her aversion for the dehumanizing absolutism her sovereign represents; his humiliation of her ultimately is a political reaction that provokes other latent forces in the state to reject him. The individualist extremism of Tristan's characters may amaze us in its destructiveness. Yet, curiously, when this psychological absolutism of the sovereign individual appears in Lohenstein's Ambre and can be generalized as rebellion, it counters and, at least momentarily, remedies a failed political absolutism.[11] The final glory in Tristan's world is anarchic striving. In the world according to Lohenstein, the dark question is whether the unstoppable life of the state, seen in the immediate coronation of Ibrahim's son, can permit any permanent accommodation for our strutting and fretting.

Notes

1. Amédée Carriat, *Tristan ou l'éloge d'un poète* (Limoges: Rougerie, 1955); Daniela Dalla Valle, *Il teatro di Tristan L'Hermite, saggio storico e critico* (Torino: Giappichelli, 1964); Claude K. Abraham, *The Strangers: The Tragic World of Tristan L'Hermite* (Gainesville: University of Florida Press, 1966).

2. No mention of the Lohenstein relationship has yet been made in *Cahiers Tristan L'Hermite*, published since 1979 under the direction of René Rougerie as the yearbook of the association Amis de Tristan L'Hermite. Bernhard Asmuth, *Lohenstein und Tacitus: Eine quellenkritische Interpretation der Nero-Tragödien und des "Arminius"-Romans* (Stuttgart: Metzler, 1971), pp. 49–63.

3. Gerald Gillespie, "Lohenstein's *Epicharis:* The Play of the Beautiful Loser," in *Studien zum Werk Daniel Caspers von Lohenstein anläßlich der 300. Wiederkehr des Todesjahres,* ed. Gerald Gillespie and Gerhard Spellerberg (Amsterdam: Rodopi, 1983), pp. 127–57 (= *Daphnis* 12 [1982]: 343–75).

4. See, for example, the comparison of Tristan's *La Mort de Sénèque* and Webster's *White Devil*, by Nicole Bonvalet in " 'The compleat woman,' ou l'affirmation de la dignité féminine," in *Douze nouvelles études sur l'image de la femme dans la littérature française du dix-septième siècle,* ed. Wolfgang Leiner (Paris: Jean-Michel Place, 1984), pp. 45–54.

5. Judith Popovich Aikin, *The Mission of Rome in the Dramas of Daniel Casper von Lohenstein: Historical Tragedy as Prophecy and Polemic* (Stuttgart: Hans-Dieter Heinz, 1976).

6. References to *Osman* are by line number, following the edition by Claude K. Abraham, Jerome W. Schweitzer, and Jacqueline Van Baelen, with introduction by Amédée Carriat, *Le Théâtre complet de Tristan L'Hermite* (University: University of Alabama Press, 1975); translations are my own.

7. Maiolino Bisaccioni, *Vite, e Fatti D'alcuni Imperatori Ottomani*, published, with separate pagination, as part of *Historia Vniversale dell'Origini, Gverre, et Imperio de Turchi. Raccolta da Francesco Sansovino; . . . Accresciuta con le vite di tutti gl'Imperatori Ottomanni fino alli nostri tempi, Dal Conde Maiolino Bisaccioni* (Venice: Sebastiano Combi, & Gio: La Noù, [1654]). It is emphasized in Bisac-

cioni's account that the Mufti was the crucial political activist who brought the conspiracy to a head; in fact, only the Mufti rates being cited in Bisaccioni's index as the chief machinator: "Muftì offeso da Ibraino gli macchina la despositione." For greater dramatic effect, Lohenstein brings closer together two separate crises within the seraglio: (1) the strangulation of Ibrahim's favorite by the jealous Kiosem, and (2) Sechierpera's attempt to recruit the Mufti's daughter while the Sultan neglects the war for Candia (Cyprus), thus precipitating his fall. Bisaccioni treats these events as distinct episodes on pp. 493–97 and 517–21, respectively. References to *Ibrahim Sultan* are by act and line, following the edition by Klaus Günther Just: Daniel Casper von Lohenstein, *Türkische Trauerspiele* (Stuttgart: Hiersemann, 1953).

8. Claude Abraham, *Tristan L'Hermite* (Boston: Twayne, 1980), pp. 100–101, believes that Tristan probably read about Osman in Vittorio Siri's *Mercurio politico* (1646) and Michel Baudier's *Histoire générale du sérail* (1624) and heard about affairs in Turkey from M. de Cézy, French ambassador to the Porte. Bisaccioni, Lohenstein's main source, was himself an eyewitness in Constantinople in the fatal year 1622 and portrays the conflicting character traits and situation of the deposed Sultan with considerable sympathy: "Era Osmanno orgoglioso, & capace di macchine strane, ma non haueua i talenti per maneggiarle (compatabile, perche era poco più che fanciullo) l'acutezza dell'ingegno ha bisogno della flemma, e della prudenza per maturare i pensieri vasti" (*Vite*, p. 336). Tristan's play anticipates Bisaccioni's view in stressing Osman's youth, beauty, impetuousness, aristocratic disdain, religious idealism, and warrior nature, as well as citing his plan to reform the military and to shift the seat of empire and his incautious rejection of the Mufti's rulings, but he omits the odd discrepancy of Osman's avariciousness—for example, his despoiling his father's tomb and thereby further alienating the military—which Bisaccioni duly notes (p. 338).

9. The work of Paul Rycaut (or Ricaut), Count of Winchelsey, Charles II's ambassador to Mohammed IV, in the French translation by Pierre Briot, *Histoire de l'Etat présent de l'Empire Ottoman*, 2 vols. (Amsterdam: Abraham Wolfgang, 1671), was Lohenstein's most likely source for the name of the Dowager Queen, Kiosem. After treating the situation of the court and Turkish politics in general terms in book 1, ch. 3, Rycaut proceeds in ch. 4 to dwell on the crisis that unfolded as Kiosem plotted to eliminate her grandson.

10. In book 1, ch. 3, Rycaut cites the case of the lesbian relationship of Mohammed IV's mother with Mulki Kadin, who became such a powerful figure behind the throne "par l'amour & par la faueur que la Reine mère luy portait" (*Histoire*, 1:30) that military and political leaders had to move against this influential servant. In ch. 9, expatiating on the role of homoeroticism in Turkish society, Rycaut includes lesbianism: "Cette passion règne de la mesme sorte parmy les femmes. Elles meurent avec l'amour & de la tendresse les unes pour les autres. Mais les vieilles sur tout font la cours aux jeunes" (1:91–92). As Asmuth has already acknowledged, Philip Wadsley Lupton, in his unpublished dissertation, "Die Frauengestalten in den Trauerspielen Daniel Casper von Lohensteins" (Vienna, 1954), is the first critic to

have stressed that Lohenstein's character Ambre is anything but naive; rath-
ᴗr she is a "Barockmensch," capable of manipulating Sechierpera's lesbianism for a more important goal (Lupton, p. 217).

11. In examining the political constitution of the Turks in book 1, ch. 1, Rycaut notes the amazing durability in view of the violence, cruelty, severity,
and seeming arbitrariness of this system of government, but he posits as the
probable explanation that the Sultan's absolute power derives from the military origins of the Ottoman Empire and the military discipline of its ruling
caste before they reached the confines of Europe: "Durant ces temps-là, dis-
je, la condition de ces peuples n'estoit autre chose, qu'une suite de guerres"
(*Histoire*, 1:13).

6. Versuch einer Typologie des "spanischen Narren" zwischen 1613 und 1787

Gerhart Hoffmeister

Wenn keine Narren auf der Welt wären, was wäre die Literatur und vor allem die Literaturwissenschaft? Diesem etwas abgewandelten Goethe-Wort möchte ich mich durchaus nicht entziehen, denn der ist nicht ganz weise, der nicht einmal ein Narr sein kann. Dies Zugeständnis muß ich schon machen, da der Faber-du-Faur-Schüler Christoph Schweitzer in seiner Dissertation von 1954 an diesem Ort bereits über mein Thema gehandelt hat.[1] Was er allerdings rezeptionsgeschichtlich darstellte, soll hier typologisch neu aufgerollt werden, indem ich den sogenannten "spanischen Narren" mit seinen verschiedenen Fazetten aus dem europäischen Kontext vorstellen möchte.

Der Kontrast zwischen Shakespeares Fool und dem spanischen Narren

Analog zum griechischen Chor darf der weise Hofnarr Shakespeares der törichten Welt die Wahrheit sagen. Er unterscheidet sich beachtlich von dem rustikalen, ungezogenen Clown, der schließlich mit seiner grotesken Komik im Zirkus landet, denkt man an den dummen August der Pantomime, den Tölpel der Englischen Komödianten und noch Bölls Akrobaten Schnier (*Ansichten eines Clowns*). Viola charakterisiert Feste in *Twelfth Night* folgendermaßen:

> This fellow's wise enough to play the fool,
> And to do that well craves a kind of wit:
> He must observe their mood on whom he jests,
> The quality of persons, and the time;
>
> (3.1.62–65)

Lears Fool ist gelehrt, weise, rätselhaft und sagt die bittere Wahrheit. Er führt zur Selbsterkenntnis und hält der Welt einen satirischen Spiegel vor. An Touchstone in *As You Like It* enthüllt sich die Seichtheit von Monsieur Jacques. Schließlich liefert Hamlet das überzeugenste Beispiel für die entscheidende Rolle und Hochschätzung des Shakespeareschen Narren in der Symbiose von Prince und Fool, mit dem wir über die aus den Fugen geratene Welt lachen oder weinen.

Diesem Hofnarren läßt sich in der spanischen Literatur kaum eine entsprechende Figur an die Seite rücken, denkt man nur an den pikaresken Gracioso der spanischen *comedia*, den bauernschlauen Diener bzw. Schalksnarren, der bei Lope de Vega und Calderón seinen Herrn parodiert, indem er gleichsam als dessen Echo ähnliche Situationen erlebt und ad absurdum führt. Von einem europäischen Echo dieses Gracioso kann jedoch keine Rede sein, da er von Harlekin und Hanswurst völlig verdrängt wurde. Doch da gab es noch den hirnverbrannten Ritter von der traurigen Gestalt, der in das entstandene Vakuum aufrückte. Denn im 17. Jahrhundert faßte man Don Quijote als Narren auf, der die Wirklichkeit mit der Welt der Phantasie verwechselte, während sich erst der deutschen Romantik die idealistische, ja mythologische Komponente dieser durchaus poetischen Gestalt entdeckte, wodurch Don Quijote Hamlet und Faust ebenbürtig wurde. Erst seit Schlegel, Schelling und Hegel lacht man nicht mehr über den verrückten Ritter, sondern erkennt die edle Natur in ihm, die mit der verkehrten Welt kontrastiert.

Der Hauptunterschied zum Fool besteht darin, daß man über Don Quijote als Entartung des Ritterideals im Barockjahrhundert spottete. Die Diskrepanz von Schein und Sein, Fiktion und Realität war konstitutiv. Der ausländische Charakter des Narren kam hinzu. Aus dem Gegensatz zum Fool ergeben sich jedoch nicht alle Aspekte des spanischen Narren. Darum sind der spanische Ursprung und die europäische Rezeption zu berücksichtigen.

Der spanische Ursprung

Am Anfang der spanischen Tradition steht offenbar der Edelmann im *Lazarillo de Tormes* (1554), der in der deutschen Übersetzung von 1614 als "Hoffauffwaerter vom Adel" bezeichnet wird, der "ziemlich gekleydet, wol auffgebutzet vnd gekämpelt, der gang war grauitetisch vnd gleich wie abegecirckelt vndt nach dem gewichte"[2]. Verzweifelt versucht er seine äußere Ehre zu retten, indem er seinen Hunger durch Mantel und Degen verdeckt und den Zahnstocher scheinheilig benutzt (S. 69). Lazarillo nimmt sich mitleidig des "armen Schluckers" (S. 72) an, der sich als großer Herr ausgibt und schließlich seinen

Gläubigern und selbst seinem Diener entläuft (S. 80). Damit beginnt sicherlich die literarische Tradition vom dürren, verhungerten spanischen Edelmann, der aus der Perspektive von unten und in der Reaktion auf den heroischen Amadís als bemitleidenswerter, aber aufgeblasener Narr erscheint—und zwar bereits im Zenit der spanischen Herrschaft in Europa und Übersee. Zwischen dieser literarischen Figur und der Verelendung des Volkes besteht insofern ein früher Zusammenhang, als im Kielwasser der Welteroberungen der Import des "spanischen Goldes" zum wirtschaftlichen Ruin des Landes führte. Auf den gleichen Kontext weist der Ursprung der *leyenda negra* hin, die nach den Forschungen von S. Arnoldsson auf die spanischen Feldzüge in Italien zurückzuführen ist[3], wo sich die spanische Soldateska grausam, unchristlich und arrogant benahm. Die Größe der spanischen Nation und ihrer adligen Repräsentanten entlarvten selbst spanische Schriftsteller wie Las Casas, González Montes und Antonio Pérez bereits vor 1600 als Mythos, aber auch Calderón spottet noch über den scheinheiligen *hidalgo* (Don Menudo) in *El Alcalde de Zalamea* (1643).

Europäische Rezeption

Christoph Schweitzer war es nicht möglich gewesen, "auf die Grundlagen, die zu dem deutschen Spanienbild . . . geführt hatten, genauer einzugehen"[4]. Soviel ist allerdings seiner Dissertation zu entnehmen, daß Impulse für das "verrückte" schwarze Spanienbild im außerspanischen Europa vielfacher Natur sind. Die Politik verquickt sich dabei genauso mit der Literatur, wie sich in der Rezeption verschiedene Kontaminationen herausbildeten.

Die europäische Antipathie, die zur Verspottung der Spanier führte, geht auf die spanische Hegemonialpolitik zurück, die nach Ansicht der Protestanten damals die katholische Universalmonarchie in Europa durchsetzen wollte. "Ein katholisches Universalreich spanischer Nation konnte ja nur auf Kosten der protestantischen Freiheit gehen. Darum nahm die . . . Flugschriftenliteratur aggressiv gegen alle spanischen Einmischungen vor und während des Dreißigjährigen Krieges Stellung"[5], angefangen mit der Erneuerung der Inquisition (1481) und der Ausbreitung des Jesuitenordens über den Schmalkaldischen Krieg (1547) bis zur Eroberungspolitik in Italien (nach 1556), in den Niederlanden (Aufstand 1568), gegenüber England (Armada 1588) und Deutschland (Spinola in der Pfalz 1620). In allen unterdrückten und bedrohten Ländern entstanden darum Schmähschriften, neben den anonymen Flugblättern auch die Werke der humanistisch Gebildeten, ob man nun an A. Arnaulds *Anti-Espagniol* (1590) oder Wilhelm von Oraniens *Apologie* (1581) denkt, an Sebastian Münsters *Cosmographia* (deutsch 1544) oder Fischarts *Jesuitenhütlein* (1580). Alle machten sie auf die spanische Grausamkeit, den spanischen Ehrgeiz, die Vorliebe für spanische Luftschlösser und spanische Heuchelei aufmerksam.

Auf diesem Hintergrund ist die Rezeption des spanischen Narren in der schönen Literatur zu sehen, wobei das Theater der internationalen Wandertruppen offenbar eine hervorragende Vermittlerrolle spielte. Zum Beispiel entstand die Commedia dell'arte im 16. Jahrhundert aus Anregungen italienischer Farcen, Dialektstücke und literarischer Renaissancekomödien, wobei sich der feststehende Typ des bramarbasierenden *capitano* aus der von Plautus herleitbaren mittelalterlichen *miles gloriosus*-Tradition nährte und größte Heiterkeit beim Publikum auslöste, weil diese Figur aus der Zeit der herumziehenden *condottieri* allzusehr bekannt war. Daß man auf die Arroganz der spanischen Heerführer besonders allergisch reagierte, geht aus der Umwandlung des *capitano* in Skaramuz hervor, der in schwarzer spanischer Tracht die althergebrachte Aufschneiderrolle im 17. Jahrhundert übernahm. Seit 1568 führten italienische Wandertruppen ihre Improvisationskünste nördlich der Alpen vor höfischen und städtischen Zuschauern auf, z. B. in Wien, Dresden und Leipzig. Die literarische Nachwirkung der Commedia dell'arte läßt sich das ganze Jahrhundert hindurch nachweisen, sowohl bei Shakespeare und Molière als auch in Deutschland, wobei sich die Wege der Vermittlung verzweigten und überlagerten. Symptomatisch dafür sind die Englischen Komödianten, deren Repertoire in der zweiten Jahrhunderthälfte die gesamte abendländische Dramatik umfaßte: die Antike, Shakespeare, die Italiener, Spanier, Franzosen und deutsche Barockbearbeitungen.

Kontaminationen und Fazetten des spanischen Narren

Die Schwarze Legende (*leyenda negra*) entstand in Spanien und spiegelt sich in der Literatur, die ihrerseits auf die heroischen Ritterromane reagierte. Don Quijote parodiert den Amadís und steigert so die im Edelmann von *Lazarillo* angelegte Literatur- und Sozialkritik. Als närrische, bis zum Wahnsinn die Realität mit der Phantasie verwechselnde Gestalt dient er mir als Paradigma für die Rezeption des verrückten Spaniers in der deutschen Literatur. Da er als symbolische Figur unausschöpfbar ist, lassen sich nämlich an ihr die wesentlichen

Fazetten des spanischen Narren aufzeigen: der *miles gloriosus*, der Liebes- und der Büchernarr.

Miles gloriosus

Don Quijote parodiert den Helden der spanischen Geschichte von der *Reconquista* bis zur Armada sowie die heroischen Protagonisten der Ritterromane. Indem Cervantes seinen Helden über Riesen, Armeen und wilde Tiere siegen läßt, die in Wirklichkeit Windmühlen, Schafherden und Zootiere sind, führt er die antike *miles gloriosus*-Tradition zu ihrem Höhepunkt. Als Don Quijote 1613 in Heidelberg anläßlich der Hochzeit des Winterkönigs Friedrichs von der Pfalz erstmalig in einem öffentlichen Festzug erschien, entlarvte seine Maske hinter dem Ritteranspruch den verrückten Prahlhans, der an wilden Einbildungen litt. Man verlachte ihn als Possenreißer und als theatralische Bestätigung der seit Luther und Fischart verbreiteten Vorstellung vom hochmütigen aufgeblasenen Spanier, ein Image, das sich nach dem Untergang der Armada mit Schadenfreude mischte.[6] Seit 1613 gaukelt Don Quijote in direkter oder vermittelter Anlehnung an das spanische Original immer wieder durch die deutsche Literatur, ob es sich um Flugblatt[7], Drama oder Roman handelt.

Die ersten Beispiele stehen allerdings noch unter dem stärkeren Einfluß des Edelmanns aus *Lazarillo* und der stereotypen *capitano*-Tradition, bis sich spätestens bei Rist ein deutlicher Übergang zu Don Quijote selbst ergibt (s. u.). Bezeichnend ist anfangs Herzog Heinrich Julius' Vincentius Ladislaus, "Sacrapa von Mantua", der bereits 1594 gravitätisch mit Knebelbart einherschreitet, sich seiner heroischen Abstammung und seiner Heldentaten brüstet und in eine Jungfrau verliebt, die sich über ihn amüsiert.[8] Vincentius steigert sich in die Rolle des *capitano* hinein, während für Don Quijote Rolle und Existenz untrennbar sind. Auch in dem von Christoph Schweitzer untersuchten Flugblatt von *Signor Spangniol* (1609) spiegelt sich noch eher der adlige Herr Lazarillos, der freilich mitleidlos als "Ein Pfaw auff der Gassen" (Str. 5) und "Ein Ehrgeiziger" (Str. 11), der hochtrabende Parallelen zu Achilles zieht, angeprangert wird. Zum Beispiel rühmt er sich seiner Herkunft, "ob schon sein geschlecht kommen sey / Von eim Negro auß Barbarey"[9]. Mit dem besagten Zahnstocher täuscht er über seinen Hunger hinweg. Hier mischt sich mit dem literarischen Muster deutlich die Schwarze Legende, die die historischen Ereignisse zu ihren Gunsten ausschlachtet. Aus demselben Grunde bearbeitete wahrscheinlich der Holländer G. A. Bredero den *Lazarillo* in seinem *Spaanschen Brabander* (1618) für die Amsterdamer Bühne, indem er dem *hidalgo* den Namen Jerolimo gab. Der Name mag auf eine Reminiszenz an Jeronimo, Marschalk von Hispanien zurückgehen, den Wanderbühnenhelden von Thomas Kyds *The Spanish Tragedy* (ca. 1584).[10] Jedoch ersetzte Bredero den grausamen Spanier durch den Aufschneider, der allein auf den hohlen Schein baut, weil ihm die äußere Ehre über alles geht. So schreitet er als Prahlhans und gespreizter Pfau über die Bühne, um in den aufgeführten Picaroszenen immer wieder sein *desengaño* zu erleben.[11]

Einen Höhepunkt dieser antispanischen Rezeptionslinie bildet Johann Rists aus dem Französischen übertragenes Gedicht "Capitan Spavento oder Rodomontades Espagnolles, das ist: Spanische Auffschneidereyen" (1635). Im Vorwort bezieht sich Rist auf Plautus und die europäische Komödie, die es erlaube, die Fehler anderer Nationen ungestraft zu attackieren. Mit diesem Büchlein wandte er sich gegen die "Maranen", d. h. die ungläubigen Spanier, die schon Opitz in seinem "Gebet, daß Gott die Spanier widerumb vom Rheinstrom wolle treiben" (1620) angegriffen, da sie sich durch ihre Grausamkeit und ihre Großmannssucht unbeliebt machten. Den Capitan läßt Rist etwa zu seinem Famulus sagen: "Hör Junger / wo ich dich soll mit dem Stabe schlagen / so werd ich dich sechs fuß tieff in die Erde jagen" (Str. 2)[12], oder es heißt:

> Als ich mit grosser macht bin Ostend gelegen /
> Spatziert ich einst hinauß / mich etwas zu bewegen /
> So kompt eine Kugel her von 45 Pfund /
> Vnd fleugt mir eben recht gantz fewrig in den Mund /
> Sie traff zwo breite Zahn / doch hab ichs nie empfunden /
>
> . . . .
>
> Ich nam die eussern Nuß / warff sie mit aller macht /
> Der Stadt Ostende zu / das Mawr vnd Thor erkracht /
>
> (Str. 42)[13]

Rist kommt insofern besondere Bedeutung zu, als er 1635 an einem Schnittpunkt der Rezeptionslinien die *leyenda negra* vom spanischen Aufschneider aus dem Französischen übernahm, dadurch gleichzeitig die *capitano*-Tradition wiederbelebte und mit den Rodomontaden die Lügenhelden Schelmuffsky und Münchhausen antizipierte. Ist es verwunderlich, daß Christian Reuter zur Parodie kleinbürgerlicher Adelssucht auf die überlieferte *capitano*-Figur rekurrierte, die ihm aus Molière und Rist bzw. Gryphius (*Horribilicribrifax* 1663) vertraut sein mußte?

Der spanische Prahlhans tritt auch in der Inkarnation Don Quijotes auf, in dem der verarmte Edelmann des *Lazarillo* gleichsam traurig wiederauferstand. Man sehe sich Opitz "hochtrabenden Iberier" in *Anderer Theyl der Argenis* nach Mouchemberg an. Dieser edle Ritter "war so haeger / daß man ihn alle Gebeine im Leibe zaehlen koennen . . . Die Wangen eingefallen als Vogelnester . . . vnd ob er wohl sehr hungrig außsahe / so gab doch sein Antlitz kein ander Zeichen als deß Ruhmes von sich"[14]. Auf die Anrede des Erzählers mit "edler Ritter" streichelt er seinen gabelichten Knebelbart und fragt, "soltet jhr niemahls gehoeret haben erwehnen meiner?" (S. 626). Darauf prahlt er wie Capitan Spavento, daß der Feind sich bereits vor seinem Gesicht entsetzt hätte. Sein Degen könne ihm mehr Reichtum verschaffen "als alle Goldgruben in Peru" zusammen (S. 629). Man erkennt hier, wie Don Quijote aus einer französischen Zwischenstufe in die deutsche Literatur einzieht, und zwar als belachenswerter, bis in groteske Einzelheiten ausgemalter Phantast.

Kurz nach der ersten deutschen Teilübersetzung des *Don Quijote* durch Joachim Caesar im Jahre 1648, die den Helden im Vorwort ebenfalls als Narren bezeichnet, erschienen Rists Friedensdramen, worin Monsieur Sausewind auftaucht. Zunächst scheint er eher als Capitan Spavento angelegt, der mit all seinen Fecht-, Reit- und Redekünsten auf Schelmuffsky vorausdeutet[15], doch zieht Rist in seiner Vorrede zum *Friedejauchzenden Teutschland* (1635) selber eine Parallele zu Don Quijote, indem er auf die französische Version von Sorels *Le Berger extravagant* (1627) verweist.[16] Mit Sausewind, der allerlei "poetische Windmühlen" im Kopf hat und sich in Rosemund verliebt, meinte Rist seinen literarischen Feind Zesen, der in seinem Drama "eine Narrenkappe mit Schellen" erhält.[17]

Interessant ist meines Erachtens, wie aus der *miles gloriosus*-Tradition die literarische Karikatur entsteht, die sich des über Frankreich vermittelten spanischen Kostüms bedient. Aber ich möchte noch ein anderes Beispiel bringen, woraus sich eine weitere Schlußfolgerung ziehen läßt, nämlich den geizigen Dragoner in *Simplicissimus* (Buch 2, Kap. 29), den sechsten Herrn des Simplex, der ebenfalls an Lazarillos Edelmann gemahnt, denn "sein gantzes Thun war fern von Fressen, Sauffen, Spielen und allen Duellen"[18]. Wollte Simplex besser essen, "so mochte . . . [er] stelen, aber mit außtrücklicher Bescheidenheit, daß [sein Herr] nicht darvon innen würde" (S. 181). Gleichzeitig sind die quixotischen Anklänge nicht zu übersehen: der alte Dragoner reitet auf seinem verhungerten Pferd so daher, gefolgt von dem zu Fuße hinterherlaufenden Simplex. Das ist, mit Günther Weydt zu reden, "echter Don Quijote"[19] und zugleich die Inversion der *miles gloriosus*-Tradition: der Herr schlendert einher "wie ein alt Weib am Stecken" und "betrübte im übrigen kein Kind" (S. 181).

Der Liebesnarr

Der Übersichtlichkeit halber haben wir bisher den schwärmerisch-schmachtenden Liebesnarren spanischer Provenienz ausgespart. Im Grunde verhält es sich aber so, daß sich die "Rodomontades Espagnolles" gleich stark im militärischen und erotischen Bereich austoben. Typisch dafür ist Brederos spanischer Brabanter, der in seiner Wirklichkeitsverblendung zwei Straßenmädchen für Göttinnen hält (Akt 2, Szene 5, Z. 627–35) und anschließend wie Lazarillos *hidalgo* vor ihnen ausreißt, als es ans Bezahlen geht. So enthüllt sich hinter dem großmäuligen Auftritt der armselige Wicht. Zu erinnern ist auch an Rists Capitan Spavento, der den Reigen fortsetzt. Seiner militärischen Angeberei korrespondiert die Prahlerei mit seiner Männlichkeit. Zum Beispiel ward ihm die schöne Venus zur Köchin gegben (Str. 38) oder er schwört seiner Dame:

> Daß / werdet jhr euch mir zum Ehgemahl ergeben /
> Ich euch die ersten Nacht wiewol fein sanfft vnd still /
> Ein gantzes Regiment Soldaten machen will /
>
> (Str. 45)

Vor lauter Begeisterung über sich selbst bricht er in einen Schönheitspreis nach dem bewährten Prinzip der insistierenden Nennung aus:

> O Fürstin meiner Arm / O Gräffin meiner Brust /
> O Hertzens Hertzogin / O meine Frewd vnd Lust /
> . . . .
> Euch dank ichs / daß ich so behertzt in Waffen bin /
>
> (Str. 46)

Diese Art amourösen Bramarbasierens, das hier gleichsam die Mode des petrarkistischen Verfahrens ad absurdum führt, erhält seit dem Auftauchen des Don Hylas zusätzliche satirische Möglichkeiten, da bei ihm das ritterliche Kostüm in Anlehnung an Sorels *Berger extravagant* erstmals durch das Schäferhabit verdrängt ist und seine Rede die Alamodesprache karikiert. Hylas geht nach den Forschungen von Schweitzer und Weydt auf Sorels Lysis zurück, den "wahnwitzigen Schäfer" in der Don-Quijote-Nachfolge, wodurch Sorel nicht Cervantes direkt, sondern d'Urfés preziöses Landleben in der *Astrée* verspotten wollte.[20] Der im Deutschen 1645 im Nürnberger Pegnitzkreis zuerst vorkommende Name Hylas stammt bezeichnenderweise aus d'Urfés Roman. Harsdörffer rückte in seinen fünften Teil der *Frauenzimmer Gesprächspiele* ein makkaronisches Gedicht von Hylas ein[21] und lieferte später eine Inhaltsangabe von Sorels Roman[22], während Birken Don Hylas als Parodie der Alamoderede und der Liebesnarretei in der *Fortsetzung der Pegnitz-Schäferey* (1645) auftreten läßt: er erscheint dort mit dem *accoutrement* des Don Quijote, "dürres Sceleton" mit Knebelbart und altem Roß und aufgeblasen wie ein "Kalkutischer Hahn". Er übertrifft Rists Capitan Spavento bei weitem, wenn er die Schäferin Neride folgendermaßen anredet:

> Maistresse meines Leibs / Princesse meiner Glieder /
> Altesse meines Glükks / Duchesse meiner Lieder /
> Lucerne meines Thuns / Artzt meiner nullitet,
> Die meinem sensitif ein güldnes Cabinet,
>
> .   .   .   .
>
> Mein brave Kammerkatz / ich lieb euch incredibel,
> Euch adorirt mon-coeur / acht diß für infallibel,
> Mavie das hangt allein an eurer Huld und Gnad /[23]

Kein Wunder, die häßliche Dulcinea läßt ihn kalt abblitzen, und die lauschenden Pegnitzschäfer lachen sich tot. Ähnlich verachtet Rosemund den Narren Sausewind in Rists Drama *Das Friedejauchzende Teutschland* (1653): während er sie maßlos ins Göttliche erhebt, sorgt sie dafür, daß er tüchtige Bauernprügel erhält.[24] Und Schließlich, hält nicht Leoriander der Hure Perelina Treue bis zum letzten Blutstropfen, weil er zu viele Anstandsbücher gelesen (*Die verwüstete vnd verödete Schäferey*, 1642)? In der Vorrede zu seiner Übersetzung der Thomas-Corneilleschen Bühnenbearbeitung des *Berger extravagant* (1663) weist Gryphius auf den wunden Punkt hin, den diese Narren miteinander teilen: "Die Hirten Namen gehen bereits unter uns in dem schwange, und zuweilen beginnet sich das Leben den Namen zu vergleichen"[25], d. h., die Übergänge zwischen Literatur und Leben zerfließen, was die drastische Reaktion der erdnahen Schäferinnen erklärt, die diejenigen närrischen Liebhaber verlachen, die glauben, schon im Anschauen und Reden der Liebe Genüge zu tun und sich bei alledem noch für die verwegensten Liebhaber halten.

Der Büchernarr

So erstaunt es kaum, wenn sogar die Mitspieler in den Schwarmreden des quixotischen Liebhabers den Keim des Wahnsinns entdecken. Zum Beispiel fragt sich Gryphius' Clarimund (*Der schwermende Schäfer*): "Woher / wie / wo und wann . . . [Lysis] in dem Haupt verwirrt | [Er] find in diesem Schwarm ein wunderseltzam Wesen" (Aufzug 1, Z. 200–201), worauf der Kaufmann Adrian erwidert: "Das ist die recht Frucht von dem verfluchten Lesen!"(1.202). Der Büchernarr ist seit Sebastian Brants *Das Narrenschiff* (1494) in der deutschen Literatur bekannt. Doch ist "Lysis" durchaus nicht mit dem sündigen Narren zu verwechseln, der sich mit ungelesenen Büchern umgibt, um sich den Anschein der Gelehrsamkeit zu geben. Brants Büchernarr ist vielmehr Gegentyp zu dem "spanischen Narren", weil er vor der Lektüre zurückschreckt, womit Lysis Ernst macht: "Wer viel studiert, wird ein Phantast!" (*Das Narrenschiff*, Kap. 1). Titel wie "Der wahnwitzige Schäfer" machen auf diesen Zusammenhang aufmerksam, der nicht aus dem Gesamtbild des spanischen Narren hinwegzudenken ist, dessen "spanische Luft im Kopf"[26] nicht nur auf den übertriebenen Stolz, sondern auf die verrückten Luftschlösser anspielt, die seit Don Quijotes Erstauftritt in Heidelberg 1613 wie Windmühlen darin herumgehen, weil man sich "überstudiert" hat. Auf den wahnsinnigen Don Quijote führt G. Weydt bekanntlich Jupiters partielle Narrheit im *Simplicissimus* zurück, indem er auf die Nürnberger als Vermittler zwischen Cervantes, Sorel und Grimmelshausen und auf die Möglichkeit von dessen *Don Quijote*-Lektüre in der deutschen oder niederländischen Fassung hinweist.[27] Jedenfalls führt Simplicissimus den Jupiter als "Phantasten" vor, "der sich überstudirt und in der Poeterey gewaltig verstiegen" (Buch 3, Kap. 3, S. 209) quixotische Weltreformpläne entwickelt.

"Das verfluchte Lesen" und der Unterricht nach Büchern haben auch nachweisbare Auswirkungen auf Simplex und darüber hinaus auf seinen Autor. Simplex, der Narr in Christo, schließt nämlich von der Bibel auf die Wirklichkeit, indem er der Illusion von dem wirklichen Leben der Bibelholzschnitte verfällt und das "schön illuminierte" Hiobs-Feuer löschen möchte (1.10); darauf wendet er sein Bibelwissen auf die Wirklichkeit an, weil er als unschuldiger Gottesnarr nichts von der Welt weiß und sie zunächst töricht mit der in der Bibel erweckten Illusion von einer heilen Realität verwechselt und dann daran mißt. Fragt er sich doch, ob er "nicht auch auff des Apostels Wort offenhertzig schließen dörffen" (1.24, S. 67). Auf seine Weise folgt er somit dem Schlußverfahren der edlen Narren Don Quijote und Jupiter. Erst am Ende des Lebens, nachdem er als "schlimmer Gesell" durch die Welt gegangen, findet der schiffbrüchige Simplicius auf der "Insul" zum Buch zurück, diesmal allerdings ohne Scheuklappen einfältiger Verblendung, sondern erleuchteten Geistes, da er nach dem Vorbild eines "heiligen Mannes" in Ermangelung von Büchern die Welt zum Buch Gottes umdeutet (6.23) und sich von quixotischem Wahnwitz um sein Seelenheil besorgt distanziert (6.25).[28]

Nun dürfte Grimmelshausen selbst aufgrund seiner überdurchschnittlichen Lesewut auf die offenbar spanische Praxis des *mantea-*

miento, des Herumschleuderns junger Leute in Laken gestoßen sein, die in ursprünglicher Form in *Guzmán de Alfarache* (Teil 1, Buch 3, Kap. 1) und im *Don Quijote* (Teil 1, Kap. 17) vorlag. Diese Szene, als Simplicissimus den *manteamiento* (2.5) über sich ergehen lassen muß, damit er stirbt und als Kalbsnarr wiederaufersteht, liefert den Initiationsritus für den Hofnarren in Hanau, der spanischen Ursprungs ist und zugleich an Shakespeares Fool erinnert. Die ihn zum Narren machten, mußten nun seine Narren sein (2.5), und indem er der Welt die bittere Wahrheit sagt, fungiert er als "ein Oracul oder Warnung Gottes" beim Gubernator (2.13, S. 133).[29]

Rezeption im 18. Jahrhundert

Mir kommt es nun darauf an, die Rezeptionslinie des spanischen Narren noch etwas weiter in das 18. Jahrhundert hinein zu verlängern. Da ist an der Jahrhundertwende zunächst die aus dem Französischen übertragene *Don Quijote*-Fortsetzung von 1696 zu nennen, *Der spanische Waghalß*, ein Sammelsurium von Abenteuern, eingelegten Novellen und Unterhaltungen aus frühaufklärerischem Geiste, worin Don Quijote in unverminderter partieller Verrücktheit über die Ungerechtigkeit der Welt spintisiert und von Amadís inspiriert alle Räuber und Teufel von der Erde verjagen möchte. Deutlich setzt er mit seinen Rodomontaden die *capitano*-Tradition fort, als er eine Schmiede attackiert, die er für die Hölle hält.[30] Nur periphere Bedeutung erlangt Don Quijote als irrender Ritter und verlachter Phantast in dem zusammengewürfelten "Spanischen Roman" *Die Verliebte Verzweifflung* von 1728.[31] Daß die spanische Lesewut auch das schöne Geschlecht befallen konnte, beweisen einige um die Jahrhundertmitte entstandene Romane, deren Heldinnen die Wirklichkeit durch die Sonnenbrille ihrer Lektüre sehen, z. B. "Donna Quichotte" in *Der unsichtbare Robinson* (1752) und *Don Quixote im Reifrock* (1753).[32] Einige Bedeutung erlangte jedoch erst Wilhelm Neugebauers *Der Teutsche Don Quichotte oder die Begebenheiten des Marggraf von Bellamonte Komisch und satyrisch beschrieben* (1753), ein Werk, das Cervantes' "Thematik und Konfiguration . . . konsequent auf deutsche Verhältnisse überträgt"[33] und bereits auf die Wielandsche und die romantische Rezeption *Don Quijotes* vorausweist[34], habe dieser doch nach F. Schlegel "die ganze Gattung der neueren Romane mit veranlasst"[35]. Nach Lessings Urteil ist Neugebauers "Nachahmung . . . keine von den schlechtesten." Wie es in seiner Rezension in der *Berlinischen Zeitung* von 1753 heisst, ist

> Sein Don Quixote, . . . ein deutscher Kaufmannsdiener, dessen Einbildung die Lesung der französischen Romane verrückt hat, so dass er nichts geringer als ein Graf zu seyn glaubt, und nichts begieriger sucht als Abentheuer, die ihm seine Tapferkeit und seine edlen Gesinnungen zu zeigen Gelegenheit geben. Sein Sancho Panza ist ein Diener, der die Einfalt selbst ist, und dem sein Herr den romanhaften Namen du Bois gegeben hat. Seine Dulcinea ist ein gutes Dorffräulein, deren Verstand an einem gleichen Fieber krank liegt, und die sich eine Gräfin von Villa-Franka zu seyn einbildet.[36]

Soweit Lessing, der nicht darauf eingeht, daß der anonyme Verfasser auf der Titelseite behauptet, sein Roman sei "aus dem Französischen übersezt." Das ist insofern wichtig, als der Literaturnarr vor Tiecks Eindeutschung des *Don Quijote* (1799–1800) weitgehend über französische Vermittlung herumschwärmte. So auch im Falle Bellamontes, der "die Artigkeit der Franzosen", wie sich der Erzähler ausdrückt, aus "den neuesten Romanen" Marivaux' erlernte.[37] Cervantes à la Marivaux konnte nur zu *marivaudages* führen, also zur psychologischen Analyse von Empfindungen am kaum vorhandenen Leitfaden amadesker Abenteuer in einem affektierten Stil, den Neugebauer nun satirisch entlarvt. Am Romanende vollzieht sich unter Ablegung der Adelsnamen die Hochzeit der zwei Paare wie in einem Marivauxschen Lustspiel, aber erst, nachdem die "Roman-Grillen" der Einsicht in die "Ausschweiffungen" der Phantasie gewichen sind.[38] Gefunden ist der "wahre Mittelweg der gesunden Vernunft", die nun die "zärtlichen Empfindungen" kontrollieren wird.[39]

Etwa ein Jahrzehnt später sollte Wieland noch einmal die spanische Narrheit im *Don Sylvio von Rosalva* (1764) in den Mittelpunkt rücken und auch eine ähnliche Lösung anstreben. Zum letzten Mal gelangen ihm hier Parodien zweier hirnverbrannter Helden, Don Sylvios und Prinz Biribinkers, die nicht zwischen Fiktion und Wirklichkeit unterscheiden können, denn die deutsche Romantik wird Don Quijote zur mythologischen Idealgestalt uminterpretieren. Wieland ging es darum, der "Dummheit, Schwärmerei und Schelmerei ihre betrüglichen Masken" abzuziehen, "die Menschen mit ihren Leidenschaften und Torheiten in ihrer wahren Gestalt, weder vergrößert noch verkleinert" abzuschildern (Buch 2, Kap. 1). Es war seine Absicht, mit dem Typ des durch französische Vermittlung verbreiteten Schwärmers abzurechnen, in dessen Kopf die "poetische und bezauberte Welt" die wirkliche verdrängt hatte (1.3). Don Sylvio, "eine Art von einem jungen Don Quichotte", wird im zweiten Teil deshalb desillusioniert und schließlich aus dem Stande des Narrentums zur Weisheit geführt.

Die Lesewut empfindsamer Provenienz herrscht in der Literatur parallel zum Sturm und Drang bis in die achtziger Jahre, genährt von Rousseaus *Nouvelle Helöise* (1761), Sternes *Sentimental Journey* (1768) und Johann Millers *Siegwart* (1776), so daß es kaum verwundert, Goethe in Weimar diesem ganzen Zauber zumindest für seine Generation den Todesstoß versetzen zu sehen. Prinz Oronaro, die Hauptfigur in *Der Triumph der Empfindsamkeit* (1777, gedr. 1787), umgibt sich mit einer artifiziellen Natur in der Stube, damit er den Mond und die Geliebte als ausgestopfte Puppe auf dem Hintergrund einer Wandtapete je nach Laune anbeten kann. Als man die "Zauberbücher" findet, die ihm den Blick für die Wirklichkeit verrückt haben, heißt es wie bei Cervantes: "Nur ins Feuer damit!" (Akt 5). Das bedeutete zugleich Goethes Abschied von seinem von Ossian geschlagenen Werther und der gesamten Werthermanie der Zeit.

Die barocke Phase des spanischen Narren war damit vorbei, jedoch lassen sich die Symptome seiner "partiellen Verrücktheit" (G. Weydt) noch bis in die Romantik verfolgen, als Cervantes' *Don Quijote* eingedeutscht und der Romanproduktion integriert wurde. Ja, das Problem von Literatur und Leben, oder anders ausgedrückt, der zu fatalen Konsequenzen führende Ersatz des Lebens durch die Literatur erhält erst in der Nachromantik etwa bei Puschkin und Flaubert zentrale Bedeutung, obgleich das spanische Milieu dann keine Rolle mehr spielt.

Zusammenfassung

Sind wir nun wie Don Sylvio einem blauen Schmetterling nachgejagt? Ist der spanische Narr nur ein Hirngespenst, ein Luftschloß der Forschung? Sollte ich vielleicht, um Storms Wort über Heyses Falken abzuwandeln, diesen Vogel getrost wieder fliegen lassen? Ich glaube nicht, es handelt sich vielmehr im Unterschied zu dem weisen englischen Hofnarren um einen eigenen Typ, der sich deutlich in der Barockliteratur abzeichnet.

Er leitet sich historisch her von der *leyenda negra*, die in den von dem spanischen Imperialismus bedrohten Ländern grassierte und den Typ des prahlenden *capitano* auf antiker Basis wiederbelebte, zunächst in der Commedia dell'arte, darauf im Capitan Spavento Frankreichs und Deutschlands. Die von der spanischen Großmachtpolitik ausgelösten polemischen Reaktionen schufen eine eigene literarische Tradition, die nach dem Ende der "spanischen Gefahr"[40] weiterwirkte und nicht nur mit der Alamodekritik, sondern auch mit der Rezeptionslinie des närrischen Ritters von *Lazarillo* und *Don Quijote* verschmolz. Beispiele dafür liefern der Signor Spangniol und der geizige Dragoner.

Der spanische Narr manifestiert sich in dem *miles gloriosus*, dem Liebes- und dem Büchernarren (s. Jupiter) mit vielfachen Übergängen. Je nach Situation kehrt der Narr die eine oder andere Seite hervor. Worauf es den Autoren ankam, war die komische Verwirrung von Fiktion und Realität, von Schein und Sein aufzuzeigen und diesen Narrentyp dem Gespött der Leser auszuliefern. Denn man lacht nicht *mit* dem spanischen Narren, man lacht *über* ihn. Der Autor darf wie der Fool mit Lachen die Wahrheit sagen, während sein spanischer Narr die Wahrheit erleiden muß; der Fool hält den Spiegel, der spanische Narr erscheint im Spiegel; jener ist englischer Hofnarr, dieser wird im Kielwasser der *leyenda negra* vorwiegend im Ausland rezipiert; er wird Gegenstand der Kritik nicht nur in politischen Flugschriften und in der schönen Literatur, sondern auch in der Musik bis in das frühe 18. Jahrhundert hinein.[41] Auf dem Hintergrund der antiken *miles gloriosus*-Tradition zeichnet sich seit Herzog Heinrich Julius' "Sacrapa von Mantua" (1594) die gleichsam leitmotivische Wiederkehr des spanischen Narren ab, wobei der Edelmann Lazarillos allmählich in Don Quijote übergeht (Rist!). Mit zum Teil stereotypen Merkmalen ausgestattet ergibt sich für diesen Narren eine gewisse Kontinuität von dem "Sacrapen" über Don Hylas bis zu Don Sylvio. Eine Mischung von Hofnarr und "spanischem Narr" kommt, soweit festgestellt, vor der Romantik zuerst bei Simplicius in Hanau vor.

Simplicius ist es auch, der auf Grund seines Vagantentums und seiner "Kostumköpfigkeit" (Thomas Mann) pikareske Züge annimmt, ganz zu schweigen von der Adelskritik und der Ichperspektive des Erzählers. Diese Tatsache dient mir jedoch eher als Beweis für die Mehrschichtigkeit des Grimmelshausenschen Werkes und seine Unausschöpfbarkeit denn als Zeugnis für eine zwar vorstellbare, aber in der Literatur sonst kaum anzutreffende Verquickung zweier zu trennender Leitfiguren, des spanischen Narren und des Picaro bzw. Schelms. Bekanntlich gelten für diesen Typ ganz andere konstitutive Merkmale, nämlich die dunkle Abkunft, der bis zur Sünde und Kriminalität gesteigerte Kampf ums Überleben, die sozialkritische Erzählperspektive von unten usw.[42] Offenbar ist die französische Vermittlung, deren Grund man in der antispanischen Haltung Frankreichs zu suchen hat, für die deutsche Rezeption des spanischen

Narren vielfach entscheidend gewesen, während der Picaroroman direkt aus Spanien importiert wurde.

Anmerkungen

1. Christoph E. Schweitzer, "Spanien in der deutschen Literatur des 17. Jahrhunderts", Diss. Yale University, 1954.

2. Hermann Tiemann, Hrsg., *Leben vnd Wandel Lazaril von Tormes* (Glückstadt: Maximilian-Gesellschaft, 1951), Kap. 3. Weitere Seitenangaben im Text beziehen sich auf diese Ausgabe.

3. S. Arnoldsson, *La leyenda negra: Estudios sobre sus orígenes* (Stockholm: Almqvist und Wiksell, 1960), S. 115–16.

4. Schweitzer, "Spanien in der deutschen Literatur", S. 51.

5. Siehe den Verfasser, *Spanien und Deutschland. Geschichte und Dokumentation der literarischen Beziehungen*, Grundlagen der Romanistik, Bd. 9 (Berlin: Erich Schmidt, 1976), S. 34.

6. Siehe Fischarts "Siegdank oder Triumpffspruch" (1588); J. Weiss, "Don Quijote am kurpfälzischen Hofe 1613, sein öffentlicher Einzug in Deutschland", *Das Bayerland* 27 (1961): 143–44.

7. Siehe z. B. das holländische Spottblatt auf den Bischof von Galen von 1665 (FM 2339 B. St. 2450 im Landesmuseum und Stadtarchiv Münster), dazu den Verfasser, "Grimmelshausens *Simplicissimus* und der spanische Schelmenroman", *Daphnis* 5 (1976): 275–94.

8. Dazu siehe *Lazarillo de Tormes*, Kap. 3.

9. Str. 11, vgl. Schweitzer, "Spanien in der deutschen Literatur", S. 230–31; das Flugblatt ist in mehreren Fassungen abgedruckt in John Roger Paas, *The German Political Broadsheet 1600–1700*, 2 Bde. (Wiesbaden: Harrassowitz, 1985–86), 1:215–16; 365–66.

10. Im deutschen Repertoire seit 1626, siehe W. Flemming, Hrsg., *Jeronimo, Marschalck in Hispanien* (Hildesheim: Olms, 1973).

11. Siehe Robbeknol in Akt 2, Szene 5, Z. 536–37 in der Ausgabe G. A. Bredero, *The Spanish Brabanter*, übertr. v. H. D. Brumble III (Binghamton, N.Y.: Center for Medieval and Early Renaissance Studies, 1982).

12. Johann Rist, *Capitan Spavento, Oder Rodomontades Espagnolles. Das ist: Spanische Auffschneidereyen . . . Zum Drittenmahl Gedruckt bey Johann Guttwasser* (o. O.: Tobias Gundermann, 1640), Sig. A8r.

13. Ebd., Sig. C5r.

14. Martin Opitz, *Anderer Theyl der Argenis* (Breslau: David Müller, 1631), Buch 2, Kap. 6, S. 625. Exemplar: George Schulz-Behrend (University of Texas, Austin).

15. Johann Rist, *Sämtliche Werke*, 7 Bde., hrsg. v. E. Mannack, (Berlin: de Gruyter, 1972), 2:129–30; 142.

16. Rist, *Sämtliche Werke*, 2:227; siehe auch Schweitzer, "Spanien in der deutschen Literatur", S. 118.

17. Rist, *Sämtliche Werke*, 2:449; Schweitzer, "Spanien in der deutschen Literatur", S. 59; 119.

18. H. J. C. von Grimmelshausen, *Der abentheurliche Simplicissimus Teutsch* . . ., hrsg. v. Rolf Tarot (Tübingen: Niemeyer, 1967), S. 181. Die Seitenangaben im Text beziehen sich auf diese Ausgabe.

19. Günther Weydt, *Nachahmung und Schöpfung. Studien um Grimmelshausen* (Bern: Francke, 1968), S. 149.

20. Schweitzer, "Spanien in der deutschen Literatur", S. 116; Weydt, *Nachahmung und Schöpfung*, S. 143.

21. Schweitzer, "Spanien in der deutschen Literatur", S. 115.

22. Teil 7 (1647), Nr. 257.

23. Abgedruckt in E. Mannack, Hrsg., *Die Pegnitz-Schäfer. Nürnberger Barockdichtung* (Stuttgart: Reclam, 1968), S. 236; 238.

24. Rist, *Sämtliche Werke*, 2:389.

25. *Der schwermende Schäffer*, in Andreas Gryphius, *Lustspiele 2*, hrsg. v. Hugh Powell (Tübingen: Niemeyer, 1972), S. 108. Weitere Angaben beziehen sich auf diese Edition.

26. Harsdörffer, zitiert nach Schweitzer, "Spanien in der deutschen Literatur", S. 60.

27. Weydt, *Nachahmung und Schöpfung*, S. 148.

28. Simplicius sieht z. B. einen tollgewordenen holländischen Matrosen: "Da stund einer mit plosem Degen vor einem Baum / fochte mit demselbigen und gab vor / er hätte den allergrößten Risen zubestreiten" (6.25, S. 574).

29. Zum spanischen Einfluß siehe den Verfasser, wie Anm. 7; zum Narrenmotiv siehe Paul Gutzwiller, "Der Narr bei Grimmelshausen", Diss. Basel 1959; zum *manteamiento* siehe z. B. Ursula Mahlendorf, "Child Brainwashing in Two Pre-Romantic Novels", *American Journal of Social Psychiatry* 4 (1984): 45–51.

30. *Der Spanische Waghalß: Oder des von Liebe bezauberten Ritters Don Quixott von Quixada gantz neue Ausschweiffung auf seiner Weissen Rosinante* (Nürnberg, 1696), S. 229–33.

31. *Die Verliebte Verzweifflung In einem anmuthigen Spanischen Roman vorgestellet; Nebst gantz neuen Abentheuern deß Berühmten Ritters Don Quichotte. Aus dem Frantzösischen ins Teutsche übersetzet und mit Kupffern gezieret*. Frankfurt und Leipzig In Verlag Daniel Walders (Augsburg, 1718). [Nach *Le Desespoir amoureux avec les nouelles visions de Don Quichotte. Histoire espagnole* (Amsterdam: Josué Steenhouwer, 1715).]

32. Lucian Tannenbaum [Pseudonym], *Hilarius Goldsteins Leben und Reisen oder Der unsichtbare Robinson* (Frankfurt/Leipzig, 1752); *Don Quixote im Reifrocke, oder die abentheuerlichen Begebenheiten der Romanheldin Arabella* (Hamburg/Leipzig, 1754 [1753]).

33. Wilhelm Neugebauer, *Der Teutsche Don Quichotte oder die Begebenheiten des Marggraf von Bellamonte Komisch und satyrisch beschrieben*, hrsg. v. L. E. Kurth und H. Jantz (Berlin: de Gruyter, 1972), S. 405.

34. Siehe den Verfasser, *Spanien und Deutschland*, S. 124–25.

35. Friedrich Schlegel, *Geschichte der alten und neuen Literatur*, Kritische Friedrich-Schlegel-Ausgabe, Bd. 6, hrsg. v. Hans Eichner (Paderborn: Schöningh, 1961), S. 274.

36. Zitiert nach dem Realienteil von Kurth-Jantz, wie Anm. 33, dazu S. 392–93.

37. Neugebauer, *Der Teutsche Don Quichotte*, S. 16.

38. Ebd., S. 245.

39. Ebd., S. 248.

40. Etwa nach der Schlacht von Nördlingen von 1634.

41. Dazu siehe z. B. das populäre Lied von A. Corelli (1653–1713), "Folla di Spagna."

42. "Zur Problematik der pikarischen Romanform" siehe den Verfasser, Hrsg., *Der deutsche Schelmenroman im europäischen Kontext*, Chloe, Bd. 5 (Amsterdam: Rodopi 1987), Einleitung.

Part III. Emperors and Princes: Society and Politics in Early Modern German Literature

7. The Eagle of the Empire

George C. Schoolfield

Of late, Balde scholarship has called attention to the complexity and, sometimes, the ambiguity of the odes of the greatest of Germany's seventeenth-century Latinists, the Jesuit Jakob Balde. The intention of this essay, however, is to comment on a Balde ode that shines by its apparent simplicity and by the apparent directness of its aims, the ode (Odes 1:38) to the eagle of the Empire.[1]

Ad Aquilam Romani Imperii

Surge, Romani Iovis et trisulci
Fulminis custos aviumque Caesar;
Praeliaturas acies minatur
    Ala rebellis;

Vulturi Sueco sociant frequentes
Signa bubones, acuuntque rostra.
Totus hostili legione circum-
    texitur aether.

Stringe iam notos, neque differ, ungueis.
Arma concussa sonuere nube.
Sistit in caelo veterem tibi Phar-
    salia campum.

Pelle Finlandos, age, pelle corvos:
Ora Stymphali vacuetur Hunnis:
Milviis ningat, lacerisque Lappis
    Fluctuet aer.

Victor optantem redeas Viennam,
Alitum sacra comitante turma.
Impleat Mavors spoliis volantum
    Castra Quiritum.

At the outset, to be sure, we might come across a small difficulty if we asked ourselves a question about the title: is it in fact not directed to the eagle but to the eagle's master? And, if so, which master is it?

The possibilities, obviously, are Ferdinand II and Ferdinand III. The elder Ferdinand passed away in 1637, and the collected odes did not appear until 1643, so that the contemporary purchaser of them might well have concluded that it was pointed at the new monarch. Yet it is altogether possible that many of the odes were circulated in manuscript before 1643, and, long ago, Georg Westermayer proposed that some of them had been written as early as 1630; a simple case in point is 2:26, written for a ceremony in 1638.[2] Thus 1:38 could be an exhortation to Ferdinand II to be up and doing. It could likewise be a heartier and more direct form of the appeal made (it has been assumed)[3] to Ferdinand III in the chess-ode, 3:13, where "King Adrastus"—the king of Argos, the hesitant participant in the campaign against Thebes —is told to get himself to the front: "Incauto nocuit credere militi / Maiestatis onus. qui residet domi, / Absens plurima nesciet" [It has done harm to entrust the burden of majesty to the reckless soldier; whoever stays at home, absent (from the scene of battle), will not know most things]. Perhaps the problem of the identity of the man behind the eagle is insoluble; the case is altogether different from that of M. C. Sarbiewski's ode to Ferdinand II (2:12).[4] There the recipient is named and then showered with praise, rather hopefully, as the bringer of peace and plenty, "Magne pacati Moderator orbis" [Oh great governor of a pacified world]. Reading this long and unambiguous ode to Ferdinand II, from the Sarmatian Horace, we may wonder why Balde—the devoted subject of Habsburg—never expressly addressed an ode to the one or the other of the emperors who reigned during the gestation of the *Carmina Lyrica*.[5] And we may wonder why we are left only with the little ode to the Imperial eagle, five strophes, seventy-four words.

From the outset of the writing of commentary on the ode, the eagle was taken as a simple incorporation of the Imperial nation's splendor and strength, "die alte Kaiserherrlichkeit," as Anton Heinrich said.[6] Heinrich wrote in 1915, a time given to patriotic rhetoric, and things had not changed since Georg Westermayer had come up with his opinion of 1868: that the poem was an address—a passionate one, "stürmisch," to the Empire itself, in eagle's form, "bei seinem Auszuge zum heiligen Kampfe," a going-forth accompanied with "heissen Segenswünschen" on the poet's part.[7] Martin Heinrich Müller likewise sees the eagle as a sign of the continuity from Roman antiquity to the Catholic-Christian present, "Wächter des antikrömischen Jupiter" and "Wappentier des Habsburgerreichs."[8] Dieter Breuer, in 1980, also seems at first to take the eagle as spiritual-political symbol and not as the representative of a single emperor or concerned with a special situation. In the course of his cogent main argument—that Balde is by no means as faithful a servant of the electoral prince, Maximilian of Wittelsbach, as his biographers have assumed but, conversely, remains forever the exiled Habsburg Alsatian—Breuer offers the ode in question as evidence: "Nicht den bayrischen Löwen sondern den römischen Reichsadler des 'Teutonicus' bzw., 'Austriacus' 'Jupiter' [as in Odes 1:36, and *Silvae* 4, Threnody 2] bemüht er als Retter in der Kriegsnot."[9] Yet Breuer continues with the altogether reasonable thought that an emperor stands behind the eagle, sets him loose, gets him flying. This fact—which Breuer calls "der politisch-konkrete Gedanke" of the poem—is revealed in the final strophe; the bird may fly home, as a victor, to Vienna, "Victor optantem redeas Viennam."

Still, the word "Vienna" turns up only in the last strophe; before that, apparently, Balde has done his best to make the reader believe that his ode is directed at Imperial power, not a specific emperor. The bird itself is the recipient of the basic verbal structure of the poem. The ode is built on a series of imperatives, injunctions more likely to be addressed to a bird, however regal, than to an emperor. These imperatives are spaced out quite regularly through the poem: the single imperative "Surge," which is followed by the finite verbs describing the dangerous situation at hand ("minatur," "sociant," "acuunt," "texitur"); then the double imperative of line 9 ("Stringe . . . neque differ"), followed by the present perfects, with their description of what has already taken place, to create the crisis situation; and then the triple imperatives of line 13, "Pelle . . . age, pelle," followed by the urgings and promises of what is to come if the eagle bestirs itself ("vacuetur," "ningat," "fluctuet," "redeas" and, finally, "Impleat"). With his customary verbal skill, Balde has made a crescendo, a *klimax*, from one command to two or three, leading the bird from stage to stage; at the same time, even as he tells the bird not to hesitate, he has in fact delayed the action, increased the tension, which is released, then, in the jussives and the flurry of feathers of the penultimate strophe.

Yet, in his artfulness, Balde never lets the readers forget that they are witnessing an avian event, a bird battle. The words beginning with *a* ("avium," "acies," "Ala") move line by line toward the left margin of the page in the first strophe, and two of them, plainly, are bird-words, the middle a war-word. The dullest eye will see that the strophe's Adonic, "Ala rebellis," is meant as the clincher of the chain of alliterative words: the rebel wing (of a bird and an army) has been set up opposite the Caesar of birds. The device, of course, is a time-honored one; in Germany's political poetry, Petrus Lotichius Secundus had used it in the concluding vision of his elegy on the mid-sixteenth-century siege of Magdeburg, where the poet—vaguely anti-Imperial on religious grounds yet anxious that the Empire be preserved—sees how the Imperial eagle attacks the white swan of the brave town.[10] In turn, the eagle is held off by the watchful bird, the Gallic cock, which summons the dawn with songs: "vigil, auroram qui cantibus evocat, ales." The circumspect Lotichius does not tell how the fight ends. His vision stops with the abrupt and unexplained restoration of peace after the threat of awful catastrophe: he does not want to see the swan of Magdeburg killed, but it likewise is unthinkable that the eagle of the Empire should be bested by the rooster of France. Balde, of course, the thoroughgoing Imperialist of the next century, knows no such constraints. He sees a clear threat to his "Rome" in this heavenly Pharsalia, where the whole sky is filled with hostile birds sharpening their beaks. It is a passage in which Balde turns around a typical element of Protestant propaganda in the Thirty Years War. The anti-Imperial forces liked to present themselves as a gallant little band, a David opposing an Imperial Goliath—the suggestion made by "Gustaf Adolf's field-psalm" in its three languages, "Verzage nicht, du Häuflein klein," "Förfäras ej, du lilla hop," "Pois pelko, joukko pienoinen." Here, the eagle is briefly the underdog, or more accurately, the underbird. But only briefly: the poet knows that the moment of greatest peril, the battle of Pharsalia, in which Julius Caesar routed Pompey, can be turned into the moment of greatest triumph; the eagle will make short work of its numerous opponents—as is predicted in strophe four, where there are still more bird-allusions and bird-jokes.

Like a Hercules, the eagle will rid the Stymphalian lands of the "Hunnish birds," the air will snow with the feathers of those birds of prey, the kites (a dark snow, since kites are dark gray, or black),[11] and swirl with the fragments of lacerated Lapps—an outrageous but visually suggestive pun on the German-Latin "lappi" from "der Lappe, der Lappen," "rag," and its resemblance to "Lappi" (or "Lappones"), that is, people from Lapland.[12] Then, the bird-battle having been won, the winged victor will return with his squadrons to Vienna; the triumphant flight is emphasized (a counterpart to the ominous *a*-words of strophe one and the equally ominous *s*-words of strophe two: "Sueco," "sociant," "Signa") by the triple alliteration on *v*: "Victor," "Viennam," "volantum." The alliterations, like the climax of imperatives, are devices obviously meant to catch and sway the reader. After all, this is propaganda poetry.

In his commentary to the odes, Benno Müller saw something very grand in this procession of the bird-army back to Vienna; it reminded him of the flight of angels.[13] (We might ask, of course, what sort of booty the angels were bearing, and why they were bound for Vienna instead of heaven.) Father Müller—like Westermayer and Heinrich after him—wanted to put the poem in a noble light, to see it as a general statement about threats to and victories of the Empire. In this connection, Müller identified the "bubones" of the gathering foe in the second strophe as the Turks, threatening the Empire from one side as the Swedes of Gustaf Adolf—the Swedish vulture—did from the other. He neglected to say who the Huns were; but Max Wehrli, following Müller's Turkish lead, identified them in a note to his translation as, again, Turks: "die Hunnen sind die Türken."[14] Although these Turkish explanations give the poem an added geographical-historical dimension, they are wrong. In the poems touching upon the depredations of the Swedish forces in Bavaria, Balde calls the Swedish troops—or their Finnish contingents—Huns, because of their less-than-admirable conduct, while Gustaf Adolf is Attila. In 2:26, on Maximilian's dedication of the statue of the Virgin Mary in Munich's main square in 1638, Balde recalls the Swedish occupation of the city six years before; as might be expected, Munich was under the special protection of the Blessed Virgin Mother, so that the efforts of Gustaf Adolf's wretched guest, Frederick of the Palatinate, to set the place afire came to naught. Yet matters were bad enough; the thunder of Mars echoed in the marketplace, and "Hic epulans ululavit Hunnus" [Here, roistering, the Hun howled]. Or, in 2:17, the "Paean Parthenius Boicarum virginum, quae pro defendenda castitate contra Suecorum irruentium furias viriliter decertarunt," Balde tells how Bavaria's virgins, having manfully defended their chastity against the furies of the raging Swedes, died rather than to submit to a fate worse than death from these "Huns." In the same poem, the Lapps are mocked—they are cheated of their prey and called weaklings to boot: "o bene Lappia / Delusa mollis." Balde talks of real events, the sack of Landsberg by the Swedes and Finns under Torstenson in 1633, and of Landshut by the troops of Horn in 1634. As for those particular companions of the Swedish vulture, the "bubones," Balde has likewise made use of a standard element of Catholic propaganda, directed at the forces under the Swedish flag. The "bubones" are, again, the Finns, who come from the realm of midnight. Forty-odd years after Balde wrote, the Capuchin monk-poet Laurentius von Schnüffis (Johann Martin) had not forgotten their terrible behavior and gave them a special place in his description of the night of the human soul:

Sehet die nächtigen, / immer schattächtigen Finnen doch an /
Wie sie in dünsteren / dicken und finsteren
Nebel und Düfften / Schatten und Lüfften
     Seynd eingethan:
     Die Sonne sehen sie
     Auch etlich Monat nie.[15]

The "bubones" are the birds of midnight, specifically horned owls, with their giant tufts of ear-hair, and they may have seemed altogether appropriate to Balde for suggesting the Finnish troops who served together with those of the Swedish vulture.

The very appearance of the Finns caused horror and loathing among their opponents, a reaction of which rich use was made. There exists, for example, a rhymed dialogue from 1631, in which a conversation is held between the two wildest contingents in the Swedish army, the Lapps (i.e., the Finns) and the Irishmen (i.e., the Scots).[16] Erich Kunze has demonstrated that there were no Lapps as such in the Swedish army; propagandists used the Lapp-word because of the familiar story that Lapps were wizards, as is shown in the rhymed "Gespräch zwischen Lappländern und kaiserlichen Soldaten," where Tilly's pious trooper says: "Das hab ich schon lange hören sagen / Mit schwarzen Künsten thust du es wagen" and "Die Lappländer sind nicht rechte Christen / Denn sie nur in der Wildnuss nisten."[17] (Does the trooper, like Balde, think of the Lapps as evil birds?) Now, the rhymed dialogue between the Lapp-Finn and the Irish-Scot pays particular attention, in its accompanying etching and its descriptive text, to the appearance of the "Lapp," who in fact is illustrated twice, as "der lappe" and "der Finlander."[18] The two look quite alike; both have the old-fashioned Finnish winter cap of fur with giant ear-flaps. (The principal difference between them, in fact, is that the Lapp carries a bow and arrow, the Finn a musket, sword, and bandolier—the Finns were the much feared mounted infantry, or light cavalry, the *agmen horribile haccapelitorum*, of the Swedish army.)[19] And, to make matters of appearance worse, and more horned-owl-like, the Finns did not cut their hair. In the former of the broadsheets just mentioned, the Tilly soldier says: "Hast so viel Haar, der Wind dich jagt," whereas in another, "Der wolerfaren Schleifer," the Finns brag about their long hair: "Drum tragen wir Finnen so lange Haar."[20]

It should be plain by this time that Balde's poem is directed solely against the Swedish forces and, especially, toward that particularly thankful object, the Finns—whether they be called "bubones," "Hunni," "Lappi," or straight out "Finlandos . . . corvos." They were hated and feared, all the more because of their record of torturing and killing priests. Indeed, the Laplander, in the conversation with the Irish-Scot, says that, although he is somewhat baffled as to why he is in Germany, he nonetheless bears a special hatred for Tilly and, then, for the Jesuits:

> Es ist ein Kerl, soll Tylli Heissen,
>   Den solln wir helffen abschmeissen,
> Ein Teil heissen auch Jesuiter,
>   Das sind die rechten ehrlichen Blüter.[21]

The detestation was mutual. Balde himself had seen the Finns at close hand and had recorded the fact. He was engaged in the study of theology at Ingolstadt when the Swedish army used its Finnish shock troops to make the bridgehead across the Lech River at Rain on 15 April (n.s.), 1632, opening Bavaria to Gustaf Adolf—the engagement in which Tilly, Balde's idol, was mortally wounded: the field marshal was brought to Ingolstadt, where he died on 30 April. The work that grew out of his death was Balde's long valedictory, *Magni Tillii Parentalia;* it includes, early on, the diary Balde kept during the siege of Ingolstadt by Gustaf Adolf and his Swedes and Finns. Quite naturally, Balde was not a little anxious about what went on outside the beleaguered city's walls. He saw (or implies that he saw) an attack of Gustaf Adolf's cavalry against the southern sector of the Imperial lines. "Six squadrons of *hippocentauri* (it may be allowed to call them infantrymen, bearing musket on horseback; the Swedes call them *tragones*)" suddenly appear; they charge and drive the defenders back into the palisades.[22] The garrison of Ingolstadt has been taken aback by the "furor and the howling of the horsemen"—"tanto . . . furore turmalique ululatu." The attackers mean to cross the pontoon bridge into the city, but are foiled, since the foresighted Governor Tilly—Werner von Tilly, the dying commander's nephew—has had it removed. Finally, they are repulsed by three squadrons of Croats, who (though tired from their long ride, having come from afar to the city's defense) gallop out with drawn sabers and chase the attackers away; these Croats, Balde tells us, are the "tonsores," ready to cut the hair of the enemy cavalry. Thus the latter will be robbed of their strength, as in the case—Balde cannot resist the temptation to use classical allusion, however real the events he describes—of King Nisus, whose regal lock of hair was cut off by his daughter Scylla. (The fighting at Ingolstadt entailed severe losses for the Swedish forces, and the commander of the Finnish mounted-infantry squadron at the crossing of the Lech, Göran Wrangel, was numbered among the slain.)[23]

What Balde had witnessed was the assault of Gustaf Adolf's Finnish horse. Whether his application of the half-animal (and grudgingly flattering) "hippocentauri" term to them has any significance, cannot be determined. It may be that he was sufficiently aware of Swedish army nomenclature to interject the new term "tragones," that is, Swedish "dragoner" (dragoons), into his description.[24] These mounted troopers, called "palantes hippocentauri," again form the rear guard when, suddenly, Gustaf Adolf lifts the siege and goes away, leaving rich booty behind. Balde proudly reports that the trusty Croats captured or killed—or captured and killed, "captos, occisos"— a number of the "hippocentauri." After all, they were hardly human. Indeed, they were so rough a lot that the Swedes themselves were scared of them, respecting their bravery even as they made fun of their stupidity. Samuel Columbus, in his book of anecdotes, *Mål-roo eller Roo-mål*, tells how, when the Finns had come to Ingolstadt and Munich, they asked if it was very far to Rome.[25] Gustaf Adolf, in another anecdote in Columbus's collection, finds a Finn sharpening his saber and asks him what he is doing. He gets the reply, in a broken mixture of Finnish and Swedish: "I polishing rapier, I slaughter tomorrow," a nice summing up of Finnish single-mindedness.[26] Valorous and limited of mind, they were like Johan Ludvig Runeberg's Sven Dufva.[27] In Columbus's collection, for example, a lame Finn is in the infantry; an officer orders him to the cavalry, so that he may ride, but he retorts, "I wish to stand in war and not flee."[28]

Balde likes to mock the Swedes themselves as barbarians by making fun of their names. In a verse-letter in the *Magni Tillii Parentalia*, sent by a ravaged but still poetically gifted Bavaria to her sister Austria, Bavaria tells how the Swedes suddenly appeared at the walls, causing confusion within. At the same time, she catalogues their silly names, the signs of their excessive savagery:

Stella bovis, Cornu, Lethum, Gustavus, Adolphus,
   Nomina sunt Scythico barbara nonne sono?[29]

(The references are to Axel Oxenstierna, Gustaf Horn, Åke Henriksson Tott, whose name is misunderstood, and Gustaf Adolf; the parts of the king's name are supposedly also quaint-sounding to Bavaria's refined ears, and so are separated by a comma.) And Balde found something else strange about the nomenclature of the foes, particularly the most barbaric of them, the Finns—namely their battle cry, the famous or infamous *hakkaa päälle* which got them the name, honored in Finnish history if not elsewhere, of *hakkapeliitat* or, in Swedish, *hackapeliter*, the *agmen horribile haccapelitorum* mentioned in passing earlier. The readership of the once popular historical novellas of Zacharias Topelius knew them well (and in Topelius they cut off the ears of a rascally Jesuit).[30] They have been given a scholarly treatment in two volumes by Arvi Korhonen.[31] It is useful to know that their contemporaries called these howling demons, with their *ululatus*, their fur caps, and their long hair, by their cry, or what their contemporaries perceived the cry to be. There are at least two contemporary accounts of them in the English language.[32] *The Swedish Intelligencer*— the yearly report for the English public on the activities of the Swedish army in the field—tells of an engagement at Höxter on the Weser.[33] The general called "Klein Ia'acob" attempts an attack on an Imperial position and is repulsed.[34] Then two Dutch regiments of horse try an attack and "ranne quite out of the field." "Then it came the Fins or Hackapells turnes to goe on; of whom there being but 4 troopes, yet shewed they a farre better resolution. So well they seconded little Ia'acob that the fight was restored and the better gotten of it." In a marginal commentary, the author of the *Intelligencer* says: "Both Armyes (of the Swedes and the Imperialists) usually call these Finlanders Horse, by the name of Hackapells; and that from the word *Hackapell*, which they use when they fall on. It signifies *Knock them downe*, for they look for no Quarter, to give or take any." So intrepid were the Hackapells that they even got praise from a Scot, Colonel Robert Monro of Fowles.[35] After telling his readers that the Finnish horsemen are called "Hagapells," Monro goes on to say that Gustaf Adolf "did principally under God ascribe the glory of the victory [of Leipzig] to the *Sweds* and *Fynnes* horsemen, who were led by the valorous Feltmarshall Gustavus Horne." These horsemen were the equals, Monro goes on with some astonishment, in their bravery to his own infantry: "It was the Scots Briggades fortune to have gotten the praise for the footservice, and not without cause."

Bearing the "hackapells" or "hagapells" in mind, the reader of Balde may return to the line that opens the fourth strophe of the poem, the description of the defeat of the hostile birds at the hands— or rather the claws—of the Imperial eagle, the point at which Balde reaches the peak of his extended imperative construction. "Pelle Finlandos, age, pelle corvos." There is the battle cry, plain as day, but directed against its users, those Finnish ravens, those Huns, those kites, those "Lapps." It is the most stirring of the instructions to the eagle, which is charged then with the Herculean task of chasing away the bad birds from the Stymphalian lands, from Arcadia. (Note that Arcadia is the word that Balde uses elsewhere [Odes 3:45, in an address to Albert Sigismund, the ecclesiastical brother of Maximilian] to describe the good, rich, and simple realm in which he, Balde, lives, and for whose safety he fears.)[36] It is a witty turnaround. The Finns are hoist with their own petard, with their own terrifying battle cry. They are called by their other name, Lapps, and they are subjected to the very transformational magic for which they are famous and feared—changed into the snow, the dark snow of black birds' feathers and shredded rags. The pun in the last word of line 15 may also have another element; these dwellers of the North, for all their infernal knowledge and equally infernal energy, are also to be taken as "Lappen," "fools, milksops, sluggards." In his German-Latin dictionary of 1691, Caspar Stieler says under "Lappe" that the word means a *homo ignavus, agrestis, timidus, meticulosus, incultus,* and the usage survives in the modern German "läppisch," "foolish."[37] In this penultimate strophe with its heaping of insults and jokes on the heads of the Finns (and Lapps), Balde shows himself once more to be the consummate propagandist: he knows full well that the loathsome auxiliaries are not the prime enemy but only the best target.[38] The pro-Imperial Silesian Protestant, Daniel von Czepko, tried the same ploy (but without Balde's merciless jokes) when, in his *Corydon und Phyllis,* he advanced the Finns to the rank of archenemy; he predicts that peace will come to Germany when the Finns are exhausted: "Endlich, wenn der Finnen Macht, / ausgedonnert, ausgekracht."[39]

The Finns, and through them the Swedes, are not the only victims of Balde's cleverness. At the outset of the poem, the eagle has been called "Romani Iovis . . . custos," the guardian of the Jove who dwells in the new Rome of Vienna. Balde substitutes "Rome" most strikingly for Vienna at the opening of his fourth threnody in the fourth book of the *Silvae,* where "Rome"—that is, Vienna—is threatened by Gustaf Adolf as it has been twice before by chieftains from a wild "northern" world, Attila the Hun and Alaric the Goth:

> Plerumque nostram Mars Aquilonibus
> Turbavit auram. Frigora tertium
>   Expavit Arctoa, et sub armis
>   Roma tuas, ALARICE, pelleis.[40]

But the situation, in fact, is the other way around: the Roman Jove, the "Jupiter Teutonicus," the "Jupiter Austriacus" (as Balde calls the emperor elsewhere), is himself the bird's keeper, and it is he who can set it free to save the Stymphalian lands—the Stymphalian lands that are Arcadia. And Arcadia, as Balde identifies it in Odes 3:45, is Bavaria. Seen in this way, as a request to Ferdinand to protect Bavaria, the poem could take on the air of an oblique chiding of Maximilian, the ruler unable to protect his own realm. Balde regarded the defense of Ingolstadt, planned by the Tillys and successfully carried out by them after Maximilian had marched away to the safety of Regensburg with the bulk of his army, as the single glorious event in the whole Bavarian disaster of 1632. (Maximilian would then surrender Munich without a fight.) Had it not been for brave Ingolstadt, Balde says, Ingolstadt which alone of the Bavarian towns defended itself, then the Baltic flood would have reached Vienna itself:

Ac ni feroceis ANGLIPOLOS minas
Fregisset Hostias: jam Stephani supra
    Turrim, coronatas VIENNAE
        Despiceret metuandus arceis.[41]

In this second threnody there is not a hint of Maximilian; the late Tilly is the unmentioned hero.

Finally, it is also possible that Balde, in his apparently triumphant close, has not been altogether respectful toward the emperor either, that distant Jove, who needed urging to unleash the Imperial eagle.[42] The poem's ending may not be so very noble after all; what the eagle, or his keeper, will get out of the victory in the Pharsalia of the sky is rich booty—like the booty that the Croats, riding out from Ingolstadt, found in the abandoned Swedish camp. A certain snideness may lie, then, in the suggestion that material rewards are necessary to make the eagle of Empire save Bavaria. In illumination of this snideness, it will be helpful to notice the placing of Ode 38 within the first book. After a series of odes to friends, Balde, in Ode 36, adduces his curiously wistful lament at an Imperial defeat in the west, the capture of Breisach. Then, in Ode 37, he excoriates the Germans for celebrating Shrovetide while the Swedes lay their country waste; the Germans are called, collectively, "peior avis nepos," a degenerate breed. After the address to the Roman eagle, there follow "Tres heroes," three odes (39, 40, 41) to leaders who have fought the Turks out of idealism: Scanderbeg, Don Juan of Austria, and John Hunyadi. Ode 42 is addressed to Willibald Ehrenmann, but tells of the poet's decision to be the bard and encomiast of the Virgin Mary; Ode 43 is directed to the Virgin Mary herself. Ode 42 consists mainly of her instructions to her poet—to sing first of her, and then of the greatest hero of them all, Tilly, who had succumbed to his wound at Ingolstadt. It is the climax of her commission:

Noster es, nostris agitande flammis,
Nos canes primum. celebris sequetur
TILLIAS, magnam meditata famam, et
  Arma Virumque.[43]

As Dieter Breuer has hinted, Balde was a slippery customer to have as
a Bavarian court poet, and Maximilian may well have wriggled a little
as he pondered "Ad Aquilam Imperii Romani," after having laughed
at the insults to the Finns. And his cousin Ferdinand, if he saw the
first book of the odes in manuscript, may likewise have felt vaguely
uneasy. Balde's Ode 38 is as close as Balde gets to Imperial praise—
and the tribute may be barbed.

Notes

1. Jacobus Balde, *Opera Poëtica Omnia Magnam Partem nunquam edita*, 8 vols.
(Bibliopol. Monachij: Typis Joannis Lucae Straubij, 1729), 1:47. The poem has
been included in Jacob Balde, *Dichtungen* (lateinisch und deutsch), ed. and
tr. Max Wehrli (Cologne: Jakob Hegner, 1963), pp. 24–45:

> An den römischen Reichsadler

> Wächter du des römischen Zeus und seines
> Dreigezackten Blitzes, der Vögel Caesar:
> Auf! Dem kampfgerüsteten Heere droht die
>   Schar der Empörer.

> Zu dem Geier Schwedens geselln sich manche
> Dunkle Eulen, wetzen sich ihre Schnäbel.
> Von des Feindes Truppen umsäumt ist ringsum
>   Gänzlich der Himmel.

> Zück nun—zögere nicht—die berühmten Klauen.
> Waffen dröhnen aus der erregten Wolke.
> Dir sind nun am Himmel bereitet neu die
>   Felder Pharsaliens.

> Auf, verjag, verjag nun die Raben Finnlands,
> Von den Hunnen säubre das Land Stymphalien.
> Geier soll es schnein, von zerfetzten Lappen
>   Woge der Luftraum!

> Komm nach Wien zurück als ersehnter Sieger
> In Begleitung heiliger Flügelscharen!
> Mavors aber fülle der Luftquiriten
>   Burg mit der Beute!

Wehrli could have improved his impressive translation by substituting "Wei-hen" ("kites"), which he also proposes for "milviis" in his commentary (p. 124), for the "Geier" in 1:15, in order to avoid a confusion with the "Geier" of 1:5. An earlier translation by Johann Baptist Neubig, *Bavaria's Musen in Joh. Jak. Balde's Oden aus dem Latein in das Versmass der Urschrift übersetzt* (Munich: Giel, 1828), pp. 124–25, omits the difficult fourth strophe, the climax of the poem.

2. Georg Westermayer, *Jacobus Balde: Sein Leben und seine Werke* (Munich: Lindauer, 1868), pp. 110; 256.

3. Ibid., p. 119.

4. Matthias Casimirus Sarbievius, *Lyricorum Lib. IV. Epodon Lib. Unus Alterque Epigrammata* (Rome: Apud Hermannum Scheus, 1643), pp. 55–56.

5. At least two commentators have noticed this circumstance: Eckart Schäfer, *Deutscher Horaz: Conrad Celtis, Georg Fabricius, Paul Melissus, Jacob Balde: Die Nachwirkung des Horaz in der neulateinischen Dichtung Deutschlands* (Wiesbaden: Steiner, 1976), p. 233: "Balde ist am wenigsten Panegyriker politischer Herrschaft; darin unterscheidet er sich von Sarbiewski. Das hat seinen Grund zum Teil darin, daß sich die Endphase des Dreißigjährigen Krieges, in die Baldes Lyrik fällt, denkbar weit von einer Pax Augusta entfernt war. Balde war ehrlich genug, die Herrschenden nicht, wie es andere Poeten und teilweise auch Sarbiewski getan haben, im Widerspruch zur Realität als August zu rühmen. Aber Balde hat sich überhaupt von Huldigungsoden an Herrscher zurückgehalten." Dieter Breuer, "Princeps et poeta: Jacob Baldes Verhältnis zu Kurfürst Maximilian I. von Bayern," in Hubert Glaser, ed., *Um Glauben und Reich: Kurfürst Maximilian I: Beiträge zur Bayrischen Geschichte und Kunst, 1573–1657*, 2 vols. (Munich: Piper, 1980), 2/1:341–52, esp. p. 342: "Auffällig ist auch Baldes Zurückhaltung in der politischen Panegyrik. Seine poetischen Arbeiten dieser Art beziehen sich überwiegend auf das Haus Habsburg: sein 'Maximilianus I. Austriacus' (1631); sein 'Panegyricus' auf die Krönung Ferdinands III. zum Römischen König (1636), der ein Jahr später noch einmal in stark erweiterter Fassung als 'Templum Honoris' erschien; seine 'Chorea Mortualis' auf den Tod der Kaiserin Leopoldine (1649); seine Ode auf den Erzherzog Ferdinand Karl (Lyr. IV,25)."

6. Anton Heinrich, *Die lyrischen Dichtungen Jakob Baldes*, Quellen und Forschungen zur Sprach- und Culturgeschichte der germanischen Völker, 122 (Strasbourg: Trübner, 1915), p. 68.

7. Westermayer, *Jacobus Balde*, p. 119.

8. Martin Heinrich Müller, *'Parodia Christiana': Studien zu Jacob Baldes Odendichtung* (Zurich: Juris, 1964), p. 77.

9. Breuer, "Princeps et poeta," p. 342.

10. "Ad Joachimum Camerarium. De obsidione urbis Magdeburgensis," in Harry C. Schnur, ed., *Lateinische Gedichte deutscher Humanisten* (Stuttgart: Reclam, 1966), pp. 252–58 and 453–55 (Elegies 2:4).

11. When I presented this essay as a lecture, I heard criticisms from classicists in the audience concerning Balde's "Milviis ningat," with the argument

that the noun exists only as *milvus/miluus* (nominative singular), and thus the dative plural must be *milvis* or *miluis*. Yet, Balde's dative plural "Milviis" is in all the printings; the nominative form "milvius" is supported by citations from classical antiquity: cf. the *variae lectiones* given in *Thesaurus linguae latinae* 8: Fasc. 5–8: 985–86: Ovid, *Metamorphoses* 2.716, "ut volucris visis rapidissima *miluius* extis"; *Fasti* 3.794: "stella Lycaoniam vergit declivis ad Areton / *Milvius*," 3.808: "attulit illi / *milvius*." One might wonder if Balde, writing "Milviis ningat," wanted to suggest, with his usual verbal ingenuity, the site of another Pharsalia, another epoch-making battle, at the "Pons Mulvius" or "Pons Milvius," where Constantine defeated Maxentius after having seen the heavenly inscription "In hoc signo vinces." (In his drama on Constantine's victory, *Pietas victrix* [1659], Balde's fellow Jesuit, Nicolaus Avancini, uses the form "Milvius.") No doubt Balde was also quite aware, and wanted his readers to be aware, of the word's secondary meaning as "rapacious person" or "devil."

12. Writers of the vernacular were likewise cognizant of the punning possibilities of "Lappen." In the prose introduction to "Ein schön Newe Lied welches Der König in Schweden mit einführet," there is the publisher's subheading "durch Nusuant Francen Gedruckt zu Upsal in Schweden. Im Jahr, Die LapLenDer VVollen einen graVVen LIstIgen FVchs in SaChsen reCht einLappen." See Friedrich Wilhelm von Ditfurth, *Die historisch-politischen Volkslieder des dreissigjährigen Krieges*, ed. Karl Bartsch (Heidelberg: Winter, 1882), pp. 221–22 (no. 84).

13. Jacobus Balde, *Carmina lyrica*, recognovit annotationibusque illustravit P. Benno Müller (Munich: n.p., 1844; Regensburg: Coopenrath, 1884; rpt. Hildesheim: Olms, 1977), Annotationes, p. 25.

14. Balde, *Dichtungen*, ed. Wehrli, p. 125.

15. Laurentius von Schnüffis, *Mirantisches Flötlein. Oder Geistliche Schäfferey* (Constantz: In der Fürstl. Bischöffl. Druckerey, Bey David Hautt, 1682), p. 57.

16. See Ludwig Bechstein, "Deutsche politische Pasquille aus dem 17. Jahrhundert," *Deutsches Museum für Geschichte, Literatur, Kunst und Alterthumsforschung* 2 (1843): 244–68, esp. 249–55. ("Seltzames Gespräch, So in dem Königl. Schwedischen Lager zwey frembde Nationen alsz ein Lapländer mit einem Newen ankommenden Irrländer / von den jetzigem Zustand und Kriegswesen gehalten.") Reprinted in Erich Kunze, "Lappen oder Finnen in den deutschen Flugschriften des 30-jährigen Krieges?" *Ural-Altaische Jahrbücher* 43 (1971): 65–78, esp. pp. 73–77. Neither Bechstein, who worked from a copy in the "herzogliche öffentliche Bibliothek zu Meiningen," nor Kunze, who follows Bechstein's description of the accompanying etching almost verbatim, reproduces the etching itself.

17. Ditfurth, *Volkslieder*, ed. Bartsch, pp. 177–80 (no. 64). Friedrich Spanheim, *Le Soldat suedois; ov Histoire de ce qui s'est passé en Allemagne depuis l'entrée du Roy de Suede en l'année 1630, jusques apres sa mort* (Geneva: n.p., 1633), p. 88, mentions the attribution of magical powers to the Lapps as an element

in Imperial propaganda: "Les Imperialistes eurent bonne grace de faire courir alors le bruit, que le Roy auoit des Lappons en son armée, qui charmoient ceux, auec lesquels ils auoient à faire, de sorte, qu'on ne leur pouuoit resister en façon aucune. Ce qu'on fortifioit par beaucoup de contes anciens, que ces gens auoient accostumé de coniurer les vents et les tempestes, et de se rendre arbitres de la bonne et de la mauuaise fortune."

18. I am indebted to Roger Paas (Carleton College) for generously having placed at my disposal copies of the originals of two broadsheets that bear the same title and have the same text as the broadsheet reprinted by Bechstein, "Deutsche politische Pasquille," and Kunze, "Lappen oder Finnen." One of the broadsheets from Professor Paas's collection has an etching with only two figures, "der Irrländer" on the left and "der lapp" on the right; the text is followed by the notation, "Gedruckt im Jahr / M.DC.XXXi." The other has a crude woodcut with three figures, from left to right, "Finn," "Lablenter," "Irlenter" (in Bechstein and Kunze's description of the etching in the Meiningen broadsheet, the order is reversed: "Der Irrlander," "der lappe," "der Finlander," from left to right); it closes: "Gedruckt zu Stettin bey Johen Schrötern / Im Jahr 1632." The armament and dress of the figures corresponds to that described by Bechstein and Kunze.

19. Cf. Michael Roberts, *Gustavus Adolphus: A History of Sweden 1611–1632*, 2 vols. (London: Longmans, Green, 1953–58), 2:213: "The Finnish horse, in particular—*agmen horribile haccapelitorum*—acquired a formidable reputation." Roberts refers to Arvi Korhonen's article, "Om finska rytteriet under Gustaf II Adolf," *Ny militär tidskrift* 4 (1931): 242–48, a preliminary study for Korhonen's later book (see note 31).

20. Julius Otto Opel and Adolf Cohn, *Der dreissigjährige Krieg: eine Sammlung von Gedichten und Prosadarstellungen* (Halle: Buchhandlung des Waisenhauses, 1862), pp. 417–22, esp. p. 421.

21. Bechstein, "Deutsche politische Pasquille," p. 255; Kunze, "Lappen oder Finnen," p. 75. For "Blüter," *Grimms Wörterbuch* 2:281 cites Franz Josef Stalder's *Versuch eines schweizerischen Idiotikons*, 1:191: "armer mensch, hungerleider."

22. Balde, *Opera Poëtica Omnia*, 8:44.

23. Svenska armén: Generalstaben, *Sveriges krig 1611–1632: 6: Från Lech till Lützen* (Stockholm: Generalstaben, 1936–39), pp. 17–27; Hanns Kuhn, "Die Schweden vor Ingolstadt: 1632," *Blätter des Historischen Vereins Ingolstadt* 50 (1931): 81–143. Grimmelshausen's Springinsfeld describes Ingolstadt as "eine Stadt und Vestung der Bayern / über welche ehemalen der grosse Gustavus Adolphus die Zähne zusammengebissen / dass er sie nach soviel erhaltenen herrlichen Siegen ungewonnen muste ligen lassen" (*Der seltzame Springinsfeld*, ed. Franz Günter Sieveke [Tübingen: Niemeyer, 1969], p. 62 [11. Capitel]).

24. For Balde, the master of *argutia*, and sensible to the overtones of every word, the new word "tragones" may also have had animal suggestions about it, from τράγος (goat) and, in Latin, *tragonis* (goatwort).

25. Samuel Columbus, *Mål-Roo eller Roo-mål*, ed. Bengt Hesselman, Nordiska texter och undersökningar, 6 (Stockholm: Hugo Gebers förlag, 1935), p. 3: "När Finnarne komme högt op i tyssland, op om Ingolstadt, München Hufwustaa'n i Beyern, långt på ander sijdan om Donau-strömen, til Bodensiön (*Lacus Bregantinus*) *Lemanus* frågade de om det än war långt til Rom?"

26. Ibid: "Kung Göstaf fick en gång sij en Finne satt ok brynade sin wärja, ok frågade honom hwad han giorde? Swar: mina lijpa rappire, mina lackta moron."

27. In *Fänrik Ståls sägner*, vol. 1 (1848): Runeberg's often quoted line is "Ett dåligt huvud hade han, men hjärtat, det var gott" ("A sorry head Sven Dufva had; his heart, though, that was good," in Charles Wharton Stork's translation). Dufva dies single-handedly defending a bridge against the Russians in the War of 1808–9; he has misunderstood the order to retreat.

28. Columbus, *Mål-Roo eller Roo-mål*, p. 77: "Minä vela stå i krig och inte fly."

29. Balde, *Opera Poëtica Omnia*, 8:66.

30. Zacharias Topelius, *Fältskärns berättelser* (1853–67); the first cycle of the series deals with events of the Thirty Years War.

31. Arvi Korhonen, *Hakkapeliittain historia* (Helsinki: Werner Söderström, 1939–42).

32. Noted by Gabriel Rein, *Suomi ja suomalaiset ulkomaan kirjallisuudessa 1500-luvulla ja 1600-luvun alkupuoliskolla*, Bidrag till kännedom af Finlands natur och folk, 68:2 (Helsinki: Suomalaisen Kirjallisuuden Seura, 1909), pp. 173–74. Rein's chapter 7 (pp. 157–229) contains a wealth of references to the appearance of Finns in German and Neo-Latin literature about the Thirty Years War, but does not include Balde's ode or the Laurentius von Schnüffis and Czepko passages mentioned later.

33. *The Swedish Intelligencer* 4 (1633): 148.

34. "Klein Jakob" was Jacob Mercier, a colonel in Hessian service, who had begun life as a cobbler; cf. H. J. C. von Grimmelshausen, *Simplicius Simplicissimus*, 11.17.

35. Robert Monro, *Expedition with the Worthy Scots Regiments*, 2 vols. (London: William Jones, 1637), 2:55; 2:66.

36. Balde, *Opera Poëtica Omnia*, 1: 180–182, esp. 182: "et omnes / Arcadiae sonuere montes" [and all the mountains of Arcadia have resounded].

37. Caspar Stieler, *Der Teutschen Sprache Stammbaum und Fortwachs oder Teutscher Sprachschatz*, 3 vols. (Hildesheim: Olms, 1968), 1:1071.

38. In the same fashion, German propaganda in the First World War called attention to the British and French use of black colonial troops; the Argentines, in the Falklands conflict, dwelled on the excesses of the Gurkhas.

39. *Weltliche Dichtungen*, ed. Werner Milch (Darmstadt: Wissenschaftliche Buchgesellschaft, 1968), p. 123.

40. *Opera Poëtica Omnia*, 2:96. In Westermayer's translation (p. 301):

Durch Nordorkane setzte uns Mars zumeist
Die Luft in Aufruhr. Arktischem Froste bebt

Zum drittenmale Rom und Deinen
Fellen, o Alarich, selbst in Waffen.

41. *Opera Poëtica Omnia*, 2:90–91. In Westermayer's translation (p. 295):

Und brach des Feindes wüthende Drohung nicht
An Ingolstadt, so liess' er vom Stephansturm
Längst über Wien's gekrönte Burgen
Seine verwilderten Blicke schweifen.

42. In reply to the question posed at the beginning of this chapter, it would seem, in consideration of the autobiographical elements in the poem's genesis (that is, Balde's experience of the siege of Ingolstadt), that Balde actually regarded Ferdinand II as the poem's keeper of the eagle.

43. *Opera Poëtica Omnia*, 1:53. In Neubig's translation (p. 143):

Bist ja mein, und musst auch für mich entflammt seyn.
Singe mich zuerst. Dein berühmter Tilly
Folg dann; seinen Ruhm doch bedenkend sing die
Waffen, den Helden.

8. Der Zensor als Literaturkritiker: Die Approbationsvermerke im frühneuzeitlichen Buch als literarhistorische Quelle

Dieter Breuer

Längst nicht alle Teile eines alten Druckes können die Aufmerksamkeit eines Literarhistorikers und Frühneuzeitforschers erregen. Fixiert auf seine Vorstellungen vom großen Autor und dessen Text, wie ihn Neudrucke schmucklos bieten, hat er lange Zeit gar nicht wahrgenommen, welch reiche Informationen ein alter Druck dem Leser von einst zusätzlich zum "eigentlichen" Text mitangeboten hat. Es bedurfte einer gründlichen Veränderung des Wahrnehmens und Fragens, eben der Frage nach den historisch-sozialen Kontexten des bis dahin isoliert betrachteten eigentlichen Textes. Dies wurde in dem Maße möglich, wie sich das Leitbild "literarisches Leben" oder *literary culture*, bezogen etwa auf das Heilige Römische Reich Deutscher Nation, durchsetzte. Aus der veränderten Optik springen die bisher oft auch bibliographisch übersehenen Teile eines alten Druckes förmlich ins Auge: nicht nur deshalb, weil sie meist typographisch viel sorgsamer gestaltet sind als der eigentliche Text, sondern weil sie auch eine Fülle von Daten bereitstellen, mit deren Hilfe der Text in seinen historischen Bezügen sehr viel leichter verstanden werden kann. Und darum geht es ja; Ziel der neuen Optik kann nicht sein, über der Entdeckerfreude an Kontexten den Text selbst zu vernachlässigen, sondern das ganze alte Buch, einschließlich seines alten Einbandes, als Überlieferungsträger von *literary culture* ernstzunehmen.

Kennzeichen des frühneuzeitlichen Buches ist eine Art Rahmenkomposition um den Textteil, zumindest ein umfangreicher Einleitungsteil, der den an der Drucklegung beteiligten Institutionen vorbehalten ist.[1] Da ist zunächst der Drucker bzw. Verleger, der auf der Titelseite und/oder im Schlußimpressum (Kolophon) namentlich hervortritt, in besonderen Fällen auch mit einer eigenen Widmungsvorrede oder Vorrede an den Leser, oft durch beigefügtes Druckprivileg des Landesherrn oder des Kaisers, mit dem er sich als Inhaber der Rechte gegen geschäftsschädigenden Nachdruck zu schützen sucht; diese Texte bieten Daten zum Status des Druckers und Verlegers, zu seinen Intentionen, seinem Verlagsprogramm, eventuell zum bisherigen Geschäftsverlauf, zum ökonomischen Aspekt des Buches. Dies ist aber nur ein Teilbereich des Rahmens. Inzwischen werden, auch bei der bibliographischen Titelaufnahme, die mit dem Widmungsteil zusammenhängenden Daten ernstgenommen: die eigentliche *dedicatio*, meist als Widmungsvorrede, oft auch als Widmungsgedicht, sowie die oft mitabgedruckten, dem Autor gewidmeten Lobgedichte von befreundeten Autoren. In ihren Namen wird die eigentliche Trägerschicht des literarischen Lebens greifbar, oft die Institution, der der Autor angehört, jedenfalls die Mäzene und Förderer des Autors, die eventuell seine Honorierung besorgen. Der dritte Teil der Rahmenkomposition, die *approbatio*, ist bis heute der unbekannteste; der bürgerliche Leser, auch der Bibliograph, hat ihn lange Zeit mit spitzen Fingern rasch überblättert und diese Spuren überwundener geistiger Knechtschaft mit Mißachtung und Nichtberücksichtigung bei der Titelaufnahme gestraft.[2] Gleichwohl beleuchtet die Approbation bzw. der Zensurvermerk einen wichtigen Aspekt des literarischen Lebens, den rechtlichen, und mit ihm die Normen und das Normbewußtsein der Zeit, denen Autor, Verleger, Mäzen und Leser gleichermaßen verpflichtet waren. Nach der *dedicatio* ist dieser Teil des frühneuzeitlichen Buches typographisch oft der aufwendigste. Wie auch immer dieses Phänomen zu deuten ist, zunächst einmal sollte es bibliographisch mit allen Namen und Daten festgehalten werden. Ich kann die sich aus diesen Daten ergebenden Aufgaben der Zensurforschung hier nur skizzieren. Die Namen ermöglichen Rückschlüsse auf Herkunft, Stellung und Bildungsstand der Zensoren. Man kann nicht davon ausgehen, daß die deutschen Zensoren der frühen Neuzeit gemäß Heines vormärzlicher Pointe "Dummköpfe" seien. Der uns vertraute literarische Topos des "ungebildeten, engstirnigen und bürokratischen Zensors" bezieht sich auf Zustände nach dem Ende des Alten Reiches.[3] Schon die Sprache der Zensoren, in der Regel Latein, signalisiert ihre Zugehörigkeit zur Schicht der Gelehrten.

Der Umstand, daß längst nicht alle alten Drucke Zensurvermerke aufweisen, lenkt den Blick auf die recht unterschiedliche Zensurpraxis in den einzelnen Territorien des Alten Reiches; trotz der strengen Zensurgesetzgebung des Reiches (Vorzensur, Nachzensur, Beidruck der Approbation, Beschränkung der Offizinen auf die größeren Städte, Vereidigung der Drucker usw.) hing die Praxis, auch die Art und Weise, ob und wie der Approbationsvermerk deklariert wurde, von der Zensurbehörde des einzelnen Territoriums ab. Auch scheinen hierbei gerade in der Frage des Mitabdrucks der Approbation die protestantischen Territorien anders zu verfahren als die katholischen. Diese Frage bedarf noch der Klärung. Ich beschränke mich im folgenden auf Beispiele aus den katholischen Staaten des Reiches. Dabei sind wiederum noch die Unterschiede zwischen weltlichen und geistlichen Staaten und die Sonderregelungen, die zusätzlichen Zensurinstanzen, für Publikationen von Angehörigen der einzelnen Ordensgemeinschaften zu berücksichtigen.[4]

Nicht ohne Probleme ist schließlich die Unterstellung des heutigen engeren Zensurbegriffs für die Approbationspraxis. Selbstverständlich sind die Normen religiöser, politischer und moralischer Art in zeitbedingter Modifikation die entscheidenden Kriterien.[5] Darüber hinaus umfaßt der ältere Zensurbegriff insbesondere für den Angehörigen der *nobilitas literaria*, der nebenbei das Amt des Zensors versieht, noch andere, nämlich philologische Aspekte: der Zensor als Korrektor und Kritiker des Sprachwerks. In Garzonis *Piazza Universale* (deutsch 1619) ist diese Bedeutung noch die vorherrschende: Korrektoren oder Zensoren sind hier diejenigen, "welche mit mangelhafftigen Reden vnd Schrifften vmbgehen / vnd dieselbe bey den autoribus zu bessern sich vnterstehen". Dies betrifft, so Garzoni, neben der Orthographie auch Fehler "in den materiis selbsten / in den subiectis, in den gründen vnd rationibus, in den motiuen / in den exempeln, in den Metaphoribus, vnd anderen figuris, vnd endlich auch in den Compositionibus . . . sonderlich in prosa oratione, da man sich nicht so zwingen / wie offtmals ein Poet in Versen thun muß"[6].

Träfe dies zu, so meine methodische Folgerung für die inhaltliche Erschließung der Approbationen, dann gäben die Approbationen nicht nur Auskunft über die Einhaltung der religiösen, politischen und moralischen Normen, sondern auch der sprachlichen und poetologischen. Die Approbation wäre eine besondere Erscheinungsform der Literaturkritik, Gegenstück zum Lobgedicht auf den Autor im dedikatorischen Teil der Rahmenkomposition, aber als Machtspruch um einiges verbindlicher für das öffentliche Ansehen als das Lobgedicht, und die größere Verbindlichkeit unterschiede diese Quelle der Literaturkritik auch vom Gelehrtenbriefwechsel und den Anfängen periodischer Literaturkritik in den Monatsgesprächen.[7]

I

Der Liederzyklus *Mirantisches Flötlein* des Kapuziners Laurentius von Schnüffis (1633–1702), erstmals 1682 in Konstanz gedruckt und auch in der Sammlung Faber du Faur vorhanden, soll ersten Aufschluß über Anlage und Argumentationsweise der Zensuren geben.[8] Das Buch ist im Rahmenteil mit Titelkupfer, separater Auslegung des Titelkupfers, Widmungsvorrede an den Kaiserlichen Geheimen Rat und Bischof von Wien Emmerich Sinelli, vier Approbationsvermerken und einem Privilegium Caesareum, Vorrede des Autors an den günstigen Leser und Widmungsgedicht des Autors an sein Buch sowie am Schluß mit Abschied des Autors vom geliebten Leser und einem Register reich ausgestattet. Der Textteil, dreimal zehn Lieder zu zwanzig Strophen, ist durch die jeweils beigefügten Kupferstiche und Noten ebenfalls sehr aufwendig. Die Reihenfolge der Approbationen verweist uns auf das Zensurverfahren für die Angehörigen dieses Ordens:

1. Anfrage beim Minister Generalis, der in diesem Fall sich gerade in Valencia in Spanien aufhält,
2. Einholung von mindestens zwei, hier sogar drei Gutachten bei den bestellten Bücherzensoren der Heimatprovinz des Autors, hier den Guardianen der Klöster Feldkirch, Engen und Wangen in Vorarlberg,
3. Entscheidung des Minister Generalis aufgrund der eingegangenen Gutachten und Benachrichtigung des Autors.[9]

Das Verfahren bedeutete für Autor, Drucker (hier: David Hautt aus Konstanz) und Verleger (hier: Johann Jacob Mantelin aus Lauffenburg) eine erhebliche Verzögerung des Erscheinungstermins. Die Gutachten sind in diesem Fall auf Anfang August 1681 datiert (2., 7. und 8. August), die Approbation der Ordensleitung dagegen erst auf den 28. November 1682. Man kann aber davon ausgehen, daß während der langen Wartezeit die Drucklegung vorbereitet wurde, auch hatte sich der Verleger das Werk vom zuständigen Provinzialoberen inzwischen kaiserlich privilegieren lassen (27. Februar 1682).

Der Verleger hat die Approbationen nicht nach ihren Daten, sondern nach ihrem inhaltlichen Gewicht angeordnet. Das erste Gutachten beschränkt sich auf das Notwendigste und scheint für unsere Zwecke wenig herzugeben:

Auf Geheiß der Oberen habe ich die geistliche Dichtung [*sacra Poesis*], die der verehrungswürdige Pater Laurentius von Schnüf-

fis gesangsweise verfaßt hat, gelesen und nach gehöriger Prüfung festgestellt, daß sie, mit dem großen Propheten Jesaja wetteifernd, nichts Anstößiges enthält, sondern die Herde Christi
durch die rauhen Wege der Buße [*via purgativa*] mit Salomon zu
den prächtigen Wegen der Erleuchtung [*via illuminativa*] und zu
den schmalen, stillen Pfaden der mystischen Vereinigung [*via
unitiva*] hinleitet, mit so süß klingendem Gesang, daß sie zu
Recht in den Seelen aller widerklinge und veröffentlicht werde.[10]

Der zweite Zensor stellt die zu erwartende überkonfessionelle, alle
Stände erfassende positive Wirkung des Buches heraus:

Auf Geheiß der Oberen habe ich die geistliche Schäferdichtung
[*sacrum Pastorale*] des verehrungswürdigen Paters und Predigers
Laurentius von Schnüffis durchgesehen und alles in ihr glücklich
gelungen und nützlich für jeden Stand und Beruf befunden, da
sie stärkt, was schwach ist, heilt, was krank, verbindet, was zerstritten, auf den rechten Weg bringt, was entmutigt, und sucht,
was verirrt ist. Zweifellos werden eigene wie fremde Schafe seine
Stimme hören. Da das Buch sich freien Zutritt nicht nur zu den
Hütten, sondern auch zu den Palästen der Fürsten verschafft und
dem Hirtenamt sorgfältig Genüge tut, da es auch nichts gegen
den orthodoxen Glauben enthält, sondern vielmehr nach dessen
uneingeschränkter Kraft trachtet, ist es nach meinem Urteil würdig, zur Ehre Gottes und zum Heil der Seelen publiziert zu
werden.[11]

Der dritte Zensor geht noch näher auf die Wirkweise der poetischen
Mittel dieser volkssprachlichen Lieder ein:

Auf Geheiß der Oberen habe ich diese volkssprachlichen Gedichte des ehrwürdigen Paters Laurentius von Schnüffis, Prediger im Kapuzinerorden, aufmerksam gelesen. Ich habe bestätigt gefunden, daß er, was nur gut und nützlich ist, die Zeit des
Weinens durch die Prosarede [*Philotheus*-Roman] und die Zeit
des Singens durch diese geistliche Poesie geziert hat. Denn ich
habe gespürt, daß aus diesem seinem blütenreichen Parnaß überhaupt nur der Duft des Lebens in das Leben überströmt. Andere
benutzen das Wort, um ihre eigenen Standesgenossen anzurufen
und die Sünder zur Buße einzuladen; dieser Autor spielt, dem
Ausspruch des Evangelisten gemäß, auch mit Flöten und lehrt
die auf Abwege Geratenen nach dem Gesetz des Herrn tanzen.
Ich zweifle ganz und gar nicht, daß, was einst dem Elisäus beim

öffentlichen Auftritt des Psalterspielers zustatten kam, auch den Lesern oder Zuhörern dieses geistlichen Gesangs zustatten kommen wird; sie werden nämlich deutlich spüren, wie von dorther der Geist Gottes über sie kommen wird. Das Buch ist daher nach meinem Urteil besonders würdig, daß seine Stimme durch den öffentlichen Druck in alle Welt hinausgehe.[12]

Die abschließende Approbation des Minister Generalis zieht nur noch in üblicher bürokratischer Geschäftsmäßigkeit das zustimmende Fazit, ohne auf Einzelheiten einzugehen.

Das Beispiel zeigt, was es zeigen sollte. Selbst wenn man unterstellt, daß der Verleger die Approbationen als willkommene Werbetexte verwendet (gleiches würde dann aber auch für alle anderen Rahmenteile gelten) und daß die Ordensleitung bei bekannten Autoren die durch die Approbation gegebene Möglichkeit zur Werbung für den Orden und seine Ziele nutzt, selbst dann bleibt bemerkenswert, mit welchem Einfühlungsvermögen die Zensoren über die vorgegebene juristische Formel *nihil obstat* hinaus Intentionen des Textes zu erfassen und zu deuten versuchen. Ihre Argumentation ist eine literaturkritische, keine juristische.

Der Autor war bis dahin nur mit seinem anonym erschienenen *Philotheus*-Roman (1665) hervorgetreten. Seine erste Lyriksammlung mußte die Zensoren, auch wenn sie Hermann Hugos *Pia Desideria*, dessen Übersetzung durch Andreas Presson oder Johannes Khuens geistliche Schäfereien kannten, vor erhebliche Probleme stellen. Im Rahmen der kurzen Rezensionen geben sie auch nur einige Gesichtspunkte für eine Interpretation, aber es sind die bis heute entscheidenden geblieben.[13] Es handelt sich um geistliche Dichtung (*sacra Poesis*), näherhin um die Gattung der geistlichen Hirtenlyrik (*sacrum Pastorale*), die die Etappen des mystischen Weges (*via purgativa, illuminativa, unitiva*) ausschreitet. Alle drei Zensoren argumentieren wirkungsästhetisch. Die besondere Wirkung dieser Lyrik wird einerseits auf ihre lieblichen Melodien zurückgeführt (*Melos dulcisonum*), andererseits darauf, daß der anspielungsreich ausgezierte Text (*floriferus Parnassus*) zugleich lebensnah ist und unmittelbar anspricht. Die affektive Wirkung der gesungenen und instrumental begleiteten Lieder kann nach Meinung des dritten Zensors bei Aufführenden wie Zuhörern sogar bis zu vergleichsweise ekstatischen Zuständen des Tanzens, der prophetischen Verzückung reichen, der Empfindung, vom göttlichen Geist erfaßt zu werden.

In diesem Deutungszusammenhang ist die Betonung der Breitenwirkung dieser Lieder verwunderlich. Sie sprechen, wie der zweite

Zensor unterstellt, Leser und Zuhörer aller Stände an, den gemeinen
Mann ebenso wie ein gebildetes höfisches Publikum. Die Bedeutung
des Topos "Literatur für jedermann" für die Autoren des katholischen
Kulturkreises im Zeitalter der Gegenreformation ist erst in letzter Zeit
erkannt und als ein wichtiges Unterscheidungsmerkmal gegenüber
den Autoren des protestantischen Kulturkreises gewürdigt worden.[14]
Für den Zensor handelt es sich offenbar um eine Schreibnorm, die er
in der Lyriksammlung des Laurentius bestätigt findet.

Vergleicht man die Rezensionen der drei Zensoren mit der Literaturkritik des Jenenser Professors Georg Litzel in seiner Anthologie
Deutsche Jesuiten = Poesie (1731), in der sich auch eine Probe aus dem
Mirantischen Flötlein des Laurentius findet, so wird rasch der Unterschied der literarisch-ästhetischen Normen deutlich, die die beiden
Kulturkreise trennten. Litzel kommt hauptsächlich aufgrund von
sprachlichen Kriterien zu dem Schluß: "Du wirst in dieser Sammlung
Gedichte antreffen, deren einige sehr schwach, andere mittelmäßig,
und noch andere ziemlich gut erscheinen; aber wisse, daß alle zusammen nichts taugen, und die besten nichts wert sein"[15]. Die unbese-
hene Tradierung solcher Urteile in Unkenntnis der andersartigen
Schreibnormen, wie sie sich zum Beispiel in den drei Approbationen
finden, kennzeichnet weithin die Literaturgeschichtsschreibung bis
heute.

II

Die literarischen Kurzkritiken der Approbationen entsprechen in Art,
Sprache und Abfolge durchaus nicht immer dem dargestellten Sche-
ma, und gerade die Abweichungen sind für die Frage nach dem Stand
der literaturkritischen Reflexion von besonderem Interesse. In dem
recht seltenen satirischen Roman des Schweizer Kapuziners Rudolf
von Schwyz (1646–1709) *Außforderung Mit Aller = demütigst gebottnem
Vernunft = Trutz An alle Atheisten / Machiavellisten / gefährliche Romanen /
und falsch = politische Weltkinder zu einem Zwei = Kampff Auff dem Plan
kurtzweiliger Dichtung* (Zug, 1686–88) befindet sich im umfangreichen
Rahmenteil neben den Approbationen der Ordenszensoren (hier nur
zwei Theologen und der Minister Generalis) auch noch die Approbation des Bücherzensors des zuständigen Ortsbischofs Dr. Johann Jacob Schmid. Die Zensur des Ordinarius gehört an sich zum Approba-
tionsteil des Buches. Ungewöhnlich ist in diesem Fall, daß sie in
deutscher Sprache abgefaßt ist und daß die Publikation fast ausschließlich mit den stilistischen Qualitäten dieses Romans gerechtfer-
tigt wird:

Erlaubnuß und Genehmhaltung deß ORDINARII.
Weilen Gegenwårtiger (durch verordnete Gottes = Gelehrte gut =
geheissene) Vernunffts = Trutz / denen Vermumbten Tugends =
Feinden meisterlich abbutzet / und bey Vernûnfftigen Sig =
pranget: Zumalen auch dem Leser die Begirde (den Außtrag zu
vernemmen) mit ziehrlicher Redens = Arte und annemblichister
Vorbringungs = Maniere gantz anflammet. Ists je billich / daß sel-
biger / vermittelst deß Buch = Drucks der Welt angedeutet und
wissenhafft gemacht werde / damit sich also an der Dulcelina alle
Welt erlaben kônne.[16]

Gelobt wird neben der satirischen Intention die affektive Wirkung auf
den Leser, die durch Zierlichkeit, d. h. die kunstvoll-angemessene
Art des Ausdrucks, und die angenehme "Vorbringungs = Maniere",
also die Schreibart, erzielt wird. Dies sind denn auch schon die wesentlichen stilistischen Kriterien der Zeit zur Beurteilung von Romanen; erstaunlich nur, daß sich ein Zensor und Theologe, gestützt
auf literaturkritisch-poetologische Kriterien, ein positives Urteil über
einen Roman bildet. Er bezieht sich damit übrigens auf Argumente in
der Romanpoetologie des Autors in der Vorrede.

Auch im Werk des Kapuziners Procopius von Templin (1609–80),
das wegen der großen Zahl der approbierten Bücher eine gute Möglichkeit zu Vergleichen bietet, hebt sich ein Ordinarius, der Münchner
Kurfürstliche Rat Caspar Kirmair, Doktor der Theologie und der
Rechte, der als Dekan von St. Peter zugleich oberster *censor librorum*
ist, mit seinen differenzierten Urteilen deutlich heraus. Während
nämlich die Zensoren am Hauptdruckort des Procopius, Salzburg,
gestützt auf die Ordenszensoren, meist ohne weitere Begründung die
Druckerlaubnis erteilen, nützt der Münchener Zensor die Gelegenheit zur Analyse der sprachlichen und stilistischen Qualitäten des
Procopius. Seine Approbation zur dreibändigen Münchner Gesamtausgabe (*Lignum Vitae*, München: Johann Jäcklin, 1665) mit den bis
dahin zwölf separat erschienenen Predigtsammlungen des Procopius
bestätigt zunächst, daß er in dieser Schrift nichts gegen den römisch-
orthodoxen Glauben oder die guten Sitten Gerichtetes gefunden habe,
"sondern in bequemer Gliederung und kunstvoll gefügten, eindring-
lichen Worten, die durchweg einen gepflegteren deutschen Stil at-
men, mit natürlichen und schönen Wendungen der deutschen Rede,
ein Höchstmaß an Bildung, Gelehrsamkeit, Wissenschaft, Beredsam-
keit, Wortgewandtheit und praktischem Nutzen", so daß er nicht nur
den Druck befürworte, sondern das Werk auch für überaus geeignet
halte, es öffentlich nachzuahmen und dem christlichen Volk vorzu-
stellen, was nicht ohne die schönste Frucht bleiben würde, besonders

wenn die gelehrte Bildung, der Geist, die Urteilskraft, die Haltung dieses frommen Autors hinzukomme.[17] Als er ein Jahr später die Einzelausgabe der Advents- und Weihnachspredigten zensiert, hebt er erneut "die einzigartige Gelehrsamkeit, die ingeniöse Invention, die kluge Disposition, die liebliche, deutliche, mit Würde verbundene Elokution sowie die Puritas der volkssprachlichen Rede und die eigentümliche Bedeutung und die Klarheit der Worte hervor"[18]. Kirmair benutzt für seine Stilbeschreibung die Begrifflichkeit der alten Rhetorik. Sie ist der bewährte Begriffsfundus, auch für Analyse und Beurteilung der volkssprachlichen Literatur; mit ihrer Hilfe zeichnet dieser Zensor das Bild des idealen Predigers, das ihm aus den Predigtsammlungen des Procopius von Templin entgegentritt. Es ist zugleich ein erster Versuch, die sprachlich-stilistischen Voraussetzungen für den erstaunlichen Erfolg der Schriften des Procopius zu erfassen. Dieser mußte lange, bis ins 20. Jahrhundert, warten, bis er wieder einen solch wohlwollenden Kritiker fand wie den Münchner Zensor.[19]

Procopius hat als Erfolgsschriftsteller des 17. Jahrhunderts die für ihn so günstigen Approbationen stets in aller Breite dem Leser mitgeteilt, ja er hat sie sogar als Spielmaterial betrachtet, mit eigenen Zwischentexten versehen und zu einer kleinen Historie von der Entstehung des Buches umfunktioniert. Sein *Mariale*, die Sammlung seiner Predigten zu den Marienfesten, die erstmals 1665 in Salzburg erschien[20], bringt im umfangreichen Rahmenteil nach Vortitel, 14strophigem "Trost = Reim", sprechendem Titelkupfer und engbedruckter Titelseite das Privilegium Caesareum für den Salzburger Verleger Johann Baptist Mayr, dessen Widmungsvorrede an den Bischof von Eichstätt, die "Supplex dedicatio ad B. V. Mariam" des Autors und eine "Praefatio ad benevolum Lectorem", die im Gegensatz zum Titel in deutscher Sprache abgefaßt ist, schließlich die "Censurae" und die Register. Die "Praefatio" und die Abschnitte der "Censurae" bilden hier inhaltlich eine Einheit. Procopius erläutert dem Leser zunächst die von der Erwartung abweichende Anordnung der Einzelpredigten (er hat die Texte zu einem Marienleben arrangiert), verweist auf das Schicksal der ursprünglich vorgesehenen begleitenden Liedersammlung (die Auflage ist beim Passauer Stadtbrand am 27. April 1662 vernichtet worden) und kündigt das nächste Opus an (*Sanctorale*). Dann fährt er unter der neuen Überschrift "Censurae" auf Lateinisch in seinem Bericht fort und erklärt dem Leser den Ablauf des Zensurverfahrens. Auf seinen Antrag hin hätten zwei Generalobere die Superioren seiner Provinz, insgesamt acht an der Zahl[21], mit der Durchsicht seiner Schriften beauftragt. Die Zensoren, deren Namen er in einer Liste in den Text einrückt, hätten nach der Durchsicht die Approbation erteilt, ihre Zeugnisse gesiegelt an die Generaloberen geschickt, die nach Prüfung endlich die Lizenzen für die Drucklegung bewilligt hätten. Er schiebt nun den Abdruck der beiden wie üblich knapp gehaltenen Approbationen der oberen Zensurinstanz (mit Datum vom 17. November 1660 and 16. August 1663) sowie die Approbation des Direktors des Salzburger Metropolitankonsistoriums für das *Mariale* (mit Datum vom 30. Januar 1664) ein und schließt einen längeren Kommentar an. Er wähne sich keineswegs von allem Irrtum frei, und die Zoili, Momi und Aristarchi würden schon das Ihrige finden. Auf Widerspruch sei er gefaßt, auch dem engelgleichen Doctor subtilis Duns Scotus, Bonaventura, Augustinus, Cyprianus und anderen großen Kirchenlichtern sei widersprochen worden, nicht zu reden von allen christlichen Märtyrern und Bekennern, von der Jungfrau Maria und ihrem Sohn, der doch die höchste Wahrheit und Heiligkeit selbst sei und dennoch das Zeichen, dem widersprochen werde: "Warum also nicht auch mir?" Er sei bereit, sofort besser zu denken, wenn die römische Kirche, der er sich in allem unterwerfe, ihn anders belehre. Er liebe die Jungfrau Maria, es seien Liebesexzesse, wenn er irre. Auf die vorstehenden Zensurvermerke wolle er den Leser in allen noch folgenden Teilen seines Werkes stets zurückverweisen, um diese nicht ständig wiederholen zu müssen. Das ganze Werk sei durchgesehen und für den Druck approbiert worden; daß es aufgrund seines Umfangs in einzelnen Teilen erscheine, sei für die Zensurfrage sekundär. Die Druckfehler möge der Leser mit Geduld und klugem Sinn korrigieren, die Bücher seien nicht in seiner Ordensprovinz gedruckt worden, er habe sie daher nicht selbst korrigieren können, er hoffe aber, daß der Himmel dieses Übel bald wenden werde.

Nimmt man nun die zweite vermehrte Auflage des *Mariale* (Salzburg 1667) zur Hand, dann kann man an dieser Stelle des bis dahin identischen Rahmenteils die Fortsetzung dieser *historia Procopii censurati* nachlesen:

Anno 1663, als der Pater General persönlich bei der Visitation der österreichischen Provinz nach Passau kam, erhielt ich endlich, wiewohl sehr unwillig, die Erlaubnis, zeitweilig nach Bayern überzusiedeln, zu dem im folgenden Schreiben dargelegten Zweck: dieses gab er mir aber nicht sofort, sondern schickte es wenig später. Nun also bringe ich, am Druckort persönlich anwesend, den Druck der Werke in Ordnung, wie ich es in Abwesenheit vergeblich versucht habe.[22]

Aus dem beigedruckten Schreiben des Generaloberen vom 2. Januar 1663 geht hervor, daß Procopius mit einem Begleiter sich von Passau nach Salzburg begeben dürfe, damit dort seine ausgearbeiteten Werke im Druck erscheinen könnten und unter seiner Assistenz Fehler verhütet würden; nach Abschluß des Druckes habe er unverzüglich in seine österreichische Provinz zurückzukehren. Allmählich wird dem Leser klar, was Procopius mit seiner öffentlichen Ausbreitung des Schriftverkehrs mit seinen Zensoren bezweckt: er sichert sich vor aller Öffentlichkeit ab. Aus diesem Grund druckt er auch noch die entsprechenden Bewilligungsschreiben der Oberen der österreichischen und der bayerischen Ordensprovinz (zu der Salzburg gehörte) sowie das Schreiben des Generaloberen an den Salzburger Verleger Mayr ab. Letzteres macht deutlich, daß der Verleger offenbar die treibende Kraft dieser Aktion zur Befreiung eines erfolgversprechenden Autors vom normalen Zensurverfahren war.[23] Procopius hatte eine pauschale Approbation für das Gesamtwerk erreicht, war fortan, bis zu seinem Tode 1680, sein eigener Zensor und Korrektor und fand in den Ordinariaten von Salzburg und München Zensoren, die seine literarischen Qualitäten hochschätzten. Eine Rückkehr ins Passauer Kloster kam wegen der ständig anfallenden Neuauflagen nicht mehr in Frage.

III

Die wenigen hier vorgeführten Beispiele ergeben noch keine Typologie der Approbation; dazu müßte die Textbasis noch wesentlich erweitert werden. Diese Einschränkung berührt jedoch nicht den Quellenwert der Approbationen für eine Geschichte der Literaturkritik im Zeitraum der frühen Neuzeit. Bleibt abschließend noch die bisher ausgeklammerte Frage nach der Art der Zensuren für die Bücher, die den Zensoren vorgelegt, aber von ihnen nicht approbiert wurden. Die hierzu nötige archivalische Vorarbeit steckt noch in den Anfängen. Doch zeigen die bisher bekannten Einzelfälle aus dem Jesuitenorden, daß für die Ablehnung ebenfalls sprachliche, stilistische, dispositionelle und stoffliche Kriterien angeführt wurden. Aber wie die Literaturkritik stets gerade gegenüber Autoren hilflos ist, die das Risiko sprachlich-ästhetischer Experimente eingehen, so auch die Zensoren. Im Falle Jacob Baldes und Michael Staudachers führte dies dazu, daß die nicht approbierten Manuskripte verloren gingen und nur die Zensuren die Zeiten überdauerten. Im Falle Baldes kann man bei den Zensoren über den zweiten Teil des *Poema de Vanitate Mundi* u. a. lesen[24]:

Die deutsche Sprachform ist hart, die Poetisierung noch härter, viele Ausdrücke sind minderwertig, ordinär, stammen von der Gasse.

Er will über die deutsche Sprache belehren, die er selbst nicht beherrscht, wie allenthalben dem Leser in die Augen springt.

Ähnlich erging es Michael Staudacher (1613–72) mit der deutschen Übersetzung seiner Schrift *Centum affectus amoris Divini* (Dillingen, 1647) und seinen Predigtsammlungen (3.–5. Teil). Hier bemängelten die Zensoren vor allem Staudachers volkssprachliche Versuche im hohen Stil: den "zu üppigen Ornatus", die "Tautologien", die neuen, gewählten Wendungen, die Vorliebe für Bilder und Vergleiche aus der weltlichen Liebesdichtung, die fehlende inhaltliche und moralische Substanz.[25] Zu erinnern ist in diesem Zusammenhang auch an Friedrich Spees hartes Schicksal, der seine *Cautio criminalis* nur an der Zensur vorbei, anonym publizieren konnte und die Drucklegung seiner *Trutznachtigall* und seines *Güldenen Tugendbuchs* (in der von Zensoren überarbeiteten Form) nicht mehr erlebte.[26]

In allen diesen Fällen argumentieren die Zensoren, wie eine ausführlichere Analyse ihrer Texte zeigen könnte, als literarisch Gebildete; sie sind keine Dummköpfe. Ihre positiven Kritiken wie ihre Verrisse sind kenntnisreich, ihre Gründe einsichtig. Aber es sind machtgeschützte Urteile, und ihre Verrisse lassen dem Werk keine Chance der Bewährung. Es ist Literaturkritik im dunklen Schatten der Vorzensur.

Anmerkungen

1. Zur historischen Entwicklung und Systematik der Beschreibung alter Drucke vgl. Christoph Weismann, "Die Beschreibung und Verzeichnung alter Drucke. Ein Beitrag zur Bibliographie von Druckschriften des 16. bis 18. Jahrhunderts", in *Flugschriften als Massenmedium der Reformationszeit*, hrsg. v. Hans Joachim Köhler (Stuttgart: Klett-Cotta, 1981), S. 447–614. Die bibliographische Erfassung der Rahmenteile ist noch nicht selbstverständlich und auch bei Weismann lückenhaft, ebenso im methodisch sonst vorbildlichen *Katalog gedruckter deutschsprachiger katholischer Predigtsammlungen*, 2 Bde., hrsg. v. Werner Welzig, Österreichische Akademie der Wissenschaften, Philosoph.-Histor. Klasse, Sitzungsberichte, 430, 484 (Wien: Österreichische Akademie der Wissenschaften, 1984–87).

2. Die vom Verfasser zur Zeit vorbereitete Bibliographie der Münchner Drucke (Teil 1: 1565–1651) bezieht auch die Approbationen genauer in die Buchbeschreibung mit ein.

3. Klaus Kanzog, "Zensur, literarische", in *Reallexikon der deutschen Literaturgeschichte*, 2. Aufl., 4 Bde. (Berlin: de Gruyter, 1984), 3:998–1049, hier S. 1031.

4. Zur Rechtslage vgl. Ulrich Eisenhardt, *Die kaiserliche Aufsicht über Buchdruck, Buchhandel und Presse im Heiligen Römischen Reich Deutscher Nation (1496–1806)* (Karlsruhe: C. F. Müller, 1970); Friedrich Kapp, *Geschichte des deutschen Buchhandels*, 6 Bde. (Leipzig: Börsenverein, 1886), bes. 1:782–85; Willibald M. Plöchl, *Geschichte des Kirchenrechts*, 5 Bde. (Wien: Herold, 1969), 5:371–78; Joseph Listl, Hubert Müller und Heribert Schmitz, *Handbuch des katholischen Kirchenrechts* (Regensburg: F. Pustet, 1983), S. 569–73; Karl Theodor Heigel, "Zur Geschichte des Zensurwesens in der Gesellschaft Jesu", *Archiv für die Geschichte des deutschen Buchhandels* 6 (1881): 162–67; Heinrich Friedrich Jacobsen und Emil Albert Friedberg, "Bücherzensur, Bücherverbot, Bücherapprobation", in *Real-Enzyklopädie der Protestantischen Theologie*, 3. Aufl., 24 Bde. [1897], 3:523–25.

5. Vgl. Johann Heinrich Zedler, *Grosses Vollständiges Universal-Lexikon*, Bd. 5 (Halle/Leipzig, 1733), Sp. 1817 ("Censor librorum"). Zur Entwicklung der Zensurkriterien vgl. Dieter Breuer, *Geschichte der literarischen Zensur in Deutschland* (Heidelberg: Quelle und Meyer, 1982).

6. Tommaso Garzoni, *Piazza Universale, das ist Allgemeiner Schawplatz . . . in unsere Muttersprach vbersetzt . . .* (Franckfurt an Mayn / bey Nicolao Hoffman / in Verlegung Lucae Jennis, 1619), S. 212 (30. Discurs, "Von den Correctoribus, Censoribus vnd Criticis") [Exemplar der Universitätsbibliothek Köln].

7. Über die Geschichte der frühneuzeitlichen Literaturkritik wird in Kürze Herbert Jaumanns Bielefelder Habilitationsschrift umfassend informieren.

8. Laurentius von Schnüffis *Mirantisches Flötlein. Oder Geistliche Schäfferey / In welcher Christus / under dem Namen Daphnis / die in dem Sünden = Schlaff vertieffte Seel Clorinda zu einem bessern Leben aufferwecket . . .* (Gedruckt zu Constantz / In der Fürstl. Bischoffl. Druckerey / Bey David Hautt / Anno 1682; In Verlegung Johann Jacob Mantelin Burgern / und Handelsmann zu Lauffenburg) [Exemplar des Provinzarchivs der Kapuziner, Koblenz-Ehrenbreitstein].

9. Vgl. "Approbatio I–IV". Das Verfahren innerhalb des Kapuzinerordens schildert Procopius von Templin, siehe unten.

10. "Approbatio I":

EX mandato Superiorum sacram Poesin, à M.V.P. Laurentio ex Schnüffis decantatam, pervolvi, & probè perspexi, quòd in ea cum magno Isaia currens non habeat offendiculum, sed gregem Christianum per vias asperas vitae *Purgativae*, cum Salomone ad vias Pulchras *illuminativae*, & semitas pacificas *unitivae* deducat melo tam dulcisono, ut meritò in omniú animis intonetur, & publico praelo demandetur. ita censeo. Constantiae 8. August 1681.

F. Aloysius Veldkirch. Guardianus,
Definator & Custos.

11. "Approbatio II":

EX mandato Superiorum sacrum Pastorale A.V.P. Laurentij ex Schnüffis Concionatoris perlustravi, vidíque cuncta in eo *prospera*, atque proficua omni statui, ac hominum conditioni, dum, *quod infirmum est, consolidat; quod aegrotum, sanat; quod confractum, alligat; quod abjectum, reducit; quódque perierat, quaerit.* Nec dubium, quin & propriae, & alienae oves vocem eius auditurae sint, cùm non solùm caulas, sed & principum aulas liberè ingrediens pastorali muneri suo solicitè satagat, cúmque nihil contra fidem Orthodoxam contineat, sed potiùs ejusdem sanitatem integerrimam spiret, dignum censeo, ut pro DEI gloria, & animarum salute praelo publicetur.
Lauffenbergae, 7. Augusti 1682
    F. Pancratius Engensis Guardianus
    & Custos ibidem indignus.

12. "Approbatio III":

DE mente superiorum legi attentè isthaec vernacula Poèmata M.V.P. Laurentii ex Schnüffis Concionatoris, Capucini, quem benè & utiliter *tempus flendi* per orationem, & *tempus canendi* per sacram hanc Poèsin distinxisse comperi; cùm ex hoc eius florifero Parnasso non nisi *oderem vitae in vitam* emanare senserim. Alii verbo clamant *coaequalibus suis*, & peccatores ad paenitentiam invitant ; iste secundùm Evangelistae dictum etiam *tibijs cantat*, ut aberrantes in lege Domini saltare doceat. Quandoquidem ergo, quod Elisaeo quondam *Psalte coram cassente*, hoc etiam lectoribus, vel auditoribus huius sacrae Psaldmodiae proventurum esse non ambigam, ut nempe *Spiritum Domini* inde supra se venientem percensuri sint. Ideò, ut *sonus* huius libri in omnem terram per publicum praelum exeat, dignissimum censeo. Dabam Wangae 2. Augusti 1681.
    F. Lucianus Guardianus ibid.

13. Vgl. Dieter Breuer, *Der Philotheus des Laurentius von Schnüffis. Zum Typus des geistlichen Romans im 17. Jahrhundert* (Meisenheim am Glan: Hain, 1969); Irmgard Scheitler, "Geistliche Lieder als literarische Gebrauchsform. Versuch einer Gattungsbeschreibung am Beispiel der Lieder des Laurentius von Schnüffis", *Zeitschrift für Bayerische Landesgeschichte* 47 (1984): 214–39; dieselbe, "Laurentius von Schnüffis", in *Die österreichische Literatur. Ihr Profil von den Anfängen im Mittelalter bis ins 18. Jahrhundert*, hrsg. v. Fritz Peter Knapp und Herbert Zeman (Graz: Akademische Druck- und Verlagsanstalt, 1986), S. 1191–1235.

14. Vgl. Dieter Breuer, "Oberdeutsche Erzählliteratur im 17. Jahrhundert. Gründe für eine Neubewertung", *Zeitschrift für Bayerische Landesgeschichte* 47 (1984): 197–213. Eine Präzisierung der hier und andernorts vertretenen These hat Verfasser beim Kongreß "Nation und Literatur im Europa der frühen Neuzeit" (Osnabrück, 1986) vorgetragen: "Deutsche Nationalliteratur und katholischer Kulturkreis".

15. Georg Litzel gen. Melissus, *Deutsche Jesuiten = Poesie Oder Eine Samm-lung Catholischer Gedichte, Welche Zur Verbesserung Allen Reimenschmieden wohl-meinend vorgeleget Megallissvs* (Franckfurth und Leipzig Verlegts Johann Eh-renfried Müller, 1731), Vorrede [Exemplar der Stadtsbibliothek Ulm]. Immer-hin bemüht sich Litzel in seiner historischen Darstellung (*Der Undeutsche Catholik* [Jena/Leipzig, 1730], S. 55; 77–78) um ein etwas differenzierteres Ur-teil gegenüber Laurentius.

16. Rudolf von Schwyz, *Außforderung Mit Aller demütigst gebottnem Ver-nunft = Trutz An alle Atheisten / Machiavellisten / gefährliche Romanen / und falsch = politische Welt = Kinder zu einem Zwey = Kampff Auff dem Plan kurtzwei-liger Dichtung / mit dem Schwerdt / der sonderbaren Beweißthumben: Also ein Ge-dichte / mit Warheit = besprengte Historia von Philologo einem Portugesischen Cava-lieren / Vnd Clarabella einer Käyserin in China* . . . (Gedruckt zu Zug / bey = und durch Heinrich Ludwig Muos / 1686. Zufinden bey Herrn Damian Mül-ler allda) [Exemplar des Provinzarchivs der Kapuziner, Koblenz-Ehrenbreit-stein]. Teil 1–2 dieses Werkes (1087 und 365 S.) erschienen 1686; Teil 3 (687 S.) 1688. Zu Rudolf von Schwyz vgl. Basilius a Bologna, *Lexicon Capuccinum* (Rom: Bilbliotheca Collegii Internationalis S. Laurentii Brundusini, 1951), Sp. 1483–84.

17. Procopius von Templin, *Lignum Vitae Oder Zwölff Frücht = tragender Baum deß Lebens* . . . (Getruckt vnnd Verlegt zu München / durch Johann Jäcklin / Churfürstl: Durchl: in Bayern Hoffbuchtrucker. Im Jahr Christi / 1665), Approbation [Exemplar des Provinzarchivs der Kapuziner, Koblenz-Ehrenbreitstein).

18. Procopius von Templin, *Adventvale, Ac Natale Iesu Christi, Sive Deliciae Spiritvs Hibernales. Hertzens = Frewd vnd Seelen = Lust im harten Winter* . . . (Ge-druckt vnd verlegt zu München / durch Johann Jäcklin / Churfürstl: Hoff = Buchdrucker / Im Jahr 1666), Zweite Approbation [Exemplar des Provinz-archivs der Kapuziner, Koblenz-Ehrenbreitstein].

19. Vgl. auch Kirmairs Approbation zu Procopius' Predigtsammlung *Sa-crum Epithalamium sive canticum canticorum* (München, 1678) sowie zu For-tunat Huebers Mirakelbuch *Zeitiger Granat = apfel*, hrsg. v. Guillaume van Ge-mert (München, 1671; Neudruck Amsterdam: APA-Holland Press, 1983), letztere in deutscher Sprache.

20. Procopius von Templin, *Mariale Das ist: Vber hundert und sechtzig gelehr-te / geistreiche / mit grosser Klarheit annemblichen Concepten / Biblischen Schriff-ten / bewehrten Rationen, Alten und Newen Historien vnd Exempeln / guter Con-nexion wol componirte / völlig außgeführte / diser vnd jeder Zeit nothwendige nutzliche Predigen Von . . . Maria . . .* (Saltzburg / Getruckt vnd verlegt durch / Johann Baptista Mayr / Hof = vnd Academischen Buchtrucker/ vnd Händler. Anno 1665).

21. Ebd. Bl. IC ijv–IC ivr.

22. Procopius vom Templin, *Mariale* . . . , Editio secunda auctior et correc-tior (Salzburg: Joh. Baptist Mayr, 1667) [Exemplar der Bayerischen Staatsbi-bliothek, München].

23. Der Brief hat folgenden Wortlaut: "Potestas ab Admodum R. P. Generali Ord. Min. Capuccinorum facta Typhographo Salisburgens: Joanni Baptistae Mayr. Pax Christi. Libentissime annuo, ut Scripturae P. Procopii dentur officinae vestrae potius quam aliorum, maxime quia Religio nostra [= unser Orden] humanitate Dominationis vestrae valde obstricta sit. Unde circa hoc necessaria monita P. PROCOPIO dabo, & licentiam Salisburgum veniendi mittam. Si in aliquo possum inservire, libentissime faciam, sicuti e caelo omnia bona precans me subscribo qui sum Dominationis Vestrae Servus in Christo Fr. Marcus Antonius Minister Generalis Capuccinus. Neoburgi 31. Octobris 1663."

24. Vgl. Luzian Pfleger, "Unediertes von und über Balde", *Zeitschrift für die Geschichte des Oberrheins* N.F. 19 (1909): 69–78, hier S. 73–74: "phrasis Germanica est dura, poesis durior; in versuum ac iocorum parum quandoque decentium gratiam quid libet audit et dicit; voces sunt multae viles, plebeiae, triviales . . ." – "Vult docere linguam Germanicam, quam ipse nescit, ut passim in oculos lectoris incurrit." Zu Baldes Verhältnis zu den Zensoren vgl. Dieter Breuer, *Oberdeutsche Literatur 1565–1650. Deutsche Literaturgeschichte und Territorialgeschichte in frühabsolutistischer Zeit*, Zeitschrift für bayerische Landesgeschichte, Beiheft 11, Reihe B (München: Beck, 1979), S. 242–49.

25. Vgl. Josef Eder, "P. Michael Staudacher S.J. (1613–1672). Ein Beitrag zur Erforschung der religiösen Literatur des 17. Jahrhunderts", Diss. Innsbruck 1966, S. 122; 268–77.

26. Vgl. Friedrich Spee, *Güldenes Tugend = Buch*, hrsg. v. Theo G. M. Oorschot (München: Kösel, 1968), S. 674–87 (Spees Zensoren und ihre Eingriffe in den Text).

9. Allegorische Repräsentation als Legitimation: Die Geburtstagsfestlichkeiten für Herzog August

Barbara Becker-Cantarino

Großartige theatralische Festlichkeiten sind das Zeichen der europäischen Hofkultur. "Vom 'Herbst des Mittelalters' bis zum sterbenden Rokoko rauscht ein bacchantischer Festzug durch die Gassen und Gärten, die Schlösser und Kirchen Europas", so bemerkte Richard Alewyn in seiner gehaltvollen, interpretativen Darstellung zur "Epoche der höfischen Feste"[1]. Die Höfe Europas, vom Italien der Spätrenaissance, zum Spanien Philipps IV., vom Kaiserhof in Wien bis zum Eleganz und weltstädtischen Geschmack diktierenden Sonnenkönig, werden von einem Taumel der allegorischen Repräsentation in glanzvollen Festlichkeiten erfaßt. So war etwa die Florentiner Doppelhochzeit, bei der der Großherzog Francesco I. von Toscana sich mit der altadeligen Venezianerin Bianca Capella vermählte und deren Tochter aus erster Ehe den Grafen Bentivoglio heiratete, 1579 wochenlang prunkvoll gefeiert worden: die geladenen adeligen Gäste und Abgesandten wurden mit großen Feierlichkeiten eingeholt und begrüßt, es folgten Ringelrennen, Turnier, Stiergefecht, die Krönung der Großherzogin, Messen, Jagden, Bankette und Bälle. Den Höhepunkt aber bildeten höfische Ritterspiele auf einer riesigen, im Freien errichteten Bühne und ein Wettbewerb allegorischer Aufzüge und Selbstdarstellungen.

So dauerten die Hochzeitsfeierlichkeiten anläßlich der Vermählung von Kaiser Leopold I. und der spanischen Infantin Margarita in Wien zwei Jahre lang, von 1666–68. Bekanntlich wurde dabei die Prunkoper *Il Pomo d'oro* (der goldene Apfel) mit den prachtvollen Bühnenbildern von Ludovico Burnacini aufgeführt, in der die Geschichte vom Wettstreit der Juno, Venus und Minerva um den goldenen Apfel der Schönheit glücklich und passend gelöst wird. Der goldene Zankapfel wird von Zeus der Kaiserin überreicht, als der vornehmsten Frau, der Tochter und Gemahlin der zwei größten Monarchen, die Juno an Macht, Pallas an Geist und Venus an Schönheit übertrifft. Dann läßt Zeus noch das Gemach des Fatums öffnen, wo sich das Bild der Kaiserin mit einer unendlichen Anzahl von Nachkommen zeigt. In dieser Huldigung verschmilzt die Allegorie mit der Wirklichkeit; die Legitimation der jungen Kaiserin, die für das Weiterleben des Hauses Österreich zu sorgen hat, findet statt in der allegorischen Repräsentation.

Eine besondere Attraktion bei diesen Hochzeitsfeierlichkeiten war ein allegorisches Roßballett, betitelt "Siegstreitt dess Lufft und Wassers Freuden-Fest", das eine Glorifizierung des Kaisers darstellte.[2] Der Wettstreit der Elemente endete mit der Vereinigung des goldenen Vlieses mit der deutsch-römischen Kaiserkrone. An der vierstündigen Veranstaltung mit etwa 1300 Mitwirkenden nahm der Kaiser selbst teil und spielte, d. h. er ritt seine eigene Rolle. Noch aufwendiger war das Feuerwerk, das auf einer Freilichtbühne zwischen zwei sechzig Fuß hohen Bergen—dem von Vulkan bewohnten Aetna und dem mit den neun Musen bestückten Parnaß—inszeniert wurde. Das Feuerwerk, das natürlich von Musik begleitet war, endete mit "73 000 Lustfeuer . . . zudem noch 300 dreipfündigen Raketen, wobei die Buchstaben A.E.I.O.U. (*Austria erit in omne ultimum*—Österreich wird in allem das Höchste sein) in der Luft verblieben"[3]. Hier wirkten Bild, Musik und Schrift zusammen, um in allegorischer Festvorstellung das Haus Österreich zu glorifizieren. Diese allegorische Repräsentation als Legitimation im barocken Fest soll uns im folgenden beschäftigen.

I

Auch in Deutschland, das schwer unter dem Dreißigjährigen Kriege gelitten hatte und sich nur langsam von den Verheerungen erholen konnte, waren allegorische Festveranstaltungen Höhepunkt und Mitte des höfischen Lebens in den kleinen und großen Fürstentümern. Die Anlässe bildeten jeweils für wichtig erachtete Ereignisse im Leben der fürstlichen Familie oder im Verlaufe von deren Politik: Geburts- und Todestage, eine Taufe oder Hochzeit, ein hoher Besuch, ein Friedensschluß, Staatsverträge, Einweihungen oder Grundsteinlegungen —an Gelegenheiten war kein Mangel. Diese Feste waren keineswegs Veranstaltungen für eine breite Öffentlichkeit; hier blieb der Adel unter sich und nur die bei Hofe zugelassenen Personen, unter denen allerdings an den kleineren Höfen neben dem Landadel auch bürgerliche Hofbeamte waren, bildeten die Zuschauer. Hans-Gert Roloff hat diese Exklusivität auf die knappe Formel gebracht: "Man spielte für sich und mit sich selbst"[4], denn oft rekrutierten sich aus diesem engen

Kreis, der geschlossenen Adelsgesellschaft, die Autoren wie auch die Schauspieler. Und das geschah nicht unbedingt nur aus Verlegenheit, weil keine passenden Berufsautoren, -komponisten oder -schauspieler vorhanden waren oder das nötige Geld dafür fehlte. Das Spielen einer Rolle, der eigenen Rolle in allegorischer Verkleidung, wie etwa Kaiser Leopold als "Majestät" im Roßballette mitgeritten ist, hatte die wichtige Funktion der Legitimation.

Diese Legitimation in der (Selbst-)darstellung geschah jedoch hauptsächlich auf der Ebene und im Medium des Bildes, weniger auf der des Wortes, das eindeutig eine sekundäre, stützende Funktion erfüllt. Anders ausgedrückt: die Konstitution der Person, ihre Legitimation findet in und durch das allegorische Bild statt, nur sekundär durch das Wort, durch das "sprachliche Kunstwerk". Wenn Stephen Greenblatt am Beispiel der großen Autoren der englischen Renaissance von Thomas More bis Christopher Marlowe feststellt: "Self-fashioning is always, though not exclusively, in language"[5]; dann bezeichnet er damit die Wortkultur der humanistischen Renaissance und Reformation, nicht die allegorische Bildkultur des barocken Hofes. Greenblatt betrachtet "middle-class writers"—wie problematisch auch immer diese Bezeichnung für das 16. Jahrhundert sein mag—mit der Faszination der auf "Sprache" fixierten Literaturkritik der Gegenwart und versucht, mit den Kategorien von "authority" und "alien (a threatening Other)" die Selbstbestimmung zu erklären. Ein solches Verfahren, das die Konstitution des Individuums im sozialen Kontext aus Sprache herleitet, beleuchtet den Unterschied zur Legitimation des barocken Fürsten. Eine andere Klasse und Welt, eine andere Sprache: am barocken Hof ist es die Sprache der Bilder und Allegorien. In den prunkvollen Hoffesten, in allegorischen Bildern, in denen der Adelige des Barock sich legitimiert und zur Schau stellt, wird eine allegorische Bilderwelt wiederbelebt und fortgemalt, indem sie aktuelle und gegenwärtige Bezüge in diese Bilder verlegt. Darauf hat jetzt wieder Conrad Wiedemann ausdrücklich in seinen "Beobachtungen zur Funktion der Barockallegorie" verwiesen.[6]

II

In diesen Rahmen aus Konventionen einerseits und Repräsentationsbedürfnis andererseits gehören die Geburtstagsfeierlichkeiten für Herzog August zu Braunschweig und Lüneburg (1579–1666). Die Konventionen waren die Mode prunkvoller Festlichkeiten, die zum Statussymbol eines Fürstenhofes gehörten; das Repräsentationsbedürfnis war von dem Willen getragen, die soziale Rolle des Herrschers und seines Hauses zu legitimieren, und das geschah in der Form von theatralischer Selbstdarstellung in allegorischen Bildern. In dieser Hinsicht unterscheiden sich diese Geburtstagsfeierlichkeiten grundlegend vom Schultheater, dessen große Leistung in der sprachlichen Ausformung, dem rhetorisch durchgeformten Text und dem anspruchsvollen, belehrenden Inhalt lag, und das religiöse oder weltliche Handlungsweisen problematisierte. Anders die höfischen Feste, wie an den theatralischen Festlichkeiten zum Geburtstag Herzog Augusts gezeigt werden soll, die als *repraesentatio maiestatis* dem höfischen Leben Sinn und Ausdruck verleihen sollen.

In den Jahren 1652 bis 1656 hat die literarisch und musisch tätige Sophie Elisabeth (1613–76)[7], die dritte Frau Herzog Augusts, musikalisch-theatralische Feste veranstaltet, um den Geburtstag des Herzogs, der 1654 immerhin schon 75 Jahre alt wurde, zu begehen. Sicher sind diese Festlichkeiten zunächst aus der Tradition der Geburtstagsglückwünsche und Gelegenheitsgedichte erwachsen. (Etwa 1600 gedruckte Gelegenheitsgedichte auf Herzog August und seine Familie von rund 390 verschiedenen Autoren aus allen Teilen Deutschlands sind erhalten, was die Beliebtheit und Proliferation dieser literarischen Gattung im 17. Jahrhundert nur unterstreicht.)[8] So hatte 1650 Martin Gosky, der aus Schlesien gebürtige Leibarzt und Hofpoet Herzog Augusts, seinem Fürsten einen prunkvollen Sammelband mit Lobgedichten und Bildkupfern überreicht. Auf etwa 1300 Folioseiten bringt dieser Band, der ausdrucksvoll mit *Arbustum seu Arboretum Poetice*—ein mit Bäumen und Büschen bepflanzter Garten der Poesie—betitelt ist, zumeist allegorische und emblematische Bilder und Verse zum Lob Herzog Augusts.[9] In allegorischen Bildern wird in hyperbolischer Form die Herrschergestalt Herzog Augusts gepriesen und dabei in Bilder umgesetzt. Unter dem Motto "Ex bello pax"[10] zeigt das Bild, wie "Schwerter in Pflugscharen" umgewandelt werden (Abb. 1). Oder es fährt z. B. auf einem undatierten(?) Blatt die herzogliche Familie—Herzog August mit dem charakteristischen Spitzbart ist deutlich erkennbar, neben ihm Sophie Elisabeth und fünf Kinder—in einem offenen Theaterwagen (Abb. 2). Der Wagen wird von acht Pferden gezogen und fährt vor dem Hintergrund der Stadt Wolfenbüttel, in der allerwärts Böllerschüsse abgegeben werden, auf einer mit Blumen bestreuten Straße entlang. Concordia ist die Wagenlenkerin, Pax steht im erhöhten Heck des Wagens, dessen Räder gerade über den am Boden liegenden Mars und Invidia rollen. Sieben Frauenfiguren begleiten den Wagen; ihre jeweiligen Insignien und Unterschrift weisen sie aus als Iustitia und Temperantia, Pallas (Athe-

Abb. 1. "Schwerter in Pflugscharen", aus Martin Gosky, Arbustum seu Arboretum Poetice *(Wolfenbüttel: Stern, 1650), Bl. 216r. (Herzog August Bibliothek, Wolfenbüttel)*

ne) und Fortitudo, Providentia, Charitas und Fides. Von oben strahlt die Herrscher-Sonne mit der hebräischen Inschrift "Jehova".

Es war ein wichtiges Ereignis aus dem Jahre 1643, das dieses Blatt illustriert: nach dem Sonderfrieden in Goslar räumten die kaiserlichen Truppen die Stadt Wolfenbüttel, und Herzog August konnte seine Residenz von Braunschweig nach Wolfenbüttel zurückverlegen. So trägt denn auch das Blatt die Bezeichnung: "Fröhliger Einzug auf einem Friedens- und Triumpfwagen in begleitung Der Gesamten Göttlichen Tugendgesellschaft der Durchl. Hochgebornen Fürsten und Herrn hern Augusti Hertzogen Zu Brauns. vnd Lüneb. etc. Mit allgemeinem Frolocken des gantzen Landes gehalten in Dero Residentz und Hauptvestung Wolfenbüttel"[11]. Damit die Bedeutung dieses historischen Augenblicks noch weiter festgehalten wird, erklärt das "Triumf Liedt" von Justus Georg Schottelius in acht vierzeiligen Strophen den allegorischen Einzug:

> Eile Sonn, Scheuss helle stralen
> Vnser Land wie Goldt zu mahlen

und weiter:

> Das gesamte Tugend-chor
> Samt dem Friede trit hervor

Abb. 2. Einzug der herzoglichen Familie auf einem "Friedens- und Triumpfwagen", aus Gosky, Arbustum seu Arboretum Poetice, *vor Bl. 230.*

. . . .
Ziehet ein mit triumphiren
Höchstberühmter Fürst und Held,
Schöne Sonn der Teutschen welt.

Der Fürst als Sonne, diese Herrscherallegorie des 17. Jahrhunders *par excellence* wird hier nicht macchiavellisch gedeutet, sondern mit dem "Tugend-chor", angeführt vom Frieden, als Hofstaat in theatralischem Aufzug verbildlicht. Diese theatralische Allegorie des Einzugs war eine Huldigung an den Fürsten, während der eigentliche Einzug ohne die allegorische Maskierung (am 14. oder 17. September 1643) stattgefunden hatte und auf einem entsprechenden "realistischen" Stich festgehalten worden ist (Abb. 3), der die Ankunft des Fürsten und seines Gefolges in (geschlossenen) Kutschen und den Einmarsch seiner Truppen zeigt. Auch auf diesem "realistischen" Stich schwebt ein Siegesengel mit Trompete ("victoria" steht auf dem aus der Trompete kommenden Schriftband) über dem Dach des Kirchenschiffes mit dem Bild des Herzogs in einem Medaillon.[12]

Abb. 3. Einzug Herzog Augusts in Wolfenbüttel (17. September 1643), nach Gosky, Arbustum seu Arboretum Poetice, *Bl. 282–83.*

Erst nachdem das Herzogtum nicht mehr von Kriegswirren bedroht und der Westfälische Friede geschlossen worden war, wurden die Hoffeste wieder aufgenommen. Schon für 1648 ist das erste Geburtstagsgedicht der Sophie Elisabeth für Herzog August erhalten, als wahrscheinlich die Hoffeste wieder begannen und dazu den Geburtstag des alternden, aber rüstigen und in Politik, Verwaltung und Gelehrsamkeit gleich erfolgreichen Fürsten zum Anlaß nahmen. Von 1650 bis zu Augusts Tod im Jahre 1666 hat Sophie Elisabeth alljährlich Dichtungen geliefert, die jeweils den Regenten in barocken Allegorien feiern; Höhepunkt der theatralischen Feste sind jedoch die Jahre 1652 bis 1656, für die Szenarien von insgesamt sechs allegorischen Spielen erhalten sind.[13] Unter diesen allegorischen Spielen sind Maskeraden, Ballette und musikalisch untermalte Darbietungen, die in der Musikgeschichte als Vorläufer des deutschen Singspiels betrachtet werden.[14] 1653 leitet Sophie Elisabeth die musikalisch untermalten Festlichkeiten so ein:

Als in Gedancken schwer Ich träumend saß entzücket /
Kompt mir für Augen gleich als wenn ich hätt' erblicket
    ein Jungfrau halb bekleidt und halb entblöst / die Haar
Zerstreuet hin und her / ihr Angesichte war
Erröthet / weil sie sich so sehr geeilt im gehen /
Es stund auff ihrem Häupt ein Sanduhr / auch zu sehen
    In ihrer rechten Hand ein Sichel scharff / die Linck
Sie auffhub / und mit selber mir gab einen Winck /
Sprach / steh auff / komm ich hab dir etwas news zu sagen /
Leg auff ein Zeitlang hin das schwermütige Zagen /
    Ermunter deinen Geist / ist dir dann nicht bewust?
Daß itzt die Guelfenburg erfüllet gantz mit Lust /
Dieweil ihr Häupt und Fürst / itzt die Jahrs' = Zeit begehet /
Von seinem Geburtstag / der Himmel gleichsam stehet
    Zusamt der Erd vernewt / und mit uns froelich ist /
So sey du's billich auch / weil du sein Werthes bist /
Und er deins Häuptes = Kron / dein Ehr und dein Vergnügen /
Drumb eil und bring herfür / die Geister nach Vermügen.
    Hiemit sie gleich verschwand: ich von der Sorgen = Banck
Auff stund / nam meine Leyr; stimbt / und drin also sang:[15]

Dann folgt ein Lied auf den "Vermehrer der Wölpenstadt", komponiert und gesungen von Sophie Elisabeth. Wir dürfen annehmen, daß diese Verse, die in einer gedruckten Geburtstagsschrift ebenfalls dem Herzog überreicht wurden, von Elisabeth szenisch dargeboten wurden. Die Szene (oder der so inszenierte lebhafte Vortrag) spielte zunächst als Gespräch zwischen der "eilenden Zeit" und der sitzenden, besorgt träumenden, dann sich mit der Leier in eine Muse verwandelnden Elisabeth. Die Muse wird von einem kleinen Orchester, das wahrscheinlich aus den herzoglichen Kindern bestand, begleitet. Die dem Druck beigegebene Partitur weist drei Instrumentalstimmen aus. Ein repräsentatives Ölgemälde der herzoglichen Familie mit Hofstaat von etwa 1645 zeigt die sechs Kinder sämtlich mit Beinviolinen vom Kontrabaß bis zum Diskantinstrument, die dem jeweiligen Alter angepaßt sind. In deren Mitte steht Sophie Elisabeth am Continuoklavier; aufgeschlagene Notenbücher deuten auf das aktive Musizieren der Gruppe. Der Herzog sitzt beim Brettspiel, einige Hofbeamte sind mit Kartenspiel beschäftigt, der restliche Hofstaat schaut wichtig und ein bißchen nutzlos direkt den Betrachter an.[16]

    Sophie Elisabeth spielt die Rolle der Muse, die den Herrscher und seine Tugend, seine Leistung für das Fürstentum besingt und verewigt. Es ist eine Vorschau auf die Musenhöfe des 18. Jahrhunderts, wo die Landesmutter mit ihren Hofdamen als Mäzenatin von Künstlern und Autoren fungiert, wo *repraesentatio maiestatis* und Herrscherkult allerdings in den Hintergrund getreten sind.

In einem anderen Geburtstagsspiel, der Maskerade *Der Natur Banquett* (1654), übernahm Sophie die Rolle der Natur und definierte ihre Rolle als "natura naturans", als oberstes Lebensprinzip, die dem Herzog "beständige Gesundheit und neue Kräfte" als Geburtstagsgaben bringt. Der gesamte Hofstaat verkleidete sich dabei ebenfalls in eine allegorische Rolle, in die Planeten und antike Götter jeweils mit entsprechendem Gefolge und feierte so mit Umzug, Musik, mit Versdarbietungen als Gaben, großem Essen und anschließender Theateraufführung den Geburtstag.[17] Jedem ist eine Rolle zugeteilt, jeder agiert seiner allegorischen Rolle entsprechend. Lediglich die glückwünschenden Verse waren textlich fixiert; sie sind im Szenarium der Maskerade verzeichnet, die Rollen lediglich kurz beschrieben. Ihre Gestaltung war dem einzelnen überlassen, jedoch durch die allegorische Figur vorgegeben.

In einem ganz ähnlichen Festspiel, *Der Minervae Banquett* (1655), hatte Sophie Elisabeth sich die Rolle der Minerva zugeschrieben, die von einem stattlichen Gefolge umgeben ist, den sieben freien Künsten und den neun Musen. Für diese Gruppe von immerhin siebzehn Damen war eine Kulisse des Musenberges Parnaß im Eßsaal errichtet worden, an dessen Fuß sie in zwei Halbkreisen mitsamt ihren Insignien Platz hatten. Darüber thronte leicht erhöht Sophie Elisabeth, während Pegasus sich gerade von der Spitze des Berges abzuheben scheint. Prometheus hatte Minerva mit ihren Damen zunächst zu diesem Platz begleitet, dann wurde der Herzog abgeholt und mit Musik begrüßt ("die Musica" saß "im Berge"). Herzog August wurde von Apollo geführt, in seinem Gefolge befanden sich "im ersten Gliede" (*Spiele*, S. 50) Orpheus, Arion und Amphion—drei große Sänger des griechischen Mythos, deren Gesang Wunder bewirken konnte—, dann folgten die sieben Weisen (große Staatsmänner der Antike) und die sieben unfreien Künste—Landwirtschaft, Jagdwesen, Kriegswesen, Wundheilkunde, Webkunst, Schiffskunst und Handwerkerkünste (es gibt keinen festen Kanon für diese *artes mechanicae*—Handwerkerkünste). Nachdem alle Mitspieler ihre "Wunsch-Reime" aufgesagt hatten, ließ August durch seinen Kanzler einen Dank verlesen "an die anwesende hocherleuchtete Minerva, als Vorsteherinn menschlicher Weißheit nebenst ihren beyhabenden allen Weisen / Freyen auch anderen Künsten" (*Spiele*, S. 60). Ein Festessen, eine musikalische Bilderfolge (auf die gleich noch einzugehen ist) im Saal, ein Ballett und eine Theateraufführung[18] im Komödienhaus schlossen

sich an, bis die maskierte Gesellschaft wieder im zeremoniös geordneten Zug sich in ihre Gemächer begab.

Alle Spieler in dieser Maskerade sind Angehörige der Familie oder
des Hofes; sie haben von der Autorin Sophie Elisabeth eine jeweils
ihrer eigenen Rolle entsprechende Maske aus Mythologie und antiker
Geschichte zuerteilt bekommen. Sich selbst hatte Sophie Elisabeth als
Minerva maskiert, als Göttin der Weisheit, die Jupiter am nächsten
steht; die sieben freien Künste werden von den ranghöchsten Verwandten, die neun Musen von (unverheirateten) Hofdamen dargestellt. Sophie Elisabeth und ihr Hof haben sich in Sinnbilder dessen
verwandelt, wofür sie auch im realen Leben verantwortlich sind: die
Frauen für die musische und artistische Verschönerung und die moralische Verbesserung des Lebens; die männlichen Verwandten und
Hofbeamten repräsentieren die weisen Regenten, Philosophen und
nützlichen menschlichen Tätigkeiten in diesem allegorischen Gebilde
einer "idealen" höfischen Gesellschaft. Nur der Herzog spielt seine
eigene Rolle: er ist und spielt zugleich den Regenten. Die Maskerade
repräsentiert und legitimiert dadurch seine Herrschaft: sie ist *repraesentatio maiestatis*.

III

Die Herrscherperson steht auch im Mittelpunkt des Singspieles *Glückwünschende Freudendarstellung* von 1652. Dieses Singspiel, das zweimal
aufgeführt und gedruckt wurde, nämlich in den Jahren 1652 und
1655, hat durch den Druck eine begrenzte literarische Öffentlichkeit
erreicht und gilt in der Musikgeschichte als eine Art Vorform der
deutschen Oper. Das ist insofern ungenau, als diese Freudendarstellung eine Bilderfolge von fünf lebenden Bildern war, die mit Musik
und erläuterndem Gesang jeweils begleitet wurden. Diese Bilderfolge
steht den niederländischen *vertooningen*, den lebenden Bildern, nahe,
die farbenprächtig, mit sprechenden Requisiten und Musik oft den
einzelnen Akten eines Stückes vorangestellt waren, um den kommenden Hergang zu erklären. (Es ist nachgewiesen, daß niederländische
Wandertruppen die *vertooningen* mit im niederdeutschen Raum gespielt und eingeführt haben.)[19] In der *Freudendarstellung* gibt es keine
eigentliche Handlung, sondern eine Reihe von fünf sprechenden Bildern, die das Leben und Regiment des Herzogs darstellen, also eine
repraesentatio maiestatis.

August wird in den vier Lebensaltern abgebildet, es ist "eine Beschreibung der Glückwünschenden Freudendarstellung an ihm sel-

Abb. 4. "Frühling", aus Sophie Elisabeth, Glückwünschende Freudendarstellung *(Lüneburg: Stern, 1652), Bl. A2r. (Herzog August Bibliothek, Wolfenbüttel)*

ber", wie die Unterschrift des ersten lebenden Bildes lautet (*Spiele*, S. 14; Abb. 4). Dieses "Theatrum" zeigt das Kind im Frühling seines Lebens, mit zwei Palmen im Hintergrund, einem Sinnbild von Frömmigkeit, Weisheit und Gelehrsamkeit (wie die Palme auch das Zeichen der Fruchtbringenden Gesellschaft war). Ebenfalls zu sehen ist ein römischer Brunnen, an dessen unterer Säule vier Löwenköpfe—das Wappentier der Braunschweiger—Wasser speien. Als Lebens- oder Jungbrunnen ist der Brunnen ebenso ein Zeichen, wie die beiden Figuren, die das Kind bei der Hand halten, links der Schutzengel, rechts das Glück. Die Figuren stehen in einem abgezirkelten, die Natur bezähmenden, barocken Garten, der auch noch mit Balustraden umgeben ist, Zeichen der behüteten, geordneten und vorgeschriebenen Kinderjahre. An den Bäumen hängen je drei Bilder rechts und links, die markante Szenen aus dem frühen Leben abbilden: Geburt, Taufe, das Gehenlernen im Laufstuhl, Puppenspiel, beim Kreiselspiel, beim Singen und im Schulunterricht. Während dieses "Lebende Bild" gezeigt wird, wird in sechs Strophen der glückliche

Abb. 5. "Sommer", *aus Sophie Elisabeth,* Glückwünschende
Freudendarstellung, *Bl. B1v.*

Lebensweg, den das Kind gehen wird, besungen, ohne jedoch auf die
Bilder im einzelnen hinzuweisen:

> drumb eile mit Lusten die Fürstliche Bahn /
> erhebe durch Glükke dich Himmelhoch an.
>
> *(Spiele,* S. 15)

Die Sinnbilder sprechen für sich.

Das zweite "Theatrum" zeigt "die Gestalt des Sommers" (Abb. 5),
einen jungen Mann zwischen Fleiß und Tugend (wie der Text die
beiden Frauenfiguren erläutert). Jetzt ist die Landschaft ein freies Feld
mit Ausblick auf einen Erntewagen und ein Dorf. Die Blumengirlan-
den und der Kranz sind zu Sommerblumen und Ährenkranz verändert worden, und nur die Baumreihen sind als feste Kulisse (und als
Bäume des Lebens) geblieben. An den je drei Tafeln hängen wieder
Bilder aus Augusts Leben, diesmal aus seiner Studienzeit und der
Cavalierstour: im Kolleg, als galanter Student, beim Fechten, in der
Reitschule, unterwegs zu Pferde und zu Schiff. (August wurde mit 15
Jahren als Student auf die Universität Rostock geschickt, dort zum

Abb. 6. "Herbst", aus Sophie Elisabeth, Glückwünschende Freudendarstellung, *Bl. B2v.*

Rektor gewählt, wo er bei Antritt und Abgabe des Ehrenamtes lateinische Reden hielt. Unter anderem bereiste er Sizilien, Malta, die Niederlande und England.) Das begleitende Lied thematisiert Fleiß und Tugend, die auch das "Lebende Bild" allegorisiert.

"Das dritte Mahl" stellt den Herbst mit Früchten an den Bäumen (Abb. 6) in den Girlanden dar; eine Baum- und Felderndte vor einer Stadt bilden den Hintergrund. "In der Mitte ward gesehen ein Mann / auff dessen eine Seite die Tapfferkeit / auff der ander Seiten die Gottesfurcht." Der Mann trägt jetzt deutlich den charakteristischen Spitzbart des Herzogs, die beiden allegorischen Figuren Attribute ihrer Bedeutung, abgeschlagene Säule und Lamm. Die gemalten Bilder zeigen weitere Stationen Augusts, seine Übernahme der Regentschaft, seine Bibliothek, seine drei Ehen und das Schloß (Wolfenbüttel?). Auch hier preisen die Verse ganz allgemein Tugend und Tapferkeit des guten Regenten.

Erwartungsgemäß bringt das vierte Bild den Winter (Abb. 7), der realistisch an den Bäumen mit Eiszapfen und Schnee angedeutet wird. Jetzt sitzt der Fürst als "alter Mann" mit Ehre (links) und Ruhe

Abb. 7. "Winter", aus Sophie Elisabeth, Glückwünschende Freudendarstellung, *Bl. C1v.*

(rechts) an seiner Seite, wohl im Sinne von öffentlichem Ansehen und Bedächtigkeit (Augusts Wahlspruch war "Alles mit Bedacht"). Die sechs gemalten Bilder zeigen Szenen aus seinen Regierungsgeschäften. Doch erscheinen in diesem Winterbild nicht der Tod, sondern ein helles Licht vom Himmel und eine Krone, Zeichen des Herrschers von Gottes Gnaden. "Darbey ward gleichfalls perspectiv-weiss / in dem allerhintersten Himmel mit güldenen Buchstaben gesehen: Vivat AUGUSTUS" (*Spiele,* S. 23). Die begleitenden Gesangstrophen wiederholen mehrfach das Lob des weisen, gottgefälligen Regenten.

Wir wären nicht im Barock, wenn nicht auf diese Krönung noch ein weiteres Finale folgen sollte: "Ward das Theatrum wiederumb in einen schönen Himmel verwandelt / auß welchem herfürging ein Engel / welcher Unserm Landes Fürsten nebenst einem Glückwünschendem Gesange einen Lorbeerkrantz aufsetzete und folgendes Lied sang" (*Spiele,* S. 25). Dem Lorbeerkranz, Sinnbild für den Lohn der christlichen Tugenden, folgt ein ganzer Engelschor mit abschließendem Lob des Fürstenhauses.

IV

Die Legitimation des Fürsten geschieht hier mit dem Anspruch des Herrschertums von Gottes Gnaden. Sie geschieht aber auch mit der Forderung an den Regenten, daß er weise, tugendhaft und tatkräftig sei. Es ist nicht ein Spiel um Staatsraison oder Staatsklugheit, wie es in Sophie Elisabeths *Frewden Spiell von dem itzigen betrieglichen Zustande in der Welt* (1656) oder den vielen literarischen Barockdramen zugrunde liegt.[20] Es ist vielmehr eine Folge allegorischer Bilder, eine *repraesentatio maiestatis*. Herrscherkult, Personenkult, Personifikation von Tugenden und allegorische Figuren gehören im absolutistischen Fürstenstaat zusammen: sie unterscheiden ihn von der abstrakten Staatsidee, die dem modernen Staat zugrunde liegt.

In dem Tugendkatalog und Rollenspiel spielt zugleich die Hofgesellschaft sich selbst und legitimiert sich dadurch. Das Spiel der Hoffeste ist kein dramatischer Konflikt sondern eine Bilderfolge; die Festlichkeiten reihen allegorische Bilder zum Zweck der Selbstrepräsentation und Legitimierung aneinander. Diese allegorischen Bilder stammen aus der Tradition, aus dem Fundus von antiker Mythologie, Geschichte, aus den Emblembüchern; insofern sind sie rückwärtsgewandt, imitativ. Ihre Inhalte und Funktionen sind jedoch der höfischen Gesellschaftsordnung angemessen, in der der Herrscher der ideale Mittelpunkt des Staates war.[21]

Auch sie sind eine Form der "bestrittenen Individualität", auf die Conrad Wiedemann in seiner Arbeit zur Funktion der Barockallegorie hingewiesen hat.[22] Sie sind eine Form des "self-fashioning", um den Ausdruck Greenblatts zu benutzen, die vornehmlich in Bildern, nicht in der sekundär bleibenden Sprache geschieht. Um sich selbst zu repräsentieren und damit zu legitimieren, spielte die Hofgesellschaft bei/in den Hoffesten sich selbst in allegorischer Form (oder sah sich auf dem Theater darin verkörpert). Ob sie mit den prunkvollen, aufwendigen, allegorischen Festen dem *horror vacui*, der Angst vor dem leeren Raum zu entkommen versuchte, wie Huizinga vorgeschlagen hat, oder eine "sublime Form des Müßiggangs" praktizierte, wie Alewyn meinte, oder nach Jacob Burckhardt gar "ein Übergang vom Leben in die Kunst", in ein ideales Reich der Schönheit, vollzog, ist nicht zu entscheiden.[23] Ein Zeitgenosse bemerkte: "Alles spielt, man spielt mit, man wird selbst gespielt. Ludendo ludimur"[24].

Anmerkungen

Sämtliche Abbildungen erfolgen mit freundlicher Genehmigung der Herzog August Bibliothek, Wolfenbüttel.

1. Richard Alewyn, *Das große Welttheater. Die Epoche der höfischen Feste in Dokument und Deutung* (Hamburg: Rowohlt, 1959), S. 9.

2. Aufgezeichnet vom Hofdichter des Kaisers Francesco Sbarra, *La contessa dell'aria e dell'acqua* (Wien: Matteo Cosmerovio, 1667).

3. Alewyn, *Das große Welttheater*, S. 104.

4. Hans-Gert Roloff, "Absolutismus und Hoftheater", *Daphnis* 10 (1981): 737.

5. Stephen Greenblatt, *Renaissance Self-Fashioning from More to Shakespeare* (Chicago: University of Chicago Press, 1980), S. 9.

6. Conrad Wiedemann, "Bestrittene Individualität", in *Formen und Funktionen der Allegorie*, hrsg. v. Walter Haug (Stuttgart: Metzler, 1978), S. 588.

7. Joseph Leighton, "Die literarische Tätigkeit der Herzogin Sophie Elisabeth von Braunschweig-Lüneburg", in *Europäische Hofkultur im 16. und 17. Jahrhundert*, 3 Bde., hrsg. v. August Buck et al. Wolfenbütteler Arbeiten zur Barockforschung, 8–10 (Hamburg: Hauswedell, 1981), 3:483–88.

8. Monika Hueck, *Gelegenheitsgedichte auf Herzog August von Braunschweig-Lüneburg und seine Familie (1579–1666). Ein bibliographisches Verzeichnis der Drucke und Handschriften in der Herzog August Bibliothek Wolfenbüttel*, Repertorien zur Erforschung der frühen Neuzeit, 4 (Wolfenbüttel: Herzog August Bibliothek, 1982).

9. Martin Gosky, *Arbustum seu Arboretum Poetice* (Wolfenbüttel: Stern, 1650), so der Titel des Frontispiz, der des Kupfertitels lautet etwas anders, wie auch die zweite Ausgabe den Titel etwas umformuliert. Eine schöne Auswahl hat der Band *Alles mit Bedacht. Barockes Fürstenlob auf Herzog August (1579–1666) in Wort, Bild und Musik*, zusammengestellt von Martin Bircher und Thomas Bürger (Wolfenbüttel: Herzog August Bibliothek, 1979) zugänglich gemacht.

10. *Alles mit Bedacht*, S. 71.

11. *Alles mit Bedacht*, S. 68–69; *Sammler, Fürst, Gelehrter: Herzog August zu Braunschweig und Lüneburg 1579–1660*, Ausstellung der Herzog August Bibliothek Wolfenbüttel 1979, Exponat Nr. 151.

12. *Sammler, Fürst, Gelehrter*, Exponat Nr. 150.

13. Wieder zugänglich in Hans-Gert Roloff, Hrsg., *Sophie Elisabeth, Herzogin zu Braunschweig und Lüneburg. Dichtungen. Erster Band: Spiele*, Arbeiten zur mittleren deutschen Literatur und Sprache, 6 (Frankfurt: Lang, 1980). Zitiert im folgenden als *Spiele*, Angaben im Text.

14. Hans-Gert Roloff hat die Bedeutung der Maskeraden gewürdigt: "Die höfischen Maskeraden der Sophie Elisabeth Herzogin zu Braunschweig und Lüneburg", in Buck et al., Hrsg., *Europäische Hofkultur im 16. und 17. Jahrhundert*, 3:489–96; und "Das Freudenspiel von 1656", *Daphnis* 10 (1982): 735–53.

15. *Gloria et Memoria Natalitia . . . Dn. Augusto . . .* (Wolfenbüttel: Stern, 1653), Sig. A2.

16. *Sammler, Fürst, Gelehrter,* Exponat Nr. 592.

17. Vgl. Roloff, "Maskeraden", S. 447–49.

18. Vgl. Joseph Leighton, "Die Wolfenbütteler Aufführung von Harsdörffers und Stadens Seelewig im Jahre 1654", *Wolfenbütteler Beiträge* 3 (1978): 122ff.

19. Vgl. Heinz Kindermann, *Theatergeschichte Europas,* 10 Bde. (Salzburg: Otto Müller, 1967), 3:263–67. Zeugnis und Beschreibung von Rist für Altona.

20. Vgl. Roloff, "Absolutismus und Hoftheater"; Klaus Reichelt, *Barockdrama und Absolutismus. Studien zum deutschen Drama zwischen 1650 und 1700* (Bern: Lang, 1981).

21. Vgl. hierzu Eberhard Straub, *Repräsentatio Maiestatis oder churbayerische Freudenfeste. Die höfischen Feste in der Münchner Residenz vom 16. bis zum Ende des 18. Jahrhunderts* (München: Stadtarchiv, 1969), S. 14–16.

22. Wiedemann, "Bestrittene Individualität", bes. S. 574–80.

23. Zitate nach Alewyn, *Das große Welttheater,* S. 9

24. Reichelt, *Barockdrama und Absolutismus,* S. 1–2, Anm. 4, 5.

10. Of Princes and Poets: Lohenstein's Verse Epistles on the Divorce of the Elector Palatine Carl Ludwig

Michael M. Metzger

Whatever might have been his other accomplishments, many an absolutist ruler of the seventeenth century enjoyed the status of a hero of erotic myth, in whom wealth, power, and sheer animal magnetism coalesced to a charisma of such potency that women of legendary beauty schemed to be his paramours and to undergo any sacrifice that liaison with so extraordinary a being might entail. Louis XIV of France exemplified this attribute of monarchy for his contemporaries, with the later Stuart kings of England as distant rivals. Within the German domains, aspects of the life of Elector Palatine Carl Ludwig seem to have exercised a comparable power over the literary imagination in the turbulent period following the Thirty Years War.[1] Carl Ludwig lived from 1617 until 1680, ruling in Heidelberg from 1649 onward, and achieved some contemporary renown as an innovative if not always successful ruler, but especially because two willful women vied memorably for his love. With Louis XIV, Carl Ludwig shared the distinction of having his amorous adventures celebrated in heroic epistles that appeared in the widely read Neukirch anthology of German Baroque poetry.[2]

Carl Ludwig was one of the most prominent political figures of his era in Germany, most similar in significance to Frederick William I, "Great Elector" of Brandenburg.[3] His mother was Elizabeth (1596–1662), the daughter of James I of England; his father Frederick V, the luckless "Winter King" of Bohemia (1596–1632). Born just before his father went to Prague to claim and then lose a royal crown, Carl Ludwig spent his early years as an exile in Holland and at the court of his uncle, King Charles I of England, whose execution he witnessed. As an outcome of the Peace of Westphalia, Carl Ludwig was recognized as the heir to the territorially reduced Rhenish Palatinate and awarded the dignity of being the eighth Imperial elector. The effective absolutist measures that he took to rebuild the war-ravaged Palatinate aroused admiration and controversy. Within the context of the Habsburg-Bourbon rivalry, the elector's political position was especially difficult because his territories bordered on France while he owed political allegiance to the emperor. During his reign, his lands became objects of French desires for aggrandizement and were devastated again at the end of the century during the War of the Palatine Succession.

In 1650, Carl Ludwig married Charlotte, Landgravine of Hesse (1627–86), and she bore him three children. The two who survived to adulthood were Carl (1651–85), his successor, and Elisabeth Charlotte (1652–1722), who married the Duc d'Orléans or "Monsieur," brother of Louis XIV. She later was renowned as "Liselotte von der Pfalz" for her letters to her step-sisters. On 16 March 1657, however, Carl Ludwig unilaterally decreed his first marriage to be null and void and entered into a morganatic union with Maria Susanna Loysa von Degenfeld (1634–77), one of his wife's ladies-in-waiting. In the years that followed, she was to bear Carl Ludwig eight sons and five daughters. Doubtless expressing the opinion of many contemporaries, his mother, Elizabeth, the exiled queen of Bohemia, wrote to Carl Ludwig in her native English from The Hague protesting this step and imploring him to be reconciled with Charlotte: "Your open keeping of that wench does you no small dishonor to all persons of all conditions. If everybody could quit their husbands and wives for their ill humors, there would be no small disorder in the world; it is both against God's law and Man's law, for though you be a sovereign, yet God's law is above you."[4]

The electress Charlotte refused to acknowledge the divorce and complained in a lengthy petition to Emperor Leopold on 26 July 1661, trying to enlist his good offices toward a reconciliation with the elector. We shall have more to say about this document shortly. Although a financial settlement was reached with the aid of the elector of Brandenburg, the marriage remained asunder. Charlotte withdrew to Kassel, but returned to Heidelberg after Carl Ludwig's death. She survived not only him and her rival, but also her son, the elector Carl II, upon whose death in 1685 the Palatinate passed into the hands of the Catholic line of Pfalz-Neuburg.

I

The first serial anthology of German poetry, *Herrn von Hoffmannswal-dau und andrer Deutschen* . . . *Gedichte*, was published in six parts between 1695 and 1709, each enjoying several printings, or in some cases new editions, in the course of the eighteenth century.[5] A seventh volume, published under very different auspices in 1727, represents a final break with the *galant* manner of Hoffmann von Hoffmannswaldau and other Silesians, the tradition exuberantly propagated in the earlier parts. The sixth part, edited by Gottlieb Stolle, already reflects the transition in literary taste from Marinism to the more decorous poetic style of the French Enlightenment. All the more anachronistic does it seem, therefore, that it should contain, among chiefly epigonal texts, a significant work by Daniel Casper von Lohenstein (1635–83), the most illustrious of the later Silesian poets to whose achievements the anthology itself was dedicated.

Lohenstein's four heroic epistles are printed in the sixth volume for the first time under his name and in a version relatively free from textual contaminations. In the book's first section, "Verliebte und Galante Gedichte," they occupy a place of honor immediately following three poems attributed, in this case probably wrongly, to Hoffmannswaldau. Because a degree of delicacy in their presentation was still appropriate in 1709, they appeared under the semicryptic collective title:

C. L. Ch. z. H. pf. *a*. R. &c.
mit
M. S. Degenfeldin gepflogene
liebes-handlung,
In vier briefen beschrieben, in deren

1. Er ihr seine liebe eröffnet,
2. Sie ihn ihrer gegenliebe versichert,
3. Er es seiner gemahlin berichtet,
4. Seine gemahlin ihm antwortet.[6]

The initials in the title stand, of course, for " Carl Ludwig, *C*hurfürst zu *H*eidelberg, *P*falzgraf am *R*hein." The author is identified only in the heading of the first poem: "Der erste brief von D. C. v. L."

When Lohenstein, most likely during the mid-1660s, composed his poetic account of the events at the Palatine court, he depicted with empathy the three participants in a dynastic and political scandal that raised anew in Protestant Europe questions of the sacramental nature of marriage and the prerogatives of the sovereign.[7] Given the prominence of the personages involved and considerations of his own career, it was impossible for Lohenstein to publish the work in its presumably original form. Carl Ludwig disliked having his marital affairs mentioned in print; when he met the author of one such report, the elector forced him publicly to eat the pages containing the indiscretion.[8] With or without Lohenstein's consent, numerous copies of the unprinted heroic epistles seem to have circulated widely. The survival until today of at least eight such manuscripts, some of them teeming with scribal errors, attests to a relatively wide currency of the notorious "Palatine" story among readers of the nobility and bourgeoisie. Pleasure at the piquancy and contemporaneity of the situation no doubt helped stimulate such interest, as did Lohenstein's dramatic and richly figurative language of human passion.

In 1680, Lohenstein published *Blumen*, a collection of the writings of his youth. In his preface, dated May 1680, some four months before Carl Ludwig died, the poet declared his reluctance to present these works to the public with an exceptional degree of self-protectiveness:

> Diese [nicht verlorengegangenen Jugendwerke] würden auch in ihrem Staube vollends verweset seyn / wenn ich nicht erfahren hette; daß Fremde unterschiedene Stücke hiervon nicht nur für ihre Arbeit ausgegeben / sondern auch so gar wider ihren Uhrsprung und Eigenschafft Erlauchten Personen mit Veränderung weniger Worte zugeschrieben hetten. Jedoch würde ich diese meine selbst wenig geschäzte Federn leichter . . . gönnen können / wenn nur andere nicht meinen Getichten zwar meines Nahmens Uberschrifft gelassen / selbte aber auf gantz andere Fälle und Personen / darauf ich nie gedacht / mit einer mercklichen Veränderung verkehrt; oder gantz frembde Eyer in mein Nest geleget hetten.[9]

Of all of the *Blumen*, the adaptation of the Palatine *Heldenbriefe* seems at once to require and affirm such a disclaimer. The section "Rosen" presents the poems under the title "Liebe zwischen König Petern dem Grausamen / in Castilien / und Johanna des Diego Haro Wittib" (*Blumen*, 12–37). Lohenstein transferred the action to historically and culturally more distant events at the court of King Pedro the Cruel (1334–69) of Castile in Spain.[10] The chief characters are now called Peter, Blanca of Bourbon, and Johanna Castria, and their names are conspicuously mentioned throughout, with other topical references liberally added. In the briefer "Palatine" versions, no personal names appear in the text at all.

Three of the four poems of the "Liebes-Handlung" are 100 verses in length, the second containing 104. This accords with the practice of Hoffmannswaldau, all of whose heroic epistles are 100 lines long. Also following Hoffmannswaldau's model, the verses are alexandrines set in quatrains with an *a b a b* rhyme scheme and alternating feminine and masculine endings. The length of the poems indicates that Lohenstein wrote the "Palatine" versions earlier, for the significantly augmented "Spanish" counterparts in *Blumen* contain, respectively, 120, 116, 104, and 136 lines. Each of Lohenstein's other two heroic epistles, an exchange between Philip II of Spain and Princess Eboly, has exactly 100 verses.

The reader of the "Liebes-Handlung" is confronted with three protagonists, each pleading the legitimacy of his or her moral and emotional position in a way more analogous to drama than to the epic or lyrical poetry. Lohenstein does not overtly approve or condemn any position, but rather lets readers come to their own conclusions. In the first epistle, Carl Ludwig declares his love to Maria Susanna von Degenfeld, as she is styled, complaining at length about his wife's coldness despite her beauty:

> Sie ist dem rosen-strauch im winter zu vergleichen,
> Der keine rosen trägt, und doch den dorn behält.

> (1.47–48)

Describing himself as enthralled by his new love, he promises her his hand in a morganatic marriage, dismissing her possible scruples by invoking the Bible (Abraham, Sarah, and Hagar), natural law, and, ultimately, the special rights of the sovereign:

> Kommt dir diß seltsam für, vermählten sich vermählen,
>   Weil keine Sara mehr den mann zu andern weist,
> Wo wehrts der himmel uns zwey seelen zu erwehlen,
>   Bevor wenn eine selbst das band in stücke reist?
> Was täglich nicht geschicht, ist nicht bald zu verdammen.
>   Zu dem, der gröste theil der menschen spricht es recht:
> Die vorwelt labte sich bey zwey und mehrern flammen:
>   Ein fürst ist auch nicht stracks gemeiner ordnung knecht.

> (1.85–92)

In pleading for her consent, he assures his beloved:

> An meine lincke hand wird man dich zwar nur trauen;
>   Solch kummer aber fällt, wenn sie mein schatz! versteht,

> Daß man mit mehrer pracht der rechten pflegt zu freyen,
>   Doch daß die lincke nur von treuem hertzen geht.

$$(1.97\text{--}100)$$

Despite her joy at being chosen by him, Maria von Degenfeld's reply in the second letter reveals her awareness of the perils awaiting her as the prince's mistress. The jealousy and spite of the court might very well seal her doom:

> Der anmuth paradieß wird mir ja zubereitet,
>   Wo nur mein untergang nicht hintern berge hält.
> Er reicht den braut-krantz mir vielleicht zum schmuck der bahre,
>   Wo noch mein schimpflich sarg wird werth der kräntze seyn:
> Rubin und diamant soll blühmen meine haare,
>   Ach! drückten sie mir nur nicht gar den scheitel ein!

$$(2.35\text{--}40)$$

Yet she will put her confidence in the prince's promise and his power, and looks forward to their lovemaking in an erotic passage that makes clear at least one of the reasons why these poems were so widely read, circulated, and recopied:

> Mich dünckt, ich fühle schon, wie er mit tausend küssen,
>   Die scharlach-lippen labt auf meiner lilgen-brust,
> Wie sein und meine seel wie wachs zusammen fliessen
>   Wie er mich überschwemmt mit einer see voll lust;
> Wie sein rubinen-mund nach meinen äpffeln lechset,
>   Und als ein saugend kind an den granaten zeucht.

$$(2.61\text{--}66)$$

Asserting that she seeks not a higher station in life, but only to please Carl Ludwig, Maria resolves to defy all hindrances to their love. If in his wisdom he believes that that is appropriate, she accepts the elector's offer of marriage, reminding him that this is the sole condition under which she will yield to his desires.

The fictive moment of the third epistle is the eve of Carl Ludwig's marriage to Maria; he tells his first wife of his decision, condemning her in striking imagery for attracting him with her beauty but then spurning his lovemaking. He reassures the electress, however, that her rights will not be diminished. In fact, if she is willing, a *ménage à trois* is a distinct possibility:

> Mein lincker arm soll sie, die rechte dich umfassen,
>   Du wirst zu deinem knie ihr zutritt ja verleihn!

Sie wird als halbe magd dir händ und füsse küssen,
  Ihr blödes auge kennt der Hagar hochmuth nicht.

(3.43–46)

To justify his claim to two wives, the elector cites the legendary precedent of the Graf von Gleichen, a Crusader who married the Mohammedan princess who saved his life in captivity. The count's first wife then bestowed an equal share in the marriage upon the woman who had brought about the husband's safe return, so that the three even share a tomb in Erfurt. This is, of course, the same theme that Goethe was to use in *Stella*.[11] If she will not agree to such an arrangement, Carl Ludwig, not without threatening overtones, counsels complaisance, citing again the special needs and prerogatives of the prince:

Es ist der höchste witz, dem himmel beyfall geben,
  Wer seine schlüsse stürmt, der stürtzt sich selbst in graus;
Der fürsten wolstand ist, gemäß dem stande leben,
  Obgleich die wollust sich theilt in mehr röhren aus.
Die eh ist ohne dem mit pfropffern unterstützet,
  Der fürsten stamm-baum ist, wie die, geartet nicht,
Die mit viel zweigen stehn für sonn und sturm beschützet,
  Weil den zertheilten stock der äste last zerbricht.

(3.65–72)

The appeal to the necessity for "grafts on the family tree" is almost certainly related to the dynastic situation of the house of Pfalz-Simmern; Carl Ludwig had only one son at the time, in the event of whose death the Palatinate would pass, to the detriment of Protestant interests, into the hands of the Catholic house of Pfalz-Neuburg upon Carl Ludwig's demise. Carl Ludwig promises the electress a separate household in the castle, but warns her not to intrigue against Maria, as he would punish any opposition harshly.

It is the "Gemahlin," however, who has the last word that may also reflect Lohenstein's own opinions. In sorrow and anger, she rejects Carl Ludwig's suggestions and the reasoning behind them, lamenting the fickle nature of men and the decay of morality and moderation in marriage. She reminds her husband that their union had produced children and blames his inconstancy for the crisis:

Die pflantzen unsrer eh sind zeugen meiner liebe,
  Allein der eckel ist der wollust mißgeburth.
Betränckten lippen sind die klärsten brunnen trübe,
  Für fremdes wasser stößt man eignen nectar fort.

Die üppigkeit verschmäht des ehweibs zucker-küsse,
Nicht daß sie häßlich sey, nur daß sie ehweib ist.

(4.45–50)

The electress concludes with the dire prediction that Carl Ludwig's caprices will mar the memory of his deeds as a ruler, and that he will be even more unhappy in his new marriage than she is now.

II

There is reason to believe that Lohenstein did not base these poems entirely on imaginative empathy with personages about whose actions he had heard only by word of mouth. The petition of the electress Charlotte to Emperor Leopold I appears to have been circulated rather widely. In 1693, the "Demüthigstes *Supplications*-Schreiben" was published in a biographical work, partly a *chronique scandaleuse*, on the last three Protestant electors Palatine.[12] Here, the petition was followed by an early printing of the four heroic epistles, which were, however, ascribed to Hoffmannswaldau and contaminated with excerpts of the "Spanish" version. In introducing the poems, the biographer emphasizes that they are the "Briefflein . . . nachgehend in Reimen gebracht . . . / welche wir ihrer Art und Zierlichkeit halben . . . beyfügen wollen" (*Lebens-Geschichte*, 132). The document was also included in Lünig's *Teutsche Reichs-Cantzley* of 1714, providing the source for Gustav Freytag's report on the affair in *Bilder aus der deutschen Vergangenheit*.[13] Although we can only speculate about whether Lohenstein saw the petition, he was certainly in a position, as an attorney in Breslau and later a city official there, to have access at least to surreptitious copies of such papers. Similarities between the petition and the poem, moreover, make it seem very likely that he used it at least as a starting point for his poetization of the Palatine divorce.

In the "*Supplications*-Schreiben," the electress recounts the indignities to which Carl Ludwig subjected her in 1657, culminating in his declaration that he would cast her off and remarry. These include his slapping her in the presence of guests and placing her under house arrest for a time. Charlotte clearly paid him back in kind, creating a spectacle at the Imperial Diet in Regensburg by exposing herself before the assemblage and finally attempting to end her troubles by shooting "die Degenfeldin," which she was only prevented from doing by the intervention of a courtier. The narrative is interspersed with eight letters, four of them ostensibly exchanged between Carl Ludwig and Charlotte. Four, however, are in Latin with German translations; the first is addressed by the Fräulein von Degenfeld to Carl Ludwig, the other three are written to her in his name. In reality, these are only slight adaptations of missives of the lovers Euryalus and Lucretia in the novella *De duobus amantibus historia* written by Enea Silvio Piccolomini in 1444.[14] Perhaps it is significant that the "Elector's" letters appear in the same sequence as do those of Euryalus in the *Historia*. Charlotte reports that she had gotten "Maria's" letter from a faithful servant, and that the "Elector's" had been found during a search of Maria's quarters; Charlotte's cousin, Count Johann Jacob von Eberstein had provided a "Dolmetschung" (*Lebens-Geschichte*, 107). We should entertain at least the possibility that a framer of the petition with some literary sophistication plagiarized these letters to add to the credibility of Charlotte's complaint, and that they never actually passed between Carl Ludwig and Maria von Degenfeld.

Several passages of the "Liebes-Handlung" appear to reflect motifs found in the "*Supplications*-Schreiben." This becomes evident if we compare Maria's purported missive to Carl Ludwig with the second of the *Heldenbriefe*. To show the derivation of the letters in the petition, a modern translation of the corresponding letter from Piccolomini's *Historia* is presented for comparison:

[Lucretia to Euryalus:]
Nicht länger kann ich Dir widerstehen, lieber Euryalus, und Du sollst wissen, daß auch ich Dich liebe. Du hast gesiegt, ich bin die Deine. Ich Unglückliche, daß ich je Deine Briefe annahm! Von allen Seiten lauern Gefahren auf mich, ich brauche Deine Klugheit und Deine Treue. Nun erfülle aber auch Dein Versprechen. Ich vertraue mich gänzlich Deiner Liebe an. Verläßt Du mich, so bist Du grausam, ein Verräter, ein Nichtswürdiger. Und es ist so leicht, ein Weib zu betrügen, aber je leichter, desto schändlicher. Bis jetzt ist ja noch nichts geschehen: gedenkst Du mich aber zu verlassen, so sag es bitte, ehe die Liebe unbezähmbar geworden ist. Wir wollen uns doch in nichts einlassen, was uns nachher reuen soll. Bei allem muß man das Ende bedenken. Ich bin, wiewohl die meisten Frauen, blind: Du bist ein Mann, sorg für mich und für Dich! Ich bin die Deine, ich vertrau mich Dir an; und wenn ich mich Dir gebe, so ist es für immer! Lebe wohl, mein Schützer und mein Führer.[15]

["*Supplications*-Schreiben"—Maria von Degenfeld to Carl Ludwig:]
Ich kan Ihm / Durchl. Churfürst / weiter nicht zuwider seyn /

noch demselben meine Liebe länger verhalten; Er hat überwunden / ich bin anjetzo die Seinige. Ach ich Elende / die ich seinen Brieff empfangen habe; Ich werde nemlich vieler Gefahr unterworfen seyn / dafern mir nicht seine Treu und Klugheit die Hand reichet. Er suche derohalben dasjenige zu halten was er geschrieben / dann ich gerathe jetzt in seine Liebe. Solte er mich aber verlassen wollen / wird er ein Verräther und der Aergste unter allen Menschen werden / sintemahlen ein Weibsbild zu hinterführen eine gar leichte Sache ist / allein je leichter desto schändlicher. Noch ist es Zeit / und wann er mich zu verlassen gedencket / so sag er es / bevor die Liebe mehr und mehr zu brennen anfängt / damit wir nicht etwas anheben / welches uns nachgehends gereuen möchte. Man muß in allen Sachen auff das Ende sehen / und weil ich ein Weibsbild bin / vermag ich solches nicht zu thun / und muß Er also meinet und seinethalben Sorge tragen. Ich ergebe mich ihm anietzo / und verlasse mich auff seine Treue / wil auch nicht die seinige zu seyn anfangen / sondern ewig bleiben. Er lebe wohl mein Auffenthalt und meines Lebens Führer. (*Lebens-Geschichte*, 105–6)

["Liebes-Handlung":]
Ach daß der himmel nicht gall in den zucker thu!
Er und die hoffnung speist mich ja mit himmel-brodte,
  Der zweifel und die furcht mischt aber myrrhen ein.

(2.4–6)

Jedoch ich will mein heil aufs fürsten worte gründen,
  Da wird kein fallbret seyn, wo er mich anckern heißt,
Des fürsten blosses ja muß mehrern glauben finden,
  Als die betheurung, so mit vielen eyden gleißt.

(2.41–44)

Doch denck' er, daß das nicht, wenn man ein reh erleget,
  Ein mägdgen bringt zu fall, ein meister-stücke sey;
Daß reu und untreu ihn weit mehr als mich beflecken,
  Denn finsterniß entstellt nur sonnen, keinen stern.

(2.47–50)

Doch dieses bündnis darf kein ander siegel schliessen,
  Als unverschrencktes recht und eines priesters band,
Die einfalt folget hier, er wird, obs recht sey, wissen,
  Daß er die andre frau vertraut der lincken hand.
Ich selbst bin lüstern nun nach der vermählungs-kette,
  Und folge, wenn er winckt, ihm zu dem priester nach,

Denn vom altare gehn nur stuffen in mein bette,
Und durch die kirche kommt man in mein schlaf-gemach.

(2.98–104)

The letters and Lohenstein's text share, clearly more than coincidentally, the motifs of Maria's fears, the ease of inveigling her, the base-
ness of a possible betrayal, and her placing of her fate in the elector's
hands. Similarly, Carl Ludwig/Euryalus's declaration of love has in
common with the first epistle the statements that the beloved could
have read his passion from his features and that he has learned only
from her what it means to love. The comparison of her eyes to the sun,
on the other hand, is so conventional and generalized as not to constitute conclusive evidence of a relationship between the poems and the
documents:

["*Supplications*-Schreiben"—Carl Ludwig to Maria von Degenfeld:]
Ich würde / dich meine liebe Maria Loysa / mit meinen Schreiben
öffters grüssen / wann ich die Gelegenheit darzu hätte / sintemahlen all mein Heyl und meines Lebens Hoffnung von dir han-
get. Ich liebe dich mehr als mich selbsten / und bilde mir nicht
ein / daß dir die Brunst meines hertzens verborgen seye. Es kan
dir ja mein Angesicht / und die in deiner Gegenwart gelassene
Seufftzer dessen ein Zeugnüß geben. Ich bitte gar sehr um Verzei-
hung / daß ich mein Hertz also vor dir außschütte / dann mich
deine außbündige Schönheit eingenommen und gebunden hält.
Was die Liebe sey / hab ich vormahls nicht gewust. Du hast mich
zu erst deren Gewalt unterworffen. Und daß ich von der Liebe
bißhero nichts gewust habe / soll dich nicht befremden / aller-
massen ich meine Gemahlin niemahlen so hefftig lieben können.
Die Strahlen deiner Augen haben überwunden / als welche mich
gefangen halten / und kräfftiger als die Sonne seyn. Dich liebe
ich Nacht und Tag / dich verlange ich / dich wünsche / dich erwarte ich / an dich gedencke ich / und an dir belustige ich mich.
Meine Seele ist in deiner Gewalt / und ich bin gäntzlich der Dei-
nige. Du allein kanst mich erhalten / du allein kanst mich auch
verderben; Erwehle eines von beyden / und schreibe mir dißfals
deine Meinung zurück / bezeuge dich auch mit den Worten nicht
härter gegen mich / als mit deinen Augen. Wirstu mir in meinem
Begehren willfahren / so leb ich glückselig / widrigen fals aber
tödtest du mein Hertz / welches dich mehr als mich liebet. Ich
empfehle mich dir und deiner Treue. Gehab dich wohl meine

Seele und meines Lebens Hülffe. Ich verbleibe dein Einiger / dein gantz Eigener / der ich meiner nicht mehr mächtig bin. (*Lebens-Geschichte*, 109–10)

["Liebes-Handlung":]
Was hier geheimnis ist, sind dir bekannte sachen,
    Mein antlitz hat dir längst verrathen meine last.

(1.3–4)

Ich liebe dich, mein kind! mit unzertheiltem hertzen,
    Nicht lasse dir das wort unglaublich kommen für.
Die flammen unsrer eh sind ausgeleschte kertzen,
    Ja unser' erste flamm entsteht, mein licht! aus dir.
Ich hab' erst, seit ich dir geopffert meine seele,
    Was lieb' und liebens-wehrt, mein kind! von dir gelernt.

(1.13–17)

Nicht frage, wer in mir so süsse glut erwecket,
    Dein eignes auge fühlt, wo sie den ursprung nimmt,
Weil heisse sonnen ja nicht leer vom brand seyn müssen,
    Aus kalten adern nicht ein warmer brunn entspringt.

(1.7–10)

Turning our attention now to the narrative itself, we might say that the mention by the electress in both the petition and the "Liebes-Handlung" of the children that she had borne Carl Ludwig is predictable in either genre:

["*Supplications*-Schreiben":]
So haben wir auch durch die Gnade Gottes zwey junge Fürsten und ein Fräulein mit einander in ehlicher Liebe gezeuget / daß also S. L. billicher massen sich selbsten solten gemäßiget haben / uns die *denegationem cohabitationis* unschuldiger massen anzudeuten. (*Lebens-Geschichte*, 102)

["Liebes-Handlung":]
Die pflantzen unsrer eh sind zeugen meiner liebe,
    Allein der eckel ist der wollust mißgeburth.

(4.45–46)

On the other hand, her outrage at being rejected in favor of "Mägde" may very well have provided the text for the close of the fourth epistle:

Wer geile mägde liebt, ist seines weibes hasser;
    Der aber liebet recht, der keusche seelen sucht.

(4.99–100)

["*Supplications*-Schreiben":]
Worauff unser Herr Gemahl gantz erröthet und geantwortet: Es ist nichts neues / daß meine Frau Gemahlin ohne gegebene Ursache zörnet. Wir aber konten Ehren halben solche Wort nicht unbeantwortet lassen / sondern sprachen: Diejenige / welche die Mägde lieber sehen als die Frauen / machen mich zornig. (*Lebens-Geschichte*, 115)

The motivation expressed in Carl Ludwig's letter for rejecting Charlotte and marrying another also appears to be precisely reflected in the poetic excerpt:

["*Supplications*-Schreiben":]
So werdet ihr auch wol wissen / wie ihr . . . mich beschimpffet / und als ich auß meinem billich gefaßten Zorn / wegen begangener Leichtfertigkeit . . . nur ein wenig gewehrt / mir gleich alle ehliche Beywohnung auff ein halb Jahr versagt / welches Verbrechen mich des Ehlichen Bandes gantz entlediget / bin auch gäntzlich dahin *resolviret* / mich von euch völlige durch einen öffentlichen *Actum* scheiden zu lassen. (*Lebens-Geschichte*, 123)

["Liebes-Handlung":]
Ich kan in unsrer eh nicht länger eh-los bleiben;
   Diß ist es, was in sich mein gantzes schreiben faßt.

(3.3–4)

Ich hab ein neues band der heyrath unterschrieben,
   Mit einer, die dir selbst offt viel vergnügung gab,

(3.39–40)

The themes of judicious advice, of the possible rewards for following it, and of the certain retribution that will follow any attempt to harm Maria are so similarly related in the following texts that it is hard to avoid the conclusion that Lohenstein based this passage on Carl Ludwig's letter of 14 April 1657 as quoted in the petition. That would explain, for example, the curiously precise specification in the third poem that Charlotte could reside in the "innre schloß":

["*Supplications*-Schreiben":]
Weil ich aber wol weiß / daß E. Lbd. mit mir drey Fürstl. Kinder gezeuget / als gebühret mir die Tag ihres Lebens I. Lbd. Fürstliche *Tractation* zu verschaffen / als kan E. Lbd. das halbe Schloß zu Heydelberg . . . Macht haben zu gebrauchen . . . allein sie wolle sich mit meiner jetzigen Gemahlin vertragen / und ihr

nichts Leyds zufügen / damit ich nicht verursacht werde E. L. ungünstig zu werden. (*Lebens-Geschichte*, 126)

["Liebes-Handlung":]
Auf solchen fall soll dir nichts an vergnügung fehlen:
  Ich und der Rhein wird dich als sonn und haupt verehr'n,
So lange du nur die, der wir uns itzt vermählen,
  Wirst lassen monde seyn, und sie in nichts versehr'n.
Wer aber sich auf sie wird was gelüsten lassen,
  Greifft biß zum hertzen uns den augenapffel an,
Der soll mit schimpff und ach von unsrer faust erblassen;
  Du weist wohl, was die rach erzörnter liebe kan.
Willst du der einsamkeit denn deine tage weyhen,
  Und dich von bett, und tisch, wie vormahls, scheiden ab,
Wird man das innre schloß zur wohnung dir verleihen,
  Das deiner bangsamkeit offt einen aufhalt gab.

(3.85–96)

The smoldering acquiescence of "die Gemahlin," though lacking the vehemence of Charlotte's letter to the elector of 15 April 1657, also makes central the idea of her being a widow whose husband still lives, suggesting once more a direct influence of the document upon the poem:

["*Supplications*-Schreiben":]
Auß Eu. Durchl. Schreiben hab ich gnugsam . . . vernommen / daß Ihro Durchl. mich nunmehro gantz und gar verstossen / und nicht mehr gesinnet seyn / mich vor eine Gemahlin zu erkennen / welches . . . jedoch will ichs GOtt dem gerechten Richter befehlen / und werde mich forthin so wissen zu halten / als eine Wittib / deren Mann annoch bey Leben / und durch leichtfertige Verführung einer nichtswürdigen Metzen von seiner rechtmässigen Gemahlin abgeleitet ist. . . . werde mich auch befleissigen gegen Eu. Dl. liebsten Concubin also zu verhalten / daß sie nicht wird Ursach haben über mich zu klagen. (*Lebens-Geschichte*, 126–27)

["Liebes-Handlung":]
GOtt schick es, wie er will, doch soll kein mensch erleben,
  Daß ich und meine magd solln neben-buhler seyn;

(4.73–74)

Nicht glaube, daß die magd zu dir mehr liebe trage,
  In huren steckt mehr brunst, mehr treu in keuscher brust.

Zur witwe machst du mich zwar, aber dich zum knechte.

(4.91–93)

To anyone familiar with the elaborate apparatus of commentary that Lohenstein appended to his tragedies and to *Arminius*, such recourse to an authoritative documentary source, if indeed it took place, should not be surprising. By imposing the canonic form of the *Heldenbrief* upon a singularly rancorous scandal on the historical stage, the poet causes the exceedingly human individuals involved to transcend the immediacy of their situation to a plane accessible only through art upon which their actions may be judged according to the values and ideas of a broader community.

III

Not until almost thirty years after the death of Carl Ludwig was the "Liebes-Handlung" printed under its author's name and in a form close to the original. Perhaps earlier publication would have been perfectly acceptable; perhaps the publisher, Thomas Fritsch, who apparently collected many texts for the anthology, had only recently acquired a manuscript in 1709. Because of warfare in the Palatinate between 1688 and 1697, interest in the area would still have been active, and the epistles opened a uniquely private perspective on European conflicts that were continuing under new auspices. Carl Ludwig's daughter, the duchess of Orléans, in whose name Louis XIV had waged the War of the Palatine Succession, was still alive, as was, of course, the Sun King himself.

When we consider the reasons for the appearance of the work in precisely this part of the anthology, it may not be altogether coincidental that volume 6 also contains occasional poems concerning noble families in western Germany who were at least indirectly concerned with the affairs of Carl Ludwig. Thus we find a poem by Georg Wilhelm von Hohendorff, "Auf die hoch-fürstl. Pfaltz-Neuburgische und Lubomirskysche vermählung," which celebrates the union in 1701 of Karl Philipp von Pfalz-Neuburg, who was to become elector Palatine in 1719, with the daughter of the Polish prince Joseph Carl Lubomirsky von Ostrog.[16] The "Vermischte Getichte" include a birthday poem to Karl Philipp by the same author.[17] Hohendorff, who lived from about 1670 until 1719, was a well-known diplomat and bibliophile and had served at the Palatine court for a time around 1700.[18] The appearance of two poems by him in the same volume that contains the "Palatine" epistles suggests that he played a role in providing the text of the latter to the publisher. Prominent among the "Hochzeit-Getichte" is a poem by Benjamin Neukirch that concerns the marriage of the Prussian princess Louisa Dorothea Sophia with Frederick, Crown Prince of Hessen-Kassel, the family of the electress Charlotte. The Hohenzollerns, whose court poet Neukirch very much wanted to be, had considerable territorial and political interests on the lower Rhine, which they were cementing through this union.

In any case, publishing Lohenstein's poetic version of Carl Ludwig's marital adventures hardly represented a risk in 1709, as the events involved now lay fifty years in the past. On the other hand, the renewed public interest in the Palatinate might have induced Thomas Fritsch to publish the work for commercial reasons. Last but not least, the opportunity to publish a work by Lohenstein in the authoritative "Silesian" anthology must have been an important factor in the decision. In the Holy Roman Empire of that time, whose politics were dominated by the grandiose continental machinations of the emperor Joseph I; King Frederick I of Prussia; and Augustus the Strong, Elector of Saxony and King of Poland, Lohenstein's tale of Carl Ludwig may well have been read nostalgically as a relic from an age irrevocably past, when passions and ambitions were more elemental and comprehensible.

Notes

1. See Hugo Hayn and Alfred N. Gotendorf, *Bibliotheca Germanorum Erotica & Curiosa*, 3d ed., 8 vols. with a supplementary volume (Munich: Georg Müller, 1913), "Carl Ludwig, Kurfürst von der Pfalz," 1:534–35; "Degenfeld, Maria Johanna Loysa von," 2:19–20. See also "Degenfeld, Maria Johanna Loysa von" in Wilhelm Kosch, *Deutsches Literatur-Lexikon: Biographisches und bibliographisches Handbuch*, 2d ed., 12 vols., (Bern: Francke, 1949), 1:321.

2. Angelo George de Capua and Erika A. Metzger, eds., *Benjamin Neukirchs Anthologie Herrn von Hoffmannswaldau und anderer Deutschen auserlesener und bißher ungedruckter Gedichte dritter Theil*, Neudrucke deutscher Literaturwerke, Neue Folge, 22 (Tübingen: Niemeyer, 1970): "Einige Helden-briefe. I. König Ludewich an die Gräffin de Montesp," (pp. 30–33); "II. Die Gräfin de Montespan an Ludewich den König," (pp. 34–36); "Ludewich der XIV an la Valiere," (pp. 40–42); "La Valiere an den könig Ludewich," (pp. 43–46). See also Daniel Casper von Lohenstein, "C. L. Ch. z. H. pf. a. R. &c. mit M. S. Degenfeldin gepflogene liebes-handlung . . . ," in Erika A. Metzger and Michael M. Metzger, eds., *Benjamin Neukirchs Anthologie Herrn von Hoffmannswaldau und andrer Deutschen auserlesener und bißher ungedruckter Gedichte Sech-*

ster Theil, Neudrucke deutscher Literaturwerke, Neue Folge, 38 (Tübingen: Niemeyer, 1988), pp. 20–56.

3. Eberhard Gothein, "Bilder aus der Kulturgeschichte der Pfalz nach dem dreißigjährigen Kriege," *Badische Neujahrsblätter* 5 (1895): 1–63; see also F. Aussaresses and H. Gauthier-Villars, *La Vie privée d'un prince allemand au XVIIe siècle: L'Electeur Palatin Charles-Louis (1617–1680)* (Paris: Plon-Nourrit, 1926); Gustav Freytag, *Bilder aus der deutschen Vergangenheit*, vol. 4 (Leipzig: List, 1924); Peter Fuchs, "Karl (I.) Ludwig, Kurfürst von der Pfalz," *NDB* 11:246–49 and "Degenfeld, v. Loysa (Louise) Maria Susanna, Raugräfin zu Pfalz," *NDB* 3:559–60; Karl Hauck, *Karl Ludwig, Kurfürst von der Pfalz (1617–1680)* (Leipzig: Breitkopf & Härtel, 1903); Ludwig Häusser, *Geschichte der Rheinischen Pfalz nach ihren politischen, kirchlichen und literarischen Verhältnissen*, 2 vols. (Heidelberg: Winter, 1924), 2:519–687; *Lebens-Geschichte / Der Weyland Durchleuchtigst. Churfürsten in der Pfaltz / Friederich des V. Carl Ludwig / und Carl. Worinnen die Böhmische Unruhe / der Dreyssig-jährige Krieg / die Vikariat- und Wildfangs-Sache / des Chur-Fürsten Carl Ludwig Liebes-Händel mit der Baronessin von Degenfeld / und die Langhänsische Sache Durch einen gantz kurtzen Begriff annehmlich beschrieben werden* (Cologne: n.p., 1693); Felix Joseph Lipowsky, *Karl Ludwig Churfürst von der Pfalz, und Maria Susanna Louise Raugräfin von Degenfeld, nebst der Biographie des Churfürsten Karl von der Pfalz, des letzten Sprößlings aus der Linie Pfalz-Simmern* (Sulzbach: Seidel, 1824); and Eduard Vehse, *Geschichte der Höfe der Häuser Baiern, Würtemberg, Baden und Hessen* (= *Geschichte der deutschen Höfe seit der Reformation*, vols. 23 and 24) (Hamburg: Hoffmann & Campe, 1853).

4. Elizabeth Stuart, *Briefe der Elisabeth Stuart, königin von Böhmen, an ihren sohn, den kurfürsten Carl Ludwig von der Pfalz. 1650–1662*, ed. Anna Wendland, BLVS 228 (Tübingen: Literarischer Verein in Stuttgart, 1902), p. 92 (spelling modernized).

5. On the publication history of the anthology, see the "Einleitung" to each of the following volumes: Angelo George de Capua and Ernst A. Philippson; Angelo George de Capua and Erika A. Metzger; Erika A. Metzger and Michael M. Metzger, eds., *Benjamin Neukirchs Anthologie Herrn von Hoffmannswaldau und andrer Deutschen auserlesener und bißher ungedruckter Gedichte*, 6 vols., Neudrucke deutscher Literaturwerke, Neue Folge, 1, 16, 22, 24, 29, 38 (Tübingen: Niemeyer, 1961–88). See also Franz Heiduk, *Die Dichter der galanten Lyrik, Studien zur Neukirchschen Sammlung* (Bern: Francke, 1971), pp. 15–22.

6. *Neukirch Anthologie, 6. Theil*, p. 20.

7. Bernhard Asmuth, *Daniel Casper von Lohenstein* (Stuttgart: Metzler, 1971), pp. 58–60; Gerhard Spellerberg, "Daniel Casper von Lohenstein," in *Deutsche Dichter des 17. Jahrhunderts*, ed. Harald Steinhagen and Benno von Wiese (Berlin: Erich Schmidt, 1984), pp. 651–52.

8. Vehse, *Geschichte der Höfe*, p. 106.

9. Daniel Casper von Lohenstein, *Blumen* (Breslau: Fellgibel, 1680), sig.):(3r–v.

10. Frances Exum, *The Metamorphosis of Lope de Vega's Pedro: The Treatment of*

Pedro I de Castilla in the Drama of Lope de Vega (Madrid: Playor, 1974), pp. 17–49; Prosper Mérimée, *Histoire de Don Pèdre I Roi de Castille*, ed. Gabriel Laplane (Paris: Didier, 1961).

11. Elisabeth Frenzel, *Stoffe der Weltliteratur: Ein Lexikon dichtungsgeschichtlicher Längsschnitte* (Stuttgart: Kröner, 1962), pp. 206–9.

12. *Lebens-Geschichte*, pp. 101–32. Further references to this work are cited in the text.

13. Freytag, *Bilder*, 4:238–49.

14. Lipowsky, *Karl Ludwig*, p. 97; Enea Silvio Piccolomini, *Briefe/Dichtungen*, tr. Max Mell and Ursula Abel (Munich: Winkler, 1966), pp. 241–99.

15. Piccolomini, *Briefe*, pp. 266–67.

16. *Neukirch Anthologie, 6. Theil*, p. 198.

17. Ibid., p. 338.

18. See Max Braubach, "Hohendorff, Georg Wilhelm v.," *NDB* 9:478–79.

Part IV. Early Modern Poets and Their Work

11. Poets Portrayed:
Iconographic Representations and
Allusions to the Empire

Richard Erich Schade

The portrait of the early modern poet participates in an iconographic strategy. Frequently positioned as the frontispiece, the author's picture interacts with the title page.[1] The image significantly informs the reading of the facing page, and in turn, is informed by it as part of a preinterpretive system. Neither portrait nor title stands alone, a relationship to be documented with reference to the portraits of Conrad Celtis, Justus Georg Schottel, and Daniel Casper von Lohenstein, each of whom exhibits a special sense of his position vis-à-vis the Holy Roman Empire, the center of early modern literary culture in northern Europe.

Conrad Celtis (1459–1508)

The portraits of the arch-humanist Conrad Celtis are numerous.[2] The choice of the one facing the title citation and *laudatio* to Celtis's protector Emperor Frederick III is governed by the portrait's particularly instructive makeup (fig. 1).[3] In the upper half of the frontispiece, Celtis is seated at his desk. The works of the ancients, his inspiration, are shelved above the writing surface. Aphrodite-Cytherea would seem to honor him with an offering of flowers. Pallas Minerva-Athena, the patron goddess of Athens, stands guard. The lower half of the frontispiece is similarly arranged. The crest of the poet suspended on bound laurel boughs is a logical extension of the *Fons Musarum*. Celtis is abstracted and, like the portrait, the heraldic device is flanked by significant mythological personae, Mercury (god of music and clever discourse), Hercules, Bacchus, and Phoebus Apollo, Vergil's god of vatic poetry. Celtis is, thus, both inspired by the gods and every inch an analogue to the deities. He, like Hercules and Phoebus, wears the laurel wreath, and the humanist is shown penning his self-definition

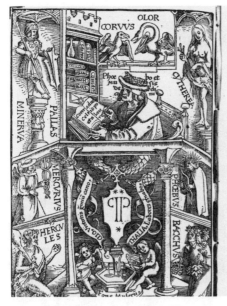

Fig. 1. Frontispiece and Title Page to Liber Primvs Carminvm *of Conrad Celtis. (Archives and Rare Books Department, University of Cincinnati Libraries)*

("Conradus Celtis poeta laure . . . "), an inscription whose validity is to be demonstrated in the poet's consummate literary creativity.[4] This Imperial poet laureate's book of songs, as the title reads, will join the others on the shelf as an equal. His Imperial patron is a latter-day Gaius Maecenas, lauded by a *Vergilius Germanicus.*

Celtis's portrait is further defined by the raucous raven and spirited swan, birds iconographically juxtaposed to the angelic instrumentalists, Clio (Muse of history) and Thalia (Muse of comic drama), flanking the *Fons Musarum.* The noisy dialogue of the birds is as poetic as the music of the Muses, for both raven and swan are associates of Phoebus. Indeed, it is the swan that defines Celtis as both the quintessential Apollo and poet for the early modern reader, a significant association later specified in the Alciatus emblem "Insignia Poetarum" (fig. 2).[5]

> Mit ruem fueren manch grosse hern
> Einn Adler, Lewen in irmm schilt,
> Etlich ein schlang, oder ein Bern,
> Oder sunst was grewlich vnd wild:

EMBLEMATA. 635
Insignia Poëtarum.
EMBLEMA CLXXXIII.

GENTILES *clypeos sunt qui in Iouis alite gestant,*
  Sunt quibus aut serpens, aut leo, signa ferunt:
Dira sed hæc vatum fugiant animalia ceras,
  Doctaq; sustineat stemmata pulcher Olor.
Hic Phœbo sacer, & nostræ regionis alumnus;
  Rex, olim, veteres seruat adhuc titulos.

Onfert insignia Poëtarum cum aliis stemmatis & sym-   *Insignia varia quid no-tent.*
bolis gentilitiis, ceu κατ᾽ ἐναντίωσιν καὶ ἀντίθεσιν. Sunt e-
nim qui Aquilam circumferant, sunt qui Vulturem, alij Dra-
conem, & alia eiusdem generis, quibus animorum diritas, im   *Insignia Poëtarum cjenia.*
manitas, rapacitas aperte declaratur. At Poëtis Olor est candi-
dus,

Fig. 2. *"Insignia Poetarum" from* Omnia Emblemata *of Alciatus.*
(Archives and Rare Books Department, University of Cincinnati Libraries)

Fig. 3. Frontispiece and Title Page to the Haubt *Sprache of Schottelius.*
(Archives and Rare Books Department, University of Cincinnati Libraries)

> Vil pas [besser] ziert die Poeten mild
> Der Schwan, in vnserm land gemayn,
> Vor iarn ein kung, vnd noch ein bild
> Lieblichs gesang, vnd sitten rayn.[6]

The imperious eagle and fierce lion are creatures appropriate to the powerful. The royal swan represents lovely song and virtuous purity (because it is monogamous), qualities no less impressive than those of "grosse hern." These characteristics, furthermore, iconographically define Celtis and other poets of the early modern era, as in the complex portrait of August Buchner, as in the name of Johann Rist's Elbschwanenorden, as in the epithet for Martin Opitz—*der Bober-Schwan.*[7]

Justus Georg Schottelius (1612–1676)

The seventeenth century, no less than the sixteenth, was given to portraying the poet.[8] Martin Bircher's *Deutsche Schriftsteller im Porträt* documents the phenomenon.[9] In this work, portrait faces biography. When no image could be located, the title page of the given poet's work was substituted, unintentionally expressing the interchangeable interaction between portrait and title. In the case of the seventeenth-century poet Schottelius, Max Wehrli states that the portrait graces the author's magnum opus, but does not specifically mention that it serves as the frontispiece to the elaborately engraved title page (fig. 3).[10]

The iconographic statement made by the Schottelius portrait appears to be simple. The scholar's visage confronts the viewer. His limbs are obscured by the robe, as if to remind the viewer that the head is the center of intellect. The simple oval frame repeats the configuration of the face. The portrait consciously refers to itself as representational art, for it is displayed as in a gallery, and the effect is enhanced by its position on a quadrilateral base, with an epitaph bearing the poet's name and defining his socioprofessional position. Interestingly, the base supports the framed portrait in much the same manner as the white collar and physically undifferentiated upper trunk of the body form the base of the poet's head. Indeed, the portrait is reducible to significantly contrasting forms (cube and sphere), which, when taken as a unit, emblematically memorialize Schottelius as QVIES personified (fig. 4)[11] or as SAPIENTIA CONSTANS (fig. 5).[12]

On the engraved facing title page, the banner of the LINGUA GERMANICA is shown suspended; it is clear that Schottelius intends to take major credit for the German language's triumph. The oval devices on the base of the columns (the palm and flower)[13] at once signal his membership in the Fruchtbringende Gesellschaft (the tree), as well as being surrogate portraits enunciating his scholarly intention (fig. 6).[14]

Die reinen dünst' ich such' / und mache sie bekant /
Die unsrer Deutschen Sprach' in ihrer art seind eigen /
Recht auf dem grunde geh' / und drin bleib unverwand
Heiß Suchend / auch wil fort / was ich drin finde zeigen /
Zu bringen frucht / die wol dem Vaterlande nutzt /
Und mit der Deutschen Zung' all' andre frembde trutzt.

These culturally patriotic goals are in significant accord with those of the Empire, for the "Erklärung des Kupfertituls" to the *Haubtsprache* reads:

Was der Gothe / Cimber / Sachs / Däne / Wahle / Franke /
    Schwabe
Vormals / nach Mundarten köhr / mit geknall geredet habe /
Suchstu das? Such Teutschen grund. Teutsche Sprache / Teutsches
    Land

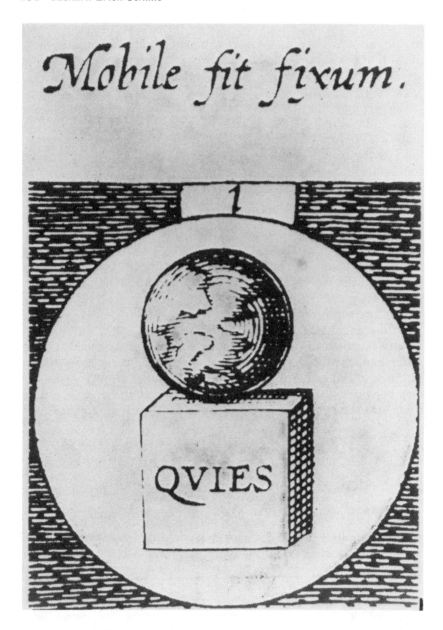

Fig. 4. "*Mobile fit fixum*" from **Emblemata** *(1624) of Otto Vaenius.*
(Heckscher, "Goethe im Banne der Sinnbilder," p. 360, item 2)

OPERVM POETICORVM

NICODEMI

FRISCHLINIPOETAE,

ORATORIS ET PHILOSOPHI
pars fcenica:in qua funt,

COMOEDIAE SEX.

REBECCA.
SVSANNA.
HILDEGARDIS.
IVLIVS REDIVIVVS.
PRISCIANVS VAPVLANS.
HELVETIOGERMANI

TRAGOEDIAE DVAE,
VENVS.
DIDO.

Ex recentißima Auctoris emendatione.

Cum Priuilegio Cæfario,

Excudebat Bernhardus Iobin,

Anno M, D, LXXXIX,

Fig. 5. *Title Page of the* Opervm Poeticorvm . . . pars scenica *of Nicodemus Frischlin. (The Beinecke Rare Book and Manuscript Library, Yale University)*

Fig. 6. "Der Suchende." The Emblem of Schottelius from Der Fruchtbringenden Gesellschaft Nahmen. *(Archives and Rare Books Department, University of Cincinnati Libraries)*

Ist der Thon und ist der Ort wo zur Kunst helt grund und stand
Die Weltweite Celtisch Sprache. Hochteutsch muß die Kunst
  hochziehen:

. . . .
Unsers höchsten Käisers Throne durchs Geschikk dis ist verliehen.
Sprachverwante Nordenleute / rahmt den Kunstweg recht mit ein:
Teutschgesinte greift mit zu / Teutsch kan wol vollkommen sein.

(fol. A3v)

In short, linguistic integrity reinforces Imperial aspirations, in much
the same way as the efforts of the portrayed poet-scholar—QVIES and/
or SAPIENTIA CONSTANS personified—are bound to bear fruit and nour-
ish the governed *Vaterland*. This is the preinterpretation suggested by
a reading of the interaction between frontispiece portrait and facing
title page.

Daniel Casper von Lohenstein (1635–1683)

The *subscriptio* to the portrait of Lohenstein emphasizes that it is first a
memorial to the poet (fig. 7).[15]

Hir zeigt im Bilde sich. der Lohen Edel-stein,
Das Kleinod Schlesiens, so, wie es ist gewesen,
Eh es der Todt geraubt. Wer noch der Folge Schein
Und Glantz wil spielen sehn, kan seine Schrifften lesen.

The closing lines point to the facing title, for it is in the novel where his
creative brilliance will continue to shine.[16] The text of *Arminius und
Thusnelda* is the ultimate memorial, a *Zeitroman* with an Imperial
program:

Vor allem aber ging es darum, seinem Arminius Züge zu verleihen, aus denen seine Zeitgenossen ohne Mühe auf eine Gleich-
setzung mit Leopold schließen mußten. Denn nur so konnte er
auf seine Landsleute einwirken und sie dahin bringen, daß sie—
und es ging hier besonders um Fürsten und hohen Adel—aus
Liebe zum großen Vaterland auf alle partikulären Interessen und
Eitelkeiten verzichteten und sich der Oberherrschaft Leopolds
willig fügten; nur so war—das ist die neue Einsicht Lohensteins
im Arminius-Roman—ein großes Römisches Reich Deutscher Nation möglich.[17]

Fig. 7. Frontispiece and Title Page to Arminius und Thusnelda *of Lohenstein. (Archives and Rare Books Department, University of Cincinnati Libraries)*

This was the Imperial literary-political program of the handsomely portrayed novelist.

The portrait itself projects a sure authority, a noble seriousness. The page of the open folio is as theatrical as the parted drape in the background. The momentous nature of literary creativity is analogous to the high historical drama being acted out on the tumultuously cluttered stage of the title engraving. Although Lohenstein's hands are at rest, they signal activity. They are the refined hands of the poet, grasping not for the sword (as on the title page), but for a small volume labeled simply "Tacitus." Lohenstein is depicted as a *Tacitus Germanicus*.[18] The intent of the complex Imperial *Zeitroman* is approximately equivalent to the critical spirit of Tacitus's *Annales*. Just as the historian Tacitus once sought to inform and advise Rome, so would Lohenstein comment on the Imperial affairs of his century. This conclusion is justified by the interpretation of the interaction between frontispiece portrait and facing title page.

Iconographic Representation and Imperial Allusions

My focus has been on only three literati, yet the documentation makes clear that each portrait participates in both an iconographic and Imperial strategy. Even as he defines himself as an Imperial *poeta laureatus*, Conrad Celtis is shown surrounded by the allegorical accoutrements of classical antiquity. The gods both justify and legitimize his position, and they indirectly sanction the Imperial convention of granting the laureate. The placing of the frontispiece across from the title and *laudatio* to Frederick III articulates the crucial symbiosis between poet and Imperial patron. In the Schottelius portrait, the allusion to QVIES and SAPIENTIA in the configuration displays a confident self-awareness. The scholar Schottelius is wisdom personified, and his membership in the Fruchtbringende Gesellschaft indicates that both poet and literary society participate in a linguistic program furthered by and furthering the hegemonic intentions of the emperor. Lohenstein's *Arminius* novel, a fiction of complex historical dynamics between Germanic-Roman past and Imperial present, is fronted by a self-possessed *Tacitus Germanicus*. Like that of Celtis, his portrait equates him to a *literatus* from antiquity; he also shares Schottelius's self-possession. Unlike Celtis and Schottelius, however, Lohenstein's noble Silesian bloodline (as recent as it may be, that is, since 1670: "der Lohen Edel-stein / das Kleinod Schlesiens") legitimizes the particular authority of the portrayed poet's literary statement.

Notes

For Christa Sammons with thanks.

1. Inasmuch as Grimmelshausen's fictional figure Courage is the formulator of her "Lebensbeschreibung," it is arguable that the novel's complex frontispiece is an authorial portrait functioning in a preinterpretive mode. See Richard Erich Schade, "The *Courasche*-Frontispiece: Gypsy, Mule, and *Acedia*," *Simpliciana* 3 (1981): 73–93, and "Thesen zur literarischen Darstellung der Frau am Beispiel der Courasche," in *Literatur und Volk im 17. Jahrhundert. Probleme populärer Kultur in Deutschland*, 2 vols., ed. Wolfgang Brückner, Peter Blickle, and Dieter Breuer, Wolfenbütteler Arbeiten zur Barockforschung, 13 (Wiesbaden: Harrassowitz, 1985), 1:227–43, and "Junge Soldaten, alte Bettler: Zur Ikonographie des Pikaresken am Beispiel des *Springinsfeld*-Titelkupfers," in *Der deutsche Schelmenroman im europäischen Kontext: Rezeption, Interpretation, Bibliographie*, ed. Gerhart Hoffmeister, Chloe, vol. 5 (Amsterdam: Rodopi, 1987), pp. 93–112. It is from such an interpretive perspective that I move to the present focus on the portraiture of "real" literati.

2. The best-known portrait of Celtis is his so-called "Sterbebild":

1507, als er sein Ende nahen fühlte, bestellte Konrad Celtis bei Hans Burgkmair sein sogenanntes Sterbebild . . . Solcher Vorsorge entspricht der Aufwand der Inszenierung. Der noch lebende Dichter erscheint im

Holzschnitt als eben Gestorbener in Halbfigur mit gesenktem Kopf, nie-
dergeschlagenen Augen und den Händen auf seinen Werken überein-
andergelegt. Entrückt hinter einer steinernen Brüstung, wird Celtis
zudem durch einen rahmenden Bogen mit Lorbeergehängen ausge-
zeichnet. Dieser Celtis ist tot. Sein vorne auf der Brüstung liegendes
Wappenschild ist zerbrochen. Die Putten links und rechts als Vertreter
der Menschheit beweinen sein Hinscheiden. Oben im Bogenwinkel
beklagen Apoll und Merkur, die göttlichen Anführer der Musen und
Künste, den Verlust.

Und doch ist dieses von Celtis sogleich an seine Freunde verschickte
Sterbebild ein Trostblatt. Denn die in seinen Büchern dargestellten
Werke des Celtis, so bekräftigen die Inschriften, werden vom Tod nicht
ungültig gemacht, sie dauern fort und verbürgen auch hinfort seinen
Ruhm.

Peter-Klaus Schuster, "Individuelle Ewigkeit: Hoffnungen und Ansprüche
im Bildnis der Lutherzeit," in *Biographie und Autobiographie in der Renaissance,*
ed. August Buck (Wiesbaden: Harrassowitz, 1983), p. 122 and fig. 1. Another
Celtis portrait by Hans Burgkmair is incorporated in the device of Celtis's
sodality; see Max Geisberg and Walter L. Strauss, *The German Single-Leaf
Woodcut: 1500–1550* (New York: Hacker, 1974), p. 485. It depicts the laurel-
crowned head of the forty-eight-year-old poet at the base of an elaborate
double-headed Imperial eagle. A laurel wreath signifying his crowning in
1487 by Emperor Frederick III is suspended from each beak. The bird's out-
spread wings depict the divine SEX OPERA DIERUM (viewer's left) and the human SEPTEM MECHANICAE (viewer's right). The enthroned figure of an emperor makes up the fowl's neck; its breast depicts the FONS MVSARVM with
the Nine Muses. An enthroned PHILOSOPHIA attended by the Seven Liberal
Arts and the Three Graces, the latter flanked by winged Mercury (left) and
horned DISCORDIA (right), make up the eagle's tail. A crowned Paris reposes
at the base of it all, as if the entire icon were the inspired dream of a humanist *literatus*. The Habsburg eagle is the protector of every creative human en-
deavor. For a discussion of the actual Imperial icons maintained in the Free
Imperial City of Nürnberg, see Gerhard Bott et al., eds., *Nürnberg 1300–1550.
Kunst der Gotik und Renaissance* (Munich: Prestel, 1986), pp. 179–81; 304–7.

3. The frontispiece portrait faces the title of one section, the *Liber Primvs
Carminvm* of the collected odes of Celtis: *Conradi Celtis . . . libri Odarum qua-
tuor* (Strasbourg: Schürer, 1513). The copy used is from the collection of the
Archives and Rare Books Department, University of Cincinnati Libraries, call
no. R.B. PA 8485/.C4802/1513. Photograph courtesy of the University of Cincinnati. The topic of self-representation in Nürnberg is discussed by Joseph
L. Koerner, "Albrecht Dürer and the Moment of Self-Portraiture," *Daphnis* 15
(1986): 409–39: "Dürer's famous 1500 *Self-Portrait . . .* fashioned in the momentous year of the half-millennium . . . was specifically produced as part of
a larger celebration of the saeculum staged by German humanists in the circle of Conrad Celtis. . . . Celtis fashioned the year 1500 into a symbol of his

own culture's advance over the past, thereby inscribing the process of history into a secular myth of progress" (p. 412). See also Dieter Wuttke, "Dürer und Celtis. Von der Bedeutung des Jahres 1500 für den deutschen Humanismus: Jahrhundertfeier als symbolische Form," *JMRS* 10 (1980): 73–129.

4. The depiction of the writer in the act of writing is an iconographic commonplace of scholarly portraiture, a topos termed "die gelehrte Hand" (see Schuster, "Individuelle Ewigkeit," pp. 137–41). A recent variation is on the dustjacket of *Das Treffen in Telgte* (Darmstadt: Luchterhand, 1979), the tale by Günter Grass. For variations see *Günter Grass. Werkverzeichnis der Radierungen* (Berlin: Anselm Dreher, 1979–80), pp. 272–75.

5. The edition consulted is from the collections of the University of Cincinnati Library, call no. R.B. PN 6349/A4/1581, titled *Omnia . . . Emblemata: Cvm Commentariis per Clavdivm Mindem* (Antwerp: C. Plantin, 1581). Photograph courtesy of the University of Cincinnati.

6. Translation by Wolfgang Hungerus of Andreas Alciatus, *Emblematum Libellus* (Paris, 1542; rpt. Darmstadt: Wissenschaftliche Buchgesellschaft, 1967), p. 237. The Latin text ("Hic Phoebo sacer . . .") links the swan specifically to Apollo. See *Spätrenaissance am Oberrhein. Tobias Stimmer 1539–1584* (Basel: Kunstmuseum, 1984), pp. 454–55, for an elaborate "Scheibenriß" (i.e., the cartoon for a glasspainting) by David Joris dated 1546: "Auf dem Entwurf steht vorne in der Mitte auf halbkreisförmig nach vorne gewölbtem hohen Sockel das für Basel kreiirte adlige Wappen mit Schwan (Emblem des Dichters), Helmzier und einem zweiten Schwan als Kleinod" (p. 454). Henceforth cited as *Tobias Stimmer*.

7. For the portrait of Buchner see Martin Bircher, ed., *Deutsche Schriftsteller im Porträt. Das Zeitalter des Barock* (Munich: Beck, 1979), p. 48. There are three swans. For Rist's Elbschwanenorden, see Karl F. Otto, Jr., *Die Sprachgesellschaften des 17. Jahrhunderts* (Stuttgart: Metzler, 1972), pp. 52–57. "Eine gemeinsame Tracht der Mitglieder war nicht vorgeschrieben; verbindlich war nur das Tragen des 'Seiden blauer BAND' mit dem 'güldin SWAN daran gehänket' " (p. 57). The portrait of Rist (Bircher, *Deutsche Schriftsteller*, p. 144) does not take up the motif. In present times the tradition is maintained in the Okerschwanorden of the Herzog August Bibliothek, Wolfenbüttel. Members receive a blue cardboard disc on which a silver swan in profile is superimposed. The epithet *der Bober-Schwan* refers both to Opitz's origins (Bunzlau on the Bober River) and to his being ennobled as "von Boberfeld" by Emperor Ferdinand II on 14 September 1627. See Marian Szyrocki, *Martin Opitz* (Munich: Beck, 1974), p. 80. The connection to the swan is made explicit in Dorothea Eleonora von Rosenthal's *Poetische Gedancken* (Breslau: n.p., 1641):

Hier ließ Martin Opitz von Boberfeld sich hören
In Deutscher Poesie / zum erstenmahl / allhier /
Wo diese Seule steht / das Zeugnus Ihm zu Ehren
Von uns gerichtet auff. Er war der Deutschen Zier /
Der Schwan der durch den Neid zum blauen Himmel drang /
Und dich / o Vaterland / in eigner Sprach' ansang.

Verse cited in Barbara Becker-Cantarino, ed., *Martin Opitz. Studien zu Werk und Person* (Amsterdam: Rodopi, 1982), p. 438; emphasis mine.

8. The passion for graphic portraiture of scholars and poets in the sixteenth century manifests itself in the works of several artists, from Albrecht Dürer and Lukas Cranach to Tobias Stimmer and Christoph Murer. Recent studies of special interest include *Der Mensch um 1500* (Berlin: Staatliche Museen Preußischer Kulturbesitz, 1977), pp. 99–115; *Köpfe der Lutherzeit* (Hamburg: Hamburger Kunsthalle, 1983); Martin Warnke, *Cranachs Luther, Entwürfe für ein Image* (Frankfurt a. M.: Fischer, 1984); *Tobias Stimmer*, pp. 223–52, and Schuster, "Individuelle Ewigkeit." The vogue in portraiture parallels one in (auto-)biographical writings. See Jozef IJsewijn, "Die humanistische Biographie," in Buck, ed., *Biographie und Autobiographie in der Renaissance*, pp. 1–19, although the entire volume deals with the phenomenon. See also James M. Weiss, "The Six Lives of Rudolph Agricola: Forms and Functions of Humanist Biography," *Humanistica Lovaniensia* 30 (1981): 19 n. 1, for information on humanist biographical writings.

9. Bircher (*Deutsche Schriftsteller*, p. 193) provides a bibliography of pertinent works. It is curious that the publisher chose to commence the series *Deutsche Schriftsteller im Porträt* with the seventeenth century, given the fact that earlier portraits abound. See, for example, Bert Nagel, *Staufische Klassik. Deutsche Dichtung um 1200* (Heidelberg: Lothar Stiehm, 1977), pp. 335–60, where Nagel interprets the statements made by selected "portraits" from the Manessische Handschrift. Of special interest is Martin Warnke, "Das Bild des Gelehrten im 17. Jahrhundert," *Res Publica Litteraria, Die Institutionen der Gelehrsamkeit in der frühen Neuzeit*, 2 vols., ed. Sebastian Neumeister and Conrad Wiedemann (Wiesbaden: Harrassowitz, 1987), 1:1–31, and John Roger Paas, *Effigies et Poesis, An Illustrated Catalogue of Printed Portraits with Laudatory Verses by German Baroque Poets*, 2 vols. (Wiebaden: Harrassowitz, 1988). Paas emphasizes that "The printed portrait in the seventeenth century was frequently a work that combined the engraver's skill in visual representation with the poet's skill in verbal communication" (1:ix–x).

10. The edition consulted is from the holdings of the University of Cincinnati Library, call no. R.B./PF 3103/.S33, titled Schottelius, *Ausführliche Arbeit Von der Teutschen Haubt Sprache* (Braunschweig: C. F. Zilliger, 1658). The explanatory subscript appears on the verso of the printed title page. For Wehrli's comments, see Bircher, *Deutsche Schriftsteller*, pp. 156–57.

11. William S. Heckscher, "Goethe im Banne der Sinnbilder," *Emblem und Emblematikrezeption. Vergleichende Studien zur Wirkungsgeschichte vom 16. bis 20. Jahrhundert*, ed. Sibylle Penkert (Darmstadt: Wissenschaftliche Buchgesellschaft, 1978), pp. 355–85, discusses the Vaenius emblem: "Das Emblem steht unter dem Motto 'Mobile fit fixum', wodurch deutlich wird, daß der Block das sich nicht Bewegende symbolisiert. Nach dem erläuternden Text soll hiermit verdeutlicht werden, daß unter dem guten Herrscher (d. h. dem Kubus) den Ausschweifungen und Verirrungen (d. h. der Kugel) Einhalt geboten wird" (p. 359). Heckscher's footnote 7 (pp. 359–60) alludes to the full

range of significances for the image in Vaenius, and he discusses other iconographic usages in order to explain Goethe's use of it as the conceptual basis for the Weimar "Altar der Agathe Tyche" (fig. 1, p. 357). Bircher (*Deutsche Schriftsteller*, p. 125) also discusses the Vaenius emblem.

12. See *Opervm Poeticorvm Nicodemi Frischlini . . . pars scenica* (Strasbourg: B. Jobin, 1589), where the device graces the title page as the mark of Jobin's printshop. The edition consulted is from the holdings of the Beinecke Rare Book and Manuscript Library, Yale University, call no. Gr4/21b. The profile bust is, of course, related to the QVIES-emblem. Bircher (*Deutsche Schriftsteller*, pp. 122–23) discusses the bronze medal of Erasmus, with its profile bust of the Roman god Terminus and the motto CONCEDO NULLI [I concede to no one, i.e., I stand fast]. He summarizes (p. 127): "Die reine Profilansicht gibt . . . nach antik platonischer Tradition die zeitlos entrückte Ansicht. Ebenso ist im Gegensatz zu dem von Empfindungen, von Freude oder Schmerz bewegten Gesicht, die reglose Physiognomie seit der Antike das auszeichnende Charakteristikum des stoischen Weisen." See *Tobias Stimmer*, pp. 62; 198, for Holbein Junior's portrait of Erasmus (1538). The humanist stands behind a bust of TERMINVS, his right hand resting on the god's head. Paul Harvey, ed., *The Oxford Companion to Classical Literature* (Oxford: University Press, 1962), p. 417, explains that "These rural *termini* had their State counterpart in the 'great God Terminus,' the sacred boundary stone which stood in the great temple of the Capitoline Jupiter." A variation in the wording is SCIENTIA IMMUTABILIS, the motto of the printer's signet of Lazarus Zeitner. It is inscribed on the cube-base of a profile bust; see W. S. Heckscher, *The Princeton Alciati Companion* (New York: Garland, 1989), p. 90. The portrait engraving of Sigmund von Birken by Jakob Sandrart is of this configuration, that is, the graphic representation of the poet's sculpted bust (Bircher, *Deutsche Schriftsteller*, p. 38).

13. Each of the magnificently baroque columns is incongruously topped by a globe. The configuration is a variation of the cube-globe iconography mentioned earlier; see Heckscher, *Alciati*, pp. 366–68: "Achille Bocchi entwirft (1555) 'ein würdiges Grabmal für einen großherzigen Mann', indem er einen mit einer Kugel bekrönten Obelisken auf einem Quaderstein setzt" (p. 367). The frontispiece of Schottelius's *Ethica* (Wolfenbüttel: Weiß, 1669; rpt. Bern: Francke, 1980) depicts an obelisk. The quadrilateral base is inscribed with title and the obelisk is topped by a small globe. The "Erklärung des KupferTituls" (sig. a8v) reads: "Mitten in dem Kupfer stehet eine Piramide . . . und ob wol Wind / Schnee / Regen und alles Ungewitter dieselbe allerseits fassen und treffen kan / so bleibt sie dennoch fest und unbeweglich stehen . . . : Anzudeuten / daß der jenige / welcher seinen Lebensbau auf gewissen festen Grund eingesenket und wol gegründet / auch nach der Kunst der Gottseligkeit und Tugend denselben recht und fest eingeschlossen / zusammengefügt und aufgeführt hat / nicht sonderlich das Ungewitter und Daherstürmen des Unglüks und der Eitelkeit achte / sondern sich fest und wol in seinem Tugendstande begreiffen / und hoch hindurch bis zu seinem Gott

dringen könne." Inasmuch as these are Schottelius's words, the columns of the *Haubt Sprache* signify the constancy of virtue. See also his laudatory figural poem "Piramide Oder Thurn = Seule" in Martin Bircher and Thomas Bürger, eds., *Alles mit Bedacht. Barockes Fürstenlob auf Herzog August (1579– 1666) in Wort, Bild und Musik* (Wolfenbüttel: Herzog August Bibliothek, 1979), p. 94.

14. The edition consulted is from the holdings of the University of Cincinnati Library, call no. R.B. PT 279/.F8/A3, titled *Der Fruchtbringenden Gesellschaft Nahmen / Vorhaben / Gemahlde und Worter* (Frankfurt a. M.: Merian, 1646). See also Klaus Conermann, *Die Mitglieder der Fruchtbringenden Gesellschaft 1617–1650* (Weinheim: Acta humaniora, 1985), pp. 466–68. Schottelius was member 397 in the Gesellschaft.

15. The edition consulted is from the holdings of the University of Cincinnati Library, call no. R.B./PT 1745/.L5A7/1689, titled *Großmuthiger Feldherr Arminius . . . Nebst seiner Durchlauchtigen Thußnelda* (Leipzig: J. F. Gleditsch, 1689), vol. 1 of 2. See Bircher, *Deutsche Schriftsteller*, p. 112, for the same portrait: "Das Porträt, gestochen von Johann Tscherning, zeigt Lohenstein im Alter von 49 Jahren und ist der Ausgabe des 'Arminius' von 1689/90 beigegeben" (p. 113). Lohenstein died in 1683.

16. The topos of pointing beyond the graphic representation to the "true" portrait of the poet, that is, to the text, is discussed by Schuster, "Individuelle Ewigkeit," in terms of the inscription (p. 124) "Vivitvr ingenio, caetera mortis ervnt" [One lives only by the intellect, all else is transitory]. The portrait of Catharina Regina von Greiffenberg, for example, bears an inscription concluding with the sentence "Wer mehr wil Ihres Ruhms mag Ihre Schrifften schauen." See Bircher, *Deutsche Schriftsteller*, p. 74.

17. Elida Maria Szarota, *Lohensteins Arminius als Zeitroman* (Bern: Francke, 1970), p. 52.

18. As far as I can determine, the presence of the Roman historian's name on the book's spine has previously gone unnoticed, although Szarota (ibid., pp. 83–86) discusses Lohenstein's Tacitus connection: "Mit sicherem Blick hat Lohenstein aus den *Annalen* die für seinen Zusammenhang wesentlichen Momente ausgewählt und wiedergegeben" (p. 84). In the notes Szarota states "Tacitus hat vermutlich achtzehn Bücher Annalen geplant = drei Hexaden. . . . Das wäre also genau die Zahl der Bücher des *Arminius*. Es ist aber höchst unwahrscheinlich, daß Lohenstein davon etwas ahnte. Und von Hexaden ist bei ihm keine Spur" (p. 448).

12. Author and Patron:
On the Function of Dedications in
Seventeenth-Century German Literature

Ulrich Maché

The dedication or *Widmungsvorrede* as we know it from Renaissance and Baroque publications is a comparative latecomer in literary history. From rudimentary beginnings in Greek and Roman antiquity it developed fully in the last half of the fifteenth century and flourished for almost two hundred years. Renaissance writers were, of course, familiar with literary patronage in the ancient world, especially with the dedicatory practices of such authors as Vergil, Horace, and Cicero.[1] In contrast to the writers of the Golden Age of Latin literature who addressed their patrons in the literary text itself, authors around 1500 celebrated their patrons through the medium of the dedicatory letter featuring hyperbolic praise and promise of immortality. The beginnings of this practice can be traced back to the third and fourth centuries A.D.[2] Medieval and early Renaissance authors have sometimes submitted letters of dedication to their patrons with their manuscripts. As a rule, these letters were written in the hope of financial reward and future support.[3]

The prevalent notion that the unprecedented frequency and sustained popularity of dedications from 1500 to 1750 was simply an outgrowth of the Renaissance spirit is historically unconvincing. It is necessary to consider the changes brought about by the printing press to explain the phenomenon. Up to Gutenberg's time, the number of copies of any manuscript book was bound to be small, and the dedication of such works would, of necessity, be known to a rather limited audience. But now, with an unparalleled boom in the publishing business, there arose an unforeseen opportunity to make literary patronage more enticing than it had ever been. To the patron this meant that his or her name was to be featured in black letter type and in immediate proximity to the title page, guaranteeing instant visibility. The patron's fame would no longer be spread through a few manuscript copies—as had been the case earlier—but through hundreds of printed volumes, each one carrying the patron's name to all parts of the civilized world; in addition, patron and author alike were firmly convinced of the immortality of literature and those connected with it. After all, the famous lines of Horace, here in Martin Opitz's version, "ICh hab' ein Werck vollbracht dem Ertz nicht zu vergleichen / Dem die Pyramides an Höhe müssen weichen," retained their glamor and credibility throughout the seventeenth century.[4]

Through the increase in the number of copies in circulation as well as through typographical innovations, the market value of dedications increased in the age of printing to an extraordinary degree. Unscrupulous authors would seize the opportunity to proffer unjustifiable praise to vain and gullible patrons or even trick them.[5] It is ironic that Erasmus of Rotterdam, who satirized the custom in his *Praise of Folly*, and who was perhaps the most influential role model for writers of dedications, eventually felt obliged to defend himself against accusations of opportunistic profiteering.[6]

Literary research on German dedications has been confined almost exclusively to the sixteenth century.[7] A study comparable to Wolfgang Leiner's monograph, *Der Widmungsbrief in der französischen Literatur (1580–1715)*, is certainly a desideratum for the German Baroque period. This chapter's preliminary analysis of dedicatory practices in seventeenth-century Germany leads to the conclusion that the function of the dedication and the conditions under which it flourished did not vary appreciably from those in France and England.[8]

By and large, prospective patrons relished the idea of being immortalized through dedications. On the other hand, to people known to be both powerful and generous the pressures of solicitation must have been troublesome. Their situation is perhaps comparable to that of today's philanthropists who are exposed to the schemes and strategies of fund raisers for charitable institutions and private colleges. There were, of course, patrons unwilling to pay or to accept dedications, and a small group of writers who abstained from dedicatory practices.[9] In addition, some authors with a delightful sense of humor (or for failure to find a patron?) decided to dedicate their works to themselves.[10]

To illustrate how the function of the dedication was largely determined by both the personality of the individual writer and his relationship to his patron, I have singled out three authors, Martin Opitz, David Schirmer, and Johann Rist: Opitz with his *Schäfferey von der Nimfen Hercinie* (1630) to demonstrate how under certain conditions a dedicatory letter can usurp the functions of a preface; Schirmer with his two anthologies to show how a poet's indigence or penchant for money can induce him to regard his dedications as a kind of money-making device; and Rist to illustrate how an author, in addition to the customary acknowledgment of his indebtedness, indulges in a rather skillful promotion of his public image.

In the somewhat brief dedication of Opitz's *Hercinie*, there is nothing that Ulrich von Schaffgotsch as a patron would have found lacking, not even the assurance that the book was to serve his "wolverdientem lobe vndt vnsterblichkeit."[11] The basic form of the dedication—the opening address to the patron, the statement of purpose, and the formal closing—is fully intact. And yet, the passages that articulate the act of offering this book to the patron amount to less than 15 percent of what appears to be a dedicatory letter. In the remaining 85 percent of the text Opitz addresses topics related to his literary reform, issues that one would expect to find in a preface. Thus, he elaborates on the controversy over the influx of foreign words into German and the difficulties involved in staying the trend. He also expresses his annoyance with unintelligent critics as well as with the ultraconservatives, those Teutonic bigots who stand in the way of cultural stimuli from abroad. Concerning the *Schäfferey* itself, Opitz presents a brief résumé of its plot, credits himself with being the first German poet to write in this genre, and determines his own position in history as a disciple of Theocritus, Vergil, Jacopo Sannazaro, and Sir Philip Sidney. In addition, he touches upon the sensitive topic of the poet's social prestige and moral reputation.[12]

It is apparent from this summary that Opitz's dedication has more to do with the promotion of literary reform than with the solicitation of monetary support. At the same time, the text clearly shows that the simple triadic form of the dedication lent itself readily to the insertion of extraneous material. Frequently, authors with less artistic discretion than Opitz used their dedications as vehicles to discuss anything and everything, from the state of their personal health to mere gossip.

In the case of the *Schäfferey von der Nimfen Hercinie* the inclusion of prefatory material in the dedication may have been the result of some serious artistic considerations. If Opitz had decided in favor of a juxtaposition of dedication and preface, it would have been necessary to extend the short dedicatory sections for the sake of balance. That, however, would have created a new aesthetic problem affecting the *Schäfferey* itself. As the reader may recall, the setting of the *Hercinie* is the territory owned by the Schaffgotsch family, and the work features a longer section devoted to the glorification of Opitz's patron and the latter's ancestors. For these reasons, the customary eulogy of the patron's forebears in the dedication would have detracted from the artistic merits of the piece. Furthermore, the slimness of the volume gave this work the appearance of a personal gift. In other words, a "Vorrede an den Leser" would have diminished the air of intimacy that the poet emphasized by introducing himself as one of the characters in the *Schäfferey*.

In contrast to Opitz, who did not suffer from lack of funds (neither in the service of Karl Hannibal von Dohna or in that of the king of Poland), David Schirmer, for about seven years, eked out an existence as an unofficial court poet on a commission basis.[13] To him, a dedication constituted both a source of income and an opportunity to emphasize the importance of patronage. To increase the likelihood of financial success Schirmer decided not to rely on one single benefactor, but to dedicate his *RosenGepüsche* (1650) to *four* patrons simultaneously.[14] This was not uncommon at the time, as the risk of being left empty-handed was a real one.[15] What gives Schirmer's first dedication its special significance is the unusual directness with which he addresses the issue of sponsorship.[16] The opening passage carries the message that even emperors and the nobility have, from early times on, been engaged in writing poetry and that, in general, poets can look back on a glorious history of financial support by the nobility as well as the wealthy—the implication being, of course, that this tradition ought to be continued. To make literary patronage particularly attractive to his audience, Schirmer describes the recent literary achievements of German poets as a culmination in European literature, closing with the remark, "wenn wir nicht an so viel Mecenaten Mangel erlitten / so würden sich gewiß mehr Marones und Horatzen blicken und sehen lassen."[17]

To document famous instances of patronage, he lists outstanding statesmen of antiquity and, in apparent contradiction of his previous statement concerning the scarcity of benefactors, Schirmer tries to raise contemporary interest in literary patronage by maintaining that even today there are "ihrer viel . . . freygebige und milde Printzen" who ("nach des Synesius Meynung") attain a godlike state of being through the act of giving.[18] And for further encouragement of prospective sponsors, Schirmer delves, once more, into history to cite some precedents worth emulating. The reader learns that even a mediocre poet such as Cherilus "bekam von Alexander dem Grossen für einen ieden guten Vers eine Krone. Die Summa / die Virgilius von Käyser Augustens Schwester empfangen / ist noch aller Welt bekant. Des Edlen Sannazars überschrift von der Stadt Venedig hat nicht mehr als 600. Dukaten getragen."[19] And according to one account which apparently impressed Schirmer greatly, Opitz was given 100 taler for a song that was a mere adaptation from Seneca.[20]

Schirmer's wishes for more generous patrons were probably shared by the majority of seventeenth-century poets, but his outspoken demand for greater support is relatively rare. From what we know about Schirmer's life there is no evidence that his style of solicitation was particularly effective. When he published the definitive edition of his *Rosen = Gepüsche* (1657), he chose a new patron for whom he wrote a versified dedicatory letter, filling the first nine pages of the book; but he also retained his original four patrons and included the old dedication for reasons of relevance, "indem darinnen von der Poesie und dero grossen Beförderern gehandelt wird."[21] We can assume that Schirmer delivered copies of this edition to at least two of his old patrons, hoping for another award.[22]

With his last voluminous publication, an anthology of occasional court poetry, *POetische RAuten = GEpüsche* (1663), Schirmer changed his dedicatory strategy.[23] Facing the title page, he had a copper engraving of Elector Johann Georg II inserted; in addition, he devoted another two pages to him, one describing the engraving of the sovereign, the other filled with dedicatory clichés such as "Dem Durchleuchtigsten / Hochgebornen Fürsten und Herrn," ending with "des Chur = Sächsischen Rauten = Krantzes Haupt = und Stamm = Herrn." Reading these first pages, one is left with the impression that Johann Georg is the sole dedicatee of this volume. Turning the pages, however, one finds that the elector was meant to share this honor with his wife, his son, his daughter, three brothers, and three sisters, as well as other relatives whose names all stand out in black letter type, followed by all their inherited and acquired titles, each page beginning the introduction of a new patron with such reassuring phrases as, "Vnd hierneben," "anderweit auch," "nichts minder auch." There is no dedicatory letter to elicit magnanimous responses, but on the other hand there is no need for it. The message is unmistakably clear: the poet has honored the elector's family with such a dedication, as well as with the content of this omnibus volume, and he intends to collect his dues from each member. It seems that Schirmer's appetite for money, as manifested in the dedications of his two collections of poetry, was not simply an outgrowth of the indigence of his early years, but inherent in his character. When his *RAuten = GEpüsche* was published in 1663, poverty was no longer Schirmer's problem since he had been the elector's librarian for about seven years; yet, to all appearances, his original proclivity for marketing his dedications in a rather clumsy fashion was still with him.

Rist's dedication for his *Musa Teutonica* (1634) also contained a strong plea for literary patronship. But in contrast to Schirmer, he did not make a lifelong practice of the solicitation of funds. Once Rist had established himself as a Lutheran minister in Wedel, he no longer stressed his financial needs. Nevertheless, this did not mean a reduction in the length of his dedicatory texts. For the sake of a more focused address to his benefactors, Rist, from about 1638 on, abandoned the practice of combining dedication and preface in the manner of Opitz's *Hercinie*. Instead, he now juxtaposed the two, using the preface to deal with such topics as poetics, literary disputes, attacks by critics, and delays in publications. Thus, the dedicatory letter could be reserved for more personal matters and for displaying to the public his personal relationships to influential people.

The warm and friendly note that Rist strikes when addressing old friends is best exemplified by his dedication for Georg Reiche, who had risen to power in the service of the Danish king. Reiche had visited Rist after many years, and to the poet's delight he had remained "derselbe alte / ehrliche teutsche Reiche . . . der er von vielen Jahren hero gewesen." [24] Genuine feelings of friendship are also evident in the dedicatory text for the Hamburg official Joachim Flagge, whose "unvermuhtete Freundschaft" had helped him to come to terms with the loss of his wife. The words of thanks that he finds for Flagge reflect his deeply felt wish to repay part of his debt through an open acknowledgment. [25]

Nevertheless, as indicated earlier, Rist often attempted to enhance his public image through his dedications. Clearly, all of them were written to impress his readers, but in addition he used dedications and prefaces as a forum to attack his critics to whom he referred as "solche Gesellen," "Meister Tadelgern," and "grobe Neidhämel" (2:222). Being extremely sensitive to criticism, Rist felt the need not only to defend himself in his dedications and prefaces, but also to compensate for any defamation by elaborating on his social and intellectual connections. A case in point is the dedicatory letter to Jaspar von Örtzen, royal *Drost* in the county of Pinneberg, to whom Rist dedicated his translation of Torquato Tasso's work *Der Adeliche Hausvater* (1650). As in other dedications, Rist reflects on his personal experiences with his patron, mentioning also their first meeting "an Jhrer Königlichen Majestät / unseres allerseits gnädigsten Königes und Herren Taffel," where von Örtzen had excelled on account of his quick-wittedness and learning. [26] The primary message to the reader is, in this instance, the poet's presence at the banquet. Social prestige seems to play a similar role when Rist mentions that von Örtzen's house still provides him with opportunities to meet "mit vortreflichen / gelehrten / tapferen Herren und Edelleuten (alß noch neülich mit dem Herren Statthalter Plessen . . . und anderen grossen Männern / welche fürwahr Eine Zier und Bluhme der hochlöblichen Meklenburgischen Ritterschafft mit gutem fuge können genennet werden)" (7:152–63). Thus, the reader was to envision Rist not as a small-time clergyman, nor as a writing hermit, but as an intellectual moving with ease and delight in high society, a man sought after by nobles and princes.[27]

In spite of Rist's repeated gestures of conventional modesty ("ich der geringste," etc.), the reader of his dedications senses the author's pride in his social standing and achievements. This is particularly evident in the dedication of his second *Monatsgespräch* to the Hamburg merchant Anthon Bilderbek, who represented the interests of the duke of Mecklenburg in the Hanseatic city.[28] As one might expect, Rist elaborates on the duke's stay at Bilderbek's house, where he "Jhrer HochFürstlichen Durchläuchtigkeit . . . fast täglich unterthänigst aufgewahrtet," and where he relished "viele hochvernünftige Unterredunge" along with "wol zugerichteten Speisen und Getränken" that were highly praised by the duke.[29]

In the case of a well-known artist, such as the son of the world-famous M. Merian, even a brief acquaintanceship sufficed to warrant a dedication.[30] Rist makes a point of stressing that his distinguished guest set aside "seine hochwichtige Geschäfte / welche er dazumahl bey fürnehmen Potentaten / Fürsten und Herren zu verrichten hatte," to visit him at Wedel. He then draws attention to the stature of his visitor as a European celebrity by mentioning the necklace which "eine grosse / weltberühmte Königin" had bestowed on Merian and uses this as an occasion to point out his own connections to high nobility.[31] Here, as in other instances, Rist's boasting was intended to enhance his own image in the minds of his readers and possibly intensify the envy of his detractors.

It is common knowledge that the popularity of the Renaissance and Baroque dedication, as exemplified here by Opitz, Schirmer, and Rist, rapidly decreased during the age of the Enlightenment. The reasons for the decline, multifaceted and complex, are convincingly dealt with by H. Kiesel and P. Münch.[32] Only two of the most obvious causes will be mentioned here. Most important was a significant rise in authorial self-esteem, fostered in part by the spectacular financial success of Voltaire and Alexander Pope. With the help of his publisher, Voltaire had been able to lay the foundation to his future wealth; and Pope, using the innovation of book subscription, had gained financial independence. At the same time, the glamor of being immortalized in literature was rapidly fading. Nevertheless, some authors, for example, Gottsched, seemed to remain oblivious to the new trend and continued to cultivate the dedicatory tradition, whereas Friedrich Peter Tacke, equally unaware of the imminent decline of the genre, published a treatise on dedicatory practices as late as 1733.[33]

Once the dedicatory letter had lost its monetary value, its rhetoric became less elevated and its typographical features unassuming. From now on, the favorite dedicatees would be what they still are today: friends, family members, and household pets. Unfortunately, in our own century a growing passion for brevity is threatening the species with extinction. Imagine the outcome, if authors decided to compress further such dedicatory morsels as, "à Jacqueline" or "for P.J."[34] But there is still hope as long as there are writers who venture beyond a two-word perimeter, for example Marcus Singer, or those who try to emulate him with such witty arcana as

TO BLANCHE
who knows—if not what it means
what it meant.[35]

Notes

1. Wolfgang Leiner, *Der Widmungsbrief in der französischen Literatur (1580–1715)* (Heidelberg: Winter, 1965), pp. 21–23.

2. Ibid., p. 23.

3. In some cases the author expected the number of readers to increase under the auspices of the patron. See also the practice of the medieval author Konrad von Würzburg whose works were frequently commissioned and who, in such cases, mentions his patrons in his texts: Inge Leipold, *Die Auftraggeber und Gönner Konrads von Würzburg*, Göppinger Arbeiten zur Germanistik, 176 (Göppingen: Kümmerle, 1976).

4. "Horatii: EXEGI monumentum," *Gedichte des Barock*, ed. Ulrich Maché and Volker Meid (Stuttgart: Reclam, 1980), p. 36.

5. Examples of abuse and fraud are given in Henry B. Wheatley, who paraphrases in detail a chapter from Thomas Dekker's *O per se O* which gives instructions for tricking a prospective patron: *The Dedication of Books to Patron and Friend: A Chapter in Literary History* (London: Stock, 1887), pp. 28–31.

6. Erasmus of Rotterdam is quoted in ibid., pp. 9–10; see also Karl Schottenloher, *Die Widmungsvorrede im Buch des 16. Jahrhunderts*, Reformationsgeschichtliche Studien und Texte, 76/77 (Münster i. W.: Aschendorf, 1953), pp. 6–8. Schottenloher quotes extensively (pp. 6–10) from Erasmus's letter to Johann Woltzheim of 30 January 1523.

7. See, for example, Schottenloher, *Die Widmungsvorrede*, and H. Junghans, "Die Vorrede bei Martin Luther," in *Lutheriana. Zum 500. Geburtstag Martin Luthers von den Mitarbeitern der Weimarer Ausgabe*, ed. Gerhard Ham-

mer and Karl-Heinz zur Mühlen (Vienna: Böhlau, 1984), pp. 39–65.

8. See Leiner, *Der Widmungsbrief;* Wheatley, *The Dedication of Books;* Junghans, "Die Vorrede"; Schottenloher, *Die Widmungsvorrede;* and Richard Firth Green, *Poets and Princeleapers: Literature and the English Court in the Late Middle Ages* (Toronto: University of Toronto Press, 1980).

9. Leiner, *Der Widmungsbrief,* pp. 264–65, 269; Wheatley, *The Dedication of Books,* pp. 163, 34.

10. Mary Elizabeth Brown, *Dedications: An Anthology of the Forms Used from the Earliest Days of Book-Making to the Present Time* (New York: Franklin, 1913), pp. 381–85; see also Wheatley, *The Dedication of Books,* pp. 23–24.

11. Martin Opitz, *Die Schäfferey von der Nimfen Hercinie* (Breslau: Müller, 1630), rpt., ed. Karl F. Otto, Jr. (Bern: Lang, 1976), p. 6.

12. By denying (as is common in seventeenth-century literature) that his beloved in his *Schäfferey* bore any resemblance to happenings in his personal life, Opitz attempted to forestall any assumptions that might be detrimental to his own reputation and damaging to that of poets in general. See Martin Opitz, *Buch von der deutschen Poeterey* (ch. 3), in his *Gesammelte Werke, Kritische Ausgabe,* ed. George Schulz-Behrend, BLVS 300, vol. 2, part 1 (Stuttgart: Hiersemann, 1978) pp. 346–54.

13. Born in 1623, Schirmer came to Dresden in 1650 hoping to obtain a permanent position. Not until 1657, after the death of Elector Johann Georg I, did he reach that goal by being appointed librarian at the elector's library.

14. Only the editions of 1653 and 1657 were available for this study. *David Schirmers Erstes RosenGepüsche* (n.p., 1653). Unless otherwise noted, all references are to the 1653 edition. For the 1657 edition, see note 21.

15. Wheatley, *The Dedication of Books,* pp. 5–6; Leiner, *Der Widmungsbrief,* pp. 265–66. A well-known story was apparently that of Ariosto's financial disappointment with his *Orlando Furioso.* His patron, Cardinal Ippolito d'Este, instead of handing him the expected reward, simply asked him, "Where did you find so many stories, Master Ludovico?" (Wheatley, *The Dedication of Books,* p. 6).

16. As a model Schirmer apparently used Rist's dedication to his *Musa Teutonica.* This is evident not only from Schirmer's passing reference to that dedication, but from the names and data given by Schirmer as well as from stylistic criteria.

17. Schirmer, *Erstes RosenGepüsche,* sig. A3–A3v. Cf. Rist, who, ten years after the publication of Opitz's *Buch von der deutschen Poeterey,* still found German literature lacking in almost every respect: *Musa Teutonica Das ist: Teutscher Poetischer Miscellaneen Erster Theil* (Hamburg: Jacob Rebenlein, 1634), sig. A5ff.

18. Schirmer, *Erstes RosenGepüsche,* sig. A5.

19. Cherilus had been previously characterized by Schirmer as "nicht sehr anmuhtig" ibid., sig. A4.

20. See Opitz's poem "Wohl dem der weit von hohen Dingen" in his *Weltliche Poemata 1644. Zweiter Teil,* ed. Erich Trunz (Tübingen: Niemeyer, 1975), pp. 331–33.

21. *David Schirmers POetische ROsen = GEpüsche. Von Ihm selbsten aufs fleißigste übersehen* (Dresden: Andreas Löfler, 1657), sig. A7v. The dedicatory letter was now prefaced with an introductory note to the reader.

22. One patron had apparently died, and Schirmer was not sure of the whereabouts of the other. Brehme had in the meantime advanced to the position of mayor of Dresden. There seem to be fewer records in Germany than in England indicating what sums were passing from patrons to poets. Wheatley, *The Dedication of Books*, mentions numerous cases and standard fees. "From the revolution to the time of George I, the price for the dedication of a play was from five to ten guineas, but when the author and his work were equally poor the dedicatee would often strike a harder bargain" (p. 34). Leiner, *Der Widmungsbrief*, also found that in France documentary evidence was scarce; nevertheless, his chapters "Der Handelswert der Widmungsbriefe" and "Der Erfolg der Widmungsbriefe" (pp. 238–68) give valuable insights. Apparently letters are the most frequent source. See Erasmus's letter to Woltzheim of 30 January 1523, which contains a number of examples; Schottenloher, *Die Widmungsvorrede*, pp. 6–10.

23. *David Schirmers Churfürstlichen Sächsischen Bibliothecarii POetische RAuten-GEpüsche in Sieben Büchern heraus gegeben* (Dresden: Löffler, 1663).

24. Whenever possible, quotations are taken from the critical edition *Johann Rist Sämtliche Werke*, 7 vols., ed. Eberhard Mannack (Berlin: de Gruyter, 1967–82). Here: *Das AllerEdelste Leben der gantzen Welt* (1663), 4:134. Further references appear in the text.

25. "Er libet GOtt . . . wie ich den solches für meine Person / und zwahr in meiner höhesten Traurigkeit . . . würklich und in der That habe erfahren / den / mein hochgeehrter Herr Flagge / mir und den meinigen / eben dazumahl / und in solchem unseren betrübten Zustande / eine solche unvermuhtete Freundschaft hat erwiesen / welche ich zwahr nicht leicht widerum kan verschulden / jedoch aber die gantze Zeit meines Lebens höchlich zu rühmen und in steter Gedächtnisse werde zubehalten wissen" (*Werke*, 4:10–11).

26. For the sake of truth Rist later makes clear that the king was, at the time of this meeting, still a ducal prince, "dazumahlen Jhrer hochfürstlichen Durchläuchtigkeit" (*Werke*, 7:160).

27. Among Rist's dedicatees are a number of influential patrons who, over the years, supplemented his income in various ways and from whom he might not have expected any special favors for dedicating a work to them. The most notable example of this type is Vincent Möller, a high administrative official in Pinneberg, who showed his particular concern for the poet on two special occasions which Rist recounts in the dedication of *Das Friedejauchtzende Teutschland* (1653). As soon as Möller had learned of an accident in which Rist smashed his shoulder blade "mit einem hohen Wagen von einem gähen Hügel herunter stürzend," he left his office to visit Rist in Wedel and subsequently assisted him financially with the purchase "eines anderen und bequemeren Wagens . . . als wäre ich etwan sein leiblicher Bruder." His role as a Maecenas is even more remarkable after burglars

stripped Rist of all his savings, his "saur erworbene Baarschaft." At that time Möller not only restored part of the loss, but activated "andere fürnehme Herren und Freunde zu gleichmässiger freygebigkeit" (*Werke*, 2:215).

28. *Das AllerEdelste Leben der gantzen Welt* (1663). Anthon Bilderbek shared the honor of being a dedicatee with Joachim von Debbern, a colonel in the Danish army to whom Rist dedicated the book as "meinem . . . sehr wehrten liben Freunde," and with Georg Reiche, an old and close friend of the poet, chief administrator in the vicinity of Itzehoe ("Amtsverwalter zu Steinburg") (*Werke*, 4:124).

29. "Jhre Fürstliche Durchläuchtigkeit . . . pflagen zu sagen / sie wüsten schier nicht / das sie jemahlen besser tractiret, noch an jenigem Ohrte mit so wol zugerichteten Speisen und Getränke fleissiger weren versehen worden / wie den auch höchstgedachte Jhre Fürstliche Durchläuchtigkeit / Jhre Mahlzeiten / mit besonderer Lust dazumahlen hielten." And to demonstrate that his friend and patron who "in einer so weltberühmten Stad . . . zu fürnehmen Aemtern gezogen," is truly a man of breeding and aristocratic stature, he points to Bilderbek's early years in Paris, his knowledge of foreign languages, and the fact that he "bei vilen grossen Potentaten in deroselben gnädige Kundschaft gerahten / und [sich] sonderlich belibet gemachet" (*Werke*, 4:136–37).

30. See also the dedication written for Anna Eleonora, Landgräfin zu Hessen, in which Rist does not fail to mention that her son, Duke Christian Ludwig of Braunschweig, on his return from Flensburg recently tried to summon the poet, who happened to be absent from Wedel, to Pinneberg. *Der zu seinen allerheiligsten Leiden und Sterben hingeführter und an das Kreütz gehefteter Christus Jesus* (Hamburg: Jacob Rebenlein, 1648), sig. a8–a8v.

31. In this case Rist refers to the late duke Christian Ludwig of Braunschweig, also a patron of Merian, who had summoned the poet more than once "aus hertzlicher Liebe zur Kunst / zu sich an seinen Fürstlichen Hoff" (*Werke*, 5:200).

32. Helmut Kiesel and Paul Münch, *Gesellschaft und Literatur im 18. Jahrhundert. Voraussetzung und Entstehung des literarischen Markts in Deutschland* (Munich: Beck, 1977), pp. 76–104.

33. See in particular J. C. Gottsched's *Redekunst* (Leipzig, 1628) and the dedications to some of his aristocratic students in various volumes of his *Deutsche Schaubühne*, 6 vols. (Leipzig, 1740–45). Friedrich Peter Tacke, *Commentatio historica et literaria de dedicationibus librorum . . . a Friderico Petro Tackio* (Wolfenbüttel: Christoph Meisner, 1733). This publication also contains a rudimentary sketch of the historical development of dedications.

34. Leiner, *Der Widmungsbrief*, p. 5.

35. Singer's original dedication reads, "TO BLANCHE who knows what is meant if not what it means." Marcus George Singer, *Generalizations in Ethics* (New York: Knopf, 1961), p. v.

13. Zum Selbstverständnis des Dichters im 17. und frühen 18. Jahrhundert

Ferdinand van Ingen

In seiner berühmten "Grabschrifft / so er ihm selbst gemacht . . . auf seinem Todtbette drey Tage vor seinem seel: Absterben"[1] hält Paul Fleming eine Rückschau auf sein Leben, das er, kaum dreißig Jahre alt, verlassen soll:

> Ich war an Kunst / und Gut / und Stande groß und reich.
> Deß Glückes lieber Sohn. Von Eltern guter Ehren.
> Frey; Meine. Kunte mich aus meinen Mitteln nehren.
> Mein Schall floh überweit. Kein Landsmann sang mir gleich.

Dieser Anfang ist in mehrfacher Hinsicht bemerkenswert. Die Gattung legt ja Trostargumente oder Mahngedanken nahe, zumindest eine moralische Erinnerung an die menschliche Sterblichkeit, dem alten Spruch *hodie mihi, cras tibi* entsprechend. Davon findet sich keine Spur, die Eingangsverse bestimmen schon die Tonart des ganzen Gedichts, die Wilhelm Kühlmann auf den Begriff "Sterben als heroischer Akt" gebracht hat.[2] In stolzem Selbstbewußtsein erwägt der Dichter seine Leistung: er ist ein berühmter, herausragender Poet gewesen. Im zweiten Quartett wird der Gedanke noch einmal aufgenommen und dahingehend verstärkt, daß Fleming die Zeitlichkeit im Bewußtsein verläßt, sich einen unsterblichen Namen gemacht zu haben: "Man wird mich nennen hören / Biß daß die letzte Glut diß alles wird verstören." Er benennt auch die Voraussetzung seines Gelingens: die materielle Unabhängigkeit, wodurch er sich ganz seiner Kunst hat widmen können—wahrhaft "deß Glückes lieber Sohn." Aber Anlage und die Möglichkeit ihrer ungehinderten Entfaltung erklären noch nicht die künstlerische Einzigartigkeit, deren sich der Dichter ohne falsche Bescheidenheit rühmt: "Kein Landsmann sang mir gleich."

Das sind ungewöhnliche Töne in einem Gedicht, das dem Formtypus der Grabschrift angehört. Auch die Aussage selbst, das Pochen auf die unvergleichliche Eigenleistung, erstaunt. Sie ist namentlich für denjenigen verwunderlich, der in der Barockliteratur das Wesentliche lediglich in der Variation von tradierten Formen und Motiven erblickt, wie dies folgendem Zitat zugrunde liegt: "Wichtig ist die Deutung der Tradition, die Nuance der Verschiebung gegenüber dem Vorbild, die kaum wahrnehmbare neuartige Betonung bei den einzelnen Autoren"[3]. Das mag für die Mehrzahl der barocken Dichter tatsächlich zutreffen, für die Allzuvielen also, nicht aber für jene, die bewußt einen eigenen Ton anstimmen, neue Formen erproben und souverän mit dem tradierten Gut verfahren, ohne doch je die allgemein verpflichtenden Normen zu verletzen oder aus dem anerkannten Spielraum auszubrechen. Pauschalurteile werden der Gesamterscheinung der Barockliteratur nicht gerecht; sie decken sich auch nicht mit dem Selbstverständnis der Dichter, deren spezifische Leistung und Eigenart schon von den Zeitgenossen hervorgehoben wurden.

"Kein Landsmann sang mir gleich"—ohne die generelle Gültigkeit der Traditionsverpflichtung und des handwerklichen Verfahrens in vorgeschriebenen Bahnen in Frage zu stellen, gilt es offenbar doch zu differenzieren. Das Problem ist wohl deshalb aktuell, weil großräumige Studien literarische Ordnungssysteme und Sprechhaltungen erarbeitet haben, die seit dem 18. Jahrhundert in Vergessenheit geraten sind, aber doch für den Barockdichter als selbstverständliches Zuordnungsgefüge funktionierten. Die Kehrseite ist jedoch, daß das Untypische und individuell Charakteristische, worauf Flemings "Grabschrifft" verweist, nicht mehr in den Blick kommt. So gehört es zu den mittlerweile liebgewonnenen Meinungen der Literaturwissenschaft, daß die Begriffe Individualität und Eigenständigkeit dem 17. Jahrhundert unangemessen seien. Neuere Forschungsergebnisse scheinen das nur zu bestätigen. Ich nenne hier Wulf Segebrechts Darstellung der Okkasionalität in der Barocklyrik, wodurch die unzeitgemäße Kategorie des Erlebnisses endgültig ausscheidet, und Wilfried Barners umfassende Darstellung der Rhetorik in ihrer grundlegenden und die Zeit prägenden Funktion, womit sich die Intentionalität als der Grundzug der damaligen Literatur erweist.[4] Beide Studien, denen repräsentative Bedeutung zukommt, erinnern an die mehrfache Gebundenheit der Literatur des 17. Jahrhunderts und an Überbausysteme, denen sich die individuelle Arbeit fügt. Sie umreißen den Hintergrund, vor dem sich unsere Fragestellung deutlicher profiliert, denn sie sind mit ihrer Ausrichtung auf literarische Zweckformen und auf Intentionalität in der Hauptsache objektbezogen. Die Frage nach dem Selbstverständnis des Dichters muß aber an einem anderen Punkt ansetzen.

Diese Frage drängt sich verstärkt auf, wenn der einzelne Dichter derart in Systeme eingebunden ist (in das einer literarischen Gattung wie in das übergeordnete der Rhetorik), daß er generell auf Allgemeines verpflichtet wird. Anders formuliert: Inwiefern erlauben solche allgemeinen Zuordnungen dichterische Eigenständigkeit und wie verhalten sich die Selbstaussagen der Dichter dazu? Der "rhetorische Grundzug" der Barockliteratur provoziert beispielsweise spätestens dann eine Antwort, wenn man den besonderen Status der Poetik untersucht. Wenn nämlich die Poetik auf der Rhetorik aufbaut, so ist sie wie diese lehr- und lernbar, folgt sie somit dem gleichen, seit der römischen Antike bereitstehenden Redesystem, das die Dreiheit *ingenium, ars, exercitatio* voraussetzt. Ein solches Lehrsystem betont auch Barner, wenn er sagt, "daß beide, Poesie wie Rhetorik, einer *doctrina* überhaupt zugänglich sind, ja ohne sie ihren genuinen Kunstcharakter nicht entfalten können"[5]. Barner geht es um das Gemeinschaftliche, in unserem Zusammenhang kommt es dagegen auf das Verschiedene an. Gilt das Redesystem gleicherweise für die "gebundene" wie für die "ungebundene Rede", muß für den Dichter ein unterscheidendes Merkmal auszumachen sein, sollte man es nicht bei den nur für ihn relevanten Eigenheiten von Metrum und Reim belassen.

Durchmustert man daraufhin die Äußerungen von Autoren des 17. Jahrhunderts, so findet man zwar verschiedene Auffassungen, aber diese lassen sich allesamt aus der Antike herleiten. Ludwig Fischer hat 1968 versucht, sie zu rubrizieren und zu systematisieren. Es sind der "poetische Geist", der "poetische Stil", der "poetische Inhalt", das "poetische Absehen" und die "poetische Freiheit"[6]. Mit Ausnahme des "poetischen Geistes" tragen diese Unterscheidungen aber nicht zum Selbstverständnis des Dichters bei; und auch dieser, der traditionelle *furor poeticus*, reicht im 17. Jahrhundert für sich genommen nicht aus, sondern hat einen eigenen Stellenwert. Darauf wird zurückzukommen sein. Joachim Dyck ist anders verfahren als Fischer; er teilt die Elemente des Dichterverständnisses anders ein, obwohl auch er bei der Unterscheidung Redner/Dichter ansetzt. Dyck hypostasiert einen Vorrang der Rhetorik vor der Poetik und sieht in den zusammenwirkenden Elementen ein "Argumentationssystem", das als Ganzes eine Übertragung des Ciceronischen Vollkommenheitsideals auf den Dichter darstelle und auf ein "Lob des Dichters" abziele. Den Akzent legt Dyck mit Recht auf die in stetem Regelmaß wiederkehrenden Begriffspaare "Naturgabe und Kunstlehre" sowie "Bildung und Tugend"[7]. Das ist insofern bestechend, als damit die Ausgrenzung der "Pritschmeister" und "Reimeschmiede" (im Zusammenhang mit den eigentlichen Legitimationszwecken der Dichtkunst) genauer erfaßt werden kann, und zwar als Emanzipationsversuch des Dichters: "Der Poet betrachtet sich als Gelehrten und beansprucht als Mitglied einer 'nobilitas literaria' die gleiche Anerkennung und gesellschaftliche Achtung, die die 'nobilitas generis' genießt"[8]. So richtig das ist, so ist doch Barner beizupflichten, wenn er nicht nur gegen Dycks Übertragungsthese Bedenken anmeldet, sondern auch zu bedenken gibt, daß das so herausgestellte Bildungsideal als grundlegendes Element des Dichterberufs erst im Kontext der wissenschaftsgeschichtlichen Entwicklung seine einmalige historische Bedeutung erhält: "Die literarische Kunstübung der Barockepoche ist ein so fundamental gelehrtes Metier, daß sie auf ihre Weise den polyhistorischen Wissenschaftsbetrieb des 17. Jahrhunderts zu repräsentieren hat"[9]. Das ist, wie mir scheint, der bessere Weg. Wieder einmal zeigt sich, daß verwandte oder gleiche Erscheinungen zu anderen Zeiten nicht dieselbe Bedeutung haben und—in Konsequenz—eine andere Funktion erfüllen können. Ob allerdings die Erscheinung der gelehrten Elitenbildung und ihres Ideals der Polyhistorie tatsächlich Forderung und Einsatz des materiellen Vielwissens im einzelnen abdecken und befriedigend erklären, bleibt weiterhin fraglich. Deshalb sind das Begriffspaar "Naturgabe und Kunstlehre" ebenso wie der Wissensbegriff genauer zu untersuchen, um die bisherigen Ergebnisse nach Möglichkeit zu verfeinern.

Es ist zunächst daran zu erinnern, daß die hergebrachte Formel *ingenium et ars* bzw. *natura et ars* im 17. Jahrhundert einen charakteristischen Bedeutungsinhalt aufweist. Angesichts der Lehrbarkeit der Poetik wird zwar von Opitz an betont, daß Regeln allein keinen Dichter machen, aber es läßt sich doch beobachten, daß die *ars* immer stärker in den Vordergrund tritt. Sigmund von Birken ergeht sich in seiner *Rede- bind- und Dicht-Kunst* in Gemeinschaftlichkeiten und Unterschieden zwischen dem Redner und dem Dichter und streicht die Bedeutung des *ingeniums* heraus. Darauf läßt er aber sofort eine einschränkende Bemerkung folgen: "Es folget aber hieraus nicht / daß ein Poet von Natur ein Poet sey / und ganz keine Belehrung vonnöten habe." Sodann verweist er auf berühmte Dichter: "Haben sie nicht / wer weiß mit was für harter Mühe / und nach wie langer Übung / ihnen selber eine Kunstlehre . . . vorgeschrieben?"[10] Artistische Schulung ist die unabdingbare Voraussetzung, auch wenn einer ein "Naturtalent" ist. Ohne eine gewisse Veranlagung bringt es zwar keiner zum Dichter, aber die *ars*, die Kunstfertigkeit, ist so wichtig, daß ihr Fehlen wahrhafte Kunst verhindert. Darüber verbreitet sich z. B. Philipp von Zesen: "Hierbei erinnere ich noch dieses: daß viele eine sehr feurige / ja alzu feurige und alzu heftige angebohrenheit zur Dichtkunst haben . . . Solche nun verdienen den nahmen eines Dichtmeisters eben so wenig / als vorige; weil ihnen die K u n s t mangelt: und ihre Dichtereien schmäkken bloß allein nach dem brande der alzu hitzigen N a t u r; die ohne Kunst nimmermehr zur rechten volkommenheit gelangen kan." Zesen geht sogar so weit, daß er solche Dichtereien für "schlimmer und ungeschikter" hält als jene, "darinnen Kunst und übung ihr meisterstükke fast allein bewiesen." Die Zeugnisse ließen sich unschwer mehren. Hand in Hand mit der hohen Wertschätzung der *ars* geht der bekannte Universalitätsanspruch. Das schickt auch Zesen voraus; dieser sei das höchste Ziel eines jungen Mannes, "der dan erst mit allem rechte ein Dichtmeister / ja zugleich auch ein volkomner Gelehrter genennet wird"[11]. Die Zielrichtung ist denn auch nicht—was Dyck und in seiner Nachfolge Fischer entgegenzuhalten ist[12]—der vollkommene Mensch, sondern *der vollkommene Gelehrte.* In diesem Begriff ist—so wird vorausgesetzt—der universale Mensch impliziert: es ist der soziale Leitbegriff jenes "wissenschaftlichen" Jahrhunderts. Die soziale Wertschätzung des Dichters beruht deshalb nicht auf den traditionellen Voraussetzungen von *ingenium* und *ars* als Veranlagung und Beherrschung von Kunstregeln, sondern auf dem beanspruchten Status eines Gelehrten, und zwar in dem Sinn, daß der gelehrte Dichter als die höchste Steigerung des universal gebildeten Menschen betrachtet wird. Das führt zum Idealbild einer gelehrten Dichtkunst, die selber in den Rang einer alles umfassenden Wissenschaft aufsteigt. Hier wird insofern anders akzentuiert wie üblich, als mir die Einbeziehung der Gelehrtheit in Verbindung mit einer Betonung des *ars*-Prinzips über eine Gelehrsamkeitsargumentation mit werbender Funktion hinauszugehen scheint.

Seit Opitz' Wort, daß die Dichtkunst "alle andere künste vnd wissenschafften in sich helt"[13], wird dieses Axiom zum grundlegenden Gedanken der Barockpoetik, ja gestaltet sich zu einem Topos, den man als ein leicht übersteigertes Legitimationsargument ansieht und den man kaum zu hinterfragen pflegt. Dennoch ist dieser Punkt meines Erachtens von besonderer Wichtigkeit. Die Abgrenzung vom "gemeinen Mann" mit Hilfe einer herausgestellten Kunst bzw. Gelehrsamkeit hat zweifellos auch eine bedeutsame soziale Komponente, die dem Dichter in der Gelehrtenrepublik und im Kreis des Adels seinen Platz sichern soll, mit andern Worten auf Legitimation der Exklusivität im sozialen Kontext seiner Zeit gerichtet ist. Darauf haben Dyck, Barner und zuletzt Gunter Grimm hingewiesen.[14] Aber es ist kritisch anzumerken, daß die Gelehrsamkeit bei ihnen nurmehr als Zielvorstellung figuriert—von Lehrgedichten und dergleichen abgesehen, in denen gelehrtes Wissen eine ganz unproblematische Rolle spielt. Ich schlage deshalb einen anderen Weg vor und stelle die Frage ins Zentrum, ob im 17. Jahrhundert das gelehrte Wissen selbst in eine *poetologische Funktion* überführt wird, also nicht Zutat und Ausschmückung ist, sondern eine über die erlernbare *ars* hinausgehende Besonderheit der *inventio* darstellt bzw. als bestimmendes Merkmal der dichterischen Arbeit anzusehen ist. Im allgemeinen findet man davon keine Spuren in den Poetiken der Zeit. Die Tradition verlangte Rückgriff und Berufung auf Dichter und Gelehrte der Antike und der Renaissance—das formt das Dichterbild, wie es sich in den Poetiken niederschlägt. Vorreden sind schon ergiebiger, vor allem die dichterischen Werke selbst. Außerdem bleibt die Bindung der Dichtung an die Rhetorik bestehen, die eine veränderte Einstellung zum Dichterberuf eher verdeckt. Der traditionelle Zusammenhang zeigt sich nicht zuletzt in der schon von Cicero und Quintilian erhobenen Forderung der Erfahrung in den Wissenschaften und der vollkommenen Tugendbeherrschung an den Orator (Quintilian, *Institutio oratoria* 1. Prooemium 18: "Vere sapiens appellari possit, nec moribus modo perfectus . . . sed etiam scientia et omni facultate dicendi"). Aber wenn der Dichter sich einerseits an den Gelehrten bzw. den gelehrten Redner anlehnt, ihn andererseits überrundet, hätte man in der andersartigen Anwendung des Wissens in der poetischen *inventio* eine für die Barockepoche wesentliche Unterscheidung des *homo doctus* vom *poeta doctus*, und zwar durchaus auch im Sinne einer Steigerung, wie sie sich, trotz dem Verhaftetsein in der Tradition, im Selbstverständnis der Dichter ausdrückt. In diesem Punkt könnte sich ein dichterisches Selbstbewußtsein ausprägen, das—neben dem spiritualistischen Dichterbegriff—einen zeittypischen Charakter aufweist.

Wenn man Harsdörffer beim Wort nimmt, ist die Ausgestaltung eines Themas "mit einer zimlichen Erfindung" die eigentliche Leistung des Dichters: einen vorgegebenen "Inhalt zu gestalten / und mit einer zimlichen Erfindung auszubilden / ist das / was ich Dichten und Dichtkunst nenne. Sie ist aber von der Reim- und Verskunst gantz unterschieden"[15]. In der poetischen Erfindung kommen erst die auch von Harsdörffer in den Vordergrund gestellten Kategorien Kunst und Wissenschaft zum Zuge, hier treffen beide zusammen. In der poetischen Erfindung wird man mit einem Kunstbegriff konfrontiert, der sich also weiter erstreckt als die eher handwerksmäßige *ars* der Verskunst und deren Kunstfertigkeit: hier weiß der Dichter mit sicherem Griff das Zweckdienliche aus dem Wissensvorrat zu erwählen. Wenn bei Zesen auf die Frage "mus dan ein Dichtmeister so gar viel beobachten / so gar viel wissen?" die Antwort lautet, "hierinnen mus des Dichtmeisters Angebohrenheit / doch niemahls ohne Kunst / das beste tuhn"[16], so kommt hier das *ingenium* zu neuen Ehren. Vom poetischen Geist geleitet, erfaßt der Dichter intuitiv das Wesentliche für sein Gedicht, anders als der systematisch vorgehende Gelehrte.

Das herkömmliche Spannungsverhältnis von Redner und Dichter erhält im 17. Jahrhundert dadurch eine besondere Note, daß der poetische Geist und das auch dem Dichter unverzichtbare umfassende Wissen eine charakteristische Verbindung eingehen. Polyhistorische Bildung ist nach wie vor die Voraussetzung eines Dichtertums im damals modernen Sinn. Aufgrund seiner *ars* und dank seinem poetischen Geist verwendet der Dichter das Wissen aber anders als der Redner bzw. der Gelehrte. Das ist der Hintergrund von Opitz' enger Bindung der Erfindung an den poetischen Geist; Magnus Daniel Omeis ist ihm noch spät darin gefolgt: "Die Alten haben sich / um gewiße Regeln von der Poetischen Erfindung zu geben / wenig bekümmert; weil sie vermeynten / die Poeten reden nicht aus eigenem Kunst-Vermögen / sondern durch einen Göttlichen Triebe." Trotz aller Skepsis wird die Bindung nicht aufgelöst, sondern es wird lapidar formuliert: "Eine gute Erfindung ist die Seele des Gedichtes"[17].

Wenn eine begriffliche Abgrenzung von der rhetorischen *inventio* den Poetikautoren offenbar Schwierigkeiten bereitete, muß es doch eine *communis opinio* gegeben haben, die eine formale Unterscheidung von *poesis* und *oratoria* in dem spezifischen Umgang mit dem vielberufenen polyhistorischen Sachwissen (*doctrina rerum*) durch den Dichter begründet sah. Das läßt sich auch an poetologischen Texten belegen. Ich verweise auf eine bekannte Stelle in Johann Klajs *Lobrede der Teutschen Poeterey*:

> Es muß ein Poet ein vielwissender / in den Sprachen durchtriebener und allerdinge erfahrner Mann seyn: Er hebet die Last seines Leibes von der Erden / er durchwandert mit seinen Gedanken die Länder der Himmel / die Strassen der Kreise / die Sitze der Planeten / die Grentzen der Sterne / die Stände der Elementen. Ja er schwinget die Flügel seiner Sinne / und fleucht an die Stellen / da es regnet und schneiet / nebelt und hagelt / stürmet und streitet. Er durchkreucht den Bauch der Erden / er durchwädet die Tiefen / schöpffet scharffe Gedanken / geziemende zierliche Worte lebendige Beschreibungen / nachsinnige Erfindungen / wolklingende Bindarten / ungezwungene Einfälle / meisterliche Ausschmükkungen / seltene Lieblichkeiten / und vernünfftige Neurungen.[18]

Man beachte die Reihenfolge: Das Vielwissen geht vorauf; daran entzündet der Dichter seinen Geist—und schon schwebt er. Klaj sagt es Schottelius nach, daß der Dichter ein "fast göttliches" Wesen ist,

"weiln ein solcher Poetischer Geist / von anmutigen Sinnreichen Ein-
fällen / kekkes Unternemens unnachfölgig steiget / sich mit Göttli-
cher Vernunfft flügelt"[19]. Aber bei Klaj handelt es sich, wie Conrad
Wiedemann ausgeführt hat, um eine durchaus persönliche Ausprä-
gung der Inspirationslehre, die dem Dichter engelhafte Eigenschaften
verleiht. Das Engel-Dichter-Gleichnis hatte für den jungen Nürnberger wohl auch kompensatorische Funktion im sozialen Bereich.
Arm wie er war, war die Sprache in unmittelbarem Sinn seine Er-
werbsquelle, woran er—jetzt ganz Bürger mit seinen bürgerlichen
Zuhörern—am Ende seiner Lobrede erinnert: "Sie ist es / die uns
allen unser Brod und Lebensmittel verdienen muß." Die dichterische
Adaption der Engelsqualität impliziert das Eintreten für geistliche
Poesie, womit Klaj und die anderen Mitglieder des Pegnesischen Blu-
menordens Frömmigkeitstendenzen im Nürnberger Bürgertum ent-
gegenkamen.

Klajs Selbstverständnis knüpft an die in der Barockpoetik geläufi-
gen Vorstellungen des vom himmlischen Feuer inspirierten Dichters
an, hebt sich jedoch durch ein Moment der Individuation entscheidend davon ab. Ähnliches gilt für Zesen. Auch er kennt das Himmel-
ansteigen, aber er gibt dem Motiv eine eigene Prägung durch seine
Vermählung mit der himmlischen Sophia, der strahlenden Himmels-
braut, die man aus dem Salomonischen Buch der Weisheit kennt.
Vorgeprägt war die Übertragung des Bildes der Sapientia auf die
"Wohlredenheit" in Meyfarts *Teutscher Rhetorica* (1634).[20] Zesen nimmt
seinerseits eine Übertragung auf die Poesie vor (Klaj folgt ihm mit
dem "Bild der Poesis" in der *Lobrede* nach), gestaltet das Motiv aber
lyrisch aus und erweitert es zu einer eigenwilligen Liebeslyrik mit
Werbung und Liebespreis, in eine regelrechte Vermählung ausmün-
dend.[21] Es sind insgesamt sieben Gedichte, von denen einige in die
frühe Sammlung *FrühlingsLust* (1642) Eingang fanden, einige schließlich in der "Sammlung letzter Hand", dem *Dichterischen Rosen- und
Liljen-tahl* (1670), programmatisch an den Anfang gestellt wurden. Die
Tugend und Weisheit verheißende Sophia sollte Zesen zum Erbau-
ungsschriftsteller legitimieren, aber das genügte dem ehrgeizigen
Dichter keineswegs.

Schon im Roman der *Adriatischen Rosemund* (1645) gibt Zesen sich
(mit einer Anspielung auf seinen latinisierten Namen *caesius* "blau")
als der blaue Ritter ("Ritterhold von Blauen"), und auf dem Titelkupfer erscheint neben Venus die Pallas, die Zesen "Kluginne" oder
"Blauinne" zu nennen pflegt. Dieser "Als-Göttin der Weisheit" gilt ein
mythologischer Aufzug, den Mahrhold-Zesen seiner Rosemund zu
ehren veranstaltet. So ist Zesen, gleichsam durch seinen Namen prä-

destiniert, Pallas-Jünger, aber ohne daß Sophia neidisch wäre. Beide sehen sich täuschend ähnlich und agieren häufig nebeneinander. Der Dichter, der sich Sophia zu seiner Liebsten erkoren hat, muß sich Pallas zur Göttin erwählen: "Weil nun aus der Weisheit alles entstehet / und durch die alles / das einen Bestand haben sol / gehandhabet und beherschet muß werden; so hat man der Pallas / als der Göttin der Weisheit / alle Vermögen / die der Weisheit eigen sind / zugeschrieben. Und eben daher ward sie für eine Erfinderin / schier aller Künste . . . gehalten"[22]. Als Pallas-Jünger verewigt Zesen seine Rosemund: die Verbindung mit der Göttin der Kunst und der Weisheit gewährleistet einen ewigen Namen—das ist das anspruchsvolle Programm der Verewigungskunst in diesem Roman.[23]

Rosemund verkörpert zugleich die Deutschgesinnete Genossenschaft, deren Gründer und Vorsteher Zesen war. In ihrem Zeichen wurde sie gegründet, d. h. im Zeichen der "Bluhme der Liebe", die das "algemeine Zunftzeichen der gantzen Genossenschaft" wurde: "Wer mit diesem Zeichen wahrhaftig gezeichnet ist / der wird allezeit / wie . . . die Alsgöttin der Liebe / mit einem Rosenmunde reden: der wird / durch seine liebliche wohlredenheit / aller gemühter zu seiner liebe bewegen"[24]. In diesem Bild als der tragenden Idee von Zesens Dichtertum werden dessen Impulse und Wirkungsabsicht erkennbar. Im Liebesprinzip, ausgedrückt im Rosemund-Kult wie in der Vermählung mit Sophia und der Verehrung der "Blauinne", kommt alles zusammen; unter Anleitung der Liebe macht Zesen auch den Schritt zum theoretischen Werk über die Geheimnisse der Sprache, dem *Rosen-mând*, dessen Titel auf die geliebte Rosemund anspielt. Hinter dem beziehungsreichen Namenspiel erkennt man Zesens Programm als *poeta doctus*. Das dichterische Werk im engeren Sinn (Roman und Lyrik) verschränkt sich mit dem theoretischen Schrifttum. *Ein* Geist hält das gesamte Werk zusammen, der Liebestrieb weitet sich auf die Sprache und ihre Liebhaber aus: "Ich schreibe aus liebe zur sprache / aus liebe zu dier / aus liebe zu meinem Vaterlande. durch liebe werde ich getrieben; von liebe rede ich; mit liebe vermische ich meine reden: damit sie solcher gestalt verlieblicht / dier / der du Liebe liebest / zu lesen belieben möchten"[25]. Diese Liebe (das Sinnbild der Rose) vereint in der Deutschgesinneten Genossenschaft alle verwandten Geister. Sie richtet sich unverrückbar auf die Göttin der Weisheit, die deshalb neben ihrer eigenen blauen Farbe sich mit der Rosenfarbe der Liebe schmückt: "Sie trug Amazonische kleidung von sterbe-blauem sammet und atlas mit silbernen spitzen verbrähmet; . . . der sturm-huht war blau angelauffen / und mit güldenen stärnlein übertzschäkkert: oben auf trug sie einen großen busch von sterbe-blau-weiss und rosen-färbigen federn"²⁶. Deutlicher kann der Bezug des Dichtertums zum Bereich des Wissens nicht ausgedrückt werden als im Bild des Pallas-Jüngers. Zesens Privatmythologie legitimiert den traditionellen Aufschwung in die überirdischen Sphären auf originelle Weise und bekräftigt durch diesen neuen Kontext das schriftstellerische Selbstbewußtsein "daß ich nuhn im klugen Sün / himlisch und nicht irdisch bin"²⁷. Das geht weit über das Dichterbild der Poetiken hinaus. Es ist ein kunstvoll stilisiertes Selbstverständnis des gelehrten Dichters, das im Werk eine Einheit stiftet. Kein Dichter der Zeit hat so konsequent am Bild des Dichtertums gebaut wie Zesen. Wenn er hier ausführlich behandelt wird, so deshalb, weil er exemplarisch zeigt, wie unabhängig von rhetorischen Vorbildern der Dichterberuf ins Bild gefaßt und wie sorgfältig dieses nach dem zeitgemäßen Ideal modelliert wird.

Das Selbstverständnis Zesens steht (wie das Johann Klajs) in schroffem Kontrast zu einem sozialen Abenteurertum. Klaj und Zesen entwickeln geläufige Vorstellungen zu hoch emporgetriebenen Idealbildern, die den Poeten von seinesgleichen wie vom Gelehrten unterscheiden. Beide sehen den unermeßlichen Wissensfundus als Voraussetzung ihrer dichterischen Leistung an. Die Selbstverständlichkeit, mit der ein Fleming noch im humanistisch-gelehrten Geist wurzelte, an dem er mit seinen lateinischen und deutschen Gedichten teilhatte, weicht beim modernen Dichter, dem solche Zugehörigkeit schon aus Gründen der Quantität nicht in gleichem Maße sicher sein konnte, einem explizierten Bezug zum polyhistorischen Leitbild. Dieser Tatbestand schlägt sich auch in der bevorzugten Art des Wissens nieder, das nicht länger ausschließlich die sogenannten *humaniora* umfaßt.

Klajs Mentor in Nürnberg, Georg Philipp Harsdörffer, war außerordentlich erfolgreich mit der Fortsetzung von Schwenters *Deliciae physico-mathematicae Oder Mathematische und Philosophische Erquickstunden* und brachte als ein "Liebhaber deß Studii Mathematici" Franz Ritters *Sonnenspiegel* heraus. Zesen übersetzte Matthias Dögens *Kriges Baukunst* und hielt eine Rede "vom nutz und währte des Saltzes", eine Jugendarbeit, auf die er noch im Alter zurückgriff.²⁸ Johann Rist, ebensowenig ein echter Neulateiner wie Klaj und Zesen, hat sich mit den *Monatsgesprächen* deutlich den Erfahrungswissenschaften zugewandt. Im Zentrum steht die Gartenkunst mit der Behandlung von Pflanzen und Blumen, ferner hört man von "Bier und Butter, Kirchenmusik und Bühnentechnik, Mühle und Kompaß"²⁹. Bei alledem hatte Rist einen ausgesprochenen Sinn für die neuen Wissenschaften. Im Vorbericht seiner *Musa Teutonica* hebt er die "grosse vollenkommenheit / die fast in allen *scientien* vnd Wissenschafften zu spüren",

hervor, wobei er namentlich "die Schiffahrten / *Architectur*, Krieges-
kunst / vnnd dergleichen Wissenschafften" nennt, denen er die "vor-
trefliche *Scripta* in den hohen *Faculteten*, oder auch andre *Philosophische*
Bücher von *Historischen* / *Chymischen* / *Mathematischen* / vnd andren
dergleichen Sachen" an die Seite stellt. Dies alles bildet aber nur den
Hintergrund für die Wissenschaft von der Dichtung, die gleichberech-
tigt in die Phalanx jener "scientien" eingereiht wird:

> Vnter anderen nützlichen vnd dabenebenst sehr anmuthigen
> Wissenschafften / ist auch die Edle / vnnd von den Alten hoch-
> geehrte Poetery / dergestalt zu diesen letzten Zeiten wieder er-
>
> hoben / daß zu zweiffelen / ob auch in jenigem *Seculo* so vor-
> treffliche *Ingenia* gelebet / vnnd ob jemahlen so liebliche vnnd
> schöne Sachen / so wol bey den Griechen / als den Lateineren /
> hervor kommen / vnnd geschrieben worden.[30]

Wenn Rist an anderer Stelle Kritik an der Dutzendware Poesie übt—
"da machet heut zu Tage ein jeder Teutsche Verß / der kaum zehn
Wort Latein / fünf Griechische Syllaben / etwas gemein Küchen =
Teutsch / von frembden Sprachen aber / offt das geringste Wörtlein
nicht verstehet / noch in der Jugend hat gelernet"—so greift er nicht
das Argument auf, daß die Dichtkunst eine Gelehrtenkunst sei, sondern lenkt er vielmehr den Blick darauf, daß sie eine gelehrte Kunst,
folglich eine Wissenschaft sei, und man "erstlich den rechten Grund
der Kunst vnd Wissenschafft verstehen lernen" muß.[31]

Man trifft immer wieder auf die akzentuierte Wissenschaftlichkeit,
wenn von des Dichters Tun die Rede ist. Zesen verweist mit Nachdruck auf die vornehmste Aufgabe der Naturwissenschaft, "die Scheidekunst aus zu üben / und die Verborgenheiten der großen Zeuge-
mutter aller dinge zu erforschen"[32]. Er überträgt diese sofort auf die
Erforschung der Sprache, die im Sinne der Natursprachenlehre analy-
siert wird und die folglich mit ihren einzelnen lautlichen Bestandtei-
len auf das Wesen der Sprache selber zurückverweist. Seine Arbeit an
der Sprache verstand Zesen solchermaßen als "Scheidekunst", somit
als ein an der modernen Naturwissenschaft geschultes Verfahren:

> Auf solche weise werden durch die Scheide-kunst / als die rechte
> auswürkerin der natur . . . viel unzählige geheimnüsse und ver-
> borgenheiten / welche die natur angefangen / aber noch nicht
> austrükken oder ausarbeiten können / und so lange in ihrem
> schoße verborgen gehalten / täglich gefunden und durch mensch-
> liche kunst-geflissenheit und vernunft zu ihrer folkommenheit
> gebracht / und fol-end ausgewürket.[33]

Hier fand Zesens vielgeschmähte Orthographie, hier fand nicht zuletzt seine durch Lautanalogien Beziehung stiftende dichterische Praxis ihren Grund. Dichtung als Naturwissenschaft: solcherart gebührte dem Dichter mit seiner Kunst im Gesamt der Wissenschaften eine Ehrenstellung; die Dichtkunst hat sich vollends von der Rhetorik emanzipiert.

Das Bewußtsein, im Strom der modernen Wissenschaften mitzuschwimmen, hat das Selbstgefühl des Barockdichters erheblich gesteigert. Mit einiger Mühe ist das Empfinden nachzuvollziehen, daß man den höchst denkbaren Entwicklungsstand erreicht hat, "angesehen selbige *Perfection* dermassen groß / daß sehr zu zweiffelen / ob wir auch der *Posterität* . . . in denen so mancherley seltzamen *inventionibus* höher zukommen / oder auch mehr newes zu erfinden / etwas nachlassen werden"[34]. Aus der Verschränkung der Dichtkunst mit der Wissenschaft—naturgemäß mehr Idee als Wirklichkeit—leiten die Dichter ihre neubegründete Erwartung ihrer dichterischen Unsterblichkeit ab, Zesen mit Berufung auf die "volkommene kündigkeit aller wissenschafften und künste"[35], Rist mit der Gewißheit, daß die Vollkommenheit seiner Verse auf den "Legibus" beruhe, die den "Regulen" "auß der Sprachen Natur" entsprechen: "Die Früchte . . . sind unsterblich / und wird man sich derselben (ob Gott wil) so lange können bedienen / so lange noch Leute fürhanden / welche dergleichen Bücher zu lesen sich nicht lassen verdriessen"[36]. Die Dichtkunst als Wissenschaft, der Dichter als Wissenschaftler: die hochgesteckten Ziele mußten sich im frühen 18. Jahrhundert verlieren.

Die Entwicklungen in der Frühaufklärung leiten das Dichterverständnis in andere Bahnen. Zwar hält Gottsched noch am Ideal des gelehrten Dichters fest: "So wird denn ein Poet . . . sich nicht ohne eine weitläuftige Gelehrsamkeit behelfen können. Es ist keine Wissenschaft von seinem Bezirke ganz ausgeschlossen. Er muß zum wenigsten von allem etwas wissen, in allen Theilen der unter uns blühenden Gelahrtheit sich ziemlicher maßen umgesehen haben"[37]. Aber Gottscheds Kritik gilt dem formalen Einsatz der Gelehrsamkeit in *inventio* und *elocutio* der Barockdichter; dagegen begreift er das Wissen eher allgemein, um es in den Dienst der Mimesis zu stellen.[38] Das erfordert ein ganz anderes Verfahren als das rhetorische, dessen systematische Stoffindung Verfügbarkeit wie Abrufbarkeit des gesamten Wissens zur Voraussetzung hat. Parallel dazu wird das Vertrauen auf den poetischen Geist erheblich heruntergesetzt. Der "göttliche Trieb" erfährt eine Reduzierung auf ein "gutes und zum Nachahmen geschicktes Naturell"[39]. Findet man auch Übereinstimmung mit Zesen, wenn Gottsched formuliert, "eine gar zu hitzige Einbildungskraft macht unsinnige Dichter: dafern das Feuer der Phantasie nicht durch eine gesunde Vernunft gemäßiget wird"[40], so ist doch die Wertschätzung des *ingeniums* merklich gedämpft. Im Zuge der Verwissenschaftlichung der Poetik wird das *iudicium* höher eingestuft, und dafür ist umfassende Bildung unumgänglich.[41] Gottscheds Befürwortung gelehrter Bildung ist denn auch kaum mehr als eine Schutzmaßnahme gegenüber dem allzu naiven Dichter: "Begeht er nun Fehler, die von seiner Unwissenheit in Künsten und Wissenschaften zeugen, so verliert er sein Ansehen . . . Ein einzig Wort kann ihn also in Hochachtung oder in Verachtung setzen; nachdem es entweder seine Gelehrsamkeit, oder Unwissenheit an den Tag legt"[42].

Dichten ist nicht länger eine Wissenschaft, denn der poetischen Arbeitsweise geht die strenge Urteilskraft ab und das poetische Erzeugnis läßt keinen Vernunftschluß zu. Zur poetikinternen Neufundierung des Dichtertums und zur Modifizierung seines gelehrten Anspruchs gesellt sich das Bewußtsein, daß der Dichter mit den aufblühenden Naturwissenschaften ohnehin nicht hätte Schritt halten können. Es kommt noch hinzu, daß aus mannigfachen Ursachen der Gelehrtenstand an Geltung eingebüßt hatte. Wissenschaft verlor für den Dichter ein Großteil ihrer Attraktivität, sein Selbstverständnis konnte von dorther kaum noch Impulse beziehen. Obwohl der gelehrte Charakter der Dichtkunst zunächst unbestritten blieb, ist eine spürbare Ernüchterung eingetreten. Die Bedeutung des Dichters in seiner sozialen Funktion beschränkt sich (wie von alters her) auf den bildungspraktischen und den ethisch-erbaulichen Zweck; das wetteifernde Moment entfällt. Aus dieser Orientierung nährt sich beispielsweise das Selbstverständnis von Barthold Hinrich Brockes, der mit seiner umfangreichen Gedichtsammlung *Irdisches Vergnügen in Gott, bestehend in Physicalisch- und Moralischen Gedichten* (1721–48) den Geschmack der Zeitgenossen genau zu treffen wußte: "Wann ich . . . gar bald gewahr ward, daß die Poesie, wofern sie keinen sonderlichen und zwar nützlichen Endzweck hätte, ein leeres Wortspiel sey, und keine Hochachtung verdiente, als bemühete ich mich solche Objecta meiner Dichtkunst zu erwehlen, woraus die Menschen nebst einer erlaubten Belustigung zugleich erbauet werden mögen"[43]. Es fehlt jeder Hinweis auf die Kunstvollkommenheit oder den ausgezeichneten Stand der Dichtkunst; am Rande vermerkt Brockes seinen "natürlichen Trieb", es scheinen der nützliche "Endzweck" und die Versicherung, "daß selbiges Buch . . . nicht ohne Nutzen gewesen", dem Dichter ganz zu genügen. Das markiert den Abstand zur humanistisch gelehrten Tradition, wodurch auch das Selbstverständnis des Dichters bestimmt ist.

Im Vergleich zu den Wissenschaften, die auf mathematisch-astronomischer Grundlage sich anschicken den Kosmos zu erobern, hat die Dichtkunst neue Bescheidenheit gelernt. Die Eroberung des Weltraums faszinierte die Schweizer Bodmer und Breitinger in besonderem Maße:

> Die Künste und Wissenschaften sind durch den Fleiß der Menschen auf das höchste gestiegen; . . . die Welt ist jetzo unendlich weiter, als sie ehmals war, und wir sehen alles in einer andern Ordnung, und mit andern Augen an; die festen und cristallenen Himmel, vormahls die ewige Wohnung einer Menge vergötterter Hirn-Geburten, sind jetzo nichts weiters, als ein unermeßlicher und rinnender Raum, in welchem tausend neue Welten, die eben so wohl als unsere Erde bevölkert seyn können, herum schwimmen.[44]

Die Schweizer geben sich nicht zufrieden mit der Nachahmung des Wirklichen; sie schicken die Phantasie auf die Suche nach möglichen neuen Welten. Der Dichter erhält so, als Schöpfer, seine kreative Kraft wieder: "Ein jedes wohlerfundenes Gedicht ist darum nicht anders anzusehen, als eine Historie aus einer andern möglichen Welt: Und in dieser Absicht kömmt auch dem Dichter alleine der Nahme ποιητου, eines Schöpfers, zu"[45]. Hier kommen bekanntlich ältere Traditionen zum Tragen, die neu belebt und neu verstanden werden. Augustus Buchner, der Lehrer Zesens und Klajs, hatte den kreativen Aspekt der poetischen Arbeit auffällig betont, und bei seinen Schülern war das nicht vergessen worden.[46] In der "neubarocken" Periode, wie Heinz Otto Burger die Zeit zwischen 1720 und 1750 genannt hat[47], knüpfen die Schweizer, während Gottsched aus Wolffs Lehre nur den Witz als die geistreiche Kombinationsgabe entlehnt hatte, an Wolffs *facultas imaginandi* an, was die Möglichkeit bot, auch die Theorie von der himmlischen Inspiration aus der Tradition zu erneuern und die "himmelansteigenden" Dichter des 17. Jahrhunderts wieder positiv zu bewerten. Ihr Gesinnungsgenosse Jakob Immanuel Pyra läßt in seinem *Tempel der wahren Dichtkunst* (1737) unter den Dichtern, die vom himmlischen Feuer entflammt sind, u. a. Opitz, Fleming, Dach, Gerhardt, Gryphius und Rist figurieren. Für Klopstock war der Boden bereitet, als er schon in der Abschiedsrede zu Schulpforta die Kategorie der göttlichen Inspiration und den Ehrennamen des Dichters, "Schöpfer", programmatisch auf den Schild erhob. Von dieser Position aus wurde eine im wahrsten Sinn poetische Eroberung des Kosmos denkbar und konnte der inspirierte Dichter die himmlischen Gefilde durchstreifen.

Dadurch, daß Klopstock das schöpferische Moment unterstreicht und den inspirierten Dichter mit der Aura des Propheten und Priesters umgibt, ist sein Erfindungsbegriff trotz mancher Anklänge an die rhetorische Tradition doch in der Hauptsache innovatorisch bestimmt, und zwar schon deshalb, weil Dichtung in seinem Verständnis eine eigene Erkenntnisart darstellt. Ohne hier auf das komplexe Bedeutungsfeld von "Entdecken" und "Erfinden" einzugehen, darf gesagt werden, daß das "Erfinden" zu den ersten Fähigkeiten des Dichters gehört, das "Entdecken" aber die Hauptaufgabe des Wissenschaftlers ist. Dennoch gibt es im Schnittpunkt des Genialen Übereinstimmungen, die Klopstock an den vorbildlichen Naturwissenschaften entwickelt hat.[48] Die Berührungspunkte finden sich im Bereich des "Neuen", und so stehen Wissenschaftler und Künstler in Klopstocks Entwurf einer "Gelehrtenrepublik" in einer Linie. Arbeiten doch beide in diesem kreativen Sinn am Fortschritt der Nation; für beide beansprucht Klopstock soziale Unabhängigkeit und Selbständigkeit.[49] Damit ist die soziale Rangerhöhung der Dichter vollzogen. Von der Wissenschaft hat der Dichter nichts zu erhoffen; ohnehin habe die "Polyhistorey" abgewirtschaftet und sei dem neuen Übel der "Polytheorey" entgegenzutreten.[50] Die Poesie dagegen besitzt eine andere, eigene Qualität. Auf wessen Seite die Vorzüge sind, kann also nicht zweifelhaft sein: "Andres ist ganz deß Wissen und Thun, der erfindet" (Ode "Der Unterschied", 1771).

Während Rist und Zesen sich von der Erde erheben im Sinne der seligen Geister, die in Ciceros *Somnium Scipionis* zur Verewigung ans Firmament versetzt wurden, schwingt sich Klopstock, der "heilige Dichter", beseligt vom göttlichen Feuer hinauf. Er folgt der spiritualistischen Traditionslinie, in der auch Johann Klaj steht, ohne dessen Trittbretts des gelehrten Wissens zu bedürfen:

> Lernt; die Natur schrieb in das Herz sein Gesetz ihm!
> Toren, er kennt's, und sich selbst streng, ist er Täter.[51]

Die Genieästhetik favorisiert den lyrischen Aufschwung (wenn sie auch eher die Metapher des Adlers benutzt[52]), aber sie kennt keine andere Bedingung als das "glühende Herz". Bald befreit sie sich auch vom "Fünklein" des christlichen Gottes, um im Zeichen Pindars Erhebungsmomente zu zeitigen, die—sei es für Augenblicke der Begeisterung—Deukalions Flutschwamm vergessen machen. Der junge Goethe setzt mit "Wandrers Sturmlied" die neue literarische Qualität für ein Theorem, um das sich die Aufklärungspoetik und die junge Dichtergeneration mit wechselnden Akzenten eifrig bemüht hatten.[53]

Anmerkungen

1. Paul Fleming, *Deutsche Gedichte*, hrsg. v. Volker Meid (Stuttgart: Reclam, 1986), S. 112.

2. Wilhelm Kühlmann, "Sterben als heroischer Akt. Zu Paul Flemings *Grabschrifft"*, in *Gedichte und Interpretationen, Bd. 1: Renaissance und Barock*, hrsg. v. Volker Meid, (Stuttgart: Reclam, 1982), S. 168–75.

3. Ludwig Fischer, *Gebundene Rede. Dichtung und Rhetorik in der literarischen Theorie des Barock in Deutschland* (Tübingen: Niemeyer, 1968), S. 8.

4. Wulf Segebrecht, *Das Gelegenheitsgedicht. Ein Beitrag zur Geschichte und Poetik der deutschen Lyrik* (Stuttgart: Metzler, 1977); Wilfried Barner, *Barockrhetorik. Untersuchungen zu ihren geschichtlichen Grundlagen* (Tübingen: Niemeyer, 1970).

5. Barner, *Barockrhetorik*, S. 238.

6. Fischer, *Gebundene Rede*, Kap. 3; über den "poetischen Geist", S. 37–52.

7. Joachim Dyck, *Ticht-Kunst. Deutsche Barockpoetik und rhetorische Tradition* (Bad Homburg v. d. Höhe: Gehlen, 1966), S. 113–34: "Das Selbstverständnis des Dichters: ein Argumentationssystem."

8. Ebd., S. 129.

9. Barner, *Barockrhetorik*, S. 234.

10. Sigmund von Birken, *Teutsche Rede- bind- und Dicht-Kunst* (Nürnberg: Christof Riegel, 1679), S. 167–83.

11. Philipp von Zesen, *Sämtliche Werke*, Bd. 11, hrsg. v. Ulrich Maché (Berlin: de Gruyter, 1974), S. 301–2 bzw. 297.

12. Dyck, *Ticht-Kunst*, S. 125–29; Fischer, *Gebundene Rede*, S. 61–63.

13. Martin Opitz, *Buch von der deutschen Poeterey*, 6 Aufl., hrsg. v. Wilhelm Braune (Tübingen: Niemeyer, 1954), S. 10.

14. Dyck, *Ticht-Kunst*, S. 129–34; Barner, *Barockrhetorik*, S. 225–32; Gunter Grimm, *Literatur und Gelehrtentum in Deutschland. Untersuchungen zum Wandel ihres Verhältnisses vom Humanismus bis zur Frühaufklärung* (Tübingen: Niemeyer, 1983), insbes. S. 196–202.

15. Georg Philipp Harsdörffer, *Frauenzimmer Gesprächspiele*, 5. Teil, Neudruck hrsg. v. Irmgard Böttcher (Tübingen: Niemeyer, 1962), S. 20.

16. Zesen, *Sämtliche Werke*, 11:300–301.

17. Magnus Daniel Omeis, *Gründliche Anleitung zur Teutschen accuraten Reim- und Dicht-Kunst* (Nürnberg: Wolfgang Michahelles u. Johann Adolph, 1704), S. 129.

18. Johann Klaj, *Lobrede der Teutschen Poeterey* (Nürnberg: Wolffgang Endter, 1645), S. 5. Zitiert nach dem Neudruck Johann Klaj, *Redeoratorien*, hrsg. v. Conrad Wiedemann (Tübingen: Niemeyer, 1965), S. 389.

19. Klaj, *Lobrede*, S. 4 [S. 388]; Justus Georg Schottelius, *Ausführliche Arbeit Von der Teutschen HaubtSprache* (Braunschweig: Christoff Friederich Zillingern, 1663), Neudruck hrsg. v. Wolfgang Hecht (Tübingen: Niemeyer, 1967), S. 105 bzw. 106–7 ("Die siebende Lobrede"):

Es sind die Gelahrten alters her hierin überall einhellig / daß die Poesis
etwas Himlisches und uhrsprünglich von den Göttern sey. . . Dannen-
hero kan ein solcher nach Kunst und Geist recht abgerichteter Poet /
wan er nur wil / in ein Gespräch gleichsam mit den Göttern sich einlas
sen / er kan das überirrdische freymütiglich durchwanderen / das ar-
beitselige wünschen der Welt / als mit geflügelter Freiheit überstrei-
chen / sich nur in sich / und sich selbst in eine Göttliche Freudenliebe
verwikelen. Und dieses alles veruhrsachen die / so auf eine hohe liebliche Art geordnete Worte / und die in der Sprache wohnende Wollust:
daß also ein Poet meinet / er nehme die Göttinnen in seinen Schutz /
und werde hinwieder von denselben süssesten Freundinnen auf einen
Luftweg der Ewigkeit geleitet / er spatziere gleichsam durch die Blu-
menreichesten Auen der Wissenschaften / erlustige sich in den wunder-
künstlichsten Lustgarten der Natur / erhebe sich auf den Göttlichen Hügel der Weißheit / überschaue das Sorgenreiche Wesen der Eitelkeit /
und binde seine Augen und Sinnen an den Himmel.

20. Johann Matthäus Meyfart, *Teutsche Rhetorica oder Redekunst* (Coburg:
Friderich Gruner, 1634), Neudruck hrsg. v. Erich Trunz (Tübingen: Niemeyer, 1977), Ende des 1. Kap., S. 7–11.
21. Ferdinand van Ingen, "Philipp von Zesens Gedichte an die Weisheit",
in *Rezeption und Produktion zwischen 1570 und 1730. Festschrift für Günther
Weydt*, hrsg. v. W. Rasch, H. Geulen und K. Haberkamm (Bern: Francke,
1972), S. 121–36.
22. Philipp von Zesen, *Der erdichteten Heidnischen Gottheiten . . . Herkunft
und Begäbnisse* (Nürnberg: Johan Hofman, 1688), S. 479.
23. Vgl. Ferdinand van Ingen, "Philipp von Zesens *Adriatische Rosemund*:
Kunst und Leben", in *Philipp von Zesen 1619–1969*, hrsg. v. Ferdinand van Ingen (Wiesbaden: Steiner, 1972), S. 47–122, speziell 74–77.
24. Philipp von Zesen, *Das Hochdeutsche Helikonische Rosentahl* (Amsterdam:
Kristof Konraden, 1669), Vorbericht, in Zesen, *Sämtliche Werke*, Bd. 12, hrsg.
v. Ulrich Maché, George Schulz-Behrend und Karl Otto (Berlin: de Gruyter,
1985), S. 199.
25. Zesen, *Rosen-mand* (Hamburg: G. Papen, 1651), Vorrede, in Zesen,
Sämtliche Werke, 11:84.
26. Zesen, *Rosen-mand*, in *Sämtliche Werke*, 11:136.
27. Philipp von Zesen, *Adriatische Rosemund*, hrsg. v. Max Hermann Jel-
linek (Halle: Niemeyer, 1899), S. 29 (Abschiedslied an Felsensohn).
28. In seinem Geschichtswerk *Niederländischer Leue* (Nürnberg: Johan Hofman, 1677), S. 77.
29. Dieter Lohmeier und Klaus Reichelt, "Johann Rist", in *Deutsche Dichter
des 17. Jahrhunderts. Ihr Leben und Werk*, hrsg. v. Harald Steinhagen und
Benno von Wiese (Berlin: Erich Schmidt, 1984), S. 347–64; Zitat S. 348.
30. *Johannis Ristii Holsati Musa Teutonica* (Hamburg: Jacob Rebenlein, 1634),
Widmungsvorrede.

31. *Johannis Ristii Holsati Poetischer Lust = Garte* (Hamburg: Zacharias Hertel, 1638), Vorrede.

32. Zesen, *Rosentahl*, in *Sämtliche Werke*, 12:186.

33. Zesen, *Rosen-mand*, in *Sämtliche Werke*, 11:111–12.

34. Rist, *Musa Teutonica*, Sig. Ajj.

35. Zesen, *Helikonische Hechel*, in *Sämtliche Werke*, 11:297.

36. Rist, *Musa Teutonica*, Sig. Avr.

37. Johann Christoph Gottsched, *Versuch einer Critischen Dichtkunst*, 4. Aufl. (Leipzig: Bernhard Christoph Breitkopf, 1751; Neudruck Darmstadt: Wissenschaftliche Buchgesellschaft, 1962), S. 105.

38. Vgl. Grimm, *Literatur und Gelehrtentum*, S. 658–65.

39. Gottsched, *Versuch einer Critischen Dichtkunst*, S. 101.

40. Ebd., S. 108.

41. Vgl. Grimm, *Literatur und Gelehrtentum*, S. 671–75.

42. Gottsched, *Versuch einer Critischen Dichtkunst*, S. 105.

43. Barthold Hinrich Brockes, *Lebens-Beschreibung (1724–1735)*, hrsg. v. J. M. Lappenberg, *Zeitschrift des Vereins für hamburgische Geschichte* 2 (1847): 169–227, Zitat S. 201; das folgende Zitat S. 202. Dazu Günter Niggl, *Geschichte der deutschen Autobiographie im 18. Jahrhundert. Theoretische Grundlegung und literarische Entfaltung* (Stuttgart: Metzler, 1977), S. 18–19.

44. Johann Jacob Breitinger, *Critische Abhandlung von der Natur, den Absichten und dem Gebrauche der Gleichnisse*, Faksimiledruck nach der Ausgabe von 1740, mit einem Nachwort von Manfred Windfuhr (Stuttgart: Metzler, 1967), S. 286–87.

45. Johann Jacob Breitinger, *Critische Dichtkunst*, Faksimiledruck nach der Ausgabe von 1740, mit einem Nachwort von Wolfgang Bender, 2 Bde. (Stuttgart: Niemeyer, 1966), 2:60.

46. *Augustus Buchners Poet*, aus dem Nachlaß hrsg. v. O. Prätorius (Wittenberg: Michael Wenden, 1665), S. 25–47, in Augustus Buchner, *Anleitung zur deutschen Poeterey / Poet*, hrsg. v. Marian Szyrocki, (Tübingen: Niemeyer, 1966).

47. Heinz Otto Burger, "Deutsche Aufklärung im Widerspiel zu Barock und 'Neubarock' ", in *"Dasein heißt eine Rolle spielen." Studien zur deutschen Literaturgeschichte* (München: Hanser, 1963), S. 94–119.

48. Bernd Fabian, "Der Naturwissenschaftler als Originalgenie", in *Europäische Aufklärung: Festschrift für H. Dieckmann zum 60. Geburtstag*, hrsg. v. Fritz Schalk und Hugo Friedrich (München: Fink, 1967), S. 47–68.

49. Wilhelm Große, *Studien zur Klopstocks Poetik* (München: Fink, 1977), S. 72–79. Auch bei Klopstock spielt darin das soziale Element eine wichtige Rolle, vgl. Große, S. 72: "Klopstock konstruiert also seine Gelehrtenrepublik als utopischen Gegenentwurf zur bestehenden Gesellschaft."

50. *Klopstocks Sämmtliche Werke*, 12 Bde. (Leipzig: Göschen, 1823), 12:87.

51. Aus der Ode "Ästhetiker" (1782).

52. Günther Peters, *Der zerrissene Engel. Genieästhetik und literarische Selbstdarstellung im achtzehnten Jahrhundert* (Stuttgart: Niemeyer, 1982), S. 121–30.

53. Ferdinand van Ingen, "Goethes Hymnen und die zeitgenössische Poetik", in *Goethe im Kontext. Kunst und Humanität, Naturwissenschaft und Politik von der Aufklärung bis zur Restauration. Ein Symposium*, hrsg. v. Wolfgang Wittkowski (Tübingen: Niemeyer, 1984), S. 1–16.

14. Poets Addressing Themselves: An Authorial Posture in Seventeenth-Century German Poetry

Barton W. Browning

Fixed in an age that balances between the still firmly embedded personal identities of the sixteenth century and the self-proclaimed individual autonomy of the eighteenth century, German poetry of the Baroque era reflects a growing concern with the self and personal identity. In this respect, questions have often been raised as to the identity of the poetic self that appears in German Baroque poetry and especially as to the fictive quality of the *ich* that appears ever more frequently in the literature of this age.

The fictive ego, as critics have recognized even in the experiential poetry of the eighteenth and nineteenth centuries, is a literary device in which the reader equates poetic voice and authorial identity only with great peril. Even in those cases where the poet's biographical data correspond exactly to a poem's content, the argument can well be made that the author's life and circumstances are, in the final analysis, irrelevant to the fictional construct embedded in the poem's literary structure. With these caveats in mind, it may then be of interest to look somewhat more closely at the manner in which various seventeenth-century poets have dealt with the question of self-depiction and self-address.

Well known for its representative rather than individual portrayal of people and things, seventeenth-century German lyric ranges widely in its use of the poetic ego. One finds, for example, the blandly universal use of the poetic self, the poet's description of himself or herself as an object for study, the use of a poet's identity as an object of self-analysis and self-examination, and in a few cases, situations in which authors depict themselves in a dialogue with their own poetic voices, a sort of double self-portrayal, wherein the authorial voice directly addresses the fictive persona of the individual author.

Depending upon the manner in which an author employs the fictive self in the poem, a rough typology might then be established to

categorize the varied uses of the poetically embodied self in seventeenth-century German poetry. A first stage in this progression is
obviously the conventional use of the poetic ego in a naive manner
that lays little claim to any further personal connection. The poet
contrasts, for example, the sadness of the poet's own poetic *ich* with
the joy of nature in such a way as to lead to reflection on the world and
humankind's place therein. A similarly universal ego permeates most
of the Petrarchian lyric of the age. Since the beloved is depicted in
stereotypical and often mechanically replicated or "wittily" altered
metaphors, the poetic self has primarily representative rather than
individual significance. One thinks of Martin Opitz's "Ich empfinde
fast ein Grauen" or, in a more narrowly Petrarchian mode, of Christian Hofmann von Hofmannswaldau's "An Melinden," poems where
the use of the first-person singular has only a highly stylized relevance
to the individual authors themselves.[1] A third level of poetic self-
depiction derives from the traditional separation of the self into distinct spheres. Originally a topos of theological reflection, the division
of self into body and soul or separate and contrary halves finds common usage in both secular and religious verse. Catharina Regina von
Greiffenberg employed this division of the self as a means of self-
exhortation in her sonnet "In äusserster Widerwärtigkeit," when she
exhorts her heart to remain steadfast in the face of a lamentable fate:

> faß dir / mein Herz / ein Herz / und Leuen mütig steh'
> im Unglücks-mittel-punct / das jederman dann seh /
> wie deine Tugend sich in trübsal pflegt zu feinen.[2]

Opitz's well-known poem "Ich will diß halbe mich / was wir den
Cörper nennen" makes use of a similar division of the self only to
prove merely an elaborate paean to the heavenly beauty of the lady
celebrated in his poem.[3] And Paul Fleming's agonizingly convoluted
"Auf ihr Abwesen" with its characteristic line, "Ich irrte hin und her
und suchte mich in mir, / und wuste dieses nicht, daß ich ganz war in
dir," clearly betrays the manifestly impersonal delight in verbal play
and paradox that typified the Neo-Latin tradition.[4]

Coming closer to the actual forms of authorial self-address in the
narrower sense, one finds numerous examples of the poetic ego dis-
cussing experiences, concerns, or other biographically related matters. For purposes of definition, this grouping includes those poems
in which poets speak in the first person and describe themselves by
means of references with clearly biographical relevance, even though
the poem may and usually does eventuate in a conclusion embodying
a generalized and implicitly universal truth. A prime example of this

type of self-examination is Hofmannswaldau's "Gedanken bei Antretung des funffzigsten Jahres" with its rueful personal confirmation that fifty is in fact less that twenty-five: "Das funfftzig schwächer sind als fünff und zwantzig waren."[5] Despite its specifically occasional character as a commemoration of Hofmannswaldau's fiftieth birthday, the poem rapidly moves from a generalized reminder of the first personal experiences with incipient physical decay to a more representative prayer that the authorial persona be spared, or at least experience only to a modest extent the sickness and sorrow that often accompany the aging process. His prayer is further that he might avoid the melancholy, mockery, false hopes, selfishness, and envy that can burden and crush one's happiness in advancing years. The poem then concludes with the pious wish that his gravestone should bear the conventionally dualistic resolution, "Der Kern ist weg / die Schalen sind vergraben." Although Hofmannswaldau's individual fate may have provided the original impetus for the poem, the recognition contained in its final message is not singular but instead applicable to the wide range of humanity.

Similarly, Paul Fleming's famous "Grabschrift" combines the impression of personal biographical detail with the wish for a positive conclusion to his earthly sojourn. Aside from the poem's descriptive caption identifying it as a deathbed composition, the poetic *ich* of this famous poem has little that relates it precisely to Fleming himself.[6] The poetic persona has enjoyed a good family background and believes himself to have achieved distinction as a poet in his native tongue. Otherwise, his theatrically envisioned departure and his self-effacing heroism in the face of imminent death—"Was frei dem Tode steht, das tu er seinem Feinde"—confirm his participation in the universal event of human finitude. Even the concluding paradoxical self-affirmation, "An mir ist minder Nichts, das lebet, als mein Leben," is little more than a restatement of the conventional body-soul duality. In what is presented as the final summation of Fleming's earthly existence, the narrative ego moves rapidly from its individual case to the safer ground of a generalized statement of the human condition, albeit stated here with a positive emphasis. The apparent individuality implicit in the poet's use of the first-person singular does not invalidate the fictive quality of the work; the poem ultimately constitutes a descriptive celebration of the triumphs of vernacular poetry while proposing a personal stance worthy of emulation.

It was, moreover, Paul Fleming who employed the mode of poetic self-address to the greatest effect in German Baroque poetry, and it is on the basis of his efforts that one can categorize more precisely further types of poetic self-address. When Bernhard Sorg dealt with the issue of self-address in German Baroque poetry, he erroneously conflated dissimilar forms by including such poems as Fleming's "Grabschrift" in his grouping of "Selbst-Anrede" poems.[7] Although not common enough in the seventeenth century to constitute its own genre, the poem of self-address as defined here involves the narrative voice of the poem—that of the poet—engaging the persona of the poet in a truncated conversation with the self producing thereby what is, quite literally, a *Selbstgespräch*.

Fleming's "An sich"—"Sei dennoch unverzagt, gieb dennoch unverloren"—is apparently the most personal of dialogues.[8] An implied conversation takes place between the poet's narrative voice and the persona of the poet as the putative recipient of the sonnet's message. The address to the poet's persona consists of series of imperatives on how to behave in the world, how to react to the vagaries of fate, and finally how to proceed among the deceptive illusions of life's transitory show: "Laß deinen eiteln Wahn, / und eh' du förder gehst, so geh' in dich zurücke." This admonition to self-restraint and self-reliance culminates in the final couplet, which, as opposed to the earlier sections of the poem, appears in the shape of a generalized and impersonal epigrammatic formulation. The persona of the poet—the object of such repeated admonitions as "sey, gieb, nim, Tu, Schau, Laß, geh"—fades from immediate focus as the poet's narrative voice summarizes the poem's message: "Wer sein selbst Meister ist und sich beherrschen kan / dem ist die weite Welt und Alles untertan." The sequence is conventional, a series of experiences or examples followed by a comprehensive summation of the major thought to be derived from the poem. For traditional sonneteers of the seventeenth century, the normal event of such a series is the turn to God in the form of a brief prayer pleading for divine intercession to relieve the woes previously related.[9] Within the Petrarchian tradition the poet's request is, understandably, for intercession of a more worldly sort. In "An sich," the final epigram employs a third conventional alternative by expressing in compressed form a generally applicable statement of universal validity.

One of the remarkable aspects of this sonnet is the gain in both impact and verisimilitude that derives from its formulation as an implicit dialogue between the poet and his poetic self. The impression left by the poem is thus dependent not merely upon the thoughts expressed but also upon the rhetorical shape Fleming has imposed on his material. In this context Fleming's other poems can provide both a partial guide to his poetic techniques as well as an indication of the genesis of the remarkable resonance that "An sich" has enjoyed among centuries of readers.

It is first of all significant that the poem of address was one of Fleming's favorite devices. His collected works are filled with poems entitled *An* or *Auff*, for example, "An Kordelien," "An Makarien," "An Sidonien," or alternatively, "Auff der Liebsten Demant," "Auff ihr Armband," and in yet another formulation of the address poem, "Er redet ihre Hals-Perlen an."[10] His poetry of address embraces parts of the body as well as persons and objects—"An ihren Mund," "Er redet ihre Thränen an," and so on—and even includes geographical locations: "Er redet die Stadt Moßkow an." That one should find such a preponderance of address poems among Fleming's works is hardly unique or even surprising. The Neo-Latin and the Petrarchistic traditions that nourished Fleming's poetic roots abound, as Karl Otto Conrady noted, in such examples of "Anrede-Lyrik."[11] As it proves, Fleming's "An sich" is not the only poem of direct self-address among his writings. In the sonnet "Er redet sich selber an," which curiously enough is anthologized among his love poems, Fleming again adopts the pose of addressing himself.[12] Here the poet's narrative voice castigates his own poetic persona for having abandoned his university studies, and he berates himself for having given in to the fruitless wanderlust that has marred the rest of his life. With an emphatic shake of his rhetorical finger the narrative voice admonishes himself: "Tu Rechnung von dir selbst, von dir und deiner Tat!" As opposed to the positive summation at the conclusion of "An sich," the narrative voice terminates its catalogue of self-accusation with the despairing conviction that the poet's persona is doomed to failure because he is too foolish to heed his own counsel:

Doch, du bist wider dich. Die Sehnsucht fremder Sachen,
was wird sie dermaleins noch endlich aus dir machen,
weil auch dein eigner Rat bei dir selbst Stat nicht hat?

Even though "Er redet sich selber an" contains little of the stoic self-assertion characteristic of "An sich," both sonnets provoke a similar anticipation on the part of the reader as to what communication will take place between self and self within the medium of the poem. The reason for this anticipation is not inherent purely in the poem's content but resides to a great extent in the structure of the poem itself. To understand this attraction it is worthwhile to look briefly at the rhetorical roots underlying this particular authorial posture.

As classically defined, the term *apostrophe* describes an orator's shift away from the normal public to address a second public, be it an absent person, the dead, the gods, or objects.[13] Quintilian further holds that the apostrophe constitutes an appeal to the emotions in that it purportedly expresses a degree of feeling beyond that appropriate to the usual speaker–public relationship.[14] The apostrophe thus relies upon the assumption of a "normal" set of listeners that the speaker abandons in favor of a presumptive second audience. Generally speaking, in seventeenth-century German lyric poetry the reader is assumed to constitute the poet's primary audience; there is an implicit mutuality of interest between poet and reader, and it is tacitly understood that the poem will address the reader as the prime recipient of its message. An apostrophe, however, shifts the apparent focus of the poetic dialogue. Within the fictional context of the poem the reader no longer serves as the primary recipient of the poetic message but rather as an auditor to the conversation between the narrative voice and the person or object addressed. The poetic apostrophe takes place as though the reader were not actually present but rather, as it were, accidentally in a position to apprehend the communication of the narrative voice.

In the case of such poems as "An sich" or "Er redet sich selber an," Fleming's narrative voice addresses its apostrophe to Fleming's own poetic persona. The effect is that of a double distancing; the audience is privy not merely to a restricted conversation but in fact finds itself in an omniscient situation and party to that most intimate of exchanges, that between self and self. If the conventional proposal holds that modern poetry is not heard but overheard, one would need to make a historical distinction in dealing with Fleming's sonnets. "An sich" and "Er redet sich selber an" are indeed dialogues with the self overheard by the reader, but at the same time they are still creatures of their age, that is, calculated performances intended, among other things, to inculcate in the reader those values that the poet's persona is expected to learn. The author's posture is thus self-conscious in both senses of the word. At the poem's first and most literal level, the narrative voice is concerned with the weaknesses of the poetic persona, problems that need the assurance of a supportive admonition. Simultaneously, the poem's rhetorically trained creator is aware that his putative poetic self-dialogue is making an impact on an audience that, in terms of his poetic fiction, does not exist. As in the case of an actor's monologue, which supposedly reveals a character's deepest thoughts and fears, the authorial self-address employed in these poems plays with the representation of closed intimacy yet with the same structural gesture communicates the poet's message to his presumptive auditors.

Fleming's two "An sich" poems thus constitute rhetorically stylized apostrophes to the self. The poet's narrative voice assumes an authorial posture of self-confrontation and self-exhortation that departs from the normal mode of poet–reader communication and serves to plead, although somewhat less obtrusively than usual, for the poet's didactic intent. The poet's normal audience remains his actual audience just as in judicial rhetoric the judge remains the true audience even though the rhetorician's apostrophe seemingly shifts his address to another person or object. But for a brief span these poems exploit the impression of a closed dialogue with the self in order to enhance both their verisimilitude and their ultimate impact. What appear to be highly personal communications reveal themselves upon closer inspection to be so general as to be impersonal in the extreme, and the self addressed in these poems proves ultimately to be exemplary rather than individual, universal rather than personal.

Anton Ulrich von Braunschweig's "Gedult-Liedlein" provides a useful contrast.[15] Whereas the theme is almost precisely that of "An sich"—an admonishment to steadfastness in a world of pain and disillusion—Anton Ulrich employs a more conventional and ultimately less impressive poetic stratagem. In the first four strophes his narrative voice speaks in the first person relating his sorry state and reflecting upon the sorry state of his fictive ego and the misery he has been forced to bear: "MIt Unmuht schlaff ich ein / erwach mit Unmuth wieder / / Betracht mit Unmuht stets / mein Elend auff und nieder." The growing realization that patience and constancy are the sole remedies for his distress then leads to the final two strophes where the narrative voice appears to turn from the "normal" audience of the poem and takes the form of an exhortative address: "Verhön dein böses Glück / verlach sein tolles Wüten / / erwarte was es doch / wil endlich aus dir brüten." Since the poem provides no precise identification of the authority dispensing this advice, the last two strophes can be read, as in the Fleming poems, as prescriptive self-admonition. Yet the poem lacks the rhetorical punch of Fleming's effort. The putative *Selbstgespräch* that informs the structure of "An sich" is here blunted by an ineffective transition to the sphere of direct advice and counsel. The instruction may be the same, but the rhetorical impact is weaker in the absence of a clearly defined and appropriately exploited *Rollenspiel*.

Fleming seems to have found few disciples in his poetry of self-address. To be sure, rhetorical conventions changed somewhat as German poetry moved into mid-century, and the Neo-Latin tradition

of the poem of address ceded its dominance as other poetic forms
gained ascendancy. Nonetheless, one further notable example of the
poem of self-address is still to be found in the poetry of Andreas
Gryphius.

Self-description and self-analysis lie, of course, at the heart of much
of Gryphius's poetry. He uses his narrative persona again and again as
a shocked and dismayed observer communicating to his "normal"
audience his despair about the transitoriness of the world and the
blindness of those who allow themselves to be deluded by its seeming permanence. Gryphius repeatedly employs rhetorical questions,
"Was sind wir Menschen doch," and direct address to the reader, "Du
siehst wohin du siehst," as well as the all-inclusive first-person plural,
"Wir sind doch nunmehr ganz / ja mehr als ganz verheeret," to establish a sense of engagement between poem and public. And, as was the
case with Fleming and Hofmannswaldau, Gryphius uses his own fate
as a demonstration of the wantonness of time's ravaging power. One
thinks of the two "Thränen in schwerer Krankheit" poems with their
detailed recapitulations of his woeful physical condition. In the forty-
eighth poem of his first book of sonnets, however, Gryphius employs
the motif of self-address in a new and striking fashion. In this poem,
which carries the revealing title "An sich selbst," he plunges immediately into self-confrontation: "MIr grawet vor mir selbst / mir zittern
alle glieder."[16] The occasion for this shattering experience is the encounter of Gryphius's poetic persona with his own image as he con-
templates his likeness as though viewing it in a mirror. The narrative
voice expresses its overwhelming sense of revulsion:

> Wen ich die lipp' vnd naß' vnd beider augen kluft /
> Die blindt vom wachen sindt / des atems schwere luft
> Betracht / vndt die nun schon erstorbnen augen-lieder.

And in a passage of special poignancy for a poet, he further observes:
"Die zunge / schwartz vom brandt felt mitt den worten nieder / /
Undt lalt ich weis nicht was."

Gryphius varies here the pattern that Fleming had established in his
self-address poems. Gryphius's rhetorically calculated self-confrontation arises not through an impassioned apostrophe to his poetic persona but rather through a visual image epitomizing the physical disin-
tegration of his narrative ego. In "An sich selbst" Gryphius quite
literally reflects upon his own image, thereby forcing consideration of
the destructive powers of corporeal decay so readily apparent in his
own features. This visual encounter with his own physical image then
leads to a listing of the symptoms accompanying his decline, his

emaciated physique, his constant state of pain, and his inability to gain respite from physical torment. The poem's final tercet provides the epigrammatic lesson to be drawn from this self-depiction:

Was ist der hohe ruhm / vndt jugendt / ehr vnd kunst?
Wen diese stunde kompt: wirdt alles rauch vndt dunst.
Und eine noth mus vns mitt allem vorsatz tödten.

Although Gryphius's personal suffering may have provided the impetus for this sonnet, his biographical details are, in the final analysis, irrelevant to the self-encounter portrayed in the poem. As D. Jöns showed in his Gryphius study, the details of Gryphius's vision of himself have more than personal significance.[17] Writing in an age acutely sensitive to the emblematic significance of visual images, Gryphius introduces the likeness of his poetic persona as an opportunity for emblematic interpretation. The somewhat enigmatic inscription "An sich selbst" proves not to be an egotistical dedication; it reveals itself rather in the light of the subsequent self-description to be the opposite of vain self-absorption. With the narrative voice's exact delineation of the poet's visual image, Gryphius provides the reader with an emblematic *pictura*. The epigrammatic warning contained in the final tercet then serves as an *inscriptio* elucidating both the portrait embodied in the mirrored image and its accompanying titular inscription. The most personal visual aspect of human identity, an individual's own image, becomes a representative display, a universal *memento mori* well calculated to recall to the poet's fellow humans the limits of their own finitude.

One further aspect of Gryphius's approach should be mentioned. By using the mirror reflection of the self, Gryphius calls up a long-established tradition of the mirror remarkable for its seemingly self-contradictory duality.[18] The mirror on the one hand is a classical symbol of vanity, the malignant self-absorption that blinds humans to the world beyond their own identities. On the other hand, the mirror also serves as a symbol of self-recognition in the highest sense, the fruitful encounter with the truth of one's own being. In his use of the mirrored reflection Gryphius transforms a highly individual encounter into a form of self-recognition in which we all are intended to recognize ourselves.

To recapitulate briefly: seventeenth-century German lyric abounds in references to the first-person singular, whether in the sense of a nonspecific, generalized self or a presumably autobiographical reflection. In most cases a poet who speaks in the first person to describe personal appearance, health, status, concerns, and so on, is engaged in a self-analysis that rapidly deserts the personal to reassert representative connections to the larger issues inherent in human existence. Despite this proliferation of first-person references, the poetry of the age is in essence *Gesellschaftslyrik*, that is, poems based upon shared experiences accessible to a wide range of readers. Still, as the age draws to its close, one perceives an ever-growing sense of individual identity. The highly rhetorical self-address that Fleming had mastered early in the century passes from memory, and Gryphius's ingenious emblematic variation of authorial self-address seems to have found no imitators. This is not to say that poetic self-depiction dies away; if anything, it accelerates. In the painfully autobiographical self-revelations of Johann Christian Günther, one finds a preoccupation with the individual self that, strangely enough, complements Barthold H. Brockes's equally consuming desire to rehearse the minutiae of his everyday existence. Clearly, however, the rhetorical verve of the previous century was giving way to newer tones. Crossing the poetic threshold of the eighteenth century, one apprehends a different communication with the reader concerning the self of the poet, a conversation combining concrete personal detail with didactic intent. Yet as the age of Baroque self-address fades, one cannot but feel some nostalgia for the resonant authority of Fleming's rhetorically sophisticated *Selbst-Anrede* or for the emblematic sophistication of Gryphius's address to his own image, two prime examples of an eminently Baroque authorial posture, the poet addressing himself.

Notes

1. Martin Opitz, *Gesammelte Werke*, ed. George Schulz-Behrend, BLVS 301, vol. 2, part 2 (Stuttgart: Hiersemann, 1979), pp. 684–86. Christian Hofmann von Hofmannswaldau, *Gedichte*, ed. Manfred Windfuhr (Stuttgart: Reclam, 1969), pp. 25–26.

2. Ulrich Maché and Volker Meid, eds., *Gedichte des Barock* (Stuttgart: Reclam, 1980), p. 245. Hereafter cited as Maché.

3. Opitz, *Gesammelte Werke*, p. 716.

4. Paul Fleming, *Paul Flemings deutsche Gedichte*, 2 vols., ed. J. M. Lappenberg, BLVS 82–83 (1865; rpt. Darmstadt: Wissenschaftliche Buchgesellschaft, 1965), 1:219.

5. Hofmannswaldau, *Gedichte*, pp. 132–34.

6. Fleming, *Gedichte*, 1:460. "The 'I' of this poem sees itself only as a member of a social order with a certain role to play. . . . The final boast is not so much personal as societal—this 'I' will live on because it has fulfilled the role assigned to it, that of a poet." Robert M. Browning, *German Baroque Poetry*

1618–1723 (University Park: Pennsylvania State Press, 1971), p. 26. See also the arguments presented by Joseph Leighton in chapter 15 of this book.

7. Bernhard Sorg, *Das lyrische Ich: Untersuchungen zu deutschen Gedichten von Gryphius bis Benn*, Studien zur deutschen Literatur, 80 (Tübingen: Niemeyer, 1984), pp. 47–51.

8. Fleming, *Gedichte*, 1:472.

9. For a discussion of the structural anticipation associated with the seventeenth-century sonnet, see Joseph Leighton, "Deutsche Sonett-Theorie im 17. Jahrhundert," *Europäische Tradition und deutscher Literaturbarock*, ed. Gerhart Hoffmeister (Bern: Franke, 1973), pp. 27–30.

10. Consult here the index to book 4 of Fleming's sonnets: Fleming, *Gedichte*, 1:951–53.

11. "Man hat die lateinische Lyrik mit guten Gründen als "Anredelyrik" bezeichnet. Bei den Neulateinern hat die *Anrede* bedeutendes Gewicht und kann erhebliche Weite gewinnen. Sie ist eine zentrale Stelle für Preis und Lob. In der deutschen Dichtung nimmt sie keinen geringeren Platz ein." Karl Otto Conrady, *Lateinische Dichtungstradition und deutsche Lyrik des 17. Jahrhunderts*, Bonner Arbeiten zur deutschen Literatur, 4 (Bonn: Bouvier, 1962), p. 211.

12. Fleming, *Gedichte*, 1:498.

13. Heinrich Lausberg, *Handbuch der literarischen Rhetorik*, 2 vols. (Munich: Max Hueber, 1960) 1:377–79.

14. Quintilian, *Institutiones oratoriae* 4.1.62–69.

15. Maché, pp. 251–52.

16. Andreas Gryphius, *Sonette*, ed. Marian Szyrocki, Gesamtausgabe der deutschprachigen Werke, 1 (Tübingen: Niemeyer, 1963), p. 61.

17. Dietrich Walter Jöns, *Das "Sinnen-Bild": Studien zur allegorischen Bildlichkeit bei Andreas Gryphius*, Germanistische Abhandlungen, 13 (Stuttgart: Metzler, 1966), pp. 59–82. The subsequent argument is also indebted to the studies by Albrecht Schöne and in particular to his *Emblematik und Drama im Zeitalter des Barock* (Munich: Beck, 1964).

18. See also Blake Lee Spahr's discussion of the mirror as the quintessential symbol of Baroque literature: "The Mirror and Its Image in Seventeenth-Century German Literature," in his *Problems and Perspectives: A Collection of Essays on German Baroque Literature* (Frankfurt a. M.: Lang, 1981), pp. 223–42.

15. The Poet's Voices in Occasional Baroque Poetry

Joseph Leighton

Originally the formulation of my title was a product of inner opposition to the idea of authorial self-consciousness springing from a feeling that in some way a fashionable and slightly questionable concept was being applied to a period of literature where it simply did not belong. I found the subject provocative, and it was in this spirit that I deliberately chose the plural "voices" to suggest from the outset a conviction that the voice of any Baroque poem is essentially fictional, that the poet is a role player whose work invariably consists of a series of set pieces, many of which have the status of training exercises. Nowhere is the poet's assuming a fictional role more evident than in the occasional poetry of the period, where the particular pose adopted may be determined by a whole host of social as well as literary considerations. Always at the back of my mind, however, there has been a particular poem that made me uneasy, a sonnet that refused to accommodate itself readily to the pattern I was so confidently prepared to assert. It is my reflection on this poem, Paul Fleming's "Grabschrift für sich selbst," which in essence inspired this essay. And it is to this poem that I shall return at the end of my deliberations.

If we attempt to apply the notion of authorial self-consciousness to seventeenth-century German poetry a critical problem of definition arises immediately. Are we to understand the term as meaning the poets' awareness of themselves as individuals, that is, as private rather than social or representative individuals, or does the term mean rather the authors' awareness of themselves as poets, an awareness which, insofar as it expresses itself in each poet's poetry, would involve awareness not only of the writer's specific poetic role but also of the limitations of the form or genre within which the poet has chosen to operate.

In relation to the first possibility it is perhaps appropriate to refer to an excellent article by Hugh Richmond on the question of personal identity and literary persona.[1] Richmond argues that the Renaissance marks the beginning of a new self-awareness. He writes that "partly as a result of non-literary pressures in the Renaissance the human mind acquired certain possibilities for self-definition and heightened performance which were not fully recognised in the literature of previous periods, so that the study of the use of these resources in Renaissance literature is still essential to the full development of modern personal identity" (p. 209). Richmond sees this process as a psychological development that nevertheless responds to specific social stimuli, as for instance when he argues that "private personality was fostered by a growing revulsion from orthodox public roles and services" (p. 210). Indeed he is bold enough to go further and state that "it was in the often forced flight from public duties that our modern awareness came to fruition" (p. 210). The first model that Richmond takes to demonstrate this argument is John Donne, whose poems he sees as rejecting public office and rewards while attempting to vindicate the worth of private sexual satisfactions.

Interesting and exciting though this argument appears to be, for the reader more acquainted with German poetry of the period the question immediately arises: does this model allow itself to be applied to Germany in the same way? Certainly as far as occasional poetry is concerned—and for the seventeenth century this means a substantial part of the poetry produced—one can scarcely speak of rejection of public office since it is so often the product of it. Although the theme of *Amtsverdruß* might be of great importance for a tragic hero such as Papinianus, for instance, one would expect few poets to make ostentatious display of such a theme because it might affect both their public status and their potential commissions. Occasional poetry in Germany, as Wulf Segebrecht has so clearly demonstrated, remains essentially a "Poesie der Nebenstunden," by definition therefore implying an acceptance of public duty.[2]

In another sense, too, the attempt to apply Richmond's model to seventeenth-century Germany raises a significant problem, namely the notion of privacy. As far as Germany is concerned, the current orthodox view would seem to be that the modern notion of privacy has its origins essentially in the eighteenth century and that it is not appropriate to apply it to literature of earlier periods. What Jürgen Habermas refers to as "Privatisierung des Lebens" is a process that can be observed not only in literature and the arts but in the social and economic function of the family unit.[3] This development had a strong impact on the poetry of the eighteenth century.[4] Nevertheless it is perfectly possible to find occasional poems in the seventeenth century into which a note of very personal grief or misfortune intrudes, as in the following sonnet by the Hamburg pastor Michael Johanssen written on the death of a colleague in 1654:

> Was mir an Seufftzen noch / und Threnen überblieben;
>   Was so viel Sorg und Leid noch nicht erschöpffet hat;
>   Was mir der schnelle Tod / nach Gottes weisen Rath /
> Durch zweyer Kinder Raub nicht gäntzich außgetrieben;
> Das schenck ich euch mein Freund / doch wieder mein Belieben:
>   Ach nehmet von mir an / den Willen für die That.
>   Der ich in tieffster Angst schier biß zur Seelen math!
> Und durch diß Threnen-Meer zu schwimmen mich muß üben;
>   Waß kan ich anders doch als Threhnen bringen bey /
>   Das unser festen Lieb ein Pfand und Zeichen sey?
> Nehmt sie den mit; es sind der treusten und der besten.
>   Ich hatte künfftig sie auff nahes Bluth gespahrt:
>   Nun nehmet ihr sie mit auff euer Hinnefahrt.
> Es sind der besten woll / doch aber nicht die besten.[5]

Even in these circumstances, however, the situation is not unambiguous. While the very personal voice of the poem and the emphasis on personal suffering are its dominant elements, it remains true that its form and the form of publication in which it appeared emphasize the public and representative function that is also embodied in the phrase "zu schuldiger Bezeugung" in the postscript with which the poet acknowledges his sense of obligation to a professional colleague.

Even more problematical than the questions of personal identity and privacy is the idea of authorial self-consciousness in the form of self-awareness as a poet. This particular variation on the idea seems to owe its origins principally to the discussion of the novel, and here in particular I think of Robert Alter's fascinating study entitled *Partial Magic* with its subtitle "The Novel as a Self-Conscious Genre."[6] In the preface Alter speaks of the kind of literature that shows itself "acutely aware of itself as a mere structure of words even as it tries to discover ways of going beyond words to the experiences words seek to indicate" (p. ix). In a formulation such as this we have an idea that is, at least potentially, equally applicable to poetry.

There are, however, obvious difficulties in applying ideas used for the discussion of the novel to lyrical poetry. If we think of the self-conscious narrator in such works as Henry Fielding's *Tom Jones* or Laurence Sterne's *Tristram Shandy*, then it is clear that the pose adopted by the narrator is a function of the author's relationship with the reader, and the constant reminders of artifice provide a check against the illusion of reality. Such reminders are not necessary in a lyrical or occasional poem; the awareness of artifice can to some extent be taken for granted and hence the question of self-consciousness in an artistic sense would seem to be irrelevant.

In a poem, too, the relationship between poet and reader is bound to be different. The voice of the poem, particularly in the case of an occasional poem, may be directed at a specific addressee rather than at a reader, and may perhaps only be understood in relation to that addressee. Where this is the case the voice is seldom purely individual, in the sense of carrying on a private conversation, but rather a representative voice fulfilling a quite specific social role determined by the nature of the occasion. The circumscription of this role within the rhetorical tradition is such that the scope for self-awareness, for expression of individuality would seem to be severely restricted.

To illustrate these problems it is worth looking at one or two examples of the kind of voice adopted by occasional poets. The variety of situations and the range of voices that can occur have already been well documented elsewhere, and I am conscious of repeating arguments that have been more than adequately rehearsed.[7] Still, it seems to me that these ideas have an important bearing on the question under discussion and are essential to my present case.

Let us first turn our attention to a sonnet by Johann Rist dating from the year 1647:

Abschiedsreimen
In einem Klinggedichte vorgestellet.
Das / in Gott selig verstorbenes Jungfräulein
redet.

Nun Vatter / guhte Nacht / Ich far' aus diesem Leben
   Sanft / süß und sauberlich an einen solchen Ohrt
   Da weder List / noch neid / noch krankheit / krieg noch mord
Noch einige Gefahr ob unserm haubte schweben.
Nun Schwester / Ich muß dir auch guhte weile geben /
   Mein einzigs Schwesterlein / als welch' ich doch hinfohrt
   Nicht schau' in dieser Welt / dieweil ich schon den Port
Der Seligkeit erreicht und ferner nicht darff streben
   Nach dieser höchsten Lust. Nun Mutter / guhte Nacht /
   Mein Geist ist himmelann / mein Leib ins Grab gebracht.
Mein liebster Jesus hat mich freundlich angenommen /

Er nennet mich sein hertz / sein schönstes Töchterlein.
O grosse Seligkeit! Was Freude wird es seyn /
Wenn wir in seinem Arm zusammen wiedrum kommen!

Der RÜstige[8]

This poem serves to demonstrate the fictionality of the voice. The poet assumes the voice of the dead girl and speaks directly to members of her family. She offers consolation to her father and mother and to the sister who has survived her and in so doing provides a model and justification of Christian faith. Both the element of consolation and the adoption of the voice of the deceased fall within the traditional armory of the epitaph and represent publicly acceptable ways of registering and reflecting upon grief and bereavement. The use of the sonnet form is a further demonstration of the poet's conscious exploitation of a fashionable form in the service of an essentially public or social duty.

This conventional epitaph in sonnet form by Johann Rist is typical of a wide variety of different poems in which the poet fulfills his or her obligation by assuming a particular voice, whether it be the voice of a relative speaking to the bereaved family, the voice of a concerned colleague comforting a bereaved friend, or the voice of bride or bridegroom as they confront each other with their hopes and fears on their wedding day. The variety of possible situations is infinite. What is common to them all is that the poet adopts a pose, assumes a voice. It is in this context that any possibility of a personal voice must be explored.

The following sonnet, written by the Hamburg schoolmaster Dieterich Osterdorff in 1649, has an interesting ambiguity that may enable us to take the discussion a little further.

Mein Jammer ist zu groß. Mein Hertze wil mir brechen /
  Die Seele flattert noch / doch nimmer wie vorhinn
  Die Mutter die ist Todt / auff der mein gantzer Sinn
Ja Hertz und Seele rast / Es ist nicht aus zusprechen
Wie groß mein Leyden sey: Was ist ihm gleich zurechen?
  Ein grosses Flammen-Feur kan nicht so hitzig seyn
  Als meiner Sinnen Angst / und meines Hertzens Pein.
Ich steh' in Thränen gleich als in den Wasser-Bächen
  Ach! liebste Mutter Ach! Mein Leben / meine Kron /
  Wie lasst ihr uns allein / und ziehet so davon?
Zwar in eur Vaterland / da alles gläntzt und strahlet
  Von Lust und Herrligkeit. Ach nehmt mich zu euch hin /
  So kan ich sagen recht / wie traurig das ich bin /
Dann hab ich meine pflicht und letzte Schuld bezahlet.[9]

On one level it might be argued that this sonnet demonstrates a kind of self-awareness both in the element of intensely personal grief as well as in the obvious desire to find adequate poetic expression for this grief. The poet's lament in lines 4 to 7 that his emotion is too intense to be contained within the confines of the poem may be seen as awareness of the limitations of the form, but in the last analysis one has to recognize that the theme is in itself a conventional one in this type of poetry and part of the standard repartee of the occasional poet.

But of course this is already taking the poem too much at its face value. Is the poem really the unbridled grief of the bereaved son lamenting the death of his mother or is this simply another example of the poet assuming a voice that is appropriate to the occasion? In the end this is a question that does not really matter because the final couplet resolves the problem, not in the sense of identifying the speaker but identifying the function of the poem. The last two lines make it absolutely clear that the poet's true concern is not so much adequate expression of grief as the fulfillment of a personal and social obligation. The personal is generalized and formalized to conform to social and cultural norms and expectations.

The examples used so far have all been epitaphs, and it may reasonably be believed that this offers too narrow a base for the discussion of such a wide-ranging problem. There is no realistic opportunity of widening the base of my argument significantly here, but it is perhaps worth looking at one example from a different context, an anonymous sonnet written for a wedding in Bremen in 1638, to take up one or two of the points already raised. The text of the sonnet is as follows:

Sonnet

Und ich / herr Bräutigamb / soll jetzund lassen klingen
   Auch meine Leyer noch / die doch erlieget gantz /
   Untüchtig / ungeschickt zu einem frewden Tantz /
Jetz nicht mehr / wie worhin / durch *Phoebus* gunst kan singen.
Mein wille zwarn ist hie / kans aber nicht vollbringen /
   Wie ihr es würdig seydt / dann ewrer Tugend glantz
   So euch hat auffgesetzt den grünen Lorber Crantz /
Lest sich durch mein *Sonnet* nicht schliessen ein / noch zwingen.
   Je dennoch sol mein Geist Ewr Ehre zu beschreiben /
   So viel er kan und mag / einsmahls bemühet bleiben /
Vor dießmal sehet an den willen / nicht die that:
   Und hört was Lucidor der Schäffer bey den Hirten
   Und seinen Schäffelein / dort bei den schönen Myrten
Euch / und der Jungfraw Braut zu lob gesungen hat.[10]

The *Bescheidenheitsfloskel* that is central to this sonnet, the poet's sense of inadequacy to the demands of the occasion, is a very frequent device in occasional poetry. It is not my concern here to comment on the accuracy or otherwise of the poet's self-perception as revealed in the poem, however, but rather to focus on an element that might arguably be seen as authorial self-consciousness. In modern terms one might, for example, say that the concern with the constraints of the sonnet form in line 8 (possibly anticipated in the use of the verb "klingen" in line 1) show an awareness of the artifice the poet seeks to exploit as well as an element of playfulness in the exploitation of the medium to which Robert Alter also refers. Against this, though, one might equally well argue that the plea in line 11—that it is the thought, the good intentions, rather than poetic ability that count on an occasion like this—reinforces the idea that we are dealing with a commonplace of occasional poetry which in turn emphasizes the element of social obligation.

In a rather different sense one might say that the very adoption of specific forms shows a kind of authorial self-awareness that comes into operation every time a poet correspondingly denotes a poem by its specific form. As Jörg-Ulrich Fechner has pointed out in relation to the sonnet, the term *Sonnet* in the seventeenth century effectively acted as an "unbestimmtes Modeattribut."[11] When the Hamburg schoolteacher Johannes Neukrantz describes a poem as a "Trochaisches Sieben-Geschränke," or Georg Greflinger denotes a sonnet as an "Echonisches Kling Getichte," an awareness of fashion is obvious. But even here, where the parading of fashionable jargon might be seen as a symptom of authorial self-consciousness, the poem remains in essence a performance through which the poet asserts not individuality but identity as a member of a group.

In much the same way Philipp von Zesen's dactylic sonnet dedicated to August Buchner at the beginning of the *Deutscher Helicon* can be seen as a form of self-conscious experimentation with which the poet charts his course and identifies his allegiances. Indeed it seems to me that precisely the figure of Philipp von Zesen would offer the ideal opportunity to explore the notion of authorial self-consciounesss more fully. But that lies well beyond the scope of this essay, and I shall content myself here with the suggestion that reference to Zesen suggests a further dimension to the problem. It may well be that the notion of authorial self-consciousness, insofar as we can perceive it at all in Baroque poetry, may have more to do with the poets' awareness of their individual status than of themselves as individuals, to be more closely related to *Standesbewußtsein*, in the sense of belonging to a *nobilitas litteraria*, than to *Selbstbewußtsein*.[12]

But let us return from these wider fields to the more restricted confines of the immediate subject. As I indicated earlier, it seemed to me that Paul Fleming's remarkable "Grabschrift für sich selbst" provided an important testing ground for my argument, and it is to this poem that I now wish to turn.

> Ich war an Kunst und Gut und Stande groß und reich.
> des Glückes lieber Sohn, von Eltern guter Ehren,
> frei, meine, kunte mich aus meinen Mitteln nähren,
> mein Schall floh überweit, kein Landsmann sang mir gleich,
> von Reisen hochgepreist, für keiner Mühe bleich,
> jung, wachsam, unbesorgt. Man wird mich nennen hören,
> bis daß die letzte Glut dies alles wird verstören.
> Diß, deutsche Klarien, diß Ganze dank' ich euch.
> Verzeiht mir, bin ichs wert, Gott, Vater, Liebste, Freunde,
> ich sag' euch gute Nacht und trete willig ab.
> Sonst Alles ist getan bis an das schwarze Grab.
> Was frei dem Tode steht, das tu er seinem Feinde.
> Was bin ich viel besorgt, den Othem aufzugeben?
> An mir ist minder Nichts, das lebet, als mein Leben.[13]

This poem has already received a good deal of critical attention, but in its own way this sonnet represents such a critical landmark that it cannot be overlooked.[14] Certainly its confident note of self-assertion and the way in which the voice of the poet and what was earlier described as the fictional voice of the epitaph are no longer entirely separable; they seem to speak for a degree of authorial self-consciousness that my argument so far has made no allowance for. This is very much a point that Dietmar Schubert emphasizes when he writes: "In diesem Gedicht, sicher einem der mutigsten deutscher Sprache, finden wir Verse, aus denen stolzes Selbstbewußtsein und das Vertrauen des Autors in die Lebenskraft seiner Dichtung spricht."[15] Schubert goes even further and describes this "Selbstbewußtsein" in effect as one of the distinguishing features of Fleming's poetry. In a telling passage in which he attempts to summarize what it is that makes Fleming's poetry unique, Schubert presents his argument as follows:

> Neu ist nicht das Instrumentarium, das er gebraucht, es ist den Normen der Casuallyrik, der Renaissancepoesie, des Lutherischen Bekenntnisliedes verpflichtet. In seiner weltanschaulichen

Haltung wurzelt er in Humanismus and Protestantismus; er variiert in seinen Gedichten philosophische Anregungen der Antike und der Renaissance.

Bedeutsam ist, daß alle poetischen Bemühungen in einen Brennpunkt münden: das sich um Selbstbewußtsein mühende lyrische Subjekt, das dieses Selbstbewußtseins bedarf, weil es tätig werden will.[16]

Schubert attaches great significance to this idea of self-consciousness, but we are entitled to ask how well such an interpretation fits with the reality of Fleming's "Grabschrift."

As far as the poem itself is concerned, three main issues arise: the voice, the person, and the poet. It is the first of these that in the end is critical, because the way we respond to the person of the poet is determined by the voice.

On one level it is certainly possible to argue that Fleming is using the epitaph as an opportunity to make a statement about himself as a person and as a poet that indicates an awareness of his own importance. At the same time, however, his use of the epitaph would make him aware of the conventional fiction that it speaks with the voice of the deceased and, what is more, with the voice of someone who is aware of his own death (just as, for instance, in the earlier sonnet by Johann Rist the young girl speaks directly from beyond the grave). Hence, however real the situation may seem to be, it represents the conscious adoption of a literary pose, the essential fictionality of which is endemic to the genre. If we wish to see the poem as evidence of authorial self-consciousness, are we entitled to ignore the conventions of the form and its normal expectations? Are we not in danger of allowing biographical knowledge to influence our assessment of this voice in much the same way as, in the past, the element of personal experience in Fleming's love poetry was overemphasized because it was possible to identify his beloved?

Similar reservations occur when we come to consider the person, in particular the strong assertion of individuality and freedom that seems to come through in the opening quatrain. But as Urs Herzog rightly points out, this "Frei; meine" is not an assertion of individual freedom in a modern sense but essentially the reinforcement of that stoical virtue which dominates so much of Fleming's verse. As Herzog writes: "Das antike stoische Ideal der Autarkie ist gemeint."[17] Similarly, at the beginning of the sestet, when the voice turns to friends and relatives to take leave, this potentially very personal moment is treated in a manner that is conscious of the public significance of the occasion and cannot be seen in any real sense as a moment of privacy. Again this is a point that Herzog stresses in his essay when he writes: "Mit dem ersten Terzett rückt das Gedicht ab nicht ins Private, aber doch in einen engeren Kreis . . . Dennoch, und wie sehr die Rhetorik nun auch verhalten wird . . . , es ist ein barockes und also öffent-liches, "geregeltes" Sterben. Einer tritt ab von der Bühne der Welt."[18]

But what of the past? "Kein Landsmann sang mir gleich," Fleming writes of himself. Or the fictional voice asserts. For is this genuinely how Fleming sees himself or how he would wish to be seen? Is this the conviction of a poet who sees that his achievement is a landmark in its own right, the self-consciousness of a poet who believes that his life is justified by his poetry? Or is it merely another variation on a conven-tional theme, on the idea that poetry bestows immortality? This idea is fundamental to the growth of occasional poetry in the seventeenth century, and the notion of *Nachruhm* as a valid answer to the tran-sience and vanity of human existence is perhaps one of the most persistent values of Baroque poetry.[19] It is therefore not surprising that Urs Herzog gives his interpretation of Fleming's poem the title "Kunst als 'Widertod.' "

I have made no attempt to offer a consistent interpretation of the poem in question here. What is important for my argument is that a poem which on the surface seems to show an almost unique degree of self-awareness by the standards of German Baroque poetry can also be seen, at the critical points where this self-awareness seems to assert itself, to conform to or be the product of long-standing traditions that have widespread validity for the whole of the seventeenth century.

For this reason it seems to me that when we talk of authorial self-consciousness in relation to the poetry of the seventeenth century we need to do so with considerable caution. We need to be sure that we are not applying an inappropriate term to traditions and conventions that have little to do with modern aesthetics. The constraints of the rhetorical tradition, and the conventional adoption by Baroque poets of a variety of essentially fictional roles and their attendant voices make it difficult to register with any degree of confidence anything that can genuinely be described as self-consciousness. But perhaps, to use the fashionable communications model, there is just too much noise on the lines. Perhaps, too, my own attempts to discern a per-sonal voice have failed to filter out the interference.

Notes

1. Hugh M. Richmond, "Personal Identity and Literary Personae: A Study in Historical Psychology," *PMLA* 90 (1975): 209–21. Further references are cited in the text.

2. Wulf Segebrecht, *Das Gelegenheitsgedicht* (Stuttgart: Metzler, 1977), pp. 212–13.

3. Jürgen Habermas, *Strukturwandel der Öffentlichkeit: Untersuchungen zu einer Kategorie der bürgerlichen Gesellschaft* (Neuwied am Rhein: Luchterhand, 1965), pp. 55–56.

4. Joseph Leighton, "Occasional Poetry in the Eighteenth Century in Germany," *MLR* 78 (1983): 340–58.

5. Commerzbibliothek Hamburg, Pressmark: S/281 vol. 5, no. 115.

6. Robert Alter, *Partial Magic: The Novel as a Self-Conscious Genre* (Berkeley: University of California Press, 1975).

7. See Ferdinand van Ingen, *Vanitas und Memento Mori in der deutschen Barocklyrik* (Groningen: Wolters, 1966), in particular the section on pp. 276–78 titled "Die Vergegenwärtigung des Toten: Der redende Tote." See also Wulf Segebrecht, "Steh, Leser, still! Prolegomena zu einer situations-bezogenen Poetik der Lyrik, entwickelt am Beispiel von poetischen Grabschriften und Grabschriftenvorschlägen in Leichencarmina des 17. und 18. Jahrhunderts," *DVLG* 52 (1978): 430–68.

8. Commerzbibliothek Hamburg, Pressmark: S/281 vol. 4, no. 158.

9. Ibid., S/281 vol. 1, no. 110.

10. Universitätsbibliothek Bremen, Pressmark: Brem.b.1113 (19/1).

11. Jörg-Ulrich Fechner, *Das deutsche Sonett. Dichtungen, Gattungspoetik, Dokumente* (Munich: Fink, 1969), p. 24.

12. See E. Trunz, "Der deutsche Späthumanismus um 1600 als Standeskultur," *Zeitschrift für Geschichte der Erziehung und des Unterrichts* 21 (1931): 17–53.

13. Paul Fleming, *Paul Flemings deutsche Gedichte*, 2 vols., ed. J. M. Lappenberg, BLVS 82–83 (1865; rpt. Darmstadt: Wissenschaftliche Buchgesellschaft, 1965), 1:460.

14. The most recent articles on the poem are Dietmar Schubert, " 'Man wird mich nennen hören . . .' Zum poetischen Vermächtnis Paul Flemings," *Weimarer Beiträge* 30 (1984): 1687–706; Wilhelm Kühlmann, "Sterben als heroischer Akt. Zu Paul Flemings 'Grabschrift,' " *Gedichte und Intepretationen, Bd. 1: Renaissance und Barock*, ed. Volker Meid (Stuttgart: Reclam, 1982), 167–75; Urs Herzog, "Kunst als 'Widertod.' Paul Flemings 'Grabschrift,' " *Der Deutschunterricht* 37/5 (1985): 38–43. The last article provides a list of earlier studies of the poem.

15. Schubert, "Man wird," p. 1687.

16. Ibid., p. 1700.

17. Herzog, "Kunst," p. 38.

18. Ibid., p. 39.

19. Joseph Leighton, "Poems of Mortality in the German Baroque," *GLL* 36 (1983): 241–57.

16. Authorial Self-Consciousness in the Theater of Caspar Stieler

Judith P. Aikin

Authorial self-consciousness would seem to be limited to those literary genres that allow authors, either as themselves or in the guise of a persona often related to the author in an ironic way, to speak directly from the first-person perspective: the first-person narrative, the third-person narrative interrupted by the first-person comments of the narrator, and, of course, lyric poetry. Drama, the objective representation of the speech-acts of others, would seemingly not lend itself to such an injection of the author into the text. Nor would drama seem to be an appropriate vehicle for the irony created by the projection of the authorial self into a literary text, by the intrusion of a subjective perspective into an objective means of representation. Furthermore, authorial self-consciousness would appear to be able to thrive only in an aesthetic context in which author and reader (or audience) stand in a relationship of considerable intimacy to one another—usually as friendly narrator or poet speaking confidentially to a single assumed reader. In this sense, too, dramatic texts seem to provide a less likely location for references to, and thus consciousness of, the authorial self. Yet the dramatic texts of one author of the German Baroque era, at least, constantly participate in such a process and structure: the works Caspar Stieler wrote, translated, or revised for theatrical performances at several small courts in Thuringia and Saxony in the years 1665 to 1684.[1]

Without becoming (or providing) a narrator of the sort seen, for example, in the modern American play *Our Town* by Thornton Wilder, and without making the play's plot into an autobiography, as in another American play, in this case Arthur Miller's *After the Fall*, Stieler manages nevertheless to inject himself into his plays. That he can do so is dependent not on some otherwise unknown technique, but on his particular relationship with his audience. Stieler served as secretary to the count of Schwarzburg-Rudolstadt, one of the "Viergrafen des Reiches," an honorary title indicating that this count was representative of his status in the Holy Roman Empire.[2] Later, Stieler was secretary to several Saxon dukes in Eisenach and then at Weimar.[3] He was a courtier—a member of the social group that included the princely family, local landed and nonlanded gentry who resided or visited at court, high-ranking personages of the court bureaucracy, and assorted court favorites (artists, poets, musicians, tutors, historians, or librarians). Stieler himself, in addition to his official position as secretary—a subministerial position of some importance—was delegated unofficially or quasi-officially several of the functions of this latter group of talented men: he participated in musical entertainments; created, produced, and probably acted in theatrical performances; tutored the princely children, pages, and other young people in foreign languages and German stylistics; read aloud at the princely table; and wrote occasional and honorific poetry.[4] Stieler seems to have been close friends with a number of notable personages, especially at Rudolstadt; he can certainly be considered to have been an intimate of the inner circle at court.

It was for the entertainment of this inner circle that Stieler wrote and produced his plays. With this built-in intimacy—the author and his cast left the festive group to perform, and then rejoined it as friends and equals at play's end—there was no need for a first-person narrative frame or interior lyric monologue to create a close relationship with the audience. Stieler could rely on a preexisting rapport of the sort assumed not by a novelist or published poet but by a storyteller who knows all the listeners personally—for instance, a grandmother telling fairytales to a family group, or a teller of tales or singer of songs in a preliterate tribal society. But unlike these examples of oral performances, Stieler's performance texts are highly sophisticated as a direct result of the level of sophistication of his audience. The intimacy Stieler enjoyed is perhaps inherent in all courtly literature and entertainments from any age; one can certainly see similar attitudes toward, and relationships with, the audience in both lyric and narrative texts by the knights and courtiers of the German Middle Ages and in the entertainments arranged for and by the Holy Roman Emperor Leopold contemporary with Stieler's activities—likewise designed to be performed in a group setting reflecting the exclusivity and inclusivity of a class-conscious courtly society.

In Stieler's plays, more than in those of his Middle-German contemporaries, this inherent intimacy between author and audience, performer and social group, is allowed free rein.[5] The close relationship is rarely forgotten for very long in the fiction of the plot or the illusion of the performance, for Stieler continually reminds the audience—with illusion-breaking techniques and speeches addressed directly to the spectators—that playwright and players are at home in the audience, and that spectators might well feel at home in the play. For Stieler, theater has a social function dependent on the particular context of the performance for which each text is designed: to establish or reinforce a network of relationships and to restate the shared values upon which group solidarity depends. Like the dramas Goethe was to create a century later for a similar court theater in the context of another closely knit social group to which the author also belonged, the plays of Stieler can be read and played outside their original context with success. But Stieler's plays, read from a twentieth-century perspective, retain perhaps more of the personable and intimate tone poured into them by their author than do those of Goethe. What emerges is a set of plays in which the presence of the author dominates even the most convoluted of plots and the most horrific or romantic of stories.

Authorial self-consciousness appears in two forms in these plays of Caspar Stieler: in verbal and situational self-referentiality, and in the creation of the author's mouthpiece in the person of the fool Scaramutza. Both forms participate in the interplay of humor, irony, and social satire in each drama, but in these two sorts of authorial invasions of the text, the author makes himself, instead of his social betters, equals, or inferiors, the butt of the joke. These incidents of authorial self-consciousness in Stieler's plays reveal him to us today, and they revealed him to his seventeenth-century courtly audience, as an individual well aware of, and mildly critical of, his own pretensions—a far cry from the smug moralizing of many of his contemporaries. He surely would have altered the classical precepts of self-consciousness, "Philosopher, know thyself!" and "Physician, heal thyself!" to "Author, laugh at thyself!"

This humorous self-critique has little in it of that groveling self-denigration or slavish modesty which characterizes many of the utterances of other petty German bureaucrats or artists dependent on patronage during the second half of the seventeenth century. The authorial identity revealed in the self-referential passages in Stieler's dramatic texts is that of an individual who feels securely a part of his social group—which is, coincidentally, also his audience. Thus self-consciousness for Stieler is always also audience-consciousness; each instance of self-referentiality is a restatement of the essential unity of the exclusive group to which he belongs, and it becomes for today's reader or spectator a charming invitation to join in an imaginary and perhaps more temporary social group consisting of the author, the cast of characters, and the members of the audience, whether actual or hypothetical.

Self-referentiality—that is, playing on his own name, pseudonym, and professional or social roles—is a form of authorial self-consciousness in which Stieler indulges in all of his writings, whether lyric poetry, plays, or learned books. As Albert Köster pointed out in his 1897 study on Stieler's early song cycle *Die Geharnschte Venus* written under the pen name "Filidor der Dorfferer," the author played on his own names in an acrostic and several anagrams in this book of poetry.[6] And one should also be aware of the definition offered for the word "Stieler" in our author's pseudonymously published dictionary *Der Teutschen Sprachschatz Stammbaum und Fortwachs*:

> Stieler / der. / manubriorum et capularum artifex, it. petiorum creator. Der erste Stieler ist GOtt gewesen / qui omnium primus petiolos produxerit, Deus ipse suit. Stieler / stilerus, nomen est gentilitium compilatoris praesentis onomastici, cognominato Serotinus, der Spate.[7]

This internal signature, the only one in the dictionary, is couched in the facetious near blasphemy so typical of Scaramutza in the plays.

In the dramatic texts, as far as I can determine, Stieler does not play directly on his real names, although there are a number of allusions to broom- and brush-makers (albeit without the term "Stiel" or "Stieler"), particularly in the name-calling vocabulary of Scaramutza. But Stieler gives his early pen name, "Filidor," to the ardent lover in *Basilene* (1667), as well as to the musician with God-given talent who resists the adulterous blandishments of a love-crazed woman in the operatic text he adapted and produced in 1684 in Weimar, *Krieg und Sieg der Keuschheit*.[8] In both cases it is likely that the members of the audience, as close acquaintances and intimates of Stieler, would have seen this self-referentiality as humorous or even as an objectified and thus ironic self-portrait of the author. Outside of lyric poetry and first-person narrative, I know of no other use of an author's own pen name as a persona or character in a fictional or fictionalized text during this period.

The two Filidors play two of Stieler's own roles in life and art: lover (Stieler had represented himself as amorous poet in *Die Geharnschte Venus*) and musician (he wrote the music for some of the poems in that song cycle himself). Others of his roles also appear in the plays in self-referential usages. The most frequent and prominent of these is the cluster of references to secretaries. One of the young men loved by a heroine—Ferramond in *Ernelinde, Oder die Viermahl Braut*—is made her secretary, a position from which he rises to first place in her heart and a high rank in the land. In *Die erfreuete Unschuld*, the hopes for analogous advancement from Stieler's secretarial post are voiced, with a good deal of self-irony, in Scaramutza's social satire of upward mobility. (Such advancement was a real possibility: the secretary who followed Stieler at Eisenach rose soon thereafter to the post of minister.) Of the examples of persons whose pretensions would place them above their actual stations, the series containing the *secretarius* is the most ambitious and thus, in the seventeenth-century social context, the most ridiculous:

> Ein ieder will mehr seyn / als er ist / und / was er ist / wil er nicht seyn. Exempli gratia: Fragt einen Stallknecht / wer er sey? So wird er antworten: Ein Bereiter. Den Bereiter: respondet: ein Stallmeister. Ein Lackeyen? so wird er sagen / ich bin ein Kammerdiener. Ein Schreiber wil ein *Secretarius*: ein *Secretarius*, ein Raht: ein Raht / ein Cantzler: ein Cantzler der Fürst . . . seyn. (1.8; p. 19)

In a similar list in *Willmut* (1.10; p. 49), Scaramutza claims to be not only a "*Secretarius*," but also "*Auditeur*," a position that Stieler held in the military at the time he wrote *Die Geharnschte Venus*. Scaramutza, instructed to guard some prisoners, halts a suspected intruder with these words: "Steh du Hund / und gieb dich gefangen! Ich bin hier General Profos / *Auditeur*, Kanzelist / *Secretarius* und Obristerwacht-meister / du hast das Leben verwircket." Since the "intruder" is actually the king's minister Ehrlieb—as Scaramutza undoubtedly knows full well—his pretensions are all the more humorous, and perhaps equally, if less directly, satirical. In *Der Vermeinte Printz* it is another comic character, Pantalon, father of the girl Scaramutza is wooing, who professes the belief that the title *Secretarius* is not far beneath the status of nobleman: "Ich hätte gemeinet / es solte zum wenigsten ein *Secretarius*, oder ein Schlösser mein Eydam werden / wenn es ja kein Edelman hätte seyn können" (1.12; p. 36). Pantalon regrets that Scaramutza is not a secretary. Elsewhere Scaramutza claims to be a secretary already; in *Die Wittekinden* he brags: "So hör / ich bin bald / wie ein Secretar, Bey unsern Herren General" (1.5; p. 8).

Several references to Stieler's professional roles gently ridicule the lowly duties to which he had to stoop, especially in Rudolstadt. In *Der Vermeinte Printz* Scaramutza has "den besten Secretarius am Hofe" write him a speech to deliver to the princely well-wisher he expected to see at his wedding (3.25; p. 115); in *Die erfreuete Unschuld* he has "den Herrn Kapelldirektor" (Stieler's duties at Rudolstadt seem to have included this post)[9] compose a love song for his sweetheart and offers him a taler in payment (3.4; p. 43 in pagination that begins after the first act). Stieler may also be satirizing his own despised duties in *Die Wittekinden* in the figure of the broadsheet poet Michele, whose muse must serve a journalistic function and who can be bribed to write lies. Michele may be a poet of a different order than Stieler, but the self-irony is clear. Stieler, the court poet dependent on a patron for his material needs, must likewise fabricate in order to please, just as he has done in this play by adding the romantic comedy to the portrayal of the count's ancestors and perhaps in flattering the count beyond his deserts.

In the later plays these cheerful spoofs on the status of Stieler's own secretarial position give way to vituperative insult. In *Willmut* (1680) Scaramutza vehemently denies being a secretary, using a veritable catalogue of sarcastic appellations. Asked about some letters that had passed between the prince and the evil siren Scheinguda, Scaramutza replies: "das müssen die Plackscheisser die *Secretarien* wissen. Und worvor sehet ihr mich denn an? meint ihr wohl / daß ich so ein Schmierflegel und Dintenklecker sey?" (1.3; p. 20).

Such claims to high status in this position and such denials of involvement in this "dirty" job would be particularly humorous if Stieler himself played the role of Scaramutza, as I believe that he did. Similarly, Scaramutza's finale in *Willmut* would be absolutely hilarious if the secretary Stieler played the part of the character who tells the audience to hurry up and leave, since the secretaries, who are all now in the comedy, are needed to write the letters about the events in the play before the replies could be received and the ultimate outcome reported to the audience. This speech, which effectively merges the realities of the play and audience, would be all the more powerful from the lips of the secretary "in the comedy" who had written the play.

One reference in *Die Wittekinden* makes Stieler's professional territory, the chancellery, a spot for hanky-panky and seduction. Scaramutza, teasing Pantalon with veiled claims of having seduced his daughter Blonja, tells him to seek her and other girls

> . . . dar
> wor Keyser Karl zu Fuß' hingehet /
> Beym Herren *Secretar.*
> Ich mein' in jener Kantzeley /
> wo man die Pässe pflegt zu siegeln /
> Wüst' ichs / die Tühr wolt' ich verriegeln /
> Und kein' / ohn einem derben Schmauß /
> Nicht lassen aus.
>
> (1.10)[10]

The armored Venus of Stieler's wartime years has become an ink-stained Venus, but she is still at home wherever the amorous poet carries out his professional duties.

Accompanying the self-irony and satirizing of Stieler's own pretensions are many barbs directed at the members of the courtly audience, and the most bold of these emerge from the mouth of Scaramutza. This brazen braggart often expresses those rebellious and disrespectful thoughts with which Stieler must have longed to confront his ill-wishers at court but dared do only in the guise of the fool in the comedy. In *Die Wittekinden* Scaramutza clearly identifies himself with his creator:

> Jetzt lernestu mich kennen.
> Ich bin ein kluger Mann /
> Und / die mich anders nennen /
> Die kommen übel an.
> Und daß du wissest / wer ich sey / . . .
> So hör / ich bin bald / wie ein Secretar,
> Bey unsern Herren General,
> Dem schwartzen Ritter . . .
> Dem Keyser dien' ich / wann michs lüst /
> Und wann er mirs belohnet.

(1.5)

When Scaramutza's awed listener, the broadsheet poet Michele, notes that his motley appearance would hardly lead one to expect such an august personage, Scaramutza reveals his nature as that of a clown:

> Du meinst / daß ich bossierlich bin?
> Das muß ich selbst gestehen . . .
> Zu schertzen ist mein Brauch.

(1.5)

In his guise as court buffoon, perhaps off stage as well as on, Stieler attains the poetic license, or fool's freedom, to express those criticisms that in any other context could mean his dismissal. Other evidence that Scaramutza speaks for his author in all the plays is to be found in his use of slang expressions from Stieler's home dialect and student days; his behavior as lover and his bold, sensual love songs not unlike those of Filidor of *Die Geharnschte Venus;* his predilection for the same sort of sexual double entendre and innuendo that characterizes Stieler's own early love songs in this collection; and his delight in teasing and mystifying the ignorant with his expertise in foreign languages.

As one might expect, references to the name "Scaramutza" provide a rich source of verbal humor. In *Willmut*, Scaramutza pretends to misunderstand his name as the insulting appellation "Schermotz" when Scheinguda calls to him, whereupon he takes the opportunity to abuse her verbally in turn: "Du magst wol selber ein Schermotz seyn. Wer ist der Narr / der so schreyet?" (2.10; p. 93).[11] In *Basilene* he gratuitously offers the information on how to decline his name, as if it were a feminine Latin noun: "Dominam Scaramutzam (juxta regulam a primae declinationis)" (1.1; p. 6). The name is also used as a term denoting Cupid in the same passage: "das kleine Scaramützgen / den blinden Cupido" (1.1; p. 7). Elsewhere the name "Scaramutza" is used as a general term for the fool in a comedy or for the funny servant who must accompany every master.[12]

Thus by means of frequent veiled references to his own identity and social and professional roles, as well as in the persons of his alter ego Filidor in two plays and his mouthpiece Scaramutza in nearly all of his plays—including heroic or romantic comedies, tragicomedies, and a tragedy—our author writes himself into his own texts, takes part in his own works of art, and, in many cases, becomes the butt of his own jokes. This activity, as has been shown here, is not just the playfulness of *homo ludens* or even of the comic mode, but participates in the process of establishing an individual and social identity for the playwright and theatrical producer as a member of an intimate social group that is also his audience.[13] His illusion-breaking techniques as he walks in and out of his own text are no *Verfremdungseffekte* designed to estrange the audience from the text and its author, as in theater since Bertolt Brecht, but invitations to share in the intimacy of the group formed by the performance, or even by the act of reading. In enticing the audience to join him in laughing at himself, he is also preparing them in a friendly, nonthreatening manner to laugh at themselves—perhaps enabling them all, author and audience alike, to step back for the moment from their own pressing concerns, pretensions, and foibles, and to view them with a healthy objectivity and, above all, with a light-hearted chuckle that can be shared by all.

Instances of authorial self-consciousness, such as those outlined here, can offer, for the latter-day reader of literature of the past, revealing insights into the author's self-concept. In the case of the theatrical works of Caspar Stieler, this self-concept takes almost entirely the form of the configuration of the social roles the author plays in his society and the social relationships he maintains with the members of his audience. Such a socially defined view of individual identity would not be out of place in German Baroque literature. Yet this emphasis on individual identity as social role in dramatic texts could also be explained by the very nature of the one genre in which role playing provides the primary means for expression. In spite of this predominantly social definition of the self, however, the alert modern reader can perhaps also glean, from the self-referential passages in his work, some notion of Stieler's personality and character, even of character development over the twenty-year period spanned by his dramatic production. The "portrait of the artist" that emerges is that of a likable, even engaging man whose lively sense of the ridiculous is tempered with a kindly attitude toward the foibles of his fellow human beings. We see a man who likes active, assertive women; who openly enjoys his own sexuality; who delights in verbal cleverness, but who prefers the earthy expressions of folk humor to the preciosity and wit of the more mannered literary texts of his age. Caspar Stieler, who successfully preserved for more than two hundred years his anonymity as dramatist and poet by hiding behind pseudonyms, thus refusing to acknowledge his identity to those readers who did not know him personally, has nonetheless left an indelible image of himself in his works.

Notes

Short passages from this chapter appeared in my book, *Scaramutza in Germany: The Dramatic Works of Caspar Stieler* (University Park: Pennsylvania State University Press, 1989), pp. 160–64 and 173–74. This material is reprinted here with the gracious permission of the Pennsylvania State University Press.

1. Six of Stieler's plays were published in 1665–67 in Rudolstadt and Jena, in many instances bound in a collective volume titled *Filidors Trauer-Lust- und Misch-Spiele*, although none was a tragedy: *Der Vermeinte Printz. Lustspiel* (Rudolstadt: Freyschmidt, 1665); *Ernelinde, Oder Die Viermahl Braut. Mischspiel* (Rudolstadt: Freyschmidt, 1665); *Die erfreuete Unschuld. Misch-Spiel* (Rudolstadt: Freyschmidt, 1666); *Die Wittekinden. Singe- und Freuden-Spiel* (Jena: Neuenhahn, 1666); *Der betrogene Betrug. Lustspiel* (Rudolstadt: Freyschmidt, 1667); and *Basilene. Lustspiel* (Rudolstadt: Freyschmidt, 1667). These plays, currently available only in a few rare copies of the original edition in libraries in Europe and the United States (some in microfilm copies of the exemplars in the Faber du Faur Collection at Yale University are more widely available), will soon appear in a facsimile edition edited by Herbert Zeman and others in the "Deutsche Nachdrucke" series. Two theatrical texts in verse, possibly intended for operatic presentation, date from 1668–69, when Stieler was in Eisenach: *Melissa. Schäfferey* (Rudolstadt?: Freyschmidt?, 1668), and *Der göldene Apfel* (MS. Weimar, Q 580). Two plays, a tragedy and an allegory, ap-

peared in 1680 in Jena: *Bellemperie. Trauerspiel des Spaten* (Jena: Johann Nisio, 1680), and *Willmut. Lustspiel des Spaten* ("Im Jahre 1680"). In 1684 Stieler created two *Zwischenspiele* for performances in Weimar, where copies of them have been preserved (Huld. 13). All of these works should likewise appear in facsimile editions in the near future, edited by Zeman and his colleagues. Since the original pagination of the plays to be cited here should still be apparent in these new editions, I have included page numbers in citations for direct quotations in the text in addition to act and scene numbers for all plays except *Die Wittekinden*, which has no pagination.

2. On this designation, see Edmund Stengel, "Die Quaternionen der deutschen Reichsverfassung: Ihr Ursprung und ihre ursprüngliche Bedeutung," *Zeitschrift der Savigny-Stiftung*, Germanistische Abt. 74 (1957): 256–61. Occasional oblique references to Imperial politics occur in Stieler's plays written for performance at this court, but Middle-German politics, dominated by Braunschweig and Saxony, seem to have been more important during the 1660s for Stieler and his Rudolstadt patrons.

3. On Stieler's life and professional posts and patronage, see esp. Herbert Zeman, "Kaspar Stieler: Versuch einer Monographie," diss. Vienna, 1965, pp. 13–110. Zeman's monograph clears up any remaining questions regarding the identity of the author of the Rudolstadt plays; it might be noted that the present analysis of incidents of authorial self-consciousness in the plays lends support to the assumption of Stieler's authorship from yet another source.

4. On Stieler's activities, especially in Rudolstadt, see also Conrad Höfer, *Die Rudolstädter Festspiele aus den Jahren 1665–1667 und ihr Dichter: Eine literarhistorische Studie*, Probefahrten: Erstlingsarbeiten aus dem Deutschen Seminar in Leipzig, 1 (Leipzig: Voigtländer, 1904), and his "Georg Bleyer, ein Thüringischer Tonsetzer und Dichter der Barockzeit," *Zeitschrift des Vereins für Thüringische Geschichte und Altertumskunde*, Beiheft 24 (Jena: Verein für Thüringische Geschichte und Altertumskunde, 1941). Höfer, in these two studies, was the first to make an authoritative attribution of the Rudolstadt plays to Stieler.

5. I am thinking here primarily of Gryphius, Lohenstein, and Johann C. Hallmann; Christian Weise occasionally uses his comic figures to establish contact with the audience, but "intimacy" is not a word I would choose to use to describe his technique. Courtly entertainments of other authors of the times, for example Justus G. Schottel or David Schirmer, lack the characteristics I find in Stieler's dramatic works. Only in the texts of poet-princes (e.g., Anton Ulrich von Braunschweig-Lüneburg) and in the performances in which the Holy Roman Emperor Leopold I or other princely personages took active part, in emulation perhaps of Louis XIV, does this sort of interaction between performance text and audience take place—and then, of course, with a different perspective ("von oben").

6. Albert Köster, *Der Dichter der Geharnschten Venus: Eine litterarhistorische Untersuchung* (Marburg: Elwert, 1897), pp. 111–12. The anagrams are "Kar-

pas" (Kaspar) and "Peilkarastres" (Kaspar Stieler). As Köster also pointed out, the pen name, too, contains an anagram: "der Dorfferer" is "der Erfforder," a reference to Stieler's home town, Erfurt. One might even speculate that one spelling Stieler uses for his later pen name in the Fruchtbringende Gesellschaft, "der Spahte," is a clue to yet another anagram: Thaesp, for Thespus, founder of the dramatic genre in ancient Greece.

7. Caspar Stieler ("der Spate"), *Der Teutschen Sprache Stammbaum und Fortwachs oder Teutscher Sprachschatz* (Nuremberg: Hofmann, 1691; rpt. Munich: Kösel, 1968), col. 2163.

8. In *Willmut* "Caspar" appears as a folk name for the Devil, p. 34, and in *Basilene* Stieler uses the idiom "mit Strumpf und Stiel außrotten" (p. 37); but whether these are puns on his own names remains unclear. On *Krieg und Sieg der Keuschheit* and its production, see especially Conrad Höfer, "Weimarische Theaterveranstaltungen zur Zeit des Herzogs Wilhelm Ernst," Sonderdruck aus dem Jahresbericht des Großherzoglichen Sophienstiftes zu Weimar (Weimar: Hofbuchdruckerei, 1914).

9. Höfer, "Georg Bleyer."

10. Blake Lee Spahr (University of California, Berkeley) pointed out to me that there is also a scatological pun lurking in this passage, for the Kaiser's feet take him, just like any other mortal, to the toilet.

11. Scaramutza uses the term "Narr," alluding to his official role in his society and in the play, ubiquitously in Stieler's dramatic works as a source of self-referential humor. Many of these allusions refer not to himself, however, but rather to others in the play, thus becoming entirely ironic—everyone is a fool but the official fool of the piece. Other appearances of the word are to be found in slang idioms in which the figurative language is applied, in another sort of ironic twist, to the literal fool, as in *Die Wittekinden* (p. 21) where Scaramutza swears that if he does not manage to break through Blonja's virgin defenses this very night, "so solstu mich vor einen Narren schelten." The humorous use of the term "Narr" becomes a major motif in *Willmut*, where Scaramutza's foolishness is exposed at the end as something bordering on evil. In this late play the idioms based on "Narr" appear in most of the scenes dominated by Scaramutza (e.g., "einen Narren an einen haben," "jederman weyß / wer nicht gar ein Narr ist / daß. . . ," "so ein Narr wäre ich nicht"). But gone is the lighthearted license granted the fool in the earlier plays; bitter irony has replaced it. The cluster of metaphorical uses of "Narr" reaches its climax in a long monologue by Scaramutza (2.7), his key speech in the play. In the play's finale he gives the appellation "Narr," and by extension, all the criticisms he has associated with it, to the courtiers in the audience: "Das Ding nimmt ja wol ein beschissen Ende! Aber ich soll erst Narrenkleider anziehen / und bin schon ein Narr / wenn ich gleich einen sammten Rock anhätte / wie der da / und jener dort" (3.11). The tables have been turned, and fools are to be found in the highest echelons of society, among Stieler's friends and acquaintances in the audience, who are now forced to join him in his self-proclaimed foolishness.

12. *Der betrogene Betrug*, p. 57; *Die erfreuete Unschuld*, p. 28.

13. On playfulness as the primary characteristic of comedy, see the excellent study on the comic subgenre by Fritz Martini: *Lustspiele—und das Lustspiel. J. E. Schlegel, Lessing, Goethe, Kleist, Grillparzer, G. Hauptmann, Brecht* (Stuttgart: Klett, 1974). His discussion lends itself particularly well to analysis of Baroque comedy, especially that by Stieler, although Martini himself did not do so.

17. Die Anonymisierung des Buchmarktes und die Inszenierung der "Speaking Voice" in der erotischen Lyrik um 1700

Uwe-K. Ketelsen

Dem Ende des *Holy Roman Empire* hat die deutsche Literaturge-schichtsschreibung bislang keine allzu große Aufmerksamkeit ge-schenkt. Glanzvoll, aber abrupt lassen die meisten Literarhistoriker es mit dem "Barock" enden—alles in allem verschämt beginnen sie (in verschiedenen Unterabteilungen) mit der "Aufklärung" als erster Epoche ein neues, das "bürgerliche" Zeitalter, zu dem sie aber erst mit dem "Sturm und Drang" so richtig Zutrauen gewinnen. Was zwi-schen den Perioden liegt, gleichsam in einer Fuge, hat nie nachhal-tig interessiert; "Nachbarocke Klassizisten", "Galante", "Hofpoeten" sind Verlegenheitsbezeichnungen, die einen Zwischenraum füllen sollen. Schon die Väter der nationalen Literaturgeschichtsschreibung des frühen 19. Jahrhunderts wie Koberstein, Gervinus oder Hettner gossen—freilich durch die fortschrittsgläubigen Kritiker des 18. Jahr-hunderts angeleitet[1]—ihre ganze Verachtung über die Poesie der Jahr-zehnte um 1700. Es genügt, das Resümee anzuführen, das Koberstein 1837 in der dritten Auflage seines *Grundrisses* zog, nachdem er dem schaudernden Leser über eine ganze Seite hin Beweise für den nach seiner Meinung desolaten Zustand der damaligen Literatur aufge-zählt hatte: "So befand sich die deutsche Poesie gegen das Ende des siebzehnten und zu Anfange des achtzehnten Jahrhunderts in gren-zenlosen Verirrungen befangen, und ihre Ausartung schien zum Aeußersten gediehen zu sein"[2]. Selbst der knochentrockene Goedeke sprach von einem "traurigen und oft Ekel erregenden Zustande"[3].

Nun wird niemand behaupten wollen, daß in der Zeit von mehr als einem Jahrhundert, die seither verflossen ist, sich die Ansichten nicht geändert hätten und der Forschung kein neues Wissen zugewachsen sei. Das stimmt durchaus. Dennoch: Der harsche Ton in den Urteilen ist zwar verschwunden, alte Einschätzungen auf der Grundlage tra-dierter Argumentationsmuster aber findet man—in neue Töne trans-formiert—immer wieder. So heißt es z. B. 1979 in der *Geschichte der deutschen Literatur,* die ein Autorenkollektiv unter der Leitung von Werner Rieck erarbeitet hat, die Entwicklung der Literatur des 18. Jahrhunderts sei "poetischer. . . Positionsgewinn gegen die feudalabsolutistische Wirklichkeit und deren Pseudokultur oder gar Kulturignoranz"[4]. Die Folge solcher Einschätzungen ist, daß die Jahrzehnte um 1700 als eine dürre Phase der deutschen Literaturgeschichte angesehen werden und daß unsere Kenntnisse alles in allem schmal sind. Noch schwerer wiegt vielleicht, daß auch die methodischen Fragestellungen fehlen, wenn diese immerhin ein halbes Jahrhundert ausmachende Lücke zwischen Hoffmannswaldaus und Lohensteins Tod (1679 bzw. 1683) und dem Auftreten Gottscheds in Leipzig anders als mit positivistischem Datengeröll gefüllt werden soll.

Unter rein literarästhetischen Gesichtspunkten ist die Produktion dieser Jahrzehnte in der Tat nicht sehr aufregend. Erst in einer neuen Perspektive gewinnt sie Leben, wenn man nämlich jene Jahrzehnte als eine kulturgeschichtlich markante Situation[5] erkennt: Mit den Vertretern der "Zweiten Schlesischen Schule"[6] sehen wir die humanistische Standeskultur an ihr Ende gekommen und den Traum von einer *nobilitas litteraria* endgültig ausgeträumt.[7] Zwar starb der traditionell "höfische" Autor ebensowenig sofort aus wie der poetisierende "Gelehrte". Aber den literarischen Alltag prägte—davon zeugen die als neue Publikationsform in Mode kommenden Anthologien im Stile der *Neukirchschen Sammlung*[8] wie die Gebirge von in deutschen Bibliotheken lagernden Gelegenheitsgedichten[9]—der jetzt massenweise auftauchende Nachwuchsakademiker, der in die mittelbaren oder unmittelbaren Dienste des sich etablierenden absolutistischen Staates strebte.[10] Das Zerbrechen alter sozialer Gruppierungen und ihrer kulturellen Normen wie das Heraufziehen neuer Schreiber- und Leserschichten mit veränderten Attitüden bilden einen sehr komplexen Vorgang, der zudem auch regional ganz erheblich differiert. Dieser Prozeß vollzog sich nicht in einem plötzlichen, gar revolutionären Wechsel, vielmehr lief er als ein wechselvolles Gleiten ab: es zogen neue Mieter in ein altes Haus, das sie dann umbauten.[11]

Dieser Veränderungen ansichtig zu werden, bringt einige Schwierigkeiten mit sich. Sie sind sehr unterschiedlicher Natur, etwa auch literaturtheoretischer Art. Daß ein Text von jemandem sei, daß er von einer Stimme gesprochen werde, ist für uns—sieht man einmal vom "Volkslied" und ähnlichen Erscheinungen ab—ein nahezu selbstverständliches Faktum; sowohl unsere ästhetischen wie unsere juristischen Normen gehen davon aus. Paul de Man etwa urteilt: "Our claim to understand a lyric text coincides with the actualization of a speaking voice"[12]. Aber wenn wir diese "speaking voice" mit dem Terminus

"Lyrisches Ich" belegen[13], wird deutlich, daß unsere Vorstellung davon dezidiert historischer Natur ist: sie entspringt der romantischen Poetik und macht—jedenfalls wenn man den Terminus präzise faßt— nur in deren kunsttheoretischen Zusammenhängen wirklich Sinn.[14] In diesem Verständnis gehört sie spätestens seit Hegel[15] zum eisernen Bestand literaturtheoretischer Gattungslehre: in der poetischen Selbstreflexion, im Prozeß der ästhetischen Anschauung seiner selbst, sucht und findet das transzendentale "Ich" zu sich selbst.[16] Daß damit im Hinblick auf die lyrische Produktion um 1700 nichts zu gewinnen ist, versteht sich von selbst und bedarf keines Nachweises. Wie aber diese "speaking voice" dort zu bestimmen sei, bleibt damit noch ganz ungeklärt.

Die spezifische Vorstellung vom "lyrischen" Sprecher taucht nicht plötzlich am Ende des 18. Jahrhunderts in den literaturtheoretischen Debatten auf; sie ist das Ergebnis eines langen Reflexionsprozesses.[17] Allerdings wird sie auch nicht einfach in einer kontinuierlichen Genese aus älteren Vorstellungen heraus entwickelt. Der Vorgang ist vielschichtig, komplex, zuweilen sogar gegenläufig. Er speist sich aus anderen als nur literarischen Quellen, etwa von der "Irrationalismus"- problematik im Kontext der rationalistischen Erkenntnistheorie her[18], aber auch aus den Folgen des Impulses, der von der Auseinandersetzung mit Shaftesburys Genieästhetik[19] ausging oder von den Einflüssen religiöser Poesie auf die weltliche. Spätere Beobachter dieser Entwicklung haben dieses Moment der Diskontinuität als Unvereinbarkeit zweier Subjektkonzeptionen in der Lyrik dargestellt, so etwa Goethe in der Gretchen-Episode[20] in *Dichtung und Wahrheit*: in der einen sieht er das Subjekt sich mit seinen Gefühlen im Text "ausdrücken", in der anderen aber ist das Subjekt allenfalls als geschickter Textarrangeur gegenwärtig. Beide Konzeptionen läßt er in einen—auch soziokulturell konnotierten—Kontrast treten; das mag ihn später dazu verführt haben, in seiner Einschätzung Johann Christian Günthers den neuen Poesiebegriff anachronistisch in die Geschichte zurückzuprojizieren, damit eine literarhistorisch verhängnisvolle Günther-Interpretation vielleicht weniger initiierend als mit seiner Autorität legitimierend.[21] Solche Probleme beginnen bereits am Ausgang des 17. Jahrhunderts aufzutauchen.

Allerdings waren sie nicht Gegenstand einer wirklichen Diskussion, selbst dann nicht, wenn man das bescheidene Niveau damaliger poetologischer Überlegungen in Rechnung stellt. Auch nachträglich lassen sich die isolierten Bemerkungen nicht zu so etwas wie einer Theorie zusammenfassen. Die Beobachtungen bleiben vage und unzusammenhängend. Das liegt schon an dem Ort, wo einschlägige

Formulierungen zumeist anzutreffen sind: oft sind es Vorreden und merkwürdigerweise auch Gelegenheitsgedichte[22], also ein Teil der Praxis selbst, wo diese Überlegungen angestellt werden.[23] Zudem scheint den Zeitgenossen die Frage nach der Urheberschaft von Lyrik nicht vorrangig gewesen zu sein, was auch verständlich ist. Denn die Frage nach dem Ursprung der Poesie im Autor ist ein Problem der Produktionsästhetik, das in der primär wirkungsästhetisch orientierten Rhetorik keinen rechten Platz findet.

Ganz unbekannt war es den Zeitgenossen indes nicht. Sie sahen im Poeten durchaus nicht nur den geschickten, "gelehrten" Arrangeur, der sprachliches Material gemäß den Regeln und dem Maß der Vorbilder mit dem Blick auf die zu erzielende Wirkung zu Texten zusammengefügt habe. Gleich im ersten Satz seiner *Deutschen Poeterey* meint Opitz: Obwohl er sich vorgenommen habe, etwas Lehrhaftes über die Dichtkunst niederzuschreiben, sei er "doch solcher gedancken keines weges, das [er] vermeine, man könne iemanden durch gewisse regeln vnd gesetze zu einem Poeten machen"[24]. Man müsse, so führt er aus, ein "Poete von natur" sein. Diese natürliche Fähigkeit wird allerdings hier wie andernorts nur sehr allgemein bestimmt, etwa als Beweglichkeit des Geistes oder mit dem nahezu topischen Terminus *furor poeticus* belegt und nur zu bald über die *res-verba*-Problematik in den formalen Bereich der traditionellen Rhetorik eingegliedert.

Es hätte zwar mehrere Möglichkeiten gegeben, das Autorproblem im literaturtheoretischen Sinne zu diskutieren, so im Zusammenhang der zaghaften Wertungsdebatte, wenn Thomasius andeutungsweise zu historischen Kategorien (und das sind immer individuelle) greift oder wenn im Rahmen der Metapherndiskussion dem Poeten die Fähigkeit zugeschrieben wird, an *verschiedenen* Dingen Gleiches (das *tertium comparationis*) zu entdecken. Verschiedenes, die *varietas*, ist als ein Moment der Mannigfaltigkeit ein Besonderes, das der Poet in seiner speziellen (d. h. ihn auszeichnenden) Fähigkeit erkennt. Solche poetologischen Probleme weisen in der Tat auf die spätere Formulierung voraus, der Poet als das Subjekt seines Textes sei als jemand zu denken, der aufs Einzelne gerichtet und somit der Theorie nicht subsumierbar sei. Aber erst, als die erkenntnistheoretischen Bemühungen der Rationalisten um das im cartesianischen Sinne Irrationale für die Poetik fruchtbar gemacht wurden (also für unsere Frage zu spät), wurde der Poet (jetzt das "Genie") in diesem Sinne Gegenstand des Nachdenkens.[25] So müssen denn Formulierungen, in denen über den Autor gesprochen wird, und mehr noch Passagen in literarischen Werken selbst, in denen die poetische Stimme Gestalt zu gewinnen scheint, gelesen werden, ohne daß sie auf einen stützenden theoretischen Rahmen bezogen und damit eindeutig gemacht werden können.

Dieses sind weitläufige und vielfältige Fragen; die hier ausgebreiteten Beobachtungen sind ihrer Fragestellung wie des berücksichtigten Materials nach sehr begrenzt. Sie beziehen sich nur auf solche Gedichte, die—in der Terminologie der Zeit—"freyen Materien" gewidmet sind. Diese stellten in den Jahrzehnten um 1700, gemessen an Gelegenheitsgedichten und der moralischen Lehrdichtung[26], eine Minderzahl dar; die meisten dieser "freyen" Gedichte sind erotischen Themen gewidmet. Zudem bleibt meine Untersuchung auf diejenigen beschränkt, die sich in den ersten beiden Bänden der *Neukirchschen Sammlung*[27] finden. Und schließlich wird diese Beobachtung auf eine zentrale Fragestellung konzentriert: welche Konsequenzen nämlich die konstatierte Veränderung der Struktur von literarischer Öffentlichkeit für die Konzeption der "speaking voice" in Gedichten gehabt habe.

In der Gesamtvorrede, die 1679 Hoffmannswaldau seinen *Deutschen Übersetzungen und Getichten* voraussetzte, findet sich eine beiläufige, nichtsdestoweniger beachtenswerte Bemerkung. Als der Autor über die vorgenommene Auswahl seiner Werke Rechenschaft gibt, merkt er an, seine erotischen Gedichte (die später in der *Neukirchschen Sammlung* als "Verliebte Arien" gedruckt wurden) habe er, um "zu ungleichem Urtheil nicht anlaß zugeben / mit fleiß zu rücke gehalten / massen denn auch viel dergleichen meiner Poetischen Kleinigkeiten allbereit in unterschiedenen Händen seyn"[28]. (Bemerkenswerterweise stellte fast zur selben Zeit—allerdings mit entgegengesetztem Ergebnis—Lohenstein ähnliche Überlegungen an.)[29] Es gibt demnach also Arten von Gedichten, die unterschiedliche Bewertungen erwarten lassen, wenn sie *gedruckt* veröffentlicht werden. Und nicht gedruckt sein, bedeutet nicht, daß Gedichte keine Öffentlichkeit finden; sie haben in einer anders strukturierten Öffentlichkeit ihre Lebenssphäre, nämlich—so ließe sich Hoffmannswaldau ergänzen—in der Form einer spezifischen Geselligkeit. Wie die ausgesehen haben könnte, malt z. B. Anton Ulrich von Braunschweig in seiner *Aramena* (1669–73)—wenngleich sicher in idealtypischer Weise und mit Blick auf einen anderen Gedichttypus—mit einiger Farbigkeit aus.[30] Seine Schilderung gibt eine Vorstellung von der Geselligkeit, in der Texte entstanden (wenn auch nicht so kunstvolle wie die Hoffmannswaldauischen). Es ist die Geselligkeit idealer adliger Unterhaltung und Zerstreuung, die einen generell oder situativ von der Herrschaft abgegrenzten Raum angenehm, aber dennoch (etwa in Spielregeln) rituell

geordnet füllt.[31] Die "speaking voices", die hier zu hören sind, sprechen (unabhängig davon, welches ihr Thema ist) von ihrer eleganten
poetischen Kunstfertigkeit und von ihrer "politischen" Urteilsfähig-
keit. Vor allem haben alle diese Stimmen (fiktive) Namen, und auch
wenn ihre Gebilde so allgemein ausfallen, daß sie aus der Erzählung
leicht herauszulösen und zu anthologisieren sind (bzw. aus anderen
Werken eingestreute Gedichte darstellen), so sind sie für die Romanfi-
guren (und noch mehr für die Leser) applizierbar. Sie sind Teil eines
komplizierten (fiktiven) Gesellschaftsspiels.

Wie sich die Atmosphäre solcher Geselligkeit in Verse umsetzen
konnte, mag ein kurzes Refraingedicht aus Abschatz' *Anemons und
Adonis Blumen* wenigstens andeuten; es dürfte aus den 60er Jahren
stammen, erschien gedruckt aber erst 1704, also posthum:

> Ich leb ohne Ruh im Hertzen /
> Von der Zeit /
> Da zwey schöner Augen Kertzen
> Mich versezt in Traurigkeit /
> Von der Zeit
> Leb ich stets in Schmertzen /
> Fühle keine Ruh im Hertzen.
> Keine Lust war mir zu nütze
> Von der Zeit /
> Da der kleine Venus-Schütze
> Seel und Hertze mir bestreit /
> Von der Zeit
> Leb ich stets in Schmertzen /
> Fühle keine Ruh im Hertzen.[32]

Man muß sich schon konzentrieren, um überhaupt zu bemerken,
wovon das "Ich" hier spricht, so minimal, stereotyp und konventio-
nell fällt die Aussage aus: es sei von der Unruhe (unerfüllter) Liebe
gepackt. Aber eigentlich macht es mit seinen Worten etwas ganz anderes, als diese Unruhe auszudrücken: es spielt (wenn auch nicht
gerade genial, so doch leicht und elegant) mit den Worten eines aufgrund des spezifischen literarischen Reglements sehr schmalen Wort-
feldes, es bindet sie in wenige—nämlich drei—Reime, koppelt sie zu
stereotypen Zeilen, die in ein festes Wiederholungsschema geflochten
werden, so daß es nach vierzehn Zeilen zur leicht variierten Aus-
gangszeile zurückkehrt. Indem es so—semiotisch gesprochen—das
signifié von dessen *signifiants* löst, verlängert es die lange Kette von
Kombinationen einschlägiger Zeichen um ein weiteres Glied[33], ja, es
fügt sich selbst—über das "Ich", seinen grammatischen Repräsentan-

ten im Text—dieser Tradition ein. Diese Auflösung der "speaking voice" in ihrem Text—die aber, wie das Beispiel der *Aramena* zeigt, keine vollständige, nur eine verschleierte ist—bedeutet die Voraussetzung für die gesellige Leichtigkeit, der das Gedicht seine Existenz verdankt. Um es blumig auszudrücken: Die (reale oder fiktive) gesellige Situation im Stile der *Aramena* bringt Texte wie den zitierten (und mit ihnen deren "speaking voice") hervor; sie ist der Meeresschaum, der solche Lieder gebiert.

Hoffmannswaldau hatte Überlegungen darüber angestellt, was geschieht, wenn Gedichte gedruckt auf dem allgemeinen Buchmarkt erscheinen (wobei ihm die Erfolgsliteratur der Zeit, aber auch religiöse Publikationen oder Flugblattliteratur zur Anschauung gedient haben mögen). Das wurde ihm nicht generell zum Problem, sondern in einer charakteristischen Situation: Zum einen war—wie er erfahren mußte—ganz offensichtlich der Bereich, in dem seine Texte bislang zirkulierten, doch nicht mehr so persönlich und so sozial strukturiert, wie er das geglaubt haben mochte und wie es möglicherweise einer älteren Tradition entsprochen hätte; jedenfalls befürchtete er (und zwar mit Recht), seine Texte könnten ihm entgleiten. Zum anderen aber begann sich der Buchmarkt qualitativ zu verändern; er war nicht mehr nur das quantitativ erweiterte Kommunikationsorgan der "Gelehrten" oder ein Medium zwischen den literarischen Gesellschaften. Gedruckt traten die Gedichte in eine andere Art von Öffentlichkeit: eben in die Öffentlichkeit des—in jenen Jahrzehnten nicht unerheblich wachsenden, zunehmend anonymer und in seiner Teilnehmerschaft diffuser werdenden—Marktes. Das bedeutete auch für die "speaking voice" der Texte eine tiefgreifende Veränderung. Diese verloren, indem sie publiziert wurden, den geselligen Rahmen, der zu ihrer Konstituierung so Entscheidendes beigetragen hatte, ohne daß ein Ersatz sich einstellte. Sie wurden in der Druckform anonymisiert und bekamen paradoxerweise trotzdem einen Namen, den des Autors, oder in vielen Fällen auch Initialen.[34]

Der Schritt in die Öffentlichkeit des nun langsam entstehenden Buchmarktes muß die Autoren des 17. und frühen 18. Jahrhunderts ungemein beunruhigt haben. (Die von den Literarhistorikern immer wieder mit Verwunderung beobachtete Steigerung der Produktion von Gelegenheitspoesie ins nachgerade Massenhafte könnte—neben den naheliegenden literarsoziologischen—ihre literaturtheoretischen Ursachen haben: die *occasio* gab der Stimme des Textes den Handlungsrahmen, der der bürgerlichen Literaturpraxis ansonsten nur zu leicht fehlte. Ähnliches gilt für die "Hofpoeten".) Zwar war es von nachgerade zwanghafter Topik, in Vorreden diesen Schritt in die Anonymität des Marktes und die kaum zu steuernde Rezeption zu entschuldigen; und von der Verantwortung entlastende Argumente (wie Bitten von Freunden und Gönnern oder die Verwahrung gegen Verstümmelung) finden sich habituell ausgeprägt, aber das allein erklärt (so wenig wie das unsichere Rollenmuster des Poeten) nicht die unisono geäußerte Scheu vor dem Schritt auf den Markt. Hoffmannswaldau behielt ja durchaus recht, wenn er das "ungleiche Urtheil" fürchtete (und deswegen die "Lust"-Gedichte *nicht* veröffentlichte), mußte er sich doch—zusammen mit Lohenstein—noch 1751 (also noch nach über einem Jahrhundert) von Gottsched sagen lassen, beide hätten "ihrer Feder so wenig, als ihrer Begierden, ein Maß zu setzen" gewußt.[35] Dieses herbe Urteil ist insofern aufschlußreich, als es den Sprecher des Textes mit dem Autor ineins setzt und dieses synthetische Produkt dann einer heteronomen (nämlich einer moralischen) Kritik unterwirft; *moralische* Kriterien sind nach 1700 ganz selbstverständlich Bestandteil *literarischer* Kritik (wobei Moral im Sinne bürgerlicher Moralkriterien bestimmt wird). Das Gottschedsche Verdikt läßt sich überhaupt nur fällen, wenn die "speaking voice" der Hoffmannswaldauischen Gedichte aus dem Stimmengeflecht (höfisch-eleganter) Gesellligkeit herausgelöst erscheint und wenn der Autor zwar einen Namen trägt, aber ansonsten anonym bleibt. (Herrn von Hoffmannswaldau hätte Gottsched dieses Urteil ja wohl kaum ins Angesicht zu sagen gewagt.)

Ähnlich hatte Hoffmannswaldau recht, wenn er die Verschiedenartigkeit der Aufnahme seiner Gedichte auf dem vom Autor nicht zu kontrollierenden Markt fürchtete. Mit Erdmann Neumeister etwa fand er einen Leser, an den seine Gedichte überhaupt nicht adressiert waren. *Als Theologe* regte sich dieser darüber auf, daß der Autor seinen erotischen Texten biblische Redewendungen einverleibt und solcherweise heilige und profane Sprache vermengt habe.

Andere Autoren jener Jahre fingen die Irritation anders auf als Hoffmannswaldau. So erschien etwa im ersten Band der *Neukirchschen Sammlung* ein Gedicht mit dem Titel "Schwangerer Jungfern Trost-Gedancken" (1. Band, S. 307–10). In der ersten Auflage von 1695 war es mit der Sigle C. S. L. gezeichnet (die mit erheblichem gelehrten Scharfsinn als Caspar Siegmund Leschke identifiziert worden ist)[36]; in der zweiten Auflage desselben Jahres (die im übrigen eine "gereinigte" war) fehlte diese Angabe, und sie kehrte in der folgenden Auflage auch nicht wieder zurück, obwohl gestrichene Stücke klammheimlich wieder eingerückt wurden. Der Autor (wohl kaum der Verleger oder Neukirch selbst), ein Breslauer Rechtsanwalt, muß seine Initialen als Index am Text so gefürchtet haben, daß er selbst die nicht eben verräterische Buchstabenkennzeichnung gelöscht sehen wollte, um dem von Hoffmannswaldau bereits 15 Jahren zuvor anvisierten Mechanismus zu entgehen.

Die Autoren der Jahrzehnte um 1700 rechneten mit diesen Gegebenheiten. Man kann es etwa den zeitgenössischen Beiträgern zur *Neukirchschen Sammlung* ablesen, am meisten Neukirch selbst. Sie taten es allerdings auf sehr unterschiedliche, ja sogar gegensätzliche Weise. Da die literarische Produktion so unübersichtlich ist, auch feste Reaktionsschemata nicht recht zu erkennen sind, bleibt manche Beobachtung so vage, daß sie vielleicht mehr den Wünschen des Beobachters entspringt als der Sache.[37] Da alle Autoren mehr oder minder deutlich der Linie des "politischen" Programms Christian Weises oder der "galanten" Doktrin von Thomasius folgten, d. h. an der im weitesten Sinne höfischen Literatur ihrer Vorgänger orientiert blieben, sind Veränderungen ohnehin nur als Variationen zu lesen. Diese fielen unter nur literarästhetischen Gesichtspunkten in der Tat nicht zum Besten aus. Dafür ließe sich vielleicht auch die neue Marktsituation als einer der Gründe anführen.

Die Anonymität des Buchmarktes zwang die Teilnehmer zu dem Versuch, Unterscheidungen, die bislang durch das gesellschaftliche und gesellige Umfeld geleistet worden waren (und die auf dem Felde der Kasualpoesie auch weiterhin wesentlich von dort kamen), in die Texte selbst zu verlegen, also der "speaking voice" einzuverleiben. Den zeitgenössischen Stellungnahmen zur poetischen Produktion ist diese Bemühung deutlich abzulesen. So ist es sicherlich kein Zufall, daß die ersten Ansätze zu einer literarischen Kritik, die mehr zu sein beabsichtigte als nur eine normative Musterung, in jene Jahre fielen. Benjamin Neukirchs Vorwort zur *Neukirchschen Sammlung* (das seine spezifische Kontur bekommt, wenn man es parallel zum Anfang von Opitz' *Deutscher Poeterey* liest) läßt Ansätze dazu erkennen, die allerdings hilflos bleiben. Neukirch griff in seinen Argumentationen ein Moment der alten Theorie von Poesie auf, die auch Opitz schon behandelt hatte, verschärfte sie und führte sie zugleich als Argument der literarischen Kritik ein: er unterschied Poeten, die es von Natur aus zum Schreiben dränge, von solchen, die durch die Umstände— z. B. durch Schule oder gesellschaftliche Verpflichtungen—dazu verleitet würden; letztere wollte er vom Markt ausgeschlossen wissen. Damit ging er nicht nur über Opitz hinaus, sondern er formulierte auch ein Argument, das bis weit ins 18. Jahrhundert hinein in Gebrauch sein sollte. Welches Gewicht er ihm beimaß, läßt sich daraus erkennen, daß er es gleich zweimal und ausführlich vortrug. Allerdings explizierte er nicht, woran man unterscheiden könne, welche eine von Natur getriebene Stimme und welche nur eine von den Umständen verführte sei. Das theoretische Instrumentarium reichte nicht aus.

Die literarische Praxis war denn auch von anderen Techniken beherrscht. Um die Leere des anonymen Marktes zu füllen und die "speaking voice" zu situieren, setzten Autoren im Rahmen der *movere*-Konzeption an. Sie erhöhten die Lautstärke ihrer Stimmen, um bemerkt zu werden; wo der gesellige Rahmen fehlte, wurde die Stimme schrill. Besonders Benjamin Neukirch legte sich keine Hemmungen auf; die Eleganz und die Geistreichigkeit seines Vorbildes Hoffmannswaldau ersetzte er durch Grobheiten und Geschmacklosigkeiten. Indem er Hoffmannswaldau zudem zum erotischen Dichter verkürzte, retuschierte er dessen Bild im Publikum, bzw. er erzeugte überhaupt erst ein spezifisches Bild von diesem Autor, in dessen (vermeintlichen) Schatten er sich werbewirksam stellen konnte. Er machte nachgerade einen Markenartikel für erotische Poesie daraus. Er hatte Erfolg damit, denn das Hoffmannswaldau-Bild ist ja noch heute wesentlich von der *Neukirchschen Sammlung* bestimmt und nicht etwa von den *Deutschen Übersetzungen und Getichten.*

Die Rollenschemata der erotischen Gedichte blieben zunächst die alten: in petrarkistischer Manier redet der begehrende Mann; es sprechen allegorische Figuren (wie Venus, Cupido usw.) oder Frauen, die die Funktion, Objekte männlicher Begierde zu sein, aus männlicher Perspektive bestätigen. Was sich verändert, ist der Ton der im Gedicht sprechenden Stimme; so etwa, wenn dem petrarkistischen Motiv der sich der männlichen Berührung verweigernden Schönen die Variante abgewonnen wird:

"Was ursach hast du dann, daß du dich so beklagst?
Da du doch diese gunst den flöhen nicht versagst".

("An Sylvien")[38]

Das *memento mori*- und das *carpe diem*-Motiv variierend, meint der Sprecher eines anderen Neukirchschen Gedichts im Hinblick auf den Busen der angeredeten Frau:

Die spitzen lassen schon die rosen-blüthe fallen /
Die berge ziehn die stoltzen liljen ein,

und wenn sie ihre Brüste nicht entblößen wolle,

. . . so schneid sie ab / und wirff sie vor die rinder.

("Ein anders")[39]

Es fällt überhaupt auf, daß die hier Redenden gegenüber ihren Vorbildern die Richtung der gesamten Triebdynamik ändern und sich zugleich in den Ton einer ungeheuren Aggressivität steigern. Hatten in Hoffmannswaldaus und seiner Generation Poesien die Sprechenden sich selbst, also den Mann, als Opfer des Eros gesehen ("Daß Venus meiner freyheit schatz / In diesen strudel möge drehen", heißt es einmal bei ihm)[40], so wendeten die Nachahmer die Klage über versagte Triebbefriedigung oder verlorenen Seelenfrieden in offene Aggressivität gegen die Frau. Sie konnten sich bis zu Zerstückelungsphantasien steigern:

> Wie soll mich ärmsten dann nicht deine pracht entzünden /
> Die / wann man sie zertheilt / kan ihrer sieben binden?
>
> ("Über die gestalt der Sylvia")[41]

heißt es auch bei Neukirch, die topographische Zergliederung des weiblichen Körpers, wie sie das traditionelle rhetorische Beschreibungsschema kannte, allzu wörtlich nehmend. Die Autoren schreckten vor nichts zurück, wenn es galt, der "speaking voice" einen Hallraum in der leeren Anonymität des Buchmarktes zu verschaffen. So heißt es in dem schon erwähnten Gedicht des Caspar Siegmund Leschke aus dem Mund einer schwangeren Jungfer:

> Wir schätzen den verlust der jungferschafft nicht groß /
> Und fühlen immer noch das angenehme jucken /
> Als der beperlte thau in unsre muschel floß /
> Und die sich öffnete denselben einzuschlucken.
>
> ("Schwangrer Jungfern Trost-Gedancken")[42]

Die "speaking voice" wird dann wohl gar zum Lockruf des Anreißers, der—wie ebenfalls in einem Neukirch-Gedicht—Eva dem Adam unters Feigenblatt fassen läßt[43] oder den Leser—in einem insgesamt ziemlich langweiligen anonymen Lustgespräch eines Schäfers mit einer Schäferin—gleichsam hinter einer Tanne voyeuristisch zum Ohrenzeugen des Orgasmus einer "Psyche" macht.[44] Der Leser wird zum Kunden einer spätbarocken Peep-Show.

Die Sprecher solcher Gedichte, die sich nicht mehr—und sei es auch illusionär—auf eine gesellige Gruppe und deren kulturelle Standards beziehen konnten, mußten sich notwendigerweise im Dunkel des anonymen Buchmarktes thematisch sehr beschränken: sie hielten an den etablierten Genres fest, also etwa an denen der erotischen Poesie; die Propagierung "Hoffmannswaldaus" als eines Markenzeichens erfüllte zumindest für eine gewisse Zeit die Funktion, den Rahmen der Erwartungen zu stabilisieren. Ein gewisser Reiz muß darin gelegen haben, die Tabugrenzen zu suchen (die aber weniger im sexuellen Thema selbst gelegen zu haben scheinen als mehr in dessen Verknüpfung mit biblischen Motiven). Wenn man sich diesen Sprecher überhaupt in einer geselligen Gruppe vorstellen kann, dann nicht in einer solchen, in der literarische Kennerschaft herrscht oder ein differenziertes Nachdenken über menschliche (oder zumindest männliche) Triebgebundenheit gefordert wird. Man kann sich ihn am ehesten in einer Zufallsrunde vorstellen, die auf minimale Übereinkünfte verpflichtet ist, die wenig Spielräume lassen, und in der vor allem—und das scheint mir noch wichtiger—die Aggressionslenkung kanalisiert ist. Es ist fast so, als vergewissere sich die "speaking voice" in dieser einverständig gelenkten Aggression ihrer selbst. Überdeutlich wird das in einem Text wie dem schon erwähnten Lustgespräch eines Schäfers mit einer Schäferin von Leschke. Es wird die Verführung Psyches durch Thyrses dargestellt; das Gedicht endet damit, daß Psyche dem Thyrses versichert, wenn sie jetzt gehen müsse, dann seien nur die Körper getrennt, ihre Seele sei aber immer bei ihm. Worauf der befriedigte Thyrses—durchaus im traditionellen Sinne des *argutiae*-Schemas—mit der zynischen "Pointe" antwortet:

Leb wohl / und liebe wohl / und leide wohl / mein leben!
Und dencke: Treue lieb ist nimmer ohne pein.[45]

Solche thematischen Folgen der Veränderung der Publikationssituation sind noch einigermaßen deutlich festzustellen. Viel schwieriger verhält es sich dagegen im Hinblick auf die Folgen für stilistische Regularien, zumal dieser Wechsel keiner zwischen Mündlichkeit und Schriftlichkeit war, denn auch das ältere Geselligkeitsmuster war schon ein solches der Schriftkultur gewesen. Daß auf der stilistischen Ebene ein Wechsel stattfand, stellten schon die Zeitgenossen mit Genugtuung fest. Die Umorientierung vom "italienischen" Stil der "Zweiten Schlesischen Schule" über die "Galanten" auf den "Klassizismus" Opitzscher oder französischer Prägung hat die Forschung meist als einen Geschmackswandel erklärt, ohne allerdings dessen Gründe namhaft zu machen. Das ist auch einigermaßen schwierig und vielleicht gar nicht ratsam. Stattdessen sollte man sich vielleicht darauf beschränken, die Folgen für die Inszenierung des Autors, seiner Stimme im Text festzustellen. An der generellen Form der Texte änderte sich zunächst nichts, die jüngeren Autoren zumindest der ersten beiden Bände der *Neukirchschen Sammlung* orientierten sich weiterhin an der Tradition. Ein Gedicht wie Benjamin Neukirch "An die Florette"[46], das in gewisser Weise die Norm hält, zeigt das ziemlich deutlich. Die "speaking voice" führt sich nachgerade als eine zitie-

rende Stimme ein: alles, was sie sagt, könnte in seiner Formelhaftig-
keit aus dem Bestand petrarkistischer Poesie ausgekoppelt sein. Die
Stimme redet gleichsam in fremder Zunge, die Formeln strömen ihr
derart zu, daß die eigenständige Invention und die Disposition in
diesen 76 Zeilen geradezu zugeschüttet werden: daß sich nämlich eine
alte Jungfer eine "schwarze Grabschrift" einhandle, während eine
Frau, die das Liebesspiel mit "zucker-süsser krafft auff alabaster
schreibt", ins "Contrafait der zarten kinder" eingeschrieben stehe.

Es ist vielfach beschrieben worden, wie die stilistische Abwen-
dung vom Hoffmannswaldauischen Vorbild dessen vielgliedrige Me-
taphernstruktur einebne, indem sie Möglichkeiten der Bildung von
Tropen nicht mehr nutzte, also etwa Vieldeutigkeiten eliminierte, die
z. B. dadurch entstanden, daß der uneigentliche Ausdruck einmal als
Metapher, ein andermal der Metonymie benutzt wurde, daß das *signi-
fiant* der einen Trope zum *signifié* der nächsten wurde usw.[47] An die
Stelle der Kette der Tropen tritt der Pleonasmus; das Plündern der
copia verborum treibt die rhetorische Bewegung des Textes nicht voran,
vielmehr tritt sie in der Wiederholung des Immergleichen auf der
Stelle. Wenn man ein Bild benutzen will: Das Neukirchsche Gedicht
liest sich, als habe der Autor die Trümmer der Hoffmannswaldauischen Poeme zusammengesammelt und dann säuberlich aufgeschich-
tet. Wenn die Stimme, die den Text spricht, Verse wie:

Der schönheit fürniß kan nicht ewig farbe fassen /
Dein schirmend wasser wird / wie trübe flut / erblassen;
Denn iede stunde zeigt / wie sie dich trotzen kan.

("An die Florette")[48]

aneinandergereiht und variationslos immer auf dieselbe Weise immer
dasselbe sagt, dann bleibt nichts zweideutig oder gar dunkel. Die
"speaking voice" übt rhetorische Selbstdisziplin, sie mutet dem Hörer
keinen Deutungsaufschub zu; sie weiß nichts von der Lust des Ent-
und Aufdeckens des *signifiés*. Es geht Knall auf Fall. Das alte Modell
der Geselligkeit organisierte—wie Anton Ulrich in der *Aramena* sehr
kunstvoll beschrieb—die Mechanismen von Ausschließungen und
Reintegrationen über die geselligen Spielregeln sehr diffizil und am
Ende harmonisierend. Der anonyme Buchmarkt gab dafür—und
das ist (wie etwa die leidenschaftliche Diskussion gegen die "Mo-
derne" nicht nur im "Sozialistischen Realismus" zeigt) bis heute
so geblieben—aufgrund seiner spezifischen Verständigungsstruktur
kaum Möglichkeiten. Neukirchs "speaking voice" trägt dem geschickt
Rechnung. Sie will überhaupt nur integrieren. Sie schließt—indem sie
die Tradition zitiert—die Leser an das bewunderte Vorbild an, zu-

gleich aber vermeidet sie die Frustrationen des Nichtverstehens (was ja Ausschließung bedeutet). Indem sie die Sprache des beerbten Modells verständlich machte, stärkte sie ein Gruppengefühl, das sich in der Fähigkeit sicher wußte, eine gemeinsame Sprache zu verstehen. Ohne Rückgriff auf solche Mechanismen ist die Aggressivität kaum zu verstehen, mit der spätestens seit 1715–20 der "italienische" Stil und besonders seine Techniken des tropischen Sprechens attackiert wurden.

Eine solche Deutung des auffallenden Stilwandels um 1700, die literatursoziologische und literaturtheoretische Phänomene zusammenzusehen versucht, trägt möglicherweise ein wenig zum Verständnis dieses Prozesses bei, denn es ist ja nur schwer einzusehen, warum das literarische Paradigma "Barock" plötzlich reif geworden und damit erschöpft sein oder warum das rhetorisch ausdifferenzierte Poesieschema keine weiteren Varianten hergegeben haben sollte. Auch läßt sich schwer erklären, warum die Neukirchs, Bessers und wie immer sie hießen, von Hause aus gröbere Patrone gewesen sein sollen als die Poeten einer Generation vor ihnen. Wenn man die literarischen Verfahren, die Textstrukturen und auch die "Botschaften" der Texte nicht isoliert, sondern im Rahmen der historischen Umschichtungen liest (unter denen mir die Veränderung auf dem Buchmarkt eine der zentralen zu sein scheint), wenn man sie also als kulturelle Phänomene deutet, dann wird unserem Verständnis manches vielleicht deutlicher.

Anmerkungen

1. Man lese etwa Johann Christoph Gottsched, "Lob- und Gedächtnißrede auf Martin Opitzen", in *Gesammlete Reden*, 2. Aufl. (Leipzig: Breitkopf, 1749), S. 173–216.

2. August Koberstein, *Grundriß der Geschichte der deutschen National-Litteratur*, 3. Aufl. (Leipzig: Vogel, 1837), S. 378.

3. Karl Goedeke, *Grundrisz zur Geschichte der deutschen Dichtung*, 2. Aufl., 15 Bde. (Dresden: Ehlermann, 1887), 3:277.

4. *Geschichte der deutschen Literatur*, Bd. 6, hrsg. v. Werner Rieck (Berlin: Volk und Wissen, 1979), S. 33. Horst Albert Glaser, Hrsg., *Deutsche Literatur: Eine Sozialgeschichte*, Bd. 3 (Reinbek: Rowohlt, 1985), S. 394–407, täuscht insofern, als er zwar ein Kapitel "Galante Poesie" hat, darunter aber vor allem Hoffmannswaldaus vor 1650 verfaßte Gedichte versteht.

5. Eine solche Perspektive ist so erneuernd nicht; sie gewinnt vielmehr Positionen zurück, die die Forschung der 20er Jahre (M. v. Waldberg, G. Müller oder A. Hirsch) bereits eingenommen hat.

6. Daß es sich hier um keine Gruppe, Schule o. ä. handelt, ist eine literarhistorische Binsenweisheit; zur abkürzenden Verständigung taugt der Terminus indes doch.

7. Zuerst: Erich Trunz, "Der deutsche Späthumanismus um 1600 als Standeskultur", *Zeitschrift für die Geschichte der Erziehung und des Unterrichts* 21 (1931): 17–53. Umfassend: Albrecht Schöne, Hrsg., *Stadt-Schule-Buchwesen und die deutsche Literatur im 17. Jahrhundert* (München: Beck, 1976).

8. Vgl. Angelo G. de Capua, Jr., "The Series Collection. A Forerunner of Lyric Anthology in Germany", *JEGP* 54 (1955): 202–25.

9. Vgl. Dorette Frost und Gerhard Knoll, Hrsg., *Gelegenheitsdichtung* (Bremen: Universität Bremen, 1977), darin vor allem die Beiträge von Leighton und Drees; Wulf Segebrecht, *Das Gelegenheitsgedicht* (Stuttgart: Metzler, 1977).

10. Vgl. Hans-Georg Herrlitz, *Studium als Standesprivileg. Die Entstehung des Maturitätsproblems im 18. Jahrhundert* (Frankfurt a. M.: S. Fischer, 1973); Helen Liebel, "Der aufgeklärte Absolutismus und die Gesellschaftskrise in Deutschland im 18. Jahrhundert", in Walther Hubatsch, Hrsg., *Absolutismus* (Darmstadt: Wissenschaftliche Buchgesellschaft, 1973), S. 488–544.

11. Vgl. Alberto Martino, "Barockpoesie, Publikum und Verbürgerlichung der literarischen Intelligenz", *IASL* 1 (1976): 107–46.

12. Paul de Man, "Lyrical Voice in Contemporary Theory: Riffaterre and Jauss", in *Lyric Poetry Beyond New Criticism*, hrsg. v. Chaviva Hošek und Patricia Parker (Ithaca: Cornell University Press, 1985), S. 55.

13. Bernhard Sorg, *Das lyrische Ich: Untersuchungen zu deutschen Gedichten von Gryphius bis Benn* (Tübingen: Niemeyer, 1984).

14. Vgl. Karl Pestalozzi, *Die Entstehung des lyrischen Ich. Studien zum Motiv der Erhebung in der Lyrik*, (Berlin: de Gruyter, 1970).

15. Vgl. Georg Wilhelm Hegel, *Ästhetik*, 2 Bde., hrsg. v. Friedrich Bassenge (Frankfurt a. M.: Europäische Verlagsanstalt, o. J.), 2:471.

16. Vgl. Jochen Hörisch, *Die fröhliche Wissenschaft der Poesie. Der Universalitätsanspruch von Dichtung in der frühromantischen Poetologie* (Frankfurt a. M.: Suhrkamp, 1976), S. 80–82.

17. Vgl. den Beitrag von Ferdinand van Ingen in diesem Band.

18. Vgl. dazu immer noch: Alfred Baeumler, *Das Irrationalitätsproblem in der Ästhetik und Logik des 18. Jahrhunderts bis zur Kritik der Urteilskraft*, 2. Aufl. (Darmstadt: Wissenschaftliche Buchgesellschaft, 1967). Wie aktuell Baeumlers Studie noch immer ist, erkennt man, wenn man neuere Arbeiten daran mißt, etwa: Angelika Wetterer, *Publikumsbezug und Wahrheitsanspruch* (Tübingen: Niemeyer, 1981), obwohl sie mit dem—allerdings rein formal gesehenen—Publikumsbegriff ein neues und fruchtbares Moment in die Diskussion einbringt. Von einem veränderten Standpunkt, nämlich dem der Psychiatrie, geht das Problem an: Jutta Osinski, *Über Vernunft und Wahnsinn: Studien zur literarischen Aufklärung in der Gegenwart und im 18. Jahrhundert* (Bonn: Bouvier, 1983).

19. Vgl. Günter Peters, *Der zerrissene Engel: Genieästhetik und literarische Selbstdarstellung im 18. Jahrhundert* (Stuttgart: Metzler, 1982), der im übri-

gen auf das nicht nur kunsttheoretische sondern gerade soziokulturell bestimmte Ideal des Shaftesburyschen "virtuoso" aufmerksam macht.

20. Johann Wolfgang Goethe, *Dichtung und Wahrheit*, Hamburger Ausgabe, Bd. 9 (Hamburg: Wegner, 1955), S. 164–71.

21. Vgl. Harald Steinhagen und Benno v. Wiese, Hrsg., *Deutsche Dichter des 17. Jahrhunderts* (Berlin: Erich Schmidt, 1984), S. 887–921.

22. Vgl. die Beiträge von Barton W. Browning und Joseph Leighton in diesem Band.

23. Vgl. Uwe-K. Ketelsen, "Poesie und bürgerlicher Kulturanspruch. Die Kritik an der rhetorischen Gelegenheitspoesie in der frühbürgerlichen Literaturdiskussion", *Lessing Yearbook* 8 (1976): 89–107.

24. Martin Opitz, *Buch von der deutschen Poeterey*, hrsg. v. Richard Alewyn, (Tübingen: Niemeyer, 1963), S. 7, 16.

25. Vgl. Silvio Vietta, *Literarische Phantasie: Theorie und Geschichte. Barock und Aufklärung* (Stuttgart: Metzler, 1986), S. 71–147.

26. Vgl. Uwe-K. Ketelsen, "Vom Siege der natürlichen Vernunft. Einige Bemerkungen zu einer sozialgeschichtlichen Interpretation der Geschichte der Fabel in der deutschen Aufklärung", *Seminar* 16 (1980):208–23.

27. [Benjamin Neukirch, Hrsg.], *Herrn von Hoffmannswaldau und andrer Deutschen Gedichte*, 2 Bde., hrsg. von Angelo George de Capua und Ernst Alfred Philippson (Tübingen: Niemeyer, 1961; 1965).

28. Christian Hofmann zu Hofmannswaldau, "Vorrede zu Deutsche Übersetzungen und Gedichte", *Poetica* 2 (1968): 552.

29. Vgl. den Beitrag von Michael M. Metzger in diesem Band.

30. Anton Ulrich, Herzog von Braunschweig-Lüneburg, *Die Durchleuchtige Syrerinn Aramena*, Teil 3, Neudruck hrsg. v. Blake Lee Spahr (Bern: Lang, 1976), S. 337–45. Entsprechend dem anderen Personal geht es in Georg Philipp Harsdörffers Gesprächsspiel "Die Poeterey" entschieden steifer zu. Vgl. Georg Philipp Harsdörffer, *Frauenzimmer Gesprächspiele*, Teil 2, Neudruck hrsg. v. Irmgard Böttcher (Tübingen: Niemeyer, 1968), S. 255–65.

31. Vgl. Norbert Elias, *Die höfische Gesellschaft* (Darmstadt: Luchterhand, 1969); Wolf Lepenies, *Melancholie und Gesellschaft* (Frankfurt a. M.: Suhrkamp, 1969).

32. Hans Aßmann von Abschatz, *Poetische Übersetzungen und Gedichte*, Neudruck hrsg. von Erika A. Metzger (Bern: Lang, 1970), S. 279.

33. Vgl. Gerhart Hoffmeister, *Petrarkistische Lyrik* (Stuttgart: Metzler, 1973).

34. Gerhard Plumpe, "Eigentum-Eigentümlichkeit. Über den Zusammenhang ästhetischer und juristischer Begriffe im 18. Jahrhundert", *Archiv für Begriffsgeschichte* 23 (1979): 175–96.

35. Johann Christoph Gottsched, *Versuch einer Critischen Dichtkunst*, 4. Aufl. (Leipzig: Bernhard Christoph Breitkopf, 1751; Neudruck Darmstadt: Wissenschaftliche Buchgesellschaft, 1962), S. 111–12.

36. Franz Heiduk, *Die Dichter der galanten Lyrik: Studien zur Neukirchschen Sammlung* (Bern: Francke, 1971), S. 85.

37. Vgl. etwa Heiduks Urteil über Johann von Besser, ebd., S. 35: "Das persönliche Moment schlägt stärker durch, 'erfüllt' jedoch selten die Form so, daß das Gedicht überzeugt".

38. *Herrn von Hoffmannswaldau Gedichte*, 1:64.

39. Ebd., 1:65.

40. Ebd., 1:450.

41. Ebd., 1:62.

42. Ebd., 1:370.

43. Ebd., 1:158.

44. Ebd., 1:122.

45. Ebd., 1:123.

46. Ebd., 2:77.

47. Vgl. Uwe-K. Ketelsen, "Die Liebe bindet Gold an Stahl und Garn zu weißer Seyde—Zu Hoffmannswaldaus erotischem Lied 'So soll der purpur deiner lippen' ", in *Gedichte und Interpretationen, Bd. 1: Renaissance und Barock*, 2. Aufl., hrsg. v. Volker Meid (Stuttgart: Reclam, 1988), S. 346–55.

48. *Herrn von Hoffmannswaldau Gedichte*, 2:77.

Index

University of North Carolina
Studies in the Germanic Languages
and Literatures

78 OLGA MARX AND ERNST MORWITZ, TRANS. *The Works of Stefan George*. 2nd, rev. and enl. ed. 1974. Pp. xxviii, 431.

80 DONALD G. DAVIAU AND GEORGE J. BUELOW. *The "Ariadne auf Naxos" of Hugo von Hofmannsthal and Richard Strauss*. 1975. Pp. x, 274.

92 PETER BAULAND. *Gerhart Hauptmann's "Before Daybreak."* Translation and Introduction. 1978. Pp. xxiv, 87.

96 G. RONALD MURPHY. *Brecht and the Bible. A Study of Religious Nihilism and Human Weakness in Brecht's Drama of Mortality and the City*. 1980. Pp. xi, 107.

97 ERHARD FRIEDRICHSMEYER. *Die satirische Kurzprosa Heinrich Bölls*. 1981. Pp. xiv, 223.

For other volumes in the "Studies" see p. ii.

Send orders to:
The University of North Carolina Press, P.O. Box 2288
Chapel Hill, NC 27515-2288

Several out-of-print titles are available in limited quantities through the UNCSGLL office. These include:

58 WALTER W. ARNDT, PAUL W. BROSMAN, JR., FREDERIC E. COENEN, AND WERNER P. FRIEDRICH, EDS. *Studies in Historical Linguistics in Honor of George Sherman Lane*. 1967. Pp. xx, 241.

68 JOHN NEUBAUER. *Bifocal Vision. Novalis' Philosophy of Nature and Disease*. 1971. Pp. x, 196.

70 DONALD F. NELSON. *Portrait of the Artist as Hermes. A Study of Myth and Psychology in Thomas Mann's "Felix Krull."* 1971. Pp. xvi, 146.

72 CHRISTINE OERTEL SJÖGREN. *The Marble Statue as Idea: Collected Essays on Adalbert Stifter's "Der Nachsommer."* 1972. Pp. xiv, 121.

73 DONALD G. DAVIAU AND JORUN B. JOHNS, EDS. *The Correspondence of Schnitzler and Auernheimer, with Raoul Auernheimer's Aphorisms*. 1972. Pp. xii, 161.

74 A. MARGARET ARENT MADELUNG. *"The Laxdoela Saga": Its Structural Patterns*. 1972. Pp. xiv, 261.

75 JEFFREY L. SAMMONS. *Six Essays on the Young German Novel*. 2nd ed. 1975. Pp. xiv, 187.

76 DONALD H. CROSBY AND GEORGE C. SCHOOLFIELD, EDS. *Studies in the German Drama. A Festschrift in Honor of Walter Silz*. 1974. Pp. xxvi, 255.

77 J. W. THOMAS. *Tannhäuser: Poet and Legend*. With Texts and Translation of His Works. 1974. Pp. x, 202.

81 ELAINE E. BONEY. *Rainer Maria Rilke: "Duinesian Elegies."* German Text with English Translation and Commentary. 2nd ed. 1977. Pp. xii, 153.

82 JANE K. BROWN. *Goethe's Cyclical Narratives: "Die Unterhaltungen deutscher Ausgewanderten" and "Wilhelm Meisters Wanderjahre."* 1975. Pp. x, 144.

83 FLORA KIMMICH. *Sonnets of Catharina von Greiffenberg: Methods of Composition.* 1975. Pp. x, 132.

84 HERBERT W. REICHERT. *Friedrich Nietzsche's Impact on Modern German Literature.* 1975. Pp. xxii, 129.

85 JAMES C. O'FLAHERTY, TIMOTHY F. SELLNER, ROBERT M. HELMS, EDS. *Studies in Nietzsche and the Classical Tradition.* 2nd ed. 1979. Pp. xviii, 278.

87 HUGO BEKKER. *Friedrich von Hausen: Inquiries into His Poetry.* 1977. Pp. x, 159.

88 H. G. HUETTICH. *Theater in the Planned Society: Contemporary Drama in the German Democratic Republic in Its Historical, Political, and Cultural Context.* 1978. Pp. xvi, 174.

89 DONALD G. DAVIAU, ED. *The Letters of Arthur Schnitzler to Hermann Bahr.* 1978. Pp. xii, 183.

91 LELAND R. PHELPS AND A. TILO ALT, EDS. *Creative Encounter. Festschrift for Herman Salinger.* 1978. Pp. xxii, 181.

93 MEREDITH LEE. *Studies in Goethe's Lyric Cycles.* 1978. Pp. xii, 191.

94 JOHN M. ELLIS. *Heinrich von Kleist. Studies in the Character and Meaning of His Writings.* 1979. Pp. xx, 194.

95 GORDON BIRRELL. *The Boundless Present. Space and Time in the Literary Fairy Tales of Novalis and Tieck.* 1979. Pp. x, 163.

Orders for these titles only should be sent to Editor, UNCSGLL, CB# 3160 Dey Hall, Chapel Hill, NC 27599-3160.

Volumes 1–44, 46–50, 52, 60, and 79 of the "Studies" have been reprinted. They may be ordered from AMS Press, Inc., 56 E. 13th Street, New York, NY 10003.

For complete list of reprinted titles write to the Editor.